NEW EDITION

The
Publicity
Handbook

NEW EDITION

The
Publicity
Handbook

The Inside Scoop from More

than 100 Journalists and PR

Pros on How to Get Great

Publicity Coverage—in Print,

On-Line, and on the Air

David R. Yale with *Andrew J. Carothers*

McGraw-Hill

Chicago   New York   San Francisco   Lisbon   London   Madrid   Mexico City
Milan   New Delhi   San Juan   Seoul   Singapore   Sydney   Toronto

Library of Congress Cataloging-in-Publication Data

Yale, David R.
    The publicity handbook : the inside scoop from more than 100 journalists
and PR pros on how to get great publicity coverage : in print, on-line, and on
the air / David R. Yale with Andrew J. Carothers.
        p.   cm.
    Includes bibliographical references and index.
    ISBN 0-8442-3242-4
    1. Public relations—Handbooks, manuals, etc.   I. Carothers, Andrew J.
II. Title.

HD59.Y33   2001
659—dc21   00-48070

McGraw-Hill

*A Division of The **McGraw·Hill** Companies*

1 2 3 4 5 6 7 8 9 0   LBM/LBM   0 9 8 7 6 5 4 3 2 1

ISBN 0-8442-3242-4

This book was set in Bell MT by JDA Typesetting Corporation
Printed and bound by Lake Book Manufacturing

Cover design by Jeanette Wojtyla

McGraw-Hill books are available at special quantity discounts to use as premiums and
sales promotions, or for use in corporate training programs. For more information, please
write to the Director of Special Sales, Professional Publishing, McGraw-Hill, Two Penn
Plaza, New York, NY 10121-2298. Or contact your local bookstore.

This book is printed on acid-free paper.

For my daughter, Margot: You're the "bestest" and the "mostest"!

Contents

Foreword

Publicity can have far greater integrity, impact, influence, and attention value than advertising—but only when it's actually used by the media you have targeted.

Whether you're a novice or a professional, *The Publicity Handbook* tells you how to increase your chances of success, so that you don't have to rely on luck—or prayer—to get media coverage.

It's a book that's worth reading—and rereading—particularly the checklists and questions at the ends of chapters.

I own several hundred public relations and journalism books, including eight that I have written.

The Publicity Handbook is a more comprehensive and useful manual than any other book. I wish that I had had it when I started as a publicist. In fact, I wish that I had written it!

—RICHARD WEINER,
Public Relations Consultant, New York

Acknowledgments

I would like to thank the many people who helped me (directly and indirectly) with this book. To Professor Rose Zimbardo, who taught me how to write (and think) clearly; to Dale O. Johnson, who showed me how the system works; to V. Hap Smith and Peggy Voulkos, who drafted me for my first publicity job; and to Burton Weber and Virginia Lawler, who taught me to write clear and concise copy—special thanks!

Many thanks also to my friend and mentor, Bob Bly; Bob Kusano; Esther Savin; and Jim Kousoulas. My agents, Michael Larsen and Elizabeth Pomada, and NTC's editors, Anne Knudsen and Danielle Egan-Miller, were always available with thorough and thoughtful feedback and advice.

Ravelle Brickman read the entire manuscript of the first edition and provided both helpful criticism and encouragement. Leslie O'Bergin's continued votes of confidence were also important during the long task of researching and writing the first edition.

Sheila and Marc Calef, S. Lynn Diamond, Phil Douglis, Sharon Haver, Ken McEldowney, Andrew McGowan, Dan Schlesinger, Judy Luki Richard Weiner, Andrew Yale, and Jerry Pozniak all read portions o manuscript and provided helpful comments and ideas. My coauthor, Andrew Carothers, helped guide me through the complexities of Web-based publicity.

Thanks to Tom Glazer for permission to use the lyrics from his song "Precious Sight"; Phil Douglis and Cliff McGoon, editor of *IABC News* (now *Communication World*), for permission to use Phil's material on publicity photography; Cora B. Everett, executive secretary of the National Conference of Editorial Writers, for permission to quote material from *The Masthead*; Judy G. Meehan, publications manager of the National Association of Broadcasters, for permission to quote from its pamphlets; Joseph Whitfield of PRSA for permission to quote from *Public Relations Journal*; Denny Griswold, editor of *PR News*, for permission to use excerpts from a case study; Jack O'Dwyer for permission to quote from *O'Dwyer's PR Services Report* and *Jack O'Dwyer's Newsletter*; Lee Levitt for permission to quote from *The Publicist*; Regina LaPierre for permission to use material from *pr reporter*; Jeffrey Tarter for permission to quote from *Soft•Letter*; Tina Koenig of Xpress Press for permission to quote from *i-PR*; Nina Sharrif for permission to quote from *Ragan's Interactive Public Relations*; and many others, too numerous to mention.

And finally, the dozens of journalists and public relations pros who gave their time and ideas to this book have made an invaluable contribution. To each of them, a special note of appreciation.

Introduction

I designed *The Publicity Handbook* for two kinds of readers: the seasoned professional who needs a reference book to answer occasional questions about the finer points of publicity and keep up with new developments (such as Webcasting and Internet-based publications), and the beginner looking for a thorough guide to the subject.

Since the Internet influences every aspect of the publicity process, this entire book has been revised. Although there is a chapter devoted solely to the Internet, the influence of the World Wide Web permeates every page. At the same time, I have not abandoned the tried-and-true publicity basics that still apply. Given the rapid influx of new publicists into the field, and journalists' frustrations with their lack of skills, the basics are more important than ever. Publicity is a fascinating subject, and I made sure that *The Publicity Handbook* is just as interesting. Throughout this book you will find examples of both excellent and awful publicity material. The examples are in a format that has been modified to fit the book page. The correct format is specified, however, for each type of publicity material.

The good examples are almost all real ones, and they are attributed to the organizations and publicists who created them. A few, however, have been created especially for this book, to illustrate specific techniques or procedures. These are attributed to groups in a fictional place called **Plains City**.

The bad examples are based on reality. Although people do produce this sort of material, the examples here are fictitious. All bad examples are attributed to organizations in the town of **Chelm**, a fictional place in a story by the Jewish writer Sholem Aleichem. According to the story, when the angels distributed people on Earth, they had two bags each. One bag was full of dumb people; the other was stuffed with geniuses. It seems the angel flying over Chelm was too low, and one of his bags got caught on a tree branch. All the fools landed in Chelm, and it's been a pretty foolish place ever since!

Throughout the book I have used *he* sometimes and *she* other times, since both men and women are reporters, editors, public service directors, and news assignment editors. I want this book to reflect the real world.

In the chapters that follow, many journalists and publicists share their opinions about publicity—and their likes and dislikes. Some of the publicists have the letters APR after their names. This designation means they have been accredited in public relations through a voluntary program of the Public Relations Society of America. Some of the journalists have moved on to other positions, or the media outlets they work for have changed names, merged, or disappeared. Nonetheless, the opinions and insights they share are still valid and highly useful.

I have also provided thorough checklists that will help you review the material in *The Publicity Handbook* and keep your publicity campaign on target. Look for them at the end of Chapters 1 through 11.

If you find this checklist format useful, you'll want to look at my other book, *Publicity and Media Relations Checklists*, which includes 59 proven work sheets that go beyond the checklists. You can find out more about it at http://www.publicityhandbook.com, this book's website. Since this is an Internet-based book, it has a website that supports it. Go to the site for updates, clickable links to sources and services, and publicity work sheets you can download and print out.

Finally, since this is a Web-oriented book, I invite you to interact with me. Let me know how you're using the book, share your publicity successes, and please give me suggestions for improving the next edition. You can reach me at david@publicityhandbook.com.

Planning for Publicity

Your on-line business just reached a milestone—even though the bottom line is still bright red. You're under considerable pressure from your backers: they want to see some recognition for your efforts in the press. So, you have your PR agency send out a press release, you cross your fingers, and you hope. But what if the news media don't give you any ink?

Perhaps you wrote, rewrote, and edited a press release for your start-up company, about your improved new widget. You spent a fortune on slick photographs to go with it. And you mailed it to every newspaper and broadcaster west of the Mississippi. It's tough trying to break into the widget market. Your company has a limited advertising budget. A lot is riding on the results of your press release. For the company. And for you. What if nobody uses your publicity material?

You've sent publicity materials to all the media outlets in town about a special event for your organization. It took a lot of work, and you hope there will be a large crowd to gawk at that fire-eating sword swallower who volunteered to add a touch of the unusual. But you're worried. What if *nobody* comes? What will you do with 100 pounds of potato salad and 30 cases of hot dogs? Will the event really promote your product? Raise the money you need? Bring your organization the attention you want?

Both the rookie and the old pro find that getting positive publicity for products, corporations, nonprofit groups, community organizations, government agencies, trade associations, and small businesses is a major concern.

But even if you have no formal training in public relations, there *are* publicity techniques you can use to make sure your message will be heard. This book will help you learn them. And you'll have a good time in the process!

Whether you work for a large corporation seeking to supplement its advertising budget with publicity, a brand-new Web-based business in search of eyeballs—and customers, a public library that wants to let job seekers know about its vocational books, a trade organization promoting natural and organic foods, or a committee opposed to school budget cuts, your task will involve hard work, skill, a sense of humor, and a pinch of luck. But when everything goes well and your story is on the airwaves and in print, that hard work and hard-earned skill will pay handsome dividends.

Publicity Defined

What, exactly, is publicity? It involves supplying information that is factual, interesting, and newsworthy to media not controlled by you, such as radio, television, magazines, newspapers, trade journals, newsletters, E-zines (on-line magazines), and websites. Your goal is to *earn* coverage because journalists think your material will be of interest to their audiences. Your material, if it is used, may stand on its own as a separate story or show, or it may become part of a larger story that draws on information from several sources.

If you use slide shows, speeches, posters, brochures, newsletters, billboards, direct mail, and advertising, in which you can control how and when a message is used, then you have become a promoter rather than a publicist. Michelle Rapkin, publicity woman at Bantam Books, explains the difference this way: "Publicity is the front cover of *Time* magazine. Promotion is the back cover."

Publicity is not advertising, since you do not pay for time or space, nor is it public relations. Public relations is a broader task, which includes publicity but involves promotion, public affairs, advertising, and opinion making as well. These are areas you may want to branch into later on, when you have mastered publicity skills. For now, your task is to learn how to do the best possible job of presenting your message to the public, via the media.

Planning for Publicity Success

Even if you have been doing some publicity for your organization, if you don't have an overall publicity plan, you should take the time to develop one now. A carefully considered plan can save you many headaches and help you avoid bad publicity later on. Even if you're doing strictly Web-based publicity, says Jed Nitzberg, APR, vice president of interactive communications for the Arthritis Foundation, you cannot forsake traditional planning. "The Internet doesn't make [the need for it] go away."

Most important, planning will help you come out ahead in the competition for media coverage.

Determining Your Publicity Goals

Your first step in the planning process is to list a set of goals for your publicity efforts. Write them down on paper because that makes them more concrete. These objectives will, of course, dovetail with your organization's overall goals. And they should be specific. It is not enough to say that you want your product, service, cause, or point of view to be well known to the public. That isn't specific enough to help your organization reach its goals.

Your publicity should help your organization accomplish one or more of the following:

- Inform people about how to choose, buy, and use your product or service.
- Persuade consumers to buy your product or service.
- Counteract misconceptions about your product, service, organization, or cause.
- Get customers into your store or onto your website.

- Get information to the public on issues your organization is concerned about.
- Draw people to a particular event or series of events or increase attendance at your regular programs and on-line events.
- Get people to volunteer.
- Recruit highly qualified employees.
- Get people to vote for a bond issue.
- Attract shareholders and support your stock's price.
- Protect your organization from frivolous lawsuits.

If, for example, you want more people to come to your clinic for family counseling, you could develop publicity that explains what family counseling is and how families with problems can benefit from it. On the other hand, you might have found that a lot of people are coming to your clinic for emergency family counseling on weekends, when the other clinics in town are closed. Your waiting room is jammed, there are not enough offices for your counselors, and on bad weekends waiting clients overflow into the street. Your staff tells you that 85 percent of the weekend problems could be solved on the telephone. How can you get people to telephone first? Well, you could develop a publicity campaign to let people know that they don't even have to leave their homes—they don't have to spend money for gasoline or carfare—your counselors are ready to help the moment they get a call.

Or perhaps your trade organization represents resorts in the Caribbean that are booked solid in high season, from January through March. Although the weather in the fall and spring months is magnificent on the islands, neither love nor money seems to lure North American tourists during these "shoulder" seasons. An opinion survey shows that most vacationers believe that during the "shoulders" the Caribbean is hot, humid, and unpleasant, with nothing interesting happening. How can you change their perceptions? One way is to provide publicity about the lovely weather and exotic events during the shoulder seasons—and the hefty savings in store for spring and fall Caribbean vacationers.

You will be able to be more exact about some goals than others, but whenever possible, try to measure the results of your publicity. If a survey shows that only 12 percent of the vacationers you interview are aware of the lure of the shoulder season's balmy weather and stunning special events, your objective may be to increase that figure to 25 percent within a year. Setting concrete goals using figures will help you evaluate the success of your publicity program.

Establishing Priorities

Your publicity goals will help you decide which programs, events, and issues get priority. Whether you're a volunteer or a full-time, paid employee, most organizations will have more requests for publicity than you can handle. Says the former publicist for Chelm General Hospital, "Working for an organization that has no publicity priorities is hellish. You have to respond to each and every request for publicity because you don't have any basis for turning people down. You don't really have enough time to do it all, so you cut corners, and your output is never first-rate. Now that I work for an organization with clear publicity policies, the results are much better."

You must be selective. If you deluge the media with publicity material, you're like the boy who cried wolf; nobody will believe you when you have a major story. Overkill means undercoverage. Not all events call for a full-scale publicity campaign, and if you overemphasize a minor one, you may have trouble getting coverage for a genuinely newsworthy program that takes place soon afterward.

Mike Martin, the news director for KRBE-FM in Houston, Texas, puts it this way: "Remember, if you flood me with stuff that is not important, you're diluting my interest. Then I'll take anything you send me as probably not important. If you hit me with only important stuff, stuff I need, stuff I can use, that's important to the community, I'm going to pay more attention when I see your logo on the envelope."

And Gus Venditto, an executive editor of *PC Magazine*, explains, "You get to know press agents, and you get a feel for which ones will sell everything equally. You tend to ignore them. The better publicists, on the other hand, know the difference between routine announcements and a really interesting product development. They get my attention."

Analyzing Your Audience

Publicity involves selling, and like any good salesperson, you should analyze your audience before you start. You have to understand why people will or will not be receptive to your message. And because you're a publicist, your task of persuasion is a double one. First you have to persuade journalists to run your material or cover your story. Once that happens, your approach, angle, and information must be enticing enough to get the public to act.

Now, I know that some readers involved in charitable, nonprofit, and community organizations are saying, "Who, me? You want me to be a salesperson? I think selling is immoral, and salespeople are the lowest of the low. After all, I work for a group with a worthy cause. We would debase it if we 'sold.'"

You can call yourself a persuader, convincer, campaigner, or anything else you wish. I'm still going to call publicists salespeople, because the reality is that you have to make two sales pitches *every time you do publicity*: one to the journalist and another to your audience.

Figuring out precisely to whom you want to sell your ideas is an important part of your publicity plan. Can you increase sales more quickly by targeting publicity toward current customers? Or should you aim your message at people who never use your product, and provide them with reasons they should?

Are you trying to reach only the people who agree with your stand on air pollution? Are there people who are undecided, or even segments of the opposition who may be persuaded to join you, or at least engage in a dialogue? Who, exactly, are they?

As Robert Cummings, environmental reporter for the *Maine Sunday Telegram*, says, "The key to getting publicity is to have something to say, and then choosing who to say it to."

Using Misconceptions in Your Favor

If you are specific when you identify your audience, you will probably be able to make a list of the misconceptions that audience has about your organization, product, service, or industry. It may even be worth doing a survey just to get detailed information about such misconceptions, since that can be a valuable resource. It tells you exactly what people need to know about you. So, even if being misunderstood angers and annoys you, or hurts you deeply, pay close attention to those wrong ideas held by the public. For example, if you work with a group that is opposed to nuclear power and your target audience consists of trade-union members who support atomic power because they think it will create more construction jobs, you will have to find the facts and figures to demonstrate that your alternative energy program will generate more jobs than nuclear reactors will.

Or if people say, "Gold mining! Not in my state! Gold mines pollute the environment," you can develop publicity material that tells them how advanced mining-management techniques protect the environment, as well as all about your award-winning restoration of the areas around closed mines, which have become unusually productive wildlife preserves. It should be easy to place this sort of material in the media because journalists and the public are always curious about the other side of the story in a controversy.

A good example of using misconceptions as the basis for publicity material is the following 60-second radio public service announcement (PSA) by the American Foundation for the Blind:

> *Robert Klein:* The meaning of words. As a child, certain things were always couched in certain ways. For example, my mother used to say, "Go visit Max next door; he's unsighted. He must be lonely."
>
> *Announcer:* The American Foundation for the Blind presents Robert Klein.
>
> *Robert Klein:* Now Max isn't unsighted. He's blind. And he isn't lonely, either. True, my mother meant well. But what she and a lot of other people don't understand is that blind people don't want to be treated like children; they want to be treated like people. I remember I once said, "See what I mean, Max?" My mother almost fainted with embarrassment. And you know what Max said? "Look how embarrassed your mother is!" Now if he can use words like *look*, don't go around saying someone's unsighted.

Of course, you should not concentrate on the misinformation; you should emphasize the facts. "To get rid of stereotypes," says Mary Jane O'Neill, director of public relations at the New York Association for the Blind, "I would stress the positive. I would not talk about beggars with tin cups, for instance, which is the classic stereotype of the blind person. I would just ignore that. Instead I would talk about the lawyer who is on his way to becoming the first blind judge in his district, or the blind insurance man who just hit the half-million-dollar sales mark."

Motivating Your Audience

You've already decided what you want to tell your audience. Now you need to figure out why people should listen to you. How can you make them want to listen? And how can you make them want to do something after they've listened? What benefit can you provide them from their point of view?

Linnea Crowe, program manager for KSTP-TV in St. Paul, Minnesota, explains it this way: "I think not only of who I'm talking to, but also what my selling point is. Why do I want them to listen to me now? Why should they listen to me? You have to give people a reason: that it's going to make them feel better, that it's going to make them happier. If you don't include that reason in your piece, you might as well not send it out."

Audience motivation is an area where nonprofit and community organizations, special interest groups, government agencies—and many online businesses—often fall down. But the advertising world does an excellent job of pointing out product and service benefits. And whatever you think of advertising, you have to admit that it works well. So, if you work with a nonprofit organization or a business that is not experienced in the ways of advertising, it would be a good idea for you to study some advertisements that you feel are particularly effective. Ask yourself exactly how these ads are able to convince you of the product's benefits. Then try to parody the ads, substituting your product, service, or organization's name for the brand in the original and creating parallel product or service benefits to fit your case. This should help you see yourself differently and increase your ability to translate your message into your audience's terms.

It is always best to be positive. Likewise, it will help you motivate your audience if you avoid reminding people of their fears or dislikes; that approach only makes them anxious or annoyed. Would you want to go to a Fourth of July picnic at the country club if you were told that children are not allowed to run or make loud noises, no guests are allowed, and ball playing, dancing, picnic blankets, and lawn chairs are not permitted? Even if the publicity piece mentioned that there would be all the burgers and hot dogs you could eat and great old-time family games, that negative beginning is hardly alluring.

There's another trick to help you find the service or product benefits likely to appeal to your audience. John B. Rand, a partner at advertising agency Reva Korda & Associates, says, "The best discipline I know is to complete this sentence: This is the business or group or service that does _____ for you. You should promise a benefit, satisfy a need, or offer a distinctive service. The more you can make this something really different, the better. I know of no other way to do this except by doing your homework and finding out what other organizations have to offer. Then invent something you can offer that they don't."

We know that media exposure can sell products and even ideas, but can it actually motivate people to change their behavior? The answer, according to a case study discussed in *pr reporter*, is yes, if . . .

Despite "reams of research" that seemed to show that mass media can't change people's behavior, the Harvard School of Public Health "announced plans in 1988 to insert 'designated driver' messages into dialogue of popular TV shows like 'L.A. Law' and 'Cheers,' then supplement them with a battery of public service announcements." Since 1988, between 95 and 98 percent of the designated driver messages in the media have been placed there by the Harvard project.

According to the *pr reporter* article, the Harvard researchers found that "randomly rotated, arbitrarily directed" messages are not effective. But when the researchers involved media people in a partnership right from the outset, drew on research-based principles of behavioral change, and committed to a long-term process, they found they could actually measure the impact of the campaign. A progress report noted, "Seventy-eight percent of a national sample stated they'd noticed designated driver messages in . . . programming."

Researching Your Marketplace

No matter what kind of organization you work with, you have competition. There almost certainly are other businesses offering similar products or services; there may be other community organizations with different perspectives from yours; there's a likelihood that other nonprofit groups compete with yours. And there is always plenty of competition for people's time and attention.

So, even if yours is the only library in town, the only health club with Nautilus equipment north of the tracks, the only company that makes ginger beer in the state, or the only place in the county that rents power tools, people may not be convinced that they should be reading library books instead of watching TV, working out instead of hanging out, guzzling ginger beer instead of sipping champagne, or renting tools instead of buying a ready-made bookshelf. You have to convince them. And to do that, you have to *know* your marketplace well.

This is especially true if you are publicizing a product. "The number-one thing about product publicity," according to Bob Seltzer, executive vice president of Porter Novelli Public Relations in New York, "is you have to understand the marketplace and what the competition is. You must know what has been said and done already. These days, if you have Internet access, you have access to dozens of databases. So if you have a new contact lens cleaner, for example, you should be able to find literally dozens of stories that have been written on the subject of cleaning contact lenses during the last two, three, or four years."

Even though you can find a wealth of information on the Internet without charge, there will be times when it's worthwhile to use a paid database for your research. Critically important material may not be available from free websites. So, if your search for information produces no results, you should consider proprietary databases such as NEXIS or back issues of publications that charge you for access.

If you have never used fee-for-access on-line databases, you'll have to do some learning first. Some of the more complicated databases, such as NEXIS, offer one-day training sessions that teach you how to use their services efficiently. User skills are vital when you tackle databases, because you are charged by the minute. And those charges can be steep. Before you start using any database to research your marketplace, be sure you understand how and what you'll be charged for the following:

- Membership, maintenance, and minimum and monthly fees.
- The actual time you're connected to the service.
- The actual time you're connected to each database within that service. Many desirable databases have additional access fees.
- Printing out or saving information.
- "Global" searching of more than one database at the same time.
- Use of a high-speed modem, if you have one.

This may sound daunting, but it really isn't. Publicists who have used databases for marketplace research can't imagine how they ever did without them. And you may find that you actually enjoy calculating whether it's more cost-effective to subscribe to a specialized database or use a "gateway" service to access it once in a blue moon, without paying subscriber fees. Information on some of the more popular databases is listed in Chapter 13.

If you don't have access to a computer with a modem, do not despair. You can still do marketplace research at your library either the good, old-fashioned way, or on a public access computer that's connected to the Internet. Sure, library research will take longer, but it costs much less. And it gets the job done. You can also subscribe to one of the press clipping services listed in Chapter 13 and gather information about your marketplace, your competitors, and your industry from thousands of national and international publications. Or you can have one of the research services in Chapter 13 search databases for you.

Reaching Your Audience

Once you have chosen your audience, you have to decide the best way to reach it.

Less experienced publicists often take the shotgun approach and send publicity to every broadcaster and publication in the country. But if you want to get teenagers to buy your new line of grunge fashions, it would be a waste of time to direct material to a radio station with a big-band format and an over-50 audience. Why should a press release about workshops for young doctors establishing their practices be sent to a weekly community newspaper? Most readers of a community weekly will not be young doctors. This sort of release should go to a professional journal.

Says Teresa DiTore, community affairs director for WCBS-AM Newsradio in New York, "You would find it much more profitable if you took the time initially to do that little bit of research because you'd get more mileage out of your efforts. It is important to know who it is you are trying to reach, and go to that station."

You have to ask several questions before you decide which media will be best for your material. The answers, of course, will vary from one piece of publicity to another:

- Which stations, publications, or websites will reach the specific audience you want?
- How much credibility do those outlets have with their audiences?
- Will their staffs be interested in your material?
- Will their audiences be interested in your material?
- How much lead time is required?

Also keep in mind that media outlets with large and broad audiences are the most difficult publicity targets. Specialized media, on the other hand, often don't get enough material that fits their narrow focuses, so they may be eager to use yours. Since they specialize, they know enough about your material to give it knowledgeable treatment. So, it's worth searching for the highly specialized newsletters, magazines, trade journals, syndicated columns, websites, and even broadcast programs that reach exactly the audience you're targeting.

There are several ways to become familiar with the audience and format of media outlets. The directories listed in Chapter 13 are a useful source of such information and will help you send your material to only those publications and stations that reach your audience. But even though media directories are useful tools, you should go beyond them. "I put together my own media lists. I prefer to do the legwork—and the due diligence—on my own. Because media outlets change every 32.3 seconds and it is very difficult to get a list that is always up to date, unless you do it yourself," says Kimberly L. McCall, president of McCall Media & Marketing, Inc. of Freeport, Maine.

Remember that editors and broadcasters don't want you to send material they can't use. Also remember that media people respond better if you address your publicity material to them by name. A good set of media directories will give you hundreds and even thousands of names and titles. However, you need to watch out for a pitfall here. Journalists and editors change jobs, and even the best media directories start going out of date the moment they are printed. Therefore, you have to check the most important names on your media contact list periodically.

That's only the start. Mary Jane O'Neill of the New York Association for the Blind advises that you read any newspaper you are interested in and, "Find out the kind of stories it runs."

That's not as hard a task as it used to be, when you had to get physical copies of out-of-town newspapers. Kimberly McCall notes, "I have found media Web sites really helpful tools for understanding how to tailor make my publicity to each outlet's readership. It's so much easier now that I can read publications on-line rather than having a million subscriptions. In addition, I can sometimes get demographic information from a site's advertising section that gives me an even better idea of who the publication's readership is."

The same principle applies to broadcasters and magazines. There's no good reason for a publicist to waste time and effort approaching a media outlet that has no interest in the publicist's material. Yet, it happens all the time. KRBE-FM's Mike Martin says, "The publicist should take time before he sends anything or calls, to make sure that the format of the station fits the subject he's dealing with."

"*PC Magazine* has a very clear focus," according to Gus Venditto. "We cover *products* for IBM-compatible personal computers. We're not really interested in anything else." That should be clear to anyone who takes the time to read through an issue or two. But Venditto, like many other journalists, finds that often publicists don't bother: "We get a lot of calls from people who probably don't read the magazine. They often try to sell us stories about their users. We never run user stories. They're just not appropriate for us."

Selecting the Right Medium

To chose the best medium for your message, you first have to become familiar with the wide range of publicity tools available to you.

If you are going to approach your audience via the printed word, your choices will range from simple community calendar listings to full-length feature articles, from one-page press releases to short, attention-getting facts, in the form of fillers, about your organization, industry, product, service, or cause. Even letters to the editor are a good medium. All of these formats are discussed in detail in Chapter 4.

Should radio or TV be a more appropriate medium for your message, you can send out news releases and short features written especially for broadcasters, video news releases, public service announcements, or community calendar listings. Techniques for putting these together are covered in Chapter 8. Appearances on special programs and talk shows, either in person or by satellite hookup or telephone, are another important avenue for publicity, and Chapter 9 will help you prepare for them.

In addition, there are times when you will get the best publicity by having the media visit you, in which case you will want to plan a press conference or special event. Check Chapter 10 for tips on how to do this well.

Getting an Angle for Business Publicity

Throughout this book you will find examples of business publicity that got good media play. They all have one thing in common: the right angle. The angle, or news peg, is the slant that makes a story interesting. With the right angle, you can transform a situation that's not the least bit news-worthy into front-page coverage.

Developing a strong news angle for your publicity is even more impor-tant now than it used to be. There has been an explosion of press releases from Web-based and high-technology businesses—and most of them have weak news pegs or none at all. Journalists are up in arms because they are inundated with press releases that don't contain any news. If you want to get coverage, you need to have strong news pegs in *all* your publicity material.

Sometimes your business will make genuine news that stands on its own merits. If you announce that your firm is marketing a new solar water heater that sells for $50, is easy to install, and can make enough hot water for a family of four, you will get coverage, because that's news. That will have an impact on almost every person in the country.

But if you want people to replace their old TV antennae with your new model, you've got a problem. While special interest and trade magazines often *will* print a straight announcement of a new product, general inter-est and mass appeal media are harder to crack. You have to develop a "ser-vice" approach. If you provide material to editors that tells people how to install an antenna and how to solve TV reception problems, you're on the right track.

Judy Gail May, the principal of May Communications in Highland, New Jersey, did just that. Over a three-year period, she developed public-ity material for the Winegard Company, a manufacturer of TV antennae, including a regular newspaper column, TV interviews, public service spots, press releases, magazine articles, and speakers for radio talk shows. The result was a lot of coverage—*with the brand name mentioned.*

Virtually every businessperson can develop service material that will get media attention. After all, you are an expert on your product or ser-vice, so it shouldn't be too difficult for you to tell people how to choose, buy, or use it.

If you are the proud owner of a fine jewelry store, for example, you could write a short radio piece on how to invest in diamonds. A mill that produces high-quality whole-wheat pastry flour could provide the food edi-tors at newspapers across the country with a recipe for quick and easy chocolate layer cake. Since most people aren't aware that you can make a light, tasty cake from whole-grain flour, food editors will be interested.

Where do you think those recipes in the paper come from? The food editor's test kitchen? Not likely! The majority come from commercial sources, just like you. And you will probably be surprised to find that folks are waiting for your advice. This is the "how-to" era, and short, well-written material that can be read over the air or printed with minimal editing is in constant demand.

Testing and Evaluating Your Publicity

"How could they misunderstand that PSA?" moaned the publicist for the Chelm Public Library, holding his head in his hands. "It's perfectly clear. It says we have *books* that will help job seekers learn about the job market. It doesn't say we have *jobs*." Yet, misunderstand it they did. Hundreds of people who were out of work heard "job seekers." They were so desperate for work that that's all they heard, so they jammed the library switchboard with calls, asking for applications for "the job." They poured through the front doors by the dozens, asking where they could apply. The librarian got some of them to look at the collection of vocational guidance books, but most of the callers and visitors were angry. They felt they had been tricked. Whether they had been isn't the point. The point is that the publicist should have pretested his publicity material to help avoid problems like this.

Pretesting is especially important with public service announcements, but it's a good idea to pretest other kinds of publicity as well. Even the most seasoned publicist occasionally gets carried away and needs outside feedback to bring the earth back into contact with her feet.

That press release or PSA may make perfect sense to you, and even to your colleagues, but how do you know that your audience will actually get the message? After all, many people won't be familiar with your product, organization, service, or cause. This is why you should try out your message on as many people as you can find who are not acquainted with your group. If they are cynical and unsympathetic, so much the better; if you can communicate with unsympathetic cynics, you can communicate with anyone.

Of course, whenever possible, your test group should be made up of people in your target audience. The size of the group is up to you, but two dozen people will give you more accurate feedback than two or three individuals.

Once you have sent out your publicity material and it has been used by the media, make an effort to evaluate its impact. Whether you are asking people to call for more information or a free booklet, place an order, visit your store or their nearest dealer, or attend a special event, sale, or meeting, be sure you and your staff have a way to keep track of where people heard about you. It may sound simple, but there is no substitute for this information!

If your publicity calls for a response—such as phoning for a free kit, sending for a free booklet, or going to your website for free information, you can track the impact of your efforts by borrowing keying techniques from direct marketing. If you use unique key codes, you can tell exactly which publicity piece and which media outlet generated each response. While key coding takes extra work, the information you get can be worth its weight in gold!

- Use extension numbers after your telephone number—and be sure your staff records an extension number for every caller.
- Use a department number or room number in your address.
- Set up tracking pages with unique URLs on your website. (URL stands for Uniform Resource Locator, a fancy name for a website address.) The URLs for these tracking pages must be kept simple; for example: xyzwidgets/10, xyzwidgets/11, and xyzwidgets/12. Be certain you'll be able to break out traffic statistics for each unique URL.

Press Clipping Services

Press clipping bureaus are an important source of information for publicists, especially if your publicity is getting picked up by wire services and syndicates and you're getting newspaper coverage in distant cities and states.

You may want to subscribe to one or two of the press clipping services listed in Chapter 13. These services scan thousands of newspapers, magazines, and websites, and monitor hundreds of television talk shows and news programs, looking for mention of your product or organization. Or you can give them subject areas that are of interest to your group, and they will supply you with newspaper, magazine, and website clippings or broadcast transcripts mentioning the keywords or names you give them.

You may wish to use one of the software programs or clipping services to develop reports that pinpoint the quantity of media exposure you receive; the number of mentions of your product or organization; the amount of favorable, unfavorable, and mixed coverage; and the number of people your publicity reaches. One of the clipping services has the capability to index and store your clippings *and* the publicity materials that generated them on a high-density optical disk. Although this additional service is expensive, it can transmute file drawers of material into a package you can hold in your hand.

Whenever you use a clipping service, find out what *all* the fees are before you sign a contract. You'll probably pay a monthly reading fee and a charge per clipping. Ask if there are any other fees, such as minimum monthly charges.

Surveys

Counting clippings is a good start in evaluating your publicity program, but it measures quantity, not impact. Yes, it's nice to get a bundle of clippings from Peoria, Pecos, Portland, Pensacola, Pittsburgh, and Poughkeepsie, but the quantity of clippings should not be the only way you measure success. The real questions are what the clippings said about your group, how many people saw them, and what impact they had. Analyzing clippings is no problem if your publicity generates just a dozen or two. But if your organization is a major publicity player, you'll have to give some thought to how you want to organize and analyze that torrent of news clips—and how you want to measure their impact on the public.

To accomplish your purpose, you may have to conduct a survey. Surveys are most helpful when you can use numbers to make a before-and-after comparison. For example, if only 17 percent of the senior citizens in your service area knew about your special insurance products for older adults before you started your publicity efforts, but 35 percent were familiar with them after six months of publicity, you have a concrete idea of your effectiveness. Unfortunately, it isn't always possible to obtain such neat figures. But even if you can't, surveys can still be useful.

It is possible for you to do a small survey yourself on the telephone or in person. Watch out for one common mistake: If you limit your questions to the customers of your store, the buyers of your products, the people who come to your antibusing meetings, or the patrons of your library, you won't find out what noncustomers, busing proponents, or nonusers of the library are thinking. So, keep these simple rules of thumb in mind:

- Unless you are seeking the opinions of a specialized group, such as doctors, senior citizens, or people with a Hispanic background, make sure your survey includes people who are a representative cross section of the geographic area you are interested in.
- When you are looking for a cross section, set quotas and make sure your interviewers fill them. Otherwise, they will tend to interview the types of people with whom they are most comfortable.
- Always keep your questions short, and make them specific.
- Allow time and space for unstructured comments; these can be most valuable.
- Limit yourself to one topic in an interview. More than that will only confuse people.

If you are conducting a before-and-after survey, be sure to ask the same questions both times. Otherwise, you are likely to get different results from your two questionnaires even without publicity.

If you don't know anything about doing surveys and you need more information to do them on your own, look at *State of the Art Marketing Research* by George Breen, listed in Chapter 13. Although it is geared toward marketing people in firms selling products, the basic techniques for doing surveys can be adapted by sellers of services as well as by nonprofit and community organizations, special interest groups, and government agencies. If you don't have the time or the staff to do your own survey, or you need a sample that is larger than you can get on your own, you may want to contact one of the opinion research firms in Chapter 13. Many opinion research outfits have an "omnibus" plan, where you can cut costs by adding your questions to a regional or national survey.

Preparing Your Organization for Publicity

Another important aspect of your function involves setting up the structures and procedures that will make it possible for your organization to support your publicity efforts. If you are to work effectively, your authority must be clearly outlined and understood by the board of directors, top executives, and the other members of your organization. The channels of communication must be established among you, top executives, and the rest of the staff, as well as between your organization and the media. You also need to make sure that you have an adequate budget.

Defining Your Authority

Find out, first of all, exactly what your role within the organization will be:

- How much authority will you have?
- What kinds of decisions will need approval?
- Who will review your work, and at what point?
- Can you turn down requests for publicity by members or staff of your organization? Under what circumstances?
- Will you be able to write copy for publicity material yourself, or will that be done by a committee? Bear in mind that writing by committee is cumbersome and time-consuming, and you have deadlines to meet. It is possible to play four-hand piano, but four-hand word processor is not practical. Try to arrange it so that only one person writes copy.

It is tremendously important that these decisions be made ahead of time and written down to prevent confusion later on. The answers to these questions may seem apparent, but many organizations do not consider what becomes obvious only with hindsight.

In most organizations, the publicist should be responsible to the executive director, president, or vice president of marketing or communications. In smaller groups that do not have professional staffs, publicists should report directly to the governing body. The only way you can know what you need to know is by having a clear channel right to the top. Don't settle for less, or you may well find yourself hamstrung by complicated procedures for getting information and approving your work. Complicated procedures mean time wasted. And publicists, who live by deadlines, can't waste time.

There is another reason why you need access to the top. "You can't fabricate publicity with some kind of machine. You can't publicize what isn't happening," says Harry Cohn, director of public relations for the American Red Cross in Greater New York. "So you should be involved in whether your organization is carrying out its programs and services well. Because if it's not, you're in real trouble."

Increasingly, innovative corporations are integrating public relations and publicity into their marketing plans. "Publicity is a marketing tool and I think it's very foolish to try to separate it from the ongoing marketing plan," says Bob Seltzer of Porter Novelli Public Relations. Because this integration is a new strategy, some executives may not realize that they have to bring the publicist into the discussions up front, where you can make the strongest contribution. You may have to persuade them to include you.

Publicists also have to be concerned about public and media reaction to their organizations, industries, and product lines, because bad public opinion will undermine the effectiveness of even the best publicity program. Since the publicist gets continual feedback on how the public views the organization or product, she should be considered an organizational resource and have input into policy making.

Setting Up Internal Communications

Make sure that there is a systematic way for you to know what is happening in your organization or business. A publicist has to know in advance what everyone in the organization is doing. Nothing can undermine your credibility with the media faster than inaccurate or incomplete knowledge of your organization.

Another part of the publicist's task is to tell the staff, volunteers, and membership about the publicity plan and program. If the publicity effort is new, or if it has had a bad reputation in the past, you will need to convince these people that your efforts are worthwhile and worth supporting. Otherwise, you may find that the people who answer the telephone "don't know about" the program you just publicized, that the sales staff have "never heard of" the free product literature and special offer, or that the organization's staff or members make statements to the press that contradict yours.

Leslie O'Bergin, former reporter for the *Santa Cruz Independent* in California, puts it bluntly: "If the publicist is going to be contradicted by other people in the organization when I call for more information, she has no use whatsoever to that organization. She is, in fact, a liability."

Communication between the group and the publicist is not a one-way street. The publicist should meet regularly with his or her supervisor or the governing body of the organization. Since publicity involves continual deadlines, fast responses, and occasional crises, there should be a provision for quick and sudden consultation.

Always tell your supervisor, key executives, or the governing body exactly what you are doing and why—before you do it. It is particularly important that they know beforehand about material that is to appear in the media. Otherwise, they may miss that television special you worked so hard to prepare, or, even worse, the media may call them for comment and catch them by surprise. Be certain that everyone in authority in your organization gets information from you first.

"We communicate to all of our staff, nationwide, the moment we get major media coverage," says Dennis Bowman, senior vice president of communication at the Arthritis Foundation. "If an arthritis story is on the 'Today Show,' we can either alert our staff in advance, or we can immediately E-mail them a statement that's consistent for all our offices across the country. When they get calls from the public about the coverage, or local reporters are doing local angle stories, our staff in the field can respond with the facts and our organization's position. We also include typical media questions and suggested responses."

In the worst of all possible cases, the publicist for the Chelm Committee Against Air Pollution invited the press to be present at a training session that was to prepare participants for the upcoming nonviolent occupation of the nearby site for a proposed coal-fired generating plant. The publicist had been told by several members of the group that inviting the press was permissible, but there had never been any discussion within the group about who could make this sort of decision. When the television crews appeared at the training session, the participants, who had not been told the media might appear, angrily turned them away. The result was some very negative publicity.

Setting Up External Communications

When your organization approaches the media, it should not speak with many tongues. Be certain your key executives, staff, membership, volunteers, and board all know that only one person should approach the media. Not only will this make it easier for you to develop working relationships and credibility with journalists, but also it will avoid the confusion so easily caused by having two or more spokespeople.

Journalist Leslie O'Bergin expresses the preference of many media people: "I expect to work with one spokesperson from the group. I don't like it when one person calls me this week and another contacts me next week. It indicates either total incoherence or conflict within the organization."

John Canelli, news director of WAVI-FM in Dayton, Ohio, says that continually changing publicists is "the same thing as continually changing reporters. The reason why you like to give a reporter a beat is simply for the reason of contacts and knowledge. You have to build rapport and trust."

If it is absolutely necessary to split up the publicity work, try to have one person for newspapers, another handling radio, and a third working with TV. Or assign spokespeople on a regional basis. This will allow each person to develop ongoing working relationships and to learn over a period of time how to work best with individual contacts. If you decide on this plan, make sure that everyone involved communicates with the others on a regular, formal basis.

When the media come to you, however, it is better to speak with many tongues. If the publicist or the executive director or the president is the only person who can talk to callers from the media, that person will be overburdened, and other people in the organization who may have the expertise to answer questions will feel left out. You should encourage those with expertise to answer routine media questions and then to let the publicist know with whom they spoke and what they said. If there are any exceptions, such as controversial situations, disasters, or emergencies, these should be spelled out—in advance.

Having more than one person available to answer questions from newspapers and broadcasters has another benefit. Says Fred Kirsch, a reporter for the *Ledger-Star* in Norfolk, Virginia, "A lot of times you'll call an office and there's only one person who is authorized to tell you something. And they're out for the day. That can get frustrating because we always need information *now*. Newspapers never give us enough time, so we're always saying, 'Hurry up, we want the information!' The more people we can talk with in an organization, the better."

Still, there are some executive directors, board members, and officers who want the publicist to handle all calls from the media. And an occasional publicist will resent a reporter's request to talk with someone higher up. Cindy Loose, a reporter for the *Staten Island Register* in New York, explains why she needs to talk with an organization's officers: "Publicists often don't really understand the importance of quotes. You might call a public relations department and get some facts and figures. But if it's a pressing issue of the day, you have to quote somebody. You don't want to quote a publicist; you want to quote a president or a vice-president. I think publicists should be aware that sometimes, even if you've gotten all the information from them, you still need to talk with an officer of the organization because you want to quote them. It's not a slight of the publicist."

One final point: it's always wise to have written guidelines for staff, volunteers, and members on how they should deal with the media.

Staffing the Telephone

You sent out a fantastic press release on a major story, but no one from the media has called you about it. Or have they? Maybe they tried to reach you, but there was no answer. Reporters who were interested in your story could have been discouraged by endless busy signals or eternal waiting on hold. Perhaps their deadlines came and went, and they couldn't run the story without some clarification. So, it died, and it's being buried right now, in the landfill outside of town, with the rest of the rubbish. Or even worse, after they failed to reach you, they *were* able to contact your competitors or your opposition. And they wrote a major story. Without any involvement from you. It happens all the time.

Jack O'Dwyer's Newsletter mentions a media relations study in which 300 business journalists were interviewed. "According to the findings . . . 28 percent said executives either did not return their phone calls or returned them too late."

But there's no reason *you* should lose important publicity opportunities just because journalists can't reach you! You can prevent problems with a good system for receiving and answering calls from the media. Your reputation with reporters depends on it. This is particularly important for small groups that don't have a staff or headquarters, and for larger businesses where reporters can get entangled in layers of bureaucracy and red tape.

Don't expect a busy reporter to keep calling you until you finally answer. Carol Rissman, news director for WBUR-FM in Boston, speaks for most journalists when she says that she is "likely to try again with a major story. But I am not likely to try again more than once, and I am not likely to try again on another day."

If you do not have an office, or if you staff it on a part-time basis, you can get by with voice mail—if you promptly return journalists' calls. If your office is open full-time during business hours, make sure that whoever takes messages from media people is clear and complete.

Try to have a direct telephone line that bypasses the switchboard and layers of voice mail prompts that lead nowhere, so reporters don't get caught in that quagmire. The person who answers that direct line should understand the constant deadline pressure media people work with. In fact, he or she should read this book, too. Also, whether your calls are answered by machine or in person, you have to respond to your messages quickly.

"It is a very, very bad idea to issue a press release unless you, or someone else who is qualified, will be in your office for the next few days to field questions or e-mail from journalists who need more information to write stories. You also need to be prepared to handle calls from other time zones around the world. It is important to be at your desk," says Tina Koenig, the CEO of Xpress Press, a press release distribution service.

With the availability of pagers and cell phones, there is no excuse for being out of touch with the media. If you don't have these tools, your publicity efforts will be handicapped. You should include your cell phone and pager numbers on all your publicity materials.

As Dennis Bowman of the Arthritis Foundation explains, "The Internet has speeded up communications, so you have to respond more quickly to arising issues. It puts the onus on us to have our experts and spokespeople prepared and ready to go at a moment's notice. Sometimes we have to respond to new studies on arthritis instantly within an hour after they are released. It used to be we had 24 hours or even a few days to prepare a response. Now we have an almost instant process to get positions written, passed on by experts, and distributed the same day or the next day to the whole staff."

Finally, if you are doing product publicity, "Have your product ready to ship [to journalists] overnight, if necessary," says Tina Koenig. If you're publicizing high-tech products, don't assume that journalists will agree to download product samples; they may require boxed copies. Although this is changing, find out first. As Koenig explains, "Now I see many fewer requests for [boxed] evaluation copies that need to be sent by mail. Many more journalists are willing to cover products that are available strictly through downloading on the Web. [Publicists] can include a link to their Web site in the release, and the journalists can easily download the product, and get the ball rolling—especially if they are working on a tight deadline."

Being prepared for calls from the media is only one side of the coin. The other side is responding to calls from the public generated by your publicity.

Touting the new subsidized suburban industrial park with no taxes on new enterprises for the next 10 years, the Chelm Chamber of Commerce sent out a news release to every paper in the country. The release got tremendous press play, and thousands of executives read it. Unfortunately, the phone number in the press release was for a single telephone line, so most callers got a busy signal. And since the secretarial staff hadn't been told about the release, prospects who did get through found that their questions weren't answered and the secretaries had not heard about the free booklet mentioned in the release.

If you expect your publicity to generate telephone calls, remember to have enough lines available to handle the response and to brief the people who will be answering those calls! If you expect a publicity campaign to generate more response from the public than you can handle, consider hiring a telemarketing firm. Very large telemarketers are set up so they can handle the sudden spikes in call volume that come from radio and television coverage. The representatives at leading telemarketing firms have complete information about each client's campaign in front of them on their computer screens. You may even find that a telemarketing service representative does a better job of handling inquiries from the public than your own staff does.

Making a Budget

Even if you plan to do all the work yourself, you still have to spend money on your publicity. You will need funds for copying and distributing news releases, photographers' fees, film and developing costs, telephone calls, and office supplies. If your organization does not have that money, you will have to raise it, or you won't be able to do a decent job of publicity. If you are convinced that publicity is important for your organization, you'll figure out where the money will come from.

It is a good idea to make a list of every possible publicity expense and then add 25 percent to cover emergencies such as natural disasters, product recalls, controversy—or even more good news than you had planned for.

As you draw up your budget, try to project the rough cost of handling the response to your publicity. If you're sending out publicity material offering free pamphlets on how to choose, buy, and use your product, how much will it cost to handle the inquiries, print the pamphlets, and mail them? Will that cost be justified on your bottom line?

Of course, there are times when your publicity's value just can't be measured. But when it can, you will have to design a yardstick that works in your situation. Make sure you understand exactly how top management expects you to measure bottom-line success, so the yardstick you design gives you figures that are acceptable to the top executives in your organization.

Success itself can be a problem. What would you do if every radio and TV station in town ran your PSAs for the new drug addiction treatment center, and hundreds of people showed up, all wanting immediate attention? Suppose the requests for that product literature you publicized nationally are 10 times larger than you expected? What will that do to your budget? Will management look beyond the increased publicity expense and see the net result of increased sales? If they don't, you'll have to help them focus on the fattened bottom line rather than the overruns in your publicity budget. This isn't likely to happen often, but success on an unexpected scale has caused problems for some organizations.

If your publicity is going to reach large numbers of people, and you are asking for a personal response, "You should always have a contingency plan outlining how you intend to handle large numbers of responses," says Harriet S. Schimel, communications director of the United Negro College Fund. "I think your basic concern, no matter how overwhelming the response, is that you want the public to feel that you're accessible." You want to convey the message that even though you're temporarily over-whelmed by the response, you'll follow through as soon as possible—and deliver whatever it is your publicity promised.

If you work for a large organization, a carefully prepared budget will gain you management's respect and make planning easier. Your budget should probably be a functional one that explains the purpose of major expenses, along with specific goals your publicity program is moving toward, and how much each goal will cost.

The budget should include staff salaries. That helps management understand how much you're spending now and why you will need more to accomplish additional tasks. You may also calculate overhead expenses at the rate of one dollar for every dollar spent on payroll.

Once you have established a budget, it's up to you to protect it. For example, if a top executive asks you to add to a publicity plan at the last minute, tell her how much it will cost. That may stop the addition dead—or get you an increased budget. And it's less likely that you'll be left hang-ing, expected to accomplish something without the dollars you need.

So far, we have looked at ways in which you can prepare your organi-zation for the publicity effort. Before launching your campaign, you should also consider taking some precautionary measures. These include getting preventive legal advice, setting up emergency procedures in case plans go awry, and keeping good records of your own actions to protect yourself from unwarranted criticism after the fact.

Checking Legal Angles

It's wise to discuss your publicity plans with an attorney on an ongoing basis to see if there are any legal angles that may affect your campaigns. This is especially important if you plan to write material designed to influ-ence legislation. In some areas, you may be required to register as a lob-byist, and there could be legal problems if you fail to do this. Your lawyer will also be able to advise you on model releases for photographs, the use of quotations from copyrighted material, and questions connected with libel and slander.

If you work for the federal government or an organization funded with federal money, ask your counsel how your publicity program will be affected by the act of Congress, dated October 23, 1913, that forbids government employment of public relations personnel. Publicists who work for government agencies or organizations that are funded by public money should ask how public disclosure or "sunshine" laws affect their publicity programs.

An area in which you must be *very* careful when you do publicity is litigation. Never comment on a case that is on trial unless you clear it with your lawyer first, or you may be held in contempt of court. While publicity can be a useful tool for winning legal battles, particularly when it's important to explain legal issues to the public, you must work closely with your legal team.

A story reported in *PR News* describes one example of teamwork between lawyers and publicists.

"In 1988, Detroit-based Casey Communications Management, Inc. (CCM), Southfield, MI, made shareholders [of the R. P. Scherer Corporation (RPS)] aware of their own best interests and helped them win a bitter, court-contested proxy fight." When RPS's board of directors refused to sell the company, brother and sister Karla and John S. Scherer, the largest shareholders, asked CCM to work out a "communications strategy, targeted toward RPS's shareholders, securities analysts, and investment bankers. . . ." And CCM did just that.

Working closely with their clients' lawyers, CCM used publicity to get their message across to shareholders, who often don't pay much attention to mailed stockholder bulletins. Since the story involved some courtroom drama in which the Scherers's lawyers battled the company's board, it received extensive coverage.

CCM helped tilt media commentary in their clients' favor "by responding directly to reporters' questions and being available night and day to service the media. In contrast, the old guard of the company usually responded to reporters with a 'no comment.' As a result, media response was generous and articles giving [the Scherers'] position usually appeared the morning after a late-afternoon release."

In conclusion, "The campaign literally paid big dividends," according to *PR News*. "After two candidates nominated by the Scherers were elected to the Board of Directors and confirmed, the Board voted unanimously to explore options for sale of the company. In May, 1989, RPS was sold to the highest bidder . . . for a price that doubled the value of the shares."

While the Scherers might have been able to force the old board of directors to sell the company strictly with a court-ordered action, using publicity to win shareholder support made it much more likely they'd achieve their objectives.

Media publicity can also be used to help ward off frivolous lawsuits. Joel Strasser, senior vice president and managing director of Dorf & Stanton Technology Communications, explains how his firm helped inform corporations that challenging his client's patent was going to be fruitless:

"About every five years or so," says Strasser, "somebody tried to challenge Olof Soderblom's patent to the token ring technology." This was once the main method of local area networking for personal computers, and a lot of people in the computer industry thought token ring was invented by IBM.

"It wasn't," according to Strasser. "Soderblom owns the patent. And he insists on royalties. But who wants to pay the bill collector?"

Although Soderblom's company, Willemijn Holding B.V., successfully sued three companies that were withholding payment, still another business tried to challenge the validity of his patent. In order to build support in the industry, the challenger was trying to get the trade press on its side. A number of negative articles appeared about how the Soderblom patents were going to be knocked down.

"To counter this inaccurate press coverage, we booked him on a very intensive U.S. media tour, aimed at data processing publications," says Strasser.

Exhibit 1.1 on pages 30 and 31 is a sample of the press releases Dorf & Stanton sent out to dozens of high-tech publications. In addition, Strasser issued announcements every time another large corporation signed a token ring licensing agreement with Willemijn. He provided the press with a backgrounder on Soderblom's token ring invention which described in plain English how it was developed and how it works, and he offered journalists interviews with the inventor.

The resulting coverage was extensive. For example, *MIS Week*, a prestigious data processing publication, did a major personal profile on how Soderblom got the patent and what he's had to do to hold on to it. Because of this coverage, any corporation that is considering a suit to overturn the Soderblom token ring patent likely will realize that it is tackling a formidable enemy with a battle-hardened fortress. While it's true that you can't measure the number of lawsuits that won't be initiated, the savings in legal fees could be far higher than the cost of the publicity campaign.

Exhibit 1.1

Willemijn Holding BV

FOR IMMEDIATE RELEASE

Contact: Joel A. Strasser or Jim Lawler
Dorf & Stanton
(212) 420-8100
(800) 223-2121 Outside NY
George Vande Sande
(202) 331-7111
Olof Soderblom
011-44-372-378538

WILLEMIJN EXPECTS PATENT OFFICE TO UPHOLD TOKEN RING RIGHTS

ROTTERDAM, May 24—Confident of a successful conclusion, Willemijn Holding B.V., owner of the Soderblom token ring patent, today indicated that it is expediting the reexamination proceeding in the U.S. Patent and Trademark Office relating to the Soderblom patent. The reexamination proceeding based upon the request by an anonymous party, was instituted last month.

Forgoing its right to file an objection with the Patent Office, Willemijn announces that it has instead requested that the reexamination be undertaken promptly. Willemijn says it is likely that the Patent Office will issue an initial rejection of some of the patent's broad claim. This, of course, does not in any way affect the enforceability of the patent. However, such a rejection clears the way for prompt submission of a full response by Willemijn's attorneys.

Willemijn Vice Chairman and token ring inventor Olof Soderblom said, "Given the utter lack of merit of the arguments put forth by the anonymous requestor, we are confident that the Patent Office will reaffirm the broad scope and validity of the patent."

Soderblom's patent, originally issued in 1982, was reissued in 1985 following Willemijn's invitation to potential licensees to file with the Patent Office whatever protests they deemed appropriate. Six such protests were filed but each was dismissed by the Patent Office in granting the broader claims contained in the reissue patent.

MORE   MORE   MORE

To date, more than 50 companies, including such household names as IBM, NCR, Hewlett Packard, Hitachi, and Toshiba have accepted licenses from Willemijn under the Soderblom patent. Since last June, three infringement suits have been successfully settled, each resulting in a license and compensation for past infringement. Consent decrees have been entered by two Courts, acknowledging the validity of the Soderblom patent.

###

Preparing for the Unexpected

"People involved in publicity should be aware of *all* the things that can go wrong, so they can develop plans to cope with emergencies," says Harriet Schimel.

What plans do you have in case your carefully created publicity program for that super-improved widget is scooped by a competitor with an even better design? What if your volunteer publicist suddenly becomes ill: do you have people standing by who will be able to pick up where your sick volunteer stopped? Suppose the governor calls a particularly important press conference and your previously arranged television and radio programs are preempted: does this mean your event will fail? Or do you have an alternate plan for reaching the public? Part of planning publicity involves making a list of every possible thing that can go wrong, as well as what you will do when that happens. Merely drawing up such a list will help you design your plans to avoid the obvious problems.

Consider in advance who your opposition may be and how you will handle them. Let's say that your geranium fanciers group wants to donate potted plants in bloom to the local hospital to cheer the patients. No one would object to that public-spirited act of charity, right? Better think again! How will the florist across from the hospital feel about your idea? Does the proprietor have friends on the hospital's board of directors? He does? Well, you better start planning!

This is a deliberately extreme case. A geranium lovers group is perhaps the least controversial organization possible. And that is the point. There is probably no organization that will not run into hostility and opposition at some time. Your publicity efforts will be vastly more effective if you think through your plans for handling opposition before it surfaces.

At a time when you least expect it, you will have to be ready to deal with "breaking" news: events that happen suddenly and that demand media coverage, such as fires, crimes, and accidents. San Francisco journalist Nancy Dunn explains, "Even with breaking news, you can be prepared to some extent. You should know media deadlines; you should know who to contact. And you should have the telephone and fax numbers for direct lines to newspaper and broadcast newsrooms, so you can reach them when the switchboards are closed at night or on weekends." This is particularly important in crisis situations. If *you* don't provide information during an emergency, reporters and the public may speculate about what is really going on. And those speculations can be far more damaging to an organization than the facts.

You should also decide who in your organization needs to be told about a breaking news event. Reporters may call officers or board members for comment, and you will want to give your people the information they need and a chance to think through their responses.

Handling controversy and dealing with the unexpected are discussed in detail in Chapters 10 and 11.

Protecting Yourself from Criticism

You may find some important hidden attitudes emerging as you try to clarify your role and develop your publicity plan. If you are involved in a nonprofit organization, community or special interest group, or government human-services agency, your organization's executives and board of directors may look down on publicity. Says Richard Weiner, owner of a public relations firm in New York and author of eight books on public relations, "Sometimes . . . there is a feeling that public relations is sleazy, improper, and immoral, and that the organization shouldn't really be doing this."

A common hidden attitude among corporate executives is that the publicist can *make* the media print or broadcast anything—even self-serving puff and fluff with no facts, figures, or news value. If you think your colleagues have either of these attitudes, even if they don't actually say so, make sure there is an honest discussion. Otherwise, these prejudices will return to haunt and hobble you again and again.

In addition, you should take some specific precautions when you are serving as a publicist, no matter how much you trust the people you are working with:

- Get information for press releases, public service announcements, and other publicity materials in writing. This is a valuable way to avoid misunderstandings.
- Follow up all conversations, both within your organization and with the media, by writing confirming memos. This is another way to be sure that everyone involved in the publicity effort agrees on the outcome.
- If other people in your organization have to approve your publicity material, ask them to initial it. They will give it more careful consideration this way, and many problems can be avoided.
- Keep copies of everything you write, including memos and interview notes, particularly if you are quoting others.
- When you quote someone in a news release, be sure to send that person a copy ahead of time. Include a note asking him or her to initial the release and send it back to you. If someone later claims to have been misquoted, you can put an end to that potential problem very quickly.

Keep good records. Questions about publicity material can arise several years after the material has been released, and by that time your memory may be pretty foggy. Suppose that some of your ardent supporters—or disgruntled customers—turn against your organization and decide to seek revenge for a real or imagined gripe. They take you to court, alleging that you libelously misquoted them in a press release five years ago. Your defense will be much easier if you still have the notes from your interviews and the copy of the release, with their initials on it, neatly filed away.

Keeping Expectations Realistic

No matter how carefully you plan and how hard you work, it is easy to expect too much from your publicity efforts, especially at first. Says journalist Nancy Dunn, "The amateur publicist is often marked by an unreasonable expectation about what one person in a media organization can or should do for his group."

Not every event is front-page material. And not every new product is a cover story. "If it isn't a landmark product," says *PC Magazine*'s Gus Venditto, a small product review is the best you can hope for. You should be grateful for it, because it's all you can expect."

Even if you get full cooperation from a reporter, and your group is covered in a front-page story with pictures, or on prime-time TV, many people won't read the paper or watch that channel that day. And those who do read the paper may not see your story; if they see it, they may not read it. If they read it or see it on TV, they still may not absorb or remember it. Because people are bombarded with communications in newspapers, radio, TV, magazines, websites, direct mail, and billboards, it takes hundreds of repetitions of your message to break through the clutter.

Creating publicity is like weaving a fabric. Each newspaper story, each radio public service announcement, each TV appearance, is another strand. It takes a lot of strands to make the yarn that weaves the cloth. And since the fabric is constantly unraveling, as people, following that all-too-human tendency, forget previous messages, you will have to weave rapidly and continuously.

"I don't think you can say, 'This press release yields that amount of business,'" says Gary Blake of the Communication Workshop. "That's asking too much. Publicity sets the scene and indirectly leads to new business." But when your publicity is on target, it can be a fruitful scene.

You should now have a good sense of how to plan your publicity program. In the following chapters you will learn the specific skills you need to get your organization the kind of publicity it deserves. There will still be situations, however, when all the skills of Madison Avenue won't get you the time of day from the media. If your group is controversial or your product is new and innovative, you may find that the media ignore you. American newspapers and broadcasters are often heavily geared toward middle-of-the-road, noncontroversial material.

If your publicity material for newsworthy events is good and you get no play from the press or airtime from broadcasters, you have an access problem. If this is the case, your task is more complex but certainly not hopeless. Chapter 11 examines access to the media and what you can do about such blockages.

As you read through this book, some examples of situations may seem not to apply to you because your product, service, or cause is "different." Don't let the "facts" deter you from the theory. The examples are selected to illustrate problems and principles that apply to all publicity programs, no matter who runs them. It will be a good exercise for you to translate the examples to fit your situation.

Small-town publicists will find that their tasks are not as complex as those of their city cousins; media people will be easier to work with, and there will be shortcuts that just aren't possible for urban publicists. But the principles behind a good publicity program are the same in Clinton, Arkansas (population 2,213), as they are in New York City.

Checklist—Your Role as Publicist

1. What are your organization's publicity goals?
2. Have you written them down?
3. Do they include specific figures?
4. Have you set publicity priorities for your organization?
5. Do you have criteria for separating major and minor stories?
6. Who, exactly, is your intended audience?
7. Can you break it into subgroups?
8. What misconceptions do people have about your product, service, cause, or issue?
9. How can you use these misconceptions in your publicity?
10. How will you motivate your audience?
11. If you're trying to change the public's behavior, can you make a long-term commitment to do this?
12. Have you made a list of your product, service, or organizational benefits for your audience?
13. Have you made a written list of your competitors?
14. Do you know what's been written and said in the media about your product, service, and industry in the last few years?
15. Have you explored how you could use the Internet and on-line databases to research your marketplace?
16. Have you taken a few minutes to read the help file for each Internet search engine you plan to use, so your searches will be quicker and more accurate?

17. Are you aware of all the fees and charges for the paid database you've chosen?
18. Which are the best broadcast stations and publications for reaching your audience?
19. Are you familiar with their formats?
20. Have you included newsletters, trade and special interest magazines, and Web-based publications on your release list?
21. Have you figured out one or more "service" approaches for publicity material that teaches people how to choose, buy, and use your product or service?
22. How will you pretest your publicity material?
23. How will you evaluate its impact?
24. Have you got management to agree on a bottom-line yardstick for measuring the results of your publicity?
25. Do you have a system for keeping track of where people read or hear about you?
26. Have you decided how you will gather and evaluate all your press clippings?
27. How much authority will you, as publicist, have?
28. Is your role in the organization clear?
29. Will you be involved in developing marketing strategies?
30. Does your organization have a written publicity plan?
31. Who will review your work?
32. Have you determined what decisions need to be approved, and who has to approve them?
33. How will you know what is happening in the organization?
34. How will you inform the staff, membership, board, officers, and executives about the publicity program?
35. Does your organization have a written policy about who can approach the media and who can respond to questions from the media?
36. How will you receive and respond to telephone calls from the media? The public?
37. Do you have a cell phone and a pager? Will you include their numbers on all your publicity materials?
38. Have you drawn up a publicity budget?
39. Does your budget include extra funds for emergencies and unexpected response to your publicity?

40. Do you have a plan for handling a larger-than-expected response to your publicity?
41. Do you have written emergency and contingency plans?
42. Have you arranged to consult an attorney?
43. Will your publicity arouse any opposition to your organization?
44. Do you have plans to handle possible opposition?
45. Have you developed a means to measure the profitability of each publicity effort?
46. Do you know if people in your nonprofit organization have doubts about the validity of publicity?
47. If they do, have you discussed these doubts with them?
48. Do you know if executives in your organization believe that the publicist can "make" the media run anything, regardless of news value?
49. Have you addressed this attitude?
50. Are you keeping written records to document the information you use in your publicity?
51. Are you following up conversations with confirming memos?
52. Do you have approved copy for all publicity materials, with initials or signatures, particularly for copy involving direct quotes?

2

Working Effectively with the Media

M edia people need publicists. Even the largest publications and broadcasters, with the largest staffs, can't be everywhere at once. So, journalists count on publicists to help them cover the bases.

"There is no medium—not the *Journal of the American Medical Association*, not the editorial pages of the *New York Times*, not the columns of the *Catholic Digest*—that is off limits for the publicist," says public relations executive Richard Weiner. "Neophyte publicists may think that there are some areas where media people—namely columnists, editorial page writers, and radio and television commentators—do not rely on public relations assistance, or that they resent suggestions. That is absolutely not true."

On the other hand, if you listen to what many journalists are saying, publicists are a scourge that makes the 10 plagues visited on ancient Egyptians seem like a dress rehearsal. "I cannot remember the last useful phone call I've received from a PR representative," says Joel Garreau, the Features/Lifestyle assignment editor for the *Washington Post*, as quoted in *Soft•letter*, a newsletter and website serving the software publishing industry (www.softletter.com).

If journalists need publicists, how can Garreau—and dozens of other journalists *Soft•letter* interviewed—be so vehemently critical of publicists? There is an explanation, and if you understand it, you can use it to gain a competitive edge for *your* publicity efforts.

Soft•letter's editors explain the situation: "There are signs that high-tech public relations has become a victim of its own success. As budgets get fatter, the result is a glut of unread news releases." This glut impacts all fields, across the board, but it's especially severe in the high-tech and Internet business arenas. That's because competitive pressures push these companies to issue huge numbers of releases. That may be tolerable, but the demand for publicity from high-tech companies and newly minted dot-coms struggling to survive has outstripped the supply of seasoned, trained publicists.

"Because there is such a boom in new technology businesses, PR firms are finding it difficult to staff," says Tina Koenig, the CEO of Xpress Press, a press release distribution service. "So you get a lot of young and less experienced PR people. Reporters are not thrilled with having to work with these newcomers because they do not have in-depth background information on the products they're promoting. And they don't know the rules of the game. They are calling at deadline times, and they are not asking if it's a good time to talk."

There are publicists who can't write a news story. And strange as it may sound, there are publicists who can't even explain the product they're pitching. "I frequently get calls from junior account execs that cannot describe the product they are pitching, other than reading the boilerplate," says Carolyn Healey of supportindustry.com, as quoted in *Soft•letter*. David Kirkpatrick, an editor at *Fortune* magazine, concurs. "It's quite frequent that after a two-minute phone or e-mail pitch I . . . have little or no understanding of what the company does," he told *Soft•letter's* readers.

No wonder journalists are furious. They're deluged with press releases and phone calls that are not newsworthy. It makes their jobs much harder. And, as *Soft•letter* explains, "The day-to-day interaction between PR people and the media is increasingly adversarial" as a result.

The tidal wave of poorly conceived and written publicity material is infuriating to journalists, but it presents an opportunity for you. If you apply the principles you are learning in this book to your publicity, it will stand head and shoulders above the glut. Journalists will recognize that you understand what a news angle is, and they'll appreciate your efforts to give them material that is useful to them. This will help you build solid working relationships with reporters, and that means better coverage in the long run.

Approaching the Media

Even though they need you, and even if your publicity material is news-worthy, well written, and properly presented, media people won't always use it the way you would like them to.

What happens to your material depends on the judgment and taste of the individual journalist, the editorial policies of the publication, station, or website and the other events that are happening that day, week, or month. You do not control the media, and any hint that you would like to will surely raise the hackles of journalists.

Since raised hackles are most destructive to the publicity process, you should learn how to work effectively with media people. For example, when you visit journalists in person, "You should be very careful not to smoke if it's a non-smoking environment," says Bill Howard, an executive editor at *PC Magazine*. And you have to watch your manners. "Occasionally," Howard points out, "an older PR person will call a woman a 'girl' or 'honey.' That will simply turn off many women."

Good media relations also involves choosing the methods you'll use to contact the media. No one method is best: it depends on the situation, the newsworthiness of your material, and, most important, the preferences of the journalists you're working with. Some reporters love the phone. Others hate it. Some always want information by mail. Others prefer to get information by fax. There are reporters who don't mind getting publicity material by E-mail. Others despise E-mailed pitches and will hold them against you. You'll uncover these preferences as you build working relationships with journalists. With today's explosion of information technology, you have quite a choice of distribution methods. You can mail your publicity materials, use an overnight courier service when the deadline is looming, send them by fax when the journalists you're contacting don't mind that, beam live appearances by satellite, use E-mail, have a service bureau prepare a mailing for you, or pick up the telephone and handle it one-on-one.

Avoid the temptation to use all these channels at once. Journalists don't like to be bombarded, and they don't look kindly on publicists who send multiple copies of the same release using different media. "I've noticed a disturbing trend toward duplicative pitches; That is, I often get the same pitch via fax, e-mail (sometimes several e-mails) and phone," says Charles Piller, Technology Business staff writer at the *Los Angeles Times*, as quoted in *Soft•letter*. Check the listings in Chapter 13 to find out more about commercially available publicity distribution services.

Contacting the Media by Mail

Mailing your press release, tip sheet, public service announcement (PSA), or press conference announcement used to be the most common way to approach media people. Although this method often gets results, journalists still get enough mail to set off a paper avalanche. Sometimes there are so many envelopes that they don't all get opened. And even if your piece is opened and read, it remains a piece of paper, unattached to any human being. You will not be able to make personal contact with all the media people you work with because you, and they, won't have the time, and because some of them will not be conveniently located. So, you will have to use the mail at times.

One very positive aspect of mailed publicity material is that this delivery method doesn't offend most journalists, unlike faxed and E-mailed materials. To the contrary, some journalists *want* you to approach them by mail, at least at first. Even though he gets 40 to 50 pieces of mail a day, Gus Venditto of *PC Magazine* prefers to receive information that way. "If they have [a product] that interests us, I'll invite them to come give us a working demonstration. I get too many people calling me up and saying they sent me a press release. It's very annoying."

Here's a trick that will give you some feedback on mailed releases and PSAs: Include a business reply (or stamped) postcard with your material. If you're a perfectionist, you can run off a duplicate set of mailing labels and place one on each of the cards, so your media contacts don't even have to fill in their names and addresses. Ask people to check boxes to let you know the following:

- If and when they used the piece.
- If they want more like it.

- If they want you to call them to supply further information. Be sure to leave a space for comments.

The answers can help you evaluate your publicity material.

Contacting the Media by Telephone

If you are using the phone to make your initial contact, or if you are following up a mailed release with a call, find out first if the journalist is free to talk, and then be brief and to the point. Gimmy Park-Li, public service manager for KNBR Radio in San Francisco, says, "I appreciate someone who comes right to the point. I'm always pressed for time, but some people go on for five minutes. I have already determined in the first 90 seconds whether this is something for my station."

If you're calling a journalist about a story for the first time, your goal is to find out:

- If you have reached the right journalist for your story.
- If the person is free to talk with you now.
- Whether the person wants to talk about the story on the telephone or have you send written material first.

When you make an exploratory call to a journalist, Bob Seltzer of Porter Novelli advises: "Try to have three or four different story ideas so if the first one is shot down, you've got the next three ready to go. If you have only one door and it's closed, you don't have an alternative." If you're following up on material you've sent, be careful. Journalists don't like to be asked if they "got that press release." Likewise, "I am . . . very tired of people who phone to tell me they have sent me an e-mail!" says Louise Kehoe, *Financial Times* bureau chief in San Mateo, California, as quoted in *Soft•letter.*

On the other hand, if you have some new information you can offer them, there's a good possibility you can spark their interest. In fact, you may deliberately withhold some intriguing facts that aren't critical to your story but will give it an interesting twist—and use them as bait when you follow up by telephone.

Whatever the purpose of your call, Bill Howard of *PC Magazine* recommends, "Always identify yourself when you're calling—even if you talked with me this morning. Editors forget who you are very quickly, because we talk to hundreds of people. If someone just says 'Hi, this is John Jones,' I can't remember if he's looking for a job, if he's a creditor, or if he's a publicist."

You could open a follow-up call like this:

> *Hello, I'm Olga Statouras from the Plains City Real Estate Association. Is this a good time to talk, or should I call back?*
>
> *I'm calling about the press release on our new smart buyer program that teaches consumers how to inspect a home before they buy it. We just found out that Ajax Insurance Company is offering a discount on home owner's insurance to graduates of our program. I can give you figures on the savings over a 15-year period and answer any other questions you may have.*

If you have not sent a news release and are making an initial call, the journalist will probably ask you to send the material in writing. If you have already sent a news release, the journalist may tell you that it hasn't been received. Don't flinch! In either case, offer to send the written material. Ask about deadlines. If time is tight, offer to send it by messenger, overnight courier, or fax. Then take care of it the instant you get off the telephone.

When you call the media, you have to be prepared to talk with a reporter one-on-one, but you also have to be ready to make an intriguing pitch to the journalist's voice mail. According to Bob Seltzer, "That's a lot different than just saying 'Here's my phone number.' There is an art to figuring out what you're going to say in 60 seconds that will make that reporter think it's worth calling you back." Don't try to improvise. Practice both your voice mail and live pitches before you make any calls.

Contacting the Media by Fax and E-Mail

Using a fax machine or E-mail to send your publicity material to journalists often is tempting. It's fast. It's cheap. And in a matter of seconds you'll know that your material was received.

The only problem is that many journalists still don't like to receive uninvited faxes or E-mails. As Bill Howard puts it, "Don't automatically send faxed press releases. Many publications which don't handle breaking news dislike them. Faxed material should be sent by invitation only.

You should be very careful of minding your manners." And as Harry McCracken, a journalist at *PC World*, explained in *Soft•letter*, "E-mail broadcasting is a real scourge. I'm getting more mail that's clearly being spammed to every editor on the planet, which makes the personal messages targeted at me all the more difficult to spot."

Even where journalists work with hard, breaking news, uninvited faxes may not be welcomed. "Never send an unsolicited fax to the *New York Times*," warns Bob Seltzer. "They go nuts about it. For many reporters, it's an absolute policy, written in blood. We fax material to journalists if they have requested that material. The only exception is if we're faxing a media alert to an assignment desk." When you *are* invited to fax or E-mail material to journalists, take advantage of it! You'll be able to help them meet impossible deadlines. And your coverage should improve as a result.

On the other hand, there is one specialized area of publicity in which faxing is an everyday practice. According to *Public Relations Journal*, for publicists handling financial stories, "The fax . . . has emerged as one of the key tools." In a survey cited in the *Journal*, 94 percent of the financial publicists said they use faxes to transmit their stories.

The reason for the extensive use of faxes by financial publicists is that publicly traded companies have to meet strict Securities and Exchange Commission regulations when dealing with information that could impact a stock's price. Publicists have to make sure that all investors will have the opportunity to act on that news at the same time, so no one has an unfair advantage.

If you work for a corporation with publicly traded stock, you have to closely examine your publicity policies. News stories about new products, personnel changes, marketing campaigns, and emergencies, for example, can all influence the price of your stock. If your story could pump up or deflate your firm's stock prices, you'll have to meet minimum disclosure requirements. It is prudent to discuss this question with your organization's lawyer and develop written guidelines for disclosure.

According to PR Newswire (a press release distribution service), the New York Stock Exchange says a listed company is expected to release news that could bear on a stock's price by the fastest means possible, to at least the following information services and media:

- Dow Jones
- Reuters

- Moody's
- *New York Times*
- *Wall Street Journal*
- Standard & Poor's
- Associated Press
- United Press International

Since wide distribution of your financial publicity will help your corporation secure investors and lenders, you probably want to go beyond this list. For example, you should include industry analysts on your news distribution list. They are often used as sources by journalists, so they are important opinion makers.

Because of the timely notification requirement, you can't release financial news with a standard fax machine, which is too slow to deliver your news to several news outlets simultaneously. You probably need a fax service bureau or a news wire. Both types of services are listed in Chapter 13. Both fax services and news wires require a written contract in advance.

Before you sign on the dotted line for a fax service, you need to ask several questions: How many faxes can the service transmit at once? Will that be enough for your distribution list? Can the service store a digitized image of your letterhead and signature? How many times will they retry a busy fax number? For how long? If one of your recipients can't be contacted, how will the service handle it? A reliable fax service can answer all these questions, as well as several more in the checklist at the end of this chapter.

If you have determined that some of the journalists on your list will accept E-mailed publicity material, you must follow certain procedures. First of all, your E-mails should be in plain text format. There are two formats you should not use. Hyper Text Markup Language (HTML) documents are formatted for the World Wide Web, and rich text documents contain formatting codes for italics, boldface, and special characters. Many journalists can't read documents formatted in either of these ways—even at some of the high-tech publications. Some E-mail programs turn rich text formatting into attachments that require an external reader program. So, unless a journalist has specifically told you that rich text formatting or HTML is OK, stick with plain vanilla text. This subject is covered in more detail in Chapter 6.

You should also avoid attachments to your E-mails. "While I . . . prefer e-mail, I don't like attachments, particularly Word documents. They are bandwidth hogs, are a pain to open and they can transmit macro viruses (and yes, I've gotten viruses from press releases!)," explains Dwight Silverman, the Consumer Electronics Business staff writer at the *Houston Chronicle,* as quoted in *Soft•letter.* If you need to send a formatted file to a journalist, get permission first. Or include links to documents on your website if you're sending a pitch or press release to journalists you don't have working relationships with.

When you E-mail a press release or a pitch letter to a large number of journalists, don't enter all their names in the recipient field. If you do, there will be a long list of names in your E-mail, which reporters will have to scroll through before they even get to your message. This is a dead giveaway that this publicity material is not exclusive. You can enter all the names in the BCC (blind carbon copy) field to avoid putting a long list of recipients in between your message and the journalists you are sending it to. But some E-mail programs will tag E-mails prepared this way as going to an "unknown recipient." If your E-mail program does this, you may want to send a separate E-mail to each journalist on your list.

Finally, keep in mind that journalists expect E-mailed publicity materials to be very short. "No one has time to wade through huge long e-mails looking for a point. Give us a break, and get right to the point," says Carol Venezia, executive editor at *PC Magazine,* as quoted in *Soft•letter.* A good way to keep your E-mailed publicity materials short is to use links in them to background materials, photos, charts, and even sound clips on your website. Grab journalists with your pitch or release, and once you have their interest, entice them to seek out more material with a concise description of each link.

Contacting the Media by Wire Service

There are two types of wire services. The first type gathers news and is part of the media; examples are Reuters, the Associated Press, and Dow Jones Newswire. You can't buy coverage from them; you have to earn it with newsworthy material. The second type of wire service distributes press releases, media alerts, pitches, and other publicity materials for a fee. You can't earn coverage from these proprietary wire services; you have to buy it. Proprietary wire services include PR Newswire and Business Wire.

Proprietary wire services have both advantages and disadvantages. It's not possible to customize your publicity materials for each media outlet when you use a proprietary wire service to distribute them. You also lose the advantage of direct contact with journalists. But they can get your story to large numbers of journalists very quickly. And perhaps just as important, they are picked up by many websites that distribute news stories, including America Online (AOL). So they can help you reach a huge audience.

They don't have to be expensive, either, especially if you use Anne Holland's clever strategy. Holland, the CEO of MarketingSherpa.Com, will often "pop out a press release to Business Wire for the cheapest local market on their list (such as Iowa for $50) because all releases, no matter what local region they're sent to, get posted to *all* their electronic lines of distribution, which is literally hundreds of websites."

Contacting the Media in Person

There are times when you will want to deliver your publicity material in person. You should do that with the media outlets that are most important to you, and with media people who don't object. When you first start as a publicist, some journalists will be glad to spend time chatting with you. Randy McCarthy, city editor for the *Boise Statesman* in Idaho, says, "I always like to meet them in person, if they are local, just to see who they are. I like to give my scam to them: what I want, what I don't want." On the other hand, Fred Zehnder, news director for KTVU-TV in Oakland, California, says, "We're generally too busy to have conferences with people. We could not possibly talk to all the publicists who would like to talk with us."

"It's almost a catch-22 situation," says Sylvia Smith, assistant city editor for the *Journal-Gazette* in Fort Wayne, Indiana. "It is sort of confusing because the person ought to be known to the reporter or editor, but we don't take real kindly to somebody's calling up and saying, 'I'd like to meet you.'" You may have to start by using the mail and the telephone; later on, when journalists are familiar with your material and your voice, you may be invited to meet with them.

On the other hand, you may decide to use the approach advocated by public relations executive Ravelle Brickman. Once journalists are familiar with your material, she suggests, "Call reporters and editors when you don't need a favor, to find out what they need and how you can help. I like to suggest a drink or lunch, so that I can get acquainted with the journalist as a person and find out what kinds of stories she's working on. She just might be planning a series where my organization can fit right in."

Some journalists will welcome this approach. "Why don't PR people ever call me and simply ask me what I'm working on?" says Charlotte Dunlap, networking senior editor at *Computer Reseller News*, as quoted in *Soft•letter*. "Since the PR person and I are probably on similar beats, why doesn't the person go so far as to see if he can do anything to help me get data on my current feature? If someone took that approach, I'd be indebted to him and again very, very likely to establish a strong relationship with that person and be very receptive to his needs/company announcements for the rest of our careers."

And as Kimberly L. McCall, the Sell columnist for *Entrepreneur's Business Start-Ups* magazine, explains, "The Internet *has* made it easier to reach thousands of people with just a click of a button. But it has also made it harder, because there is so much more clutter out there as a result. So the real personalized relationships with reporters have become that much more important. The Internet is *not* a substitution for your communication skills."

When you deliver your publicity material in person, be brief and to the point, especially if you are dropping in without an appointment. If you are approaching a city editor, you are apt to find him listening to the police radio, typing with one hand, and holding the telephone with the other. Wait until he's free, give him a 20-second summary of your material, and hand it to him. He will probably take a few seconds to eyeball it, and he may ask a question or two. Then, you should leave. If he has any further questions, he'll call you later.

Whatever you do, do not read the release to the editor. "Give editors and reporters credit for the ability to read," says S. Griffin Singer, city editor for the *San Antonio Light*. "Nothing irritates me more than for a publicist to bring in a release and then stand there and read it to me like a first-grade teacher. I think they're unconscious of just how annoying it is to us."

Answering Questions

Although you have delivered your publicity material to the media, your job does not end. A reporter, an editor, or a news director may need more information, and you should be ready to respond to the call. If he asks you for facts and figures, if he requests details, it's your task to get them for him.

"It is the publicist's job," says journalist Nancy Dunn, "to make things as easy as possible for people in the media. If you don't have all the information, you should say, 'I'll call you back. When would be convenient? When do you need it by?' If it turns out that you can't get the information, call back and say so. Don't leave them hanging."

If you don't help journalists with more information, your story may not get covered, and you will hurt your working relationship with media people. Says Tom Callaghan, staff writer for the *Birmingham News*, "I don't like the ones you call to get more information who don't have that information on hand or don't seem willing to go to any extra trouble to get it for you."

When you're asked to send a press kit or other follow-up material, Bill Howard advises, "Stick a Post-it on the outside with a note like: 'Bill—as per our phone conversation Tuesday, here's the backgrounder on WonderCalc.'" This, he says, not only helps trigger an editor's recall, but also, "if [a] high-level editor's mail is opened by an assistant, [the note] assures that this is not an unsolicited mailing."

Avoiding Pressure and Observing Ethics

If you don't get a clear indication of interest, but you don't get turned down either, try to clarify the situation, advises Nan Hohenstein of Nan Hohenstein Public Relations in San Francisco. "Be very straightforward with journalists. Say, 'Are you interested, but just too busy to deal with it now? OK, then I'm going to call you back next Wednesday. I hope you don't think I'm pushing, but this has limited time value. If you can't get to it, quite truthfully, I want to shoot it on to someone else.'" Journalists appreciate and respond to that kind of candor.

The most important point to remember is that you have to persuade the journalist to give you coverage. "What I admire most is when I get a release that is written so that I want to cover the event," says the *Norfolk Ledger-Star*'s Fred Kirsch. And Ed Hinshaw, manager of public affairs and vice president of WTMJ in Milwaukee, advises, "A friendly tone helps to keep the door of the mind open."

You need to be persuasive, persistent, and friendly, but exercise restraint. Says KNBR's Gimmy Park-Li, "One of my pet peeves is publicists who are overly aggressive." Fred Kirsch adds, "The main thing is to come across as a person. We can get the same information from various sources, but we just enjoy it more dealing with someone we like."

Don't waste time telling media people how hard you and your staff worked to produce an event. You will only annoy your contacts. The event must stand on its own merit.

Once you have telephoned or visited and presented your material, Nan Hohenstein advises, "Keep your distance. It creates an awkwardness to assume you have a relationship with a journalist. If you get one good story, then you begin to assume that they're all going to be good, and the journalist is going to start feeling put upon."

How do you make sure the journalist writes an accurate story once you've provided the material or finished the interview? There's usually not much you can do other than trust that he's a professional and will do a competent job. But even though reporters want to be accurate in their coverage, they have continual deadline pressure. They have to work on more than one story at the same time. And since many reporters are generalists, even at some of the trade publications, they often don't have as much technical knowledge as you and your staff do.

Most journalists bristle at even the slightest suggestion that you want to approve their copy, and rightly so. Remember, you don't control the media, and journalists cherish their independence. Nevertheless, there are techniques you can use to help make sure the coverage you get is accurate, especially in a controversial situation or when specialized or technical information is involved:

- Give the journalist detailed, accurate written background information up front. If there are common misconceptions about your product, service, organization, or cause, counter them in this material. Journalists will welcome and use this kind of material, whether it's on paper or on your website.
- If you have any inkling that you may get negative or mixed coverage, ask the reporter what unfavorable observations he has. This gives you the opportunity to state—or restate—your point of view, and the result can be better coverage.
- Offer the reporter the opportunity to call you when the story is finished, to read direct quotes back to you for accuracy. Some

journalists will agree to do this if you can make yourself available when they need you.

■ If your story involves technical or specialized information, offer journalists the opportunity to review their finished copy with you for accuracy. Many journalists will welcome this chance, particularly if they are not specialists. Other reporters won't agree to it. Either way, it's worth asking about.

Whether you decide to follow Nan Hohenstein's advice and keep your distance, or take Ravelle Brickman's working-relationship approach, wait to make any friendly overtures until after your material appears.

Accurate, interesting, up-to-date information is what media people want from you. Liquor, tickets to ball games, and other freebies usually won't get you coverage. Many journalists resent publicists bearing gifts. They feel you're trying to buy their interest. Millard C. Browne, editorial-page editor of the *Evening News* in Buffalo, New York, explains changes in journalistic ethics in an issue of *The Masthead*, the magazine of the National Conference of Editorial Writers:

> *Journalism ethics have been going through a veritable revolution on the subject of "freebies" in the past two decades. Practices that were once commonplace— papering the city room with free passes to movies and sporting events, for example—are long gone. So is all the free booze that used to pour in at Christmas time from . . . press agents.*
>
> *Now the rules in every reputable newsroom are being drawn tighter and tighter. . . .*
>
> *So free trips are out, for example. But what if a newsman has a chance to cover a bona fide story he can't reach except as part of a government or company sponsored trip? Does he stay home, or does he sign in and insist that the sponsor bill his paper for a reasonable pro-rata share of the cost?*
>
> *The* News, *along with more and more major metropolitan newspapers, does the latter in almost every case.*

Ethical standards at newspapers, broadcast stations, and many magazines have been tightened even further since the *Masthead* article was written. The Radio-Television News Directors Association Code of Ethics mandates that members ". . . will decline gifts or favors which would influence or appear to influence their judgments." And concern about journalistic ethics is so keen now that there is a monthly newsletter devoted completely to news about ethical situations faced by journalists.

Talking Off the Record

No matter how well you know a journalist, even if you are friends, you should never expect to talk off the record. Says Nancy E. Karen, vice president for marketing and communications at United Way of Tri-State in New York, "The press has a job to do. Yes, there are many journalists who can be trusted to keep what you say off the record, but that's a crummy thing to do to them. You're asking them not to do their job. Well, why tell them in the first place?"

Asking to go off the record can do more than annoy reporters. You may tell a reporter about the quality-control problems you're having at your East Side assembly plant, or the morale problem that's plaguing your clerical support staff. Sure, it's off the record—and an ethical reporter won't use your information directly—but you've given the reporter a clue to something she may not have known about, and she may find another source who is willing to talk for the record. Says Cindy Loose of the *Staten Island Register*, "I'll talk to anybody off the record, and I'll use that information if I can get it and confirm it from another source. I may get a lead I would not have had if they hadn't talked off the record. Also, I've got to agree before you tell me something that you want to be off the record."

Most of the time it just isn't wise to speak off the record, but when it comes to government agencies and organizations funded with public money, you cannot even make that request. Your money comes from the public, and you are accountable to the public. Reporters are well aware of this, and they may be even better acquainted with public disclosure laws than you are. Asking to go off the record implies that information that should be public is not. Since reporters depend on free access to information, they will be angered by a request to go off the record, and your agency or organization will look as if it wants to avoid responsibility for the information.

Taking No for an Answer

When you work with the media, there will be times when you will get no for an answer. Even if it's your major story of the year, even if you think you have the most amazing photographs, an irresistible news peg, and astoundingly important information, you will have to accept a negative answer. Remember those hackles! Don't argue with journalists when they've turned you down. You'll only alienate them.

Larry Kramer, managing editor for the *Trenton Times* in New Jersey, says, "I have no problem with somebody calling me and trying to pitch me a story; I have a problem if, once I decide one way or another, they keep trying to change my mind. We basically have an understanding here with most people we deal with. They can take their shot, and we'll do what we want with it. I don't admire anybody who can't be told no."

Ed Hinshaw of WTMJ feels that this is an especially difficult area for inexperienced publicists: "They rarely recognize when a conversation has reached a natural conclusion in agreement or disagreement."

If you are turned down, ask the reporter or editor whether he would recommend anyone else at the paper or station who should get the release, tip sheet, or feature story idea. If he says no, your story is dead, at least at that media outlet. Don't try to circumvent him by going to another reporter or editor there. He'll be furious. And for good reason!

What you should do is put on your thinking cap, and see if you can dream up a whole new angle. Test it out on some colleagues and friends— and be certain it really is different. Then call the journalist who turned you down, say that you've just discovered a whole new angle on that story you mentioned, and make your pitch.

For example, if you've just been turned down on a story about your research on how high school sports influence female self-images, try a different slant. Instead of discussing how your research may affect the educational process, try describing the reaction that male coaches and players had to your report.

Asking for Advice

If you start expecting too much from media people, you will have difficulty because they will feel imposed upon. This is particularly true when it comes to asking for advice about publicity. As public relations pro Nan Hohenstein put it, "For the most part, journalists don't have time to give lessons. Also it's as if you're asking journalists to train one more pest. It's a bad idea."

"I wouldn't appreciate anyone asking me for advice," says reporter Cindy Loose. "They've got their job; I've got mine. If they don't know their business, they should go learn it and leave me alone. I'm not in the training business."

When you are working with reporters, editors, and news directors, you are trying to establish yourself as a reliable news source. Although some journalists enjoy giving advice, asking for it undermines your credibility in the long run. So, if you need advice about publicity, find other sources. Ask members of the journalism or public relations department at your local college if they can answer questions for you. Even better, join one of the professional organizations listed in Chapter 13. Then you can get to know other publicity people, and you can share your questions about—and solutions to—publicity problems.

If you are asking media people for preferences, as opposed to advice, that's different. Says Nan Hohenstein, "I think you can ask them 'Would you prefer to receive this in the form of a feature story, or would you prefer that I jot down the six issues you might deal with in your story?'" But, even with preferences, don't ask too many questions. You have to make decisions, and too many questions will make you seem indecisive.

Some reporters don't even feel that it's appropriate to discuss their preferences. Cindy Loose says that she expects a publicist "to give me something." She explains, "I'll work from there. But I think it's their job to decide how to approach me. If they send me a press release and I'd rather meet with them, I'll call them and tell them I need a meeting."

There is one exception: public service directors at radio and TV stations are sometimes willing to help nonprofit publicists learn. Some public service people run workshops and classes for publicists from community and nonprofit organizations; others work on a one-to-one basis. Asking public service directors for advice will not hurt your reputation, especially if you are a beginner, but even here, public service directors have limited time and an incredible workload, so be sensitive about how much of their time you're asking for.

You may think that if you send in public service material that is not up to par, the public service director will call to tell you. That does happen. Occasionally. But don't count on it. "We mean well," says By Napier, program director of WCCO-AM Radio in Minneapolis–St. Paul, "but there are other things to do. I guess our critique is expressed in how often we book them or use their guests [on our talk shows]."

Observing Format Preferences

One of the most important format requirements for any publicity material is that it be neatly word processed and duplicated. Editors, reporters, news directors, and public service directors have to read dozens of press releases, tip sheets, backgrounders, press conference invitations, and PSAs every day. Even though virtually all of them are typed, reading them is still a difficult task, and it would become impossible if it involved interpreting handwritten material. (When you get to know some media people, ask to see how much publicity material they receive in a day or week. You'll be amazed!)

Journalists from Alaska to Florida make it clear: they want publicity material to be neatly word processed, with no handwritten corrections.

If you have your choice of typestyles, stick to standard types. Fancy typefaces, especially script faces, are hard to read and may convince a bleary-eyed editor that your piece should be placed in the "circular file." If you're using a word processor, be sure your printer has near letter-quality capability. Sure, the printer works faster in draft mode (where you can see the little dots that make up the letters), but the results don't command the same respect.

To duplicate your publicity material, use a copying machine or photo-offset printing. As long as the copies are clear and clean, the method is not important, although using carbon copies is considered bad manners. For an annual event, however, it is unwise to use a printed or photocopied form that you fill in each year, with only the dates changed. That format announces: Stale news. Nothing new!

The standard size for news releases, PSAs, backgrounder sheets, filler sheets, press conference invitations, and other communications with the media is 8½-by-11-inch paper. Don't use legal-size paper. It is harder to handle, it doesn't fit into standard file folders, and it is too long to fit most copybooks used at radio stations. Use 20- or 24-pound bond; onionskin is too flimsy and difficult to handle.

At the top of each sheet of publicity material, include your name, your organization's name, address, and phone number, E-mail address, website address, and the date.

Don't staple two-page press releases. The editor has to separate them, and that's a nuisance. Nor should you send two or three releases stapled together. If the editor doesn't like the first one, the others will probably be tossed out without being looked at. The best idea is to send each release in a separate envelope. They'll have a better chance that way.

Releases up to five pages long can and should be folded and sent in #10 business envelopes. If the background material accompanying your release brings the total to more than five pages, then you should use a 9-by-12-inch white envelope. Postal employees give first-class treatment to white envelopes—especially if they have a border of green diamonds—but automatically treat brown kraft envelopes as third-class.

All mailed publicity material should be sent first-class, of course. Don't give in to the temptation to save money by using your bulk-mail permit to send out press releases or PSAs. It's a surefire way to miss deadlines and make certain your material is dated before it arrives.

Further details on formats for different types of publicity materials are given in Chapters 4 and 8.

Working Within Deadlines

When you work with journalists, you move in a world of continual dead-lines, in which time is tyrannical. "Sometimes the press seems arrogant because we have to have the information by an inflexible deadline. But that's reality," says Gus Venditto.

One of your first tasks as a publicist is to find out deadline times. Once you have made your media list, call each outlet and ask. You will find a wide variation. The public service people at a radio station may have three or four deadlines for locally produced programs and a four-week lead-time requirement for PSAs. For the news director, it will be quite a different story. "Deadline time for me, for a radio news operation, is every hour at the top of the hour," says WAVI-FM's John Canelli.

Web-based journalists have even more deadline pressure than their brick-and-mortar counterparts. "Internet-based journalists have to file sto-ries and meet deadlines two or even three times a day. They are constantly calling, and their needs are very pressing. You have to be ready to respond quickly. There is one Web-based news organization that calls me several times a week. When new arthritis studies come out, they have to put sto-ries online almost instantly," says Jed Nitzberg, APR, vice president of interactive communications for the Arthritis Foundation.

Nitzberg explains that Web-based journalists need expert commen-tary, and they need it now because of their deadlines: "[Internet reporters have] told me that when they find people like me, who are willing to talk to them on a regular basis, it's a lifesaver. Some publicists get tired of the constant barrage of phone calls from Web-based journalists. They are actu-ally refusing to talk to some of these reporters."

You can't predict whether a Web-based reporter will call you. Even if you limit your publicity distribution list to traditional media outlets, many of them now have Web-based counterparts with which they exchange stories and story ideas. If you're going to be a publicist, tight "Internet time" deadlines are part of your picture.

At the newspapers, the city editor has a different deadline from the Sunday and feature editors. So, you need to ask each person you'll be working with when the specific deadlines are. Then use this information—not only to get your material in on time but also to avoid interrupting your contacts when they are too busy to talk to you.

Deadline Realities

You may have the most interesting story, but it will die if you miss the deadline. The deadline is when a reporter has to hand his copy to the editor so that it can be edited and set in type in time for the printer. In order for your morning paper to be on the doorstep or at the newsstand when you're ready to go to work, it takes the cooperation of many people, and it wouldn't be possible to deliver that paper on time if they didn't all have deadlines. Radio and TV people have similar requirements; they need to meet deadlines so that their stories can be chosen, rewritten, and timed, and so that visuals can be found to go with them, tape can be edited for broadcast, and everything can be put together to fill the airtime exactly. Without deadlines, the six o'clock news might sometimes appear at 6:00 and sometimes at 6:45 or 7:00. And monthly magazines might appear every three weeks—or every seven.

According to public relations executive Richard Weiner, nonprofit organizations share a common problem: "Sometimes they will agonize over a news release for weeks, and miss the point, which is to get it out." This is a problem even at many large businesses, where executives don't understand the realities of media deadlines.

The bottom line is stark and simple: no matter how wonderful your product, no matter how worthy your cause, no matter how vital your story, you cannot be late when you are a publicist.

"Even advertising copy must be turned in by a particular time during the business day to be on the air," says KNBR's Gimmy Park-Li. "So if advertising people have to honor deadlines, I think publicists must honor them as well."

If you do not honor deadlines, you will undermine your credibility with media people. Carole Halicki, editorial director for WRAU-TV in Peoria, Illinois, says that she received a weekly newsletter from an area congressman touting the need to observe March 20 as National Agriculture Day. "The 'newsletter' was written on March 21, and I received it March 26. So even if I wanted to mark the celebration of National Agriculture Day, it was a week old and was by then probably National Pickle Day. I would think if a group goes to all the trouble to mail out their stuff, they'd do it so it would arrive before, not after, the suggested release date."

If you do miss a deadline and your material doesn't run, it is *your* fault. Don't try to blame media people for your failure. That may sound obvious, but journalist Nancy Dunn gives the following example: "Someone once called me at home and woke me up early on Christmas morning to berate me for not covering her event, which was submitted after the deadline. I was furious. I never could treat her seriously after that."

Allowing Enough Lead Time

You also need to know how much advance notice media people require. Lead time is especially important for feature material and special broadcasts.

The amount of lead time you will need to publicize your product, issue, or event will depend on the size of the publicity campaign, how much competition there is for airtime and newspaper space in your area, the deadlines and lead requirements at the media outlets you'll be working with, and even the time of year.

For the Annual California Spring Garden Show, a major event sponsored each May by the Oakland Office of Parks and Recreation, planning starts during the previous summer. And for Oakland's Children's Fairyland, which celebrated its 25th anniversary with a seven-month-long festival that involved thousands of people from dozens of cities—as well as a score of foreign nations—and got worldwide news coverage, publicist Burton Weber made the first media contact six months before the festivities started.

Another reason why you should not wait until deadline time or just before to approach media people is that they are going to want some time to check on your material, to develop a story, and to find background information. Gladys Adams, editor of the *Kansas City Voice*, says this about being approached at deadline time: "If you know anything about the operation of a newspaper, you would hardly do that. It really bothers us, especially if it's something we should be digging into, that would serve our community to know. If you call us at the last minute, our schedules are already full, and we can't do that digging."

Avoiding Last-Minute Panic

One problem for new publicists who have not planned carefully enough is last-minute panic. "Last-minute panic makes it hard to deal with a publicist," says Nancy Dunn. "Panic-stricken people tend to apply more pressure to squeeze things in after the deadline. Unprofessional publicists, either paid or volunteer, try to put responsibility on me to make the event successful. Often these are the very people who complain about bad coverage, when the real problem is they were badly prepared."

Media people generally are not sympathetic toward *any* publicist in the grip of last-minute panic. "Last-minute panic is really bad," says Mark Shepherd, feature writer for the *Columbia Daily Tribune* in Missouri. "My view is that if a person has a job cranking out releases and he doesn't get them out on time, I wouldn't have much sympathy for him."

So, write this cardinal rule in big letters, and post it over your desk: "I must get my publicity materials in to the media in plenty of time so I avoid last-minute panic and I give journalists plenty of time to do a good job."

Showing Consideration at Deadline Time

You will generally want to stay away from your media contacts right around deadline time. That charming reporter who spent an hour interviewing you about your trade association's position on new legislation will turn into a snarling beast, ready to bite your head off, at deadline time. She has other things to worry about. She has to have her stories ready by the deadline, and that's all that is important to her. "I don't want to talk to anybody at deadline time," says WBUR-FM's Carol Rissman.

On the other hand, if you have a truly major story that is hard, breaking news, she won't mind being interrupted. Let's say, for example, that the Martians have just landed on your patio and they have chosen your organization to be their official Earth representative. That's news: that's big news, and it doesn't matter if you call the media at deadline time. In fact, media people will be upset if you *don't* call about major news as soon as it happens. "If it's something that's important, that's immediate, and I would like to know about it, I don't care if it's deadline time or not," says Jim Kemp, news director for WVUE-TV in New Orleans.

Introducing Yourself to the Media

If you are handling publicity for a new business, an organization that is not well known, or one that has never done publicity before, you will have to introduce yourself to the media. After all, anybody with a word processor and some letterhead can send out a press release or a PSA claiming to represent an organization. Any reporter, editor, news director, or public service director worth his salt will want to check on your organization's background, history, and reliability. Even if they're familiar with your organization, they'll want to make sure that you, the new publicist, are authorized to represent it to the media.

As Jim Kemp explains, "If I got something from an organization I didn't know about, before I'd do anything with it, I'd certainly want to find out who they are."

Some media people will call the publicist of an unknown organization to ask for more information. Others do not have the time or the inclination, so don't gamble that they will automatically get in touch with you or check into your organization's history or company's background. "We get so much material from organizations that we do know, unless a new group informs us as to what they're about, we would not use their . . . [material]," says Jules Moreland, public service and program director for KFMB-TV in San Diego.

The easiest way to introduce a new organization to the media is by pulling together all the basic information about your products, services, and track record into one convenient backgrounder sheet.

Providing Backgrounders

With every press release, press conference invitation, request for coverage, community calendar announcement, and PSA, you should include a backgrounder sheet on your organization. According to Sylvia Smith of the *Fort Wayne Journal-Gazette*, a backgrounder for a nonprofit organization should "explain the purpose of the organization, when it was formed, who the people are on its board, where it gets its funding, and what it expects to do with its money."

A backgrounder for a business should include information about the organization's structure, capitalization, and sales volume and a two- or three-sentence discussion of its history and position in the marketplace. But don't overdo it. According to Gus Venditto, "You can go too far with introductory material. One new PC company included an SEC filing in their media kit. They looked well capitalized. So that made me suspicious. Why did they include it?"

Even after you are well known, including a backgrounder is a good idea because journalists can use it to round out a story. While a backgrounder sheet should be short—one page is ideal—you should include the URLs for more information on your website. These URLs should be the exact addresses that take journalists directly to the material, so they don't have to hunt for it. Exhibit 2.1 shows a typical backgrounder sheet.

Sending Your Organization's Publications to the Media

Unless a media person has asked you specifically to include her on your subscription list, don't send her your newsletter or magazine. If it's written well and all the stories are in the right format, it would be easy for her to use one of them, but you're asking *her* to choose which one. There are three problems with that: you're asking her to run old news; even if she were willing to do that, she may not have the time to make that choice; and *you* should be setting the priorities.

If you want the media to cover a story that will appear in your organization's publication, send out a release based on that story. Be absolutely certain to time the release so journalists get it with enough lead time to break the story just before your publication date. And be sure you let the journalists know you want to coordinate the release dates with them. Then the media will have fresh news to work with, and they may well use it.

Also, don't send media people your organization's meeting agenda or minutes unless they ask you to. Agendas are notoriously dull, and the minutes will probably not seem interesting even if the proceedings are. If your meeting is newsworthy, write a news release—and make sure it has an intriguing angle and hard facts that a journalist can bite into.

Exhibit 2.1

Back to the Basics, Inc.
1535 Roaring Brook Road
Plains City 00000

Contact: Dee Nominator, (123) 456-7890

September 30, 2002

Purpose: To advocate the return to basics in education. To convince parents, teachers, and the public that reading, writing, arithmetic, and self-discipline are the most important parts of education. To illustrate the problems faced by children who cannot read and write well, who cannot do simple arithmetic, and who have no self-discipline. To develop curricula and materials for teachers who want to go back to the basics but have forgotten how.

Board Members: Linda S. Lurie, M.D., director of Pediatric Services, Plains City Hospital; Lars T. Borgward, owner, Hill Street Restaurant; Mrs. Mary Kaapala, housewife; H. Michael Smith, member of the Plains City Board of Education; R. H. Asher, manager, Downtown Bookstore. For complete bios of board members, go to www.backtobasics.pln/boardbio.

Membership: 775.

Funding: Membership dues, 20%; contributions, 25%; grant from the Plains City Foundation, 55%.

IRS tax-exempt number: 99-999.

Plains City fund-raising number: 675.

Budget: Staff and office, 30%; curriculum materials and development, 50%; publications, 20%. For complete budgets since 1990, go to www.backtobasics.pln/budgetdata.

Accomplishments: Back to the Basics, Inc., was founded in 1979. We have developed our basic reading curriculum and distributed it, without charge, to 1,755 educators statewide. We are about to release the third revision of our basic curriculum. For a complete list of our achievements since our founding in 1979, go to www.backtobasics .pln/wedidit!

# # #

Even a lovely, new four-color brochure that tells all about your product line is not normally the kind of material you would send to the media, although there are exceptions. If you know a reporter or editor fairly well and you think he will file the brochure for future reference, then send it with a cover letter explaining that it is good background material.

You may, on occasion, be able to develop a news peg about the publication of the brochure. Send it along with a news release based on that peg. Here is a clever example by public relations executive Ravelle Brickman for the YMCA of Greater New York:

> **Consumer News Note**
>
> *The YMCA of Greater New York has been running nonprofit children's camps since 1885.*
>
> *Yet until this year, there has never been a single directory listing all the camps, sleep-away and day, serving the New York area.*
>
> *Now the Y has put together a simple folder, listing rates, dates, hours and location of every camp in the five boroughs as well as its cluster of resident camps in nearby Port Jervis, New York.*
>
> *To get your free copy of the directory, just "DIAL-A-Y," 582-2000, any time of day or night, and ask about day camp.*

Building Your Reputation for Accuracy

Reporters, editors, news directors, and public service directors know that your responsibility is to your organization and not to their newspapers or stations. They're not going to trust you completely until you establish a good reputation by proving that your facts are accurate, by keeping your promises, and by always meeting deadlines. According to Larry Kramer of the *Trenton Times,* "It takes a while to know someone well enough to know where their prejudices are."

You can never rest on your laurels. "A news source is only as good as the last time I used it," says Larry Badger, news director at KGW-TV in Portland, Oregon.

Being Known for Accuracy

A good news source provides information that is reliable and can be confirmed. For KRBE-FM's Mike Martin, material from a publicist is of interest "as long as he establishes the credibility of the information." He explains, "It could be anybody calling. And I have to be able to check out the facts before I can use them as part of the news. So if he gives me enough to cover my backside with, I'm happy."

When a publicist is considered a good source, her job is much easier because reporters and editors seek her out. If her relationship with the media has become a two-way street, her publicity material will get more attention and interest. Since reporters and editors work under constant pressure, they are likely to turn to their good sources first. The *Norfolk Ledger-Star*'s Fred Kirsch states, "I usually go to the sources that have been most cooperative in the past and seem to be able to grasp what it is I need. It's just tremendous to know that I can count on particulars, especially when I'm in a hurry."

With complete information and an honest approach, you are well on the way to earning that good reputation. "If they can give me all I need to know—if they know what they're talking about, and they haven't made me go to a lot of effort, they'll have a good reputation with me. Their reputation is as good as their information," says Randy McCarthy of the *Boise Statesman.*

A word of warning: Even if your facts are strictly accurate, media people will be furious if you try to fool them by leaving out crucial information. If your day-care center is operated by a religious cult and your release fails to mention the sponsoring organization, it doesn't matter that the rest of the release is completely truthful.

Tom Callaghan of the *Birmingham News* reflects the opinions of many journalists when he says, "We'd like you to be open and honest about who you are and what you represent." If the truth about your product, service, or cause needs to be hidden, you can't use a publicity program. You need a propaganda campaign.

"Reporters don't like to be manipulated," agrees journalist Nancy Dunn. "We have to work within an editorial perspective. We're not here to serve your goals; we're here to put out a newspaper."

Journalist Leslie O'Bergin feels the same way: "I don't like flimflamming," she says. "Flimflamming is incomplete information, concealment of purpose. It's an insult to my intelligence. I have no intention of ever knowingly writing a publicity article—in a sense, a free ad—for an organization that is lying to me, no matter what their purpose, and even if I personally agree with that purpose."

She adds, "Sometimes flimflamming is intentional. Sometimes it is a misunderstanding of what publicity is all about. But in either case, I feel it indicates a mistrust of the validity of the organization itself. If the person in charge of publicity does not trust the usefulness of that group enough to be honest not only with me but also with the public, I think there's something worth investigating about the organization from an entirely different point of view."

Puffery is similar to flimflamming, and it's just as frowned upon. The publicist blows puffs of smoke that look interesting, bringing journalists running to see what's going on. When they arrive, the puffs of smoke have dissipated into nothing. But this puff is no magic dragon; it only makes media people angry. "If the event is different from what they said and they made something out of nothing in the press release, and I get there and it's not what I was led to believe, I would remember that. And I would probably bear a grudge against them," says Randy McCarthy.

Even if you're smart enough to put one over on journalists with puffery and flimflamming, you can't fool the public, at least not for long. Publicity cannot mask bad performance. "Bear in mind," says KSTP-TV's Linnea Crowe, "that the only thing you can do with publicity is to get people to sample your product or service. If it doesn't live up to your publicity, if you have a high return at the beginning and then it peters out, the service or product is not holding up to the expectations created by the publicity. And the people you are trying to reach are going to realize that sooner or later."

Being Able to Withstand Scrutiny

If you are going to have a good reputation with the media, your publicity efforts must withstand public scrutiny. Once that press release or PSA is sent out, you cannot take it out of circulation, and you can't control its use. It has been publicly distributed, and it is probably public domain under the copyright law. Anyone who has it can use it for any purpose. It's a good idea to ask yourself the following questions about *each* piece of publicity material before you release it:

- How would I feel about defending it before a congressional committee?
- Would I be comfortable discussing it with an investigative reporter?

If you have the slightest doubt, don't send it out. Media people will often pick up on something that's not exactly as it should be. "Before a PSA goes on our air," says WCBS-AM's Teresa DiTore, "it is thoroughly researched. We even go out to community organizations and just drop in to see how they treat people. If someone sends me in copy that says 'Fees based on ability to pay,' I want to know what that means. And very often, before we put it on the air, I call the organization. And I say, for example, 'I make $150 a week. I want to come in for psychotherapy. How much do I have to pay?' And if they tell me $50 per week, I say, 'Hey, now wait a second. That is not ability to pay.' Very often we have turned people down because of things like that."

That situation is damaging and embarrassing enough, but if it should happen after the information has been published or aired, you're really hurting your organization. For example, the *Columbia Journalism Review* awarded a "Laurel" to Sally Jesse Raphael, hostess of a talk show on New York's WMCA Radio, "for exercising firm control" when a guest, having billed herself as an ordinary person who had lost a great deal of weight, turned out to be a paid lecturer for a well-known weight-loss group. When Raphael discovered the deception, she told her listeners, "I'm gonna throw the lady off the show. I thought she was a civilian. I was misled. I apologize to you. We're going to continue the program without her."

A firm in Chelm built an expensive wastewater treatment plant that allowed it to recycle chemical pollutants, instead of discharging them into the river. It wanted to let the community know that its efforts were paying off, and the river was already cleaner. Unfortunately, it took publicity photos upstream from the factory, above the former source of pollution, because it was "more scenic" there. Even in Chelm, the firm got caught, and what a time the newspapers and broadcasters had with that one!

Keeping the Media Informed of Changes

Certain procedures and taboos must be heeded when you work with the media. Whether it's a weekly paper with a circulation of 5,000 or a TV station with 10 million viewers, if the time or place of an event changes, you must notify every media outlet that got your publicity material. Failure to do this can mean that you will never get publicity again, unless you buy your own newspaper or station.

Failure to notify the media of changes can cause unexpected problems. The former publicist for the Chelm Recreation Department sent out a news release about an appreciation rally for the Chelm Soccer Team. But he got the time wrong. Instead of 8:00 P.M., he wrote 6:00 P.M. "What's the big deal?" he said to himself when he discovered the error. "So, they'll sit on the grass for two hours and have a picnic. By the time the team arrives, they'll be full of vinegar. It'll make a good rally. Besides, it's too much trouble to call all those stations and papers, and I didn't make a list of them, anyway."

The eager fans began arriving at 5:00 P.M. By 6:00 they were restless. At 6:30 they were pounding on the stadium doors, and at 7:00 a full-scale riot was broken up by the police. Soccer fans are generally not gentle folks. Dozens of people were arrested, and lots more were hospitalized. The stadium was a shambles, and damages were estimated at several hundred thousand dollars. Guess who was called on the carpet by the mayor the next day? The publicist for the Chelm Recreation Department quickly found himself in the market for another job.

When you send out publicity material about an event, keep a complete list of every media outlet you directed it to. In the rare case of a change in time or place, call each station or newspaper, and then follow up the call with a written note of the change. Journalists expect this, and they will be most unhappy if you emulate the ex-publicist from Chelm.

Jim Kemp of WVUE-TV says this about a publicist who doesn't tell him of last-minute changes: "It's not going to make him very popular. I'm going to forgive him once. After a second time, I'm going to get a little wary. And if it happens more often than that, I probably wouldn't take his calls." There are many journalists who won't even give you a second chance.

Your reputation with the media is one of your most valuable assets— or major liabilities. It will follow you from one organization to the next.

Since media people know each other, exchange information, and relocate frequently, it may grow larger than life, and it could spread to other cities and states. A bad reputation can make it almost impossible for you to get coverage.

Checklist—Basics of Good Media Relations

1. Have you included a prestamped reply card with your mailed publicity material, so you can get feedback?
2. Have you practiced your telephone or personal approach to media people, so that you can be brief and to the point?
3. When you call, do you ask your media contact whether it is a good time to talk?
4. When you make follow-up calls, do you have some good additional facts or a new angle to tempt journalists to cover your story?
5. If you're making an exploratory call, do you have several story ideas ready?
6. Unless you're handling financial publicity, do you fax publicity material by invitation only?
7. If you work for a publicly traded corporation, have you consulted your lawyer and developed a written disclosure policy for news that could affect stock prices?
8. Have you included industry analysts on your media release list?
9. Are you prepared to answer journalists' requests for additional information?
10. How many incoming and outgoing lines does your fax service have?
11. How many faxes can the service transmit simultaneously?
12. Can your service send separate messages to different lists at varying times, and do this automatically?
13. Will the fax service store and maintain your contact lists on its computer?
14. How many working days does the fax service need to make list additions and changes?
15. How does the service confirm that your faxes were received?
16. If one of your recipients can't be contacted, how many retries will the service make? Over how many hours?

17. If one of your recipients can't be contacted after repeated retries, how will the fax service handle it?

18. Can your letterhead, logo, and signature be digitized for your faxes?

19. Can the service generate cover pages that let recipients know to which person in the organization the fax is directed?

20. Can you send the service material to be faxed, by fax?

21. If so, how does the service ensure that the image will be clear enough for retransmission?

22. Can you send the service material to be faxed by E-mail?

23. Is there a setup fee?

24. Are there minimum charges?

25. Is there a minimum billing time per transmission?

26. After any minimum billing time, is time billed in full minutes or in smaller, more economical units?

27. What is the discount on overnight transmissions?

28. Does the service supply a daily accounting of on-line time billed?

29. Have you asked the journalists you work with closely if you can E-mail publicity material to them?

30. If you're thinking about delivering publicity material in person, have you made sure the journalists involved are receptive to this?

31. Do you tag all filled requests for follow-up material with a personal note reminding the journalists that they asked for it?

32. If you're not sure whether a journalist you've approached is interested in a story, do you call to clarify the situation?

33. Have you prepared a backgrounder sheet for your nonprofit organization?

34. Does the backgrounder include your purpose, the names of board members, your funding sources and budget, and your goals and achievements?

35. Have you prepared a backgrounder sheet for your business?

36. Does the backgrounder include information about the organization's structure, capitalization, and sales volume and a two- or three-sentence discussion of its history and position in the marketplace?

37. Do your backgrounder sheets include URLs to more information on your website? Are these URLs exact addresses, so journalists don't have to search for the information?

38. When journalists interview you or people who work for your organization, do you provide the reporters with written background information?

39. Does the written material include URLs to more information on your website?

40. Is it prepared especially for the story you're working on with them?

41. Does it include material that counters common misconceptions about your organization, product, or service?

42. During interviews, do you ask if the journalist has any unfavorable observations so that you can respond?

43. Do you offer journalists the opportunity to read back direct quotes to you before their stories are finished?

44. If your story involves technical or specialized information, do you offer journalists the opportunity to review their finished copy with you for accuracy?

45. Do you understand why it's not wise to go off the record in conversations with journalists, even in your "special" situation?

46. Can you gracefully accept no for an answer?

47. If you were turned down when you first pitched an important story, have you worked at developing one or more new angles?

48. Do you avoid the temptation to ask journalists for advice about how to prepare your publicity?

49. Have you found a better source for advice?

50. Is all your publicity material on 8½-by-11-inch paper?

51. Is all your publicity material neatly typed and duplicated?

52. Are you mailing all your publicity material with first-class postage?

53. Is the material you're sending to the media in the correct format?

54. Have you made a list of the deadlines faced by all the reporters and editors you'll be working with?

55. Do you know the lead times at all the media outlets you work with?

56. Have you figured out how much lead time you need for your events and publicity campaigns?

57. Do you avoid contacting the media at deadline time unless you have hard, breaking news?

58. Do you coordinate the release of stories that you want to run in your newsletter and simultaneously in the press with the journalists involved?

59. Are you being straightforward about your organization or business? Have you given journalists a complete picture?

60. Are you sure your publicity will withstand public scrutiny?

61. Do you keep a record of where all your publicity material is sent in order to issue corrections, if necessary?

3

How to Create Newsworthy Publicity

Journalists want two things from publicists: your facts have to be reliable, and your material must have a news angle or news peg that makes it different and interesting. It doesn't matter whether you're trying to get publicity from newspapers, magazines, radio, television, or websites; all journalists insist on newsworthy material. Otherwise, their readers will lose interest, their medium will lose market share, their advertisers will go elsewhere, and they won't have jobs anymore.

One of the most important things you need to know is the difference between hard news, and feature or human interest stories. Hard news has time value; it must be covered *now* or it will be stale. Disasters, crimes, lay-offs by large companies, new medical and scientific breakthroughs, and even major-league scores are all hard news. Soft news is often related to hard news events, but it doesn't have the same urgency. The media can run it today, tomorrow, or next week. It usually involves more background information and often has a human interest angle. Because it will stay fresh for a long time, soft news is sometimes called "evergreen" material.

A feature story summarizing AIDS research during the past year is "evergreen." If it doesn't run today, it can run tomorrow. Or the next day. On the other hand, a news story about the discovery of a new, highly effective treatment for AIDS is hard, breaking news. It won't keep.

Your organization may continually generate hard news. On the other hand, most of your publicity may involve feature and human interest material. Or, like most organizations, you're somewhere in between.

Where your organization falls on the hard-soft news spectrum depends on three variables:

- The type of product, service, or cause you're involved with. Bowling ball manufacturers make less hard news than oil companies.
- Whether or not your industry, organization, or cause gets caught up in controversy or tied in with trends. If it does, you're more likely to generate hard news.
- Your ability to show the media that the material is newsworthy and backed up with facts, that it's related to what's happening in the news, that it has a unique and interesting angle or news peg, and that you can be objective and informative.

You'll generate more hard news coverage if your publicity material meets these guidelines.

If you want to do a first-rate job of publicity, you must relentlessly pursue every opportunity, every possibility. Still, you have to be sure that the opportunities and possibilities are genuine and not false hopes that result in no publicity or, even worse, undermine your credibility with the media. You need to develop a sense of what is news—and what isn't.

Selecting Newsworthy Facts

Even Mary quite contrary would probably not make news these days if she didn't cultivate her message as well as her garden. When, where, why, and how does her garden grow? These are the basic questions all journalists will ask.

Before you write a single press release, you will have to work and rework your message until it is crystal clear.

First, make a list of the five *w*s and the *h*:

- Who is doing what for whom?
- When, where, and why are they doing it?
- How is it being done?
- What are the results?

For example, it's not enough to say that your product is an exciting new development based on years of research. You need to answer questions such as these:

- Why is the product exciting?
- What will it do for buyers: Save them time and money? Make them happier or healthier?
- How is it better than what's on the market now?
- What research was involved in developing it?
- What tests show its superior performance?
- Who is already using it?
- What are its specifications?
- How was the technology discovered? By whom?
- What was the *personal* impact on the team who developed it?

It's not adequate to say that your charitable organization has hundreds of volunteers who raise thousands of dollars for community activities. What are the activities? Who are the volunteers? Each of them is a living, thinking, feeling human being, and in every person there is at least one human interest story.

Perhaps you have a retired singer who volunteers as a coach for a high school drama group. She helped the youngsters raise money to buy costumes for their most recent production. A story is beginning to emerge. Probe further, and you may find that the teenagers really enjoy someone who can tell them what it was like working with Elvis. Much to everyone's delight, they are leaping clear across the generation gap. And one of the students, a quiet fellow, was cast in the role of a social butterfly. Suddenly, he is becoming more confident. His grades were borderline, but now his schoolwork is improving. That story will interest many more readers than a dull list of fund-raising quotas.

You will also have to figure out how to present statistics in an interesting way. For example, if your company has developed a new, recyclable package for microwave food products, determine which facts and figures may have visual appeal. Even without photos, a good description can create pictures in the minds of readers or listeners. How many tons of waste will *not* end up in landfills or incinerators this year as a result of your new product? What would that waste look like piled high? Ten football fields 30 feet deep? A hundred fields? More? How much paper and metal will the recycled packaging save yearly? How many books could be printed on that paper? How much energy will recycling save, and how many tankers of petroleum does that represent? The clearer and more descriptive your message, the better your media coverage will be.

Media people expect you to have clarified and developed your message before you approach them. "We don't know your organization. You know your organization," says KSTP-TV's Linnea Crowe. "And you should know what kinds of things you're trying to sell."

Editors, reporters, and public service directors want you to be specific because they need facts, not impressions, and focus, not fuzziness. "If there is a clear focus to the group, then it will be easier for their publicist to get my interest, and it will be easier for me to write about them," says journalist Leslie O'Bergin. "I couldn't even begin to count the number of people who thought their organization had a clear focus, but who could not give me the explanation I needed to write a thorough story."

Before you leap into print or onto the airwaves, ask yourself if you're prepared to be in the spotlight. "Don't publicize your organization or event until you're really ready," warns journalist Nancy Dunn. "If you're not fully prepared, you'll be stuck with an amateurish image that will be hard to live down."

Remaining Objective

The only time your publicity material should contain opinions is when you're quoting someone. "There's no way an opinionated release would ever see the light of day in our paper," says Brian Youmatz, news editor for the *Framingham Middlesex News* in Massachusetts. And although he might use the release as background material for a reporter-written story—if he thought the issues were important and he wanted to cover them—it would make him "think twice about the reliability" of that publicist's material in the future.

News releases are supposed to be objective, and that means they are written in the third person. A biased news release may do more than harm your reputation as a credible news source, since many journalists may assume you have something to hide. Such a release could, conceivably, set off an investigative-reporting effort aimed squarely at your organization. Fred Zehnder at KTVU-TV comments: "An opinionated, biased news release or news conference will result in a very zealous attempt to get the other side. It would be a cue right off the bat that somebody has an ax to grind."

No matter how passionately you feel about your product, the issues, and the information, keep that passion under control. Give facts and figures. Leave opinions for quotes, which actually help your release by giving it color and life.

The sample release in Exhibit 3.1 tells you almost nothing about the product, and the extreme hyperbole will turn editors off. Change the names of the company and the item, and it could be about almost anything! What do you do if your superiors won't listen to reason and insist you produce material like this? You could write two releases—one to satisfy them and one designed to get media coverage. You distribute only the second one to the media. It has been done.

Exhibit 3.1

Very Big Widget Company   **Contact: Ben Pupik III**
1000 Easy Street   **(123) 456-7890**
Chelm 00009
July 2, 2001

For Immediate Release

Very Big Introduces High-Powered Widget That Anticipates Market Needs
CHELM, July 2—Executives at the Very Big Widget Company, in one of the industry's most impatiently awaited maneuvers, continue to demonstrate tangibly the corporation's pledge to develop cutting-edge SOS Technology with the debut of the New, Improved HH-707 High-Powered Widget which sets new standards for widget performance.

MORE   MORE   MORE

"The HH-707 High-Powered Widget offers a higher output capacity, uses less power and ultimately gives its users a far lower cost per job," according to Chaim Trotskell, Product Manager for the 700 Series Widgets.

"With this powerful solution to the high cost of Widget usage, we have met the increasing demand for reasonably priced Widgets. We have reinforced our worldwide pledge to become the global Widget leader," Trotskell continues.

With worldwide headquarters in Chelm, The Very Big Widget Company is a recognized trailblazer in Widgets featuring the latest SOS Technology, which takes full advantage of microminiaturization. The Company, with $550 million in sales in fiscal 2000, employs 1,500 people worldwide.

###

If you are writing about your new French restaurant, it would be unwise to say, "Chef Andre Paté delights in leaving the kitchen to explain the composition of each delightful surprise to the eagerly awaiting customers." It would be much better if you wrote, "Chef Andre Paté often shares his recipes with the customers. 'I love to tell people how I make my pastries because they are so eager to learn,' he says."

The text of the release in Exhibit 3.2 is an example of slanted material without factual backing. The opinionated words and phrases and undocumented information are italicized.

The rewritten version in Exhibit 3.3 makes better news for several reasons. First, many of the opinions in the original release are now in direct quotes. Second, the opinions used are more selective, so they do not overwhelm the reader. Third, a key allegation is now supported by giving the source of the information, the Chelm Attorney General's Office. And finally, the use of proper journalistic format makes it read as news, not bombast.

The release lead in Exhibit 3.4 on page 80, which does not have a news peg, illustrates a common mistake made by publicists for websites. The fact that you have a website up and running is not news; there are literally millions of websites. A quick search of the Internet turns up more than a dozen

Exhibit 3.2

CHELM, Sept. 30—After our *victory* in the Chelm State Assembly, the *struggle to break the back* of the *parasitic* head shop trade shifted yesterday to federal court, where attorneys for the drug paraphernalia industry pulled out a last-minute temporary restraining order in a *bold* attempt to protect the *multimillion-dollar profits* of their clients from going up in smoke.

This move lays to rest the *myth* that head shops are small, innocuous businesses making a few dollars on rolling papers and water pipes. This industry is *wealthy, organized and powerful*, and it has the *money and the clout to hire high-priced* legal talent to protect its *vested* interests. In fact, a *huge war chest* was collected for their court challenges.

The constitutional issue is merely a *smoke screen* hiding a *vast empire built on the enhancement and glorification* of drug abuse. As one of the sponsors of the paraphernalia ban, I call upon the governor of Chelm to lend maximum assistance in resisting any *cynical* effort to *manipulate* the law or prevent its immediate enforcement.

Exhibit 3.3

CHELM, Sept. 30—The effort to limit the "head shop" trade shifted yesterday from the Chelm State Assembly to federal court, where attorneys for the industry got a last-minute restraining order that will delay the State's enforcement of the new laws against drug paraphernalia.

"This move lays to rest the myth that head shops are small, innocuous businesses making a few dollars on rolling papers and water pipes," says Assemblyman Ed Tichnor. "This industry is wealthy, organized and powerful. It has the money and the clout to hire the best legal talent."

MORE   MORE   MORE

The Chelm Association of Head Shop Owners has raised $785,000 for its legal defense fund in the past five months, according to figures obtained by Tichnor from the Chelm Attorney General's Office.

"The constitutional issue is merely a smoke screen hiding a vast empire built on the enhancement and glorification of drug abuse," says Tichnor, who formally asked the governor to provide legal resources to defend the new laws.

on-line purveyors of fresh seafood, all of whom ship by air courier. And yes, many of them include recipes.

If Zetz wants to get coverage from the media, the publicist has to go beyond this and develop a solid news peg. Include some of the Zetz family recipes in the release, explain why they are unique, and food editors may be interested in their story. Spell out how Zetz Seafoods' fishing fleet avoids entangling porpoises and dolphins in their nets, and Zetz has a good shot at getting coverage from science and environment reporters. If Zetz's competitors are not handling fresh fish properly, thus raising public health issues, that's a news peg for health and medicine reporters.

Exhibit 3.4

Chelm Farmers' Market Resident Opens Virtual Seafood Store
CHELM, Jan. 27—Zetz Seafoods, resident of the Historic Chelm Farmers' Market, has opened its doors to the World Wide Web. Visitors to the site, www.zetzseafoods.chl, can purchase fresh seafood along with some special gift selections. Everything is sent via air courier.

All of the Zetz Family's favorite recipes are on-line, along with color photos of each dish.

Take a virtual tour of the Chelm Farmers' Market and view the QTVR images and digital video.

Round Hole or Square, You Need a Peg

Another important news test involves uniqueness. If every other new widget has the same features yours does, if all the charities in town run garage sales and pancake breakfasts, if every other small business has crazy days sales in late August, then yours won't get much more than an events calendar listing or minor media coverage. Then again, if you come up with an unusual angle, you increase your chances for major coverage of an ordinary product or event.

With product publicity, you'll have to work closely with the marketing department to decide which aspects of their strategy will create the most usable news angles. Perhaps your new widget comes with a guarantee of satisfaction, while the other widget manufacturers "let the buyer beware." That's one way to separate your product from the crowd, give journalists a usable news angle, and get good coverage.

You can use the same approach with events. If your crazy days sale is the only one around to start with an old-fashioned tug-of-war in the middle of Main Street, just as they used to do before World War II, you have a better chance at good coverage. Should your group's garage sale feature a trunkful of historic pictures from the late 19th century, you're apt to get a nice spread in the paper if you offer to let the editor use any pictures she wants.

The most important thing in a news release is the peg. The peg is the focus, the angle, the main point, the unusual idea, the new material, the explanation of how the story will have an impact on the audience. The peg is the justification for the news release. There are some standard techniques for creating news pegs where none existed before. For instance, Americans love to celebrate holidays, anniversaries, seasons, and new world records for the biggest and the best. Tie your story to a celebration, anniversary, new record, or seasonal theme, and you have an instant peg that can make the difference between good coverage and no results at all.

Another standard technique for conjuring up a news peg is to create an award. "I've gotten coverage in the Business Section (which isn't easy to do) for an award I used to give out. I called it the Percy Award," says Gary Blake of the Communication Workshop. "It's named after that awful phrase 'pursuant to your request.' I started the Percy Awards . . . when I gave a mock award for the worst, most vague and antiquated memos, letters and reports. People heard about them on the radio and in *USA Today*. They submitted their favorite examples to me. And the Percy Awards became a regular feature, with a lot of newspapers picking up the story every year. Because of the Percy Awards, people began to identify me as a crusader for good writing. I can't say the Awards brought me business directly, but they did help my image," says Blake.

Adding new information to a major debate among consumers who buy your product, or in your industry, is another way to create a strong news peg. Copywriter Bob Bly sent out the release shown in Exhibit 3.5, which discusses the most effective techniques for creating advertising

---

Exhibit 3.5

FROM: Bob Bly, 174 Holland Avenue, New Milford, NJ 07646
CONTACT: Bob Bly—(201) 599-2277

For immediate release

New Free Fact Sheet Reveals What Engineers Like (and Don't Like) about Industrial, High-Tech, and Business-to-Business Advertising
New Milford, NJ—If your most recent industrial, high-tech, or business-to-business ad campaign didn't generate the results you'd hoped for, it may be because engineers—a key target for such campaigns—respond to advertising differently than "normal folk," according to New Milford, NJ-based copywriter and advertising consultant Bob Bly.

"Engineers look down on advertising," says Bly. "For the most part, they have a low opinion of advertising and of people who work in the field. As a result, advertising aimed at engineers must be informational and professional, not gimmicky or promotional. Avoid writing copy that sounds like 'ad copy.' Engineers will be quick to reject such material as 'fluff.'"

Among Bly's advice to industrial advertisers and agencies:

The engineer's purchase decision is more logical than emotional. "Certainly, there are emotional components to an engineer's buying decision. But for the most part, an engineer buying a new piece of equipment will analyze technical specifications," says Bly.

MORE   MORE   MORE

Engineers want to know the features, not just the benefits. "In consumer advertising classes, we are taught that benefits are everything, and that features are unimportant. But engineers are not content to know just the benefit. They also want to understand the feature that enables the product to provide the benefit," insists Bly.

Engineers are not turned off by jargon and technical language. "In fact," says Bly, "they like it. Use of technical language in ad copy shows the engineer that you speak his language and are not superficial in your understanding of his requirements."

Engineers and other technical specialists are attracted by visuals that reflect their area of expertise. "For instance, when illustrating ads aimed at electrical engineers, use circuit diagrams."

Engineers do not like a "consumer approach" to advertising. "There is a raging debate in business-to-business advertising whether engineers respond to a straight technical approach, a clever consumer-style approach, or something in between," says Bly. "Those who prefer the creative approach argue that the engineer is a human being first and an engineer second, and will therefore respond to creativity and cleverness just like everyone else.

"Unfortunately," adds Bly, "there is much evidence to the contrary." Bly says he has been involved in numerous tests of consumer vs. technical copy in ads and direct mail packages aimed at engineers, and that "the straightforward, low-key, professional approach will outpull the 'glitzy' ad or mailing virtually every time."

To receive a free copy of the "Marketing to Engineers" tip sheet, write to Bob Bly, Dept. ME, 174 Holland Avenue, New Milford, NJ 07646, or call (201) 599-2277.

aimed at engineers. Since this is a hot topic in publications specializing in advertising and public relations news, these editors will welcome this type of material.

Yet, even though a news peg is critical for good publicity, many publicists send out pegless releases. "One pet peeve" about publicists, says Tom Callaghan of the *Birmingham News*, "is when they put out a release without any news focal point just because they think it's time to put out a release. That's just a waste of our time." KTVU-TV's Fred Zehnder adds to that view, "Publicists may feel that providing coffee and doughnuts for reporters and cameramen is a good reason for us to cover an event. It isn't." Coffee and doughnuts aren't a substitute for a news peg.

Can you see why journalists would consider the sample releases in Exhibits 3.6 and 3.7 to be pegless?

The problem with the release in Exhibit 3.6 is that it is full of congratulations and self-praise. Yes, it is nice that 38 employees are Acme Champions, but what does that mean? How much did they sell? When, exactly, is the "most recent period"? And why is it news? Award ceremonies like this are held all the time. The story may be of interest to the families and friends of the honorees, but the recipients' names aren't mentioned.

We are told that interesting speeches were made, but not *why* they are of interest; we have no idea what the speakers said. In fact, change a few names and phrases, and this release could apply to almost any organization. If you came across such a release anywhere but in this book, would you bother to read it? Of course not! It's "inside stuff," of interest only to the people involved, and even they may be bored silly by the ceremonial pomposity. Ceremonial pomposity is not news, unless some very well-known people are involved.

Exhibit 3.7 is also inside stuff. If you are not one of the businessmen involved, there's nothing in it for you because this is not a public event. You cannot take part because you have not been invited, and the news was released after the event was over. So, even though the piece may have a peg when it is run in the *Chelm Chamber of Commerce Newsletter*, that peg falls apart outside Chamber of Commerce circles. That's why private events are not usually news.

"We do not serve as a bulletin board," says Paul Neely, features editor of the *St. Petersburg Times* in Florida. "It is important to have some awareness of what news value is, what makes something unusual. A stamp club meeting is not unusual. A stamp club meeting where someone from out of town is showing a stamp worth half a million dollars is unusual."

An important question you should ask before you send out any news release is: If this story were about an organization you were unfamiliar with, would you be interested in reading it?

You may think that's all fine for other people, but your product is unique and wonderful—or your website, which has just been heavily endowed with

Exhibit 3.6

CHELM, June 16—On Monday afternoon, June 15, Acme Products in Chelm honored 38 National Sales Champions who each achieved astounding sales figures for the most recent period. The audience included the justly proud spouses of the honorees as well as key employees and suppliers.

In addition to awarding Sales Champion pins, Mr. Martin Puffer, president, delivered a brief farewell address, since he is retiring in June after 54 years of distinguished service to the firm.

Corky McCorkle, vice president of Sales, was the guest speaker. Ms. McCorkle gave an interesting and unusual speech praising and congratulating the Champions after she presented them with their Acme Achievement certificates.

Mr. John Gonn, chairman of the board, was very proud to have made his 16th annual presentation of the Acme Champions induction ceremony. He extended good wishes to the honorees and thanked the entire staff of Acme.

The Chelm community should be very proud of their Acme Champions, since Acme's requirements are perhaps the highest in the nation. These employees are the key hope for Chelm's economic future.

###

Exhibit 3.7

CHELM, Jan. 7—How lucky can you get? You couldn't better the winning odds at the First Annual Golf and Field Day held by the Chelm Chamber of Commerce on Thursday, Jan. 3, at the Circular Club Golf Course, according to an announcement today by Chamber president R. J. Solfeggio.

Four hundred Chelm businessmen who attended the Chamber's popular all-day outing enjoyed a "big edge" in their chances to win. Twenty-five "superduper" awards alone, valued at $100 to $250 and more, were picked during the windup dinner, starting at 7:00 P.M.

###

venture capital funding, is "different" from your 150 competitors, or your group is a charity with a worthy cause, and *you* should be able to get publicity just by asking for it. Don't believe that for a second!

You're not asking for publicity; you're providing journalists with a story they can use. As KOOL-TV's Bill Close puts it, "Never use the word *publicity*. *Publicity* is a profane, obscene word. Don't come in here and say, 'Hey, we need some publicity.' The least the publicist can do is make an intelligent effort to camouflage it by saying, 'We have a cute little angle we think will make a good feature for you.' It's a matter of intelligent salesmanship."

Creating Newsworthy Events

Sometimes you will want to create news by staging an event that is designed to get you coverage. "We've done a lot of special events [to] which we hope to draw 80 people," says Bob Seltzer of Porter Novelli. "But that special event is in no way, shape or form directed at those 80 people. It's aimed at the media, who will then cover what you're doing."

Let's say your construction trades association has not been able to interest the local media in figures demonstrating that defense spending will produce only a few jobs in your state, but the same amount of money, if spent on rebuilding the state's infrastructure, would produce work for many more people. Although the idea of a "peace dividend" has been discussed in the national media, there's never been a local angle story from your state.

You may get coverage if you stage an event that dramatizes the controversy. It's possible for you to entice news photographers and camera crews to a rally where, for example, a dozen people are gathered in a tight group wearing jumpers and caps that look like bullets. Completely surrounding the "defense workers" would be a hundred "construction trade workers" with equally interesting and photogenic costumes. Since large groups are hard to assemble and difficult to photograph, you may use one person to symbolize each hundred—or thousand—jobs, depending on the figures your research uncovers. Photographed from a bird's-eye viewpoint, that would make quite a picture!

Perhaps you're running a halfway house that helps ex-drug addicts become part of the community again after their release from residential treatment centers. The house is across the street from a neighborhood park, and although there has never been a problem, the neighbors are worried; they're even reluctant to let their children play in the park. You're worried, too. Your permit to operate the halfway house has been issued on a trial basis. The neighbors may challenge your application for permanent status at the upcoming public hearings.

You have to create a positive image. You decide to sponsor an End of Winter Festival at the local park for neighborhood families, with residents of your halfway house serving as volunteers. Several of them have formed a band, so it will be easy for you to fill the day with live music, and there will be free hot chocolate, hayrides, and a snowball fight with the alderman—whose daughter is one of the residents.

Although skating season is over, the outdoor rink is still frozen. Hundreds of children and their parents are given buckets of tempera paint, and soon marvelous designs cover the ice, fading slowly into a swirled rainbow as the surface melts during the next week.

The ice paintings appear on the front page of the evening paper, as well as on two local TV news shows; no one has ever painted on ice before, at least not in your city. The neighborhood is buzzing. They've had a chance to see the halfway house residents as people, and they liked what they saw. They're proud that their area is page-one news, and they know that your halfway house helped create that news. You got good coverage because you provided interesting, highly visual material with human interest and a new, unusual angle. That is what the media want.

The Local Angle

Since national news magazines, as well as all-news television and radio networks, cover national news so thoroughly, many weekly and daily newspapers limit themselves to local news stories. This is especially the case with suburban newspapers. Many radio and TV newsrooms also concentrate on local news because they rely on networks and wire services to cover the national scene. So, it is often important that publicity material received from out-of-town sources is of local interest.

Localizing news releases pays handsome dividends, with placement rates five to ten times higher than releases without localization. In fact, some stories *must* be localized to get media coverage. Only about a third of the material needs to be local, and local statistics can be just as helpful as local names.

If your corporation is headquartered in Plains City, for example, but you have dealers all along the Eastern Seaboard, try to get coverage in their media outlets as well by localizing individual releases. Using a word processor, you can customize lead paragraphs for each release, and include a paragraph or two about how a customer from each community has benefited from your product.

When your organization is making an announcement, you can send out different releases attributing the announcement to local spokespeople in each community. Or you can refer reporters to an expert in their region for an interview that rounds out the material in your release.

Exhibit 3.8 provides an example of the lead paragraphs from a localized press release. They would be followed by more information about your organization and its product. How do you get the localized information? With the help of local dealers, who stand to gain a lot from press coverage in their area.

In the lead for the release in the exhibit, localized information can be plugged in for each community newspaper in the country. All the local dealer has to do is get the name and age of a local garden club member

---

Exhibit 3.8

PLAINS HEIGHTS, April 30—Plains Heights resident Mike T. Chen doesn't rake and bag grass clippings anymore—but his lawn is still neatly manicured and deep green. Thirty-eight-year-old Chen, a member of the Plains Heights Garden Club, mows his lawn the same as everyone else. But his new Mulch-O-Matic lawn mower transforms the clippings into a fine powder and blows it deep into the lawn, where it quickly turns into high-grade compost.

"Plains City residents create about 1,500 tons of grass clippings each season. With a $30 per ton fee at the Plains County Dump, grass clippings cost the city's residents about $45,000 annually," says Mulch-O-Matic's president, Melissa Fielding.

"That's a double shame," Fielding continues. "Perfectly good mulch material is going to waste. And the County Dump is running out of room."

who is a Mulch-O-Matic user, find out how many tons of grass clippings local residents produce yearly, and determine the local dump's disposal fee. The balance of the release does not have to be customized.

If you are sending out localized releases, you will want to let editors know immediately that, despite the out-of-town address, the material will be of use to them. Mark your releases "local angle story" with a red marker. If you plan to send out a great deal of localized material, you can even have a rubber stamp made up. However you do the marking, it will be appreciated by news directors and editors. "It really does help to mark a press release 'local angle story' if the material originates in another city," says Gladys Adams of the *Kansas City Voice*.

Whenever you can, include the name and telephone number of a local contact on your material. This is most important when the media outlet is far away from you.

You can use this approach in another way. If the media are covering a national story of interest to your organization, you can call news directors or editors and offer a local angle on the story.

If there's national coverage on the dangers of toxic chemicals seeping out of garbage dumps and into water supplies, and your organization has solid information about that problem at a nearby landfill, call the local media outlets and offer your story.

Or, let's say Congress has just passed new legislation that you believe will make your widgets much more expensive—and give foreign widget makers an unfair advantage. You could call local journalists and offer your facts and figures on how that decision will affect local workers. You could also contact national media outlets and offer material on how the new widget legislation will impact your area of the country. If you act fast, before there has been any "grassroots" coverage on this story, and if your facts, figures, and anecdotes are specific, you have the best chance of getting coverage.

"I would certainly welcome a call like that because we are interested in attempting to localize national stories," says WVUE-TV's Jim Kemp.

Journalist Nancy Dunn suggests that you could open a call about a local-angle story by saying, "I'm working for so-and-so and I'm trying to get some coverage of blank. Other sides of this issue have been covered, but I've never seen it covered from this angle before." Or, "This has been covered in the national press, but I haven't seen the local aspects covered yet." Then briefly tell the reporter your angle and information.

Backgrounding a News Story

Let's say there have been a dozen train wrecks in your county in the past few months. The media are running a story about the official investigation that has just been announced. You could call reporters and offer your Defend the Rails Association's information about discriminatory tax policies that favor other forms of transportation and lead to slipshod railroad maintenance—and train wrecks.

All journalists need quick and easy access to reliable background information; that's why journalists are heavy Internet users. If you offer solid, useful background information, and journalists get used to turning to you as a source, your media coverage is sure to improve. You can offer background information on an ongoing basis, using several different approaches:

- Set up a toll-free telephone hot line for journalists, and promote it regularly. Your promotional material should explain the resources you offer and your hours of operation. If it's possible, including a preprinted Rolodex card will help ensure that journalists keep your number at their fingertips. To make a hot line successful, you have to keep a healthy file of facts at your command and have a fast way to retrieve the exact information your caller is asking for, as well as a method for quickly handling inquiries that require research. You also must be prepared to staff that hot line during business hours and have a way for journalists to page you when the hot line is not staffed.

- An alternative to a staffed hot line is a voice mail system to let journalists listen to in-depth recorded presentations on topics they choose from a menu. Beware of the limitations of voice mail systems, however. More than two or three menu levels get awfully confusing. Also, limit your choices to four or five items per level, or your system will seem difficult to use. Keep your presentations short; two minutes is about the longest people can follow when they're listening on the phone. Always have a menu choice that immediately connects journalists to a live person who can answer questions. And be sure to let callers know at the end of each selection that they can find more information on your website.

- Set up a fax-back service that offers a selection of documents with background information on your industry, product line, or company.

You can purchase fax-back equipment or use an outside service. In either case, journalists call in and request the documents that interest them. The documents are delivered directly to the caller's fax machine in a matter of minutes.

- Distribute a file folder with a prelabeled tab (Widget Fact File, for example), or a loose-leaf binder, with factual material about your product, industry, or cause. Make sure that every journalist who may ever write stories about your subject gets a copy. And set up a program to update the file regularly.

- Provide in-depth background information on your website. While some journalists will find this resource on their own, it's a good idea to promote it regularly. For more information about turning your website into a resource for journalists, see Chapter 6.

- List your organization in the commercially distributed off-line and on-line expert directories mentioned in Chapter 13.

- No matter how you provide background information, keep in mind that most journalists are on-line and can research thousands of databases and websites. What will bring them to your backgrounding service, and keep them coming back, is high-quality, reliable information that is updated regularly and is easy to work with. If your information is unique and can't be found elsewhere, that's going to be even more attractive to journalists. Be sure to let the press know if you have information not available elsewhere.

Publicity for Products

Product publicity may seem simple at first glance, but a tremendous amount of thought and strategizing is involved in getting more than a mere product mention.

First you have to look at the product itself. There are two broad types of products—commodity and differentiated—and you have to decide into which category yours falls. Many products are somewhere in between.

- *Commodity products* are like every other product of their kind on the market—they all have the same basic features. Sure, yours may come in color while competitors' are all black or white, but if all the other qualities are the same, you still have a commodity product. Pack-

aged goods such as soap, peanut butter, soft drinks, and hair spray
are typical commodity products.

■ *Differentiated products* have features and benefits that are different
from the competition. Quality furniture, books, many toys, and most
heavy industrial equipment are examples of differentiated products.

If you're promoting a commodity product, you can use several strategies. "Identify product benefits that competitors have ignored—even
though their products have them as well," says Donald M. Levin, of Levin
Public Relations Marketing, Inc., in White Plains, New York. Buyers will
begin to identify that benefit with your product, even if all your competitors offer the same feature.

Another approach is to tie your commodity product to issues and
events that are of interest to consumers, such as awards and sporting
events. If you develop a clever angle and do your homework with the media,
an award program can pay handsome dividends, even with a Spartan
budget. Tournaments and sports competitions, on the other hand, have
higher visibility than awards, but they are more expensive to plan, run,
and publicize.

For noncommodity products, or products that fall in between, there
are several other options. Bob Bly suggests, "Identify either what is *new*
about the product, or the most different, unusual, newsworthy or interesting feature or aspect of the product."

You can also produce publicity material that teaches the public how to
buy, choose, and use your product. Or you can tie in to a hot issue on the
minds of consumers.

Paul Gourvitz of Gourvitz Communications, a New York video production house, solved a tough publicity challenge with an inventive
approach. Matchbox wanted to do a video news release about its new toys,
R. C. Ripskate and R. C. Radskate. "They were clever toys," Gourvitz
says, "but we needed to make the product newsworthy." Gourvitz and his
colleagues interviewed a national skateboard champion who used the toys
to demonstrate safety tips for young skateboarders. With safety as a peg,
this became an interesting news story, and, with action footage of an
actual skateboard competition, "the video news release was well-accepted
by news producers across the country," according to Gourvitz's account
in *Playthings*.

A good news peg is only the start of effective product publicity. You
have to provide solid information about your product. If you say that your

product's performance is superior, you have to be able to back it up with facts, and if the data that support your claims come from an independent source, so much the better. Moreover, whenever you deal with product claims, you have to conform to Federal Trade Commission regulations, as well as a plethora of state and local laws. It's a good idea to have your lawyer review the copy for all publicity material that contains product claims.

When you write a press release announcing a new product, be sure to include all the significant facts in the lead. The following lead paragraph, from a release prepared for Sharp by Dorf & Stanton Technology Communications, gave editors enough hard facts to know beyond a doubt that this copier was a breakthrough product.

> *ATLANTA—A full-color copier which can produce seven-color copies on letter-sized plain paper at the rate of 7.5 copies per minute will be highlighted at this year's COMDEX show by Sharp Electronics Corporation. The CX-7500 is currently being sold through Sharp's network of dedicated color copier dealers throughout the country.*

Timing Your Product Publicity

The right timing for your product publicity is critical. In addition to conforming to media lead times, you have to determine if the marketplace needs to be "conditioned" ahead of time to accept publicity for a product that people may not even have thought of. As public relations executive Bob Seltzer explains, "If you're going to come out with a new contact lens cleaner in six months, you would be very smart to get articles about the problems of cleaning contact lenses in the media—now. These stories don't even require that your product is mentioned. You're educating the marketplace about a problem, so when your product launches, you've made your audience more receptive. Publicity does not work as effectively if you wait until the product comes out to build awareness."

You can also publicize a product before it's available to create a dramatic awareness that gets the media and the public looking forward to its introduction. Seltzer notes that Porter Novelli launched the Gillette Sensor razor with an announcement in October, even though the product would not come out until January. "The object was to build anticipation and expectation. Every year *Fortune* magazine does an article on the 10 best products of the year. The Gillette Sensor was actually named one of the 10 best products for 1989, even though it wasn't even introduced until 1990," according to Seltzer.

This worked well with the Gillette Sensor partly because the story behind the product was so dramatic. It took 10 years to develop this new razor with 13 moving parts protected by 22 patents. Gillette spent about $200 million on manufacturing equipment and planned to spend $175 million on a 19-country marketing campaign. The size of the effort and expenditures alone is big news.

The publicity campaign was coordinated in 19 North American and European countries, with the kickoff at an elaborate press conference in early October 1989. A second wave of consumer publicity was launched in December and January. The campaign included the following elements:

- Special story angles and materials for trade, consumer, and business publications.
- Sensor gift packs for selected editors.
- Results from a panel of 5,000 consumers who tested and rated the product.
- A backgrounder on the history of the safety razor, which Gillette's founder invented and first manufactured in 1903.

The results of this campaign were also dramatic, with more than 800 placements internationally, including:

- Feature TV segments on "Good Morning America," "CBS Evening News," Financial News Network's "Business Tonight," and European TV.
- Hundreds of feature stories in major business, trade, and consumer publications, including *Newsweek, Forbes, Elle,* and *Mirabella.*
- Stories on all the major wire services, including three AP stories, UPI, and Reuters.
- Hundreds of feature newspaper stories, among them the *Wall Street Journal, Los Angeles Times, Boston Globe, Detroit Free Press, Philadelphia Inquirer,* and *New York Times.*
- Hundreds of European newspaper and magazine placements, including *Le Figaro, Milano Finanza,* and the *Frankfurter Allgemeine Zeitung.*

- A picture on the cover of *Fortune* and the caption ". . . literally on the cutting edge."
- A report by *USA Today* staffer James Cox, who tested the razor himself and announced that it "maneuvers well."

Recycling Your Publicity

Your press release has been written and distributed. You have organized and analyzed the clippings and got some very nice comments from your colleagues, superiors, and even the board of directors. Your task is over now, isn't it?

Not so fast! Now it's time to start recycling your publicity. Once you realize the possible return on your investment, I'm sure you'll be convinced that the effort is worthwhile. There are two ways to recycle:

- Use reprints of the most favorable clippings in your promotional material. They can give you far more credibility than even the slickest four-color brochure. In a large organization, you'll want to coordinate this effort with your sales and marketing department.
- Use reprints as the basis of further publicity, by selecting detailed articles on how to choose, buy, and use your product, repackaging them, and offering them as giveaways. This works especially well with articles written by an insider—you or someone from your organization.

In either case, you need to get permission from the publication that first printed the article, since the piece is probably copyrighted in the publication's name. This is usually a formality: write a note to either the permissions editor (at large publications) or the editorial contact (at smaller publications) explaining how you'll use the reprint, and the company will probably reply with its approval.

Gary Blake uses copies of articles about his company, the Communication Workshop, in packets of material that he sends to prospects. "They round out a prospect's way of looking at you," he says. "It gives you a lovely chance to parade your credentials without seeming self-serving—and that's the wonderful thing about publicity."

Freelance copywriter Bob Bly used the second approach with an article he had written for *Business Marketing*. The press release shown in Exhibit 3.9, which he sent to 60 advertising, public relations, sales, and marketing publications, resulted in 18 stories over the following months. Some were just short blurbs, but others were word-for-word pickups of the entire release, including one in *Nation's Business* that generated 400 inquiries. Bly didn't send his release directly to *Nation's Business*—that publication picked it up from elsewhere!

As a result of this recycling campaign, Bly received 2,000 requests for the booklet within six months. The inquiries led to sales of hundreds of copies of his books about advertising and marketing, and generated several consulting assignments. His out-of-pocket cost for the publicity was under $100.

Exhibit 3.9

FROM: Bob Bly, 174 Holland Avenue, New Milford, NJ 07646
CONTACT: Bob Bly—(201) 599-2277

For immediate release

Free Booklet Reveals 31 Ways to Get More Inquiries from Your Ads
New Milford, NJ—A new booklet, published by independent copywriter and advertising consultant Robert W. Bly, reveals 31 strategies for creating ads that generate more inquiries, leads, sales and profits for advertisers.

The booklet, "31 ways to get more inquiries from your ads," is available free of charge to business executives, entrepreneurs, advertising professionals, and students. The cost to the general public is $1.00.

Bly said he originally wrote the booklet for companies and ad agencies that need to see more of a bottom-line return from advertising campaigns originally designed purely to build "image" and awareness.

"There's no reason an image campaign can't also generate leads as well as awareness," says Bly. "High-quality inquiries mean more sales and profits. And they also provide a way of measuring response. The booklet

MORE   MORE   MORE

presents 31 ways to increase any ad's pulling power without destroying the basic concept or interfering with communication of the key message."

Some of the inquiry-producing techniques presented in the booklet include:

Offer free information—a booklet, brochure, catalog, price list, order form—in every ad you write.

Give your literature piece a title that implies value. "*Product guide* sounds better than *catalog*," notes Bly. "*Planning kit* implies greater value than *sales brochure*."

For a full-page ad, use a coupon. According to Bly, "This will increase response 25 to 100 percent."

Make the coupon large enough so that there is plenty of room for prospects to write their name and address. "Tiny coupons drive people crazy," notes Bly.

In a fractional ad, put a heavy dashed border around the ad.

"This creates a coupon-like appearance, which in turn stimulates response," explains Bly.

Offer something FREE—such as a free product sample, free report, free video or audio cassette, free analysis, free consultation, free estimate, free seminar, free demonstration, or free trial.

Says Bly: "By modifying existing ads using the techniques outlined in this booklet, advertisers can increase response to their ads 20 to 100 percent—without destroying the basic concept and theme of these campaigns."

To receive a free copy of "31 ways to get more inquiries from your ads," send a self-addressed stamped #10 envelope to: Advertising Inquiries, 174 Holland Avenue, New Milford, NJ 07646.

Bob Bly is a freelance copywriter specializing in business-to-business and direct response advertising and the author of 16 books including *The Copywriter's Handbook* (Holt).

###

Self-Liquidating Publicity

It's often worth offering a free report, article, checklist, or other inexpensive giveaway to get people to respond to your publicity so you can mail them promotions for your products or services. Sometimes, however, you can charge a small fee for the item and defray the cost of your publicity campaign, making it "self-liquidating."

Gary Blake of the Communication Workshop has done this successfully with a series called "The Excellent Writer's Posters." "The first poster we publicized was called 'No Institutionitis,'" Blake explains. "It had hundreds of stuffy institutional phrases like 'enclosed please find,' and 'under separate cover.' *USA Today* picked up the story from our release and we got about 1,000 paid requests for that poster over the next six months."

Blake adds, "I think when thousands of our posters go up on bulletin boards all across the United States, we're building for the future. A number of times a prospect has told me 'I saw your name once before. Today I saw it the second time, and that's why I'm calling you.' In fact, that's how I got my biggest client." Exhibit 3.10 shows one of the releases Blake used to publicize the posters.

Exhibit 3.10

CLIENT: CONTACT:
The Communication Workshop   Gary Blake
217 East 85th Street   (718) 575-8000
New York, NY 10028
(718) 575-8000

For Immediate Release:

New Posters Help People Learn Punctuation "At a Glance"
NEW YORK, N.Y. APRIL 23rd—What's the difference between a comma and a semicolon? A dangling modifier and a misplaced modifier? If you're like most people, you need a brush-up in the basics of punctuation and grammar.

To help people master the basics of punctuation and grammar, The Communication Workshop, a New York City consulting firm devoted to help-

MORE   MORE   MORE

ing businesspeople and technicians improve their writing, is offering 2-color posters on each of these touchy topics.

The eye-catching posters ("Punctuation at a Glance" and "Grammar at a Glance") clearly differentiate the eight most important punctuation marks and the six stickiest grammar glitches, giving rules and showing examples that are visually bold and can be understood "at a glance."

For a copy of each of these posters, suitable for displaying on bulletin boards, send $4.00 (including postage and handling) to The Communication Workshop, 217 East 85th Street, New York, NY 10028.

###

Checklist—Keys to Newsworthy Publicity

1. Have you determined whether your organization generates mostly soft news, hard news, or a mixture of the two?
2. Do you understand why your release is either hard or soft news, and how to develop an angle based on the news type?
3. Have you checked each piece of publicity material before mailing to make sure it has the who, when, where, why, how, and what?
4. Have you decided how to dramatize your statistics?
5. Are your news releases objective? Backed by facts and figures? Focused on one or two main ideas?
6. Are your news releases written in the third person, with opinions confined to quotes?
7. Is your organization ready to handle the media's questions—no matter what they ask about?
8. Is your news release unique enough to warrant media attention?
9. If your release were about an organization you were unfamiliar with, would you be interested in reading it?
10. Is there anything else you can do to make your product, service, or cause stand out from the pack?
11. What is your news peg?
12. Are there other pegs you could use to make your release, press conference invitation, or tip sheet more interesting?
13. Have you considered creating a news peg by tying your story to a seasonal theme, anniversary, award, or new record for the biggest and the best?

14. Have you thought about creating a news peg by adding new information to a debate in your industry, or among consumers who buy your product?

15. If you're doing product publicity, are you working with the marketing department to decide which aspects of the marketing strategy will make the best news pegs?

16. Has your lawyer reviewed any product claims in your publicity material to make sure they don't run afoul of FTC regulations and federal, state, and local law?

17. Is your event open to the public? If not, why are you publicizing it?

18. Do you understand why you don't ask journalists for some "publicity"?

19. If your release or press conference is about a cause or controversy, have you developed a peg that makes it news?

20. Have you thought about how your organization can create newsworthy events to further its goals?

21. Is your organization ready to offer local-angle and background material on fast-breaking national news stories?

22. Are you developing background approaches for "grassroots" local stories for the national media as well as local media?

23. Are you localizing press releases for out-of-town newspapers and broadcasters?

24. Are you using your dealer and distributor network or local chapters as sources for the information you need to localize stories?

25. Have you marked your localized releases "local angle story"?

26. How many ways can you develop to localize stories in addition to those discussed in this chapter?

27. Have you considered positioning your organization as an authority journalists can regularly turn to for information?

28. Have you promoted this backgrounder service to all journalists who can use it?

29. Will you handle this service as a hot line, voice mail system, fact file, fax-back service, or website?

30. Have you determined if yours is a commodity or differentiated product—or somewhere in between?

31. If yours is a commodity product, have you identified product benefits competitors have ignored?

32. To which issues or events can you tie your product for strong news pegs?

33. Have you provided solid information about your product?

34. Have you backed up claims about product performance with verifiable facts, preferably from an independent source?

35. Has your lawyer reviewed any product claims in your publicity material?

36. Have you determined whether there is a need to "precondition" the marketplace to prepare it to accept your product?

37. Have you worked out a timetable for your product publicity campaign?

38. If you're considering publicizing your product before it's actually available, have you made sure that the story is dramatic enough to make this approach work?

39. Are you using reprints of your media clippings to bolster your promotional material?

40. Have you thought about repackaging published articles about your product or service as giveaways and using publicity to promote them?

41. Have you considered charging a small fee to make your premium self-liquidating?

Writing for Print Media and the Web

4

If you're like most people, you feel ice crystals forming in your innards and an intense desire to run away from home when you have to write something. Writing scares many intelligent, creative, dynamic people, and many writers, too. Relax: a simple secret can help you overcome your fear of writing.

A plumber and a writer were once comparing their jobs over a round of beer. When the writer mentioned writer's block, the plumber was incredulous. "Writer's block!" he exclaimed. That's ridiculous. Did you ever hear of plumber's block? Why don't you just look at the blueprints and get started?"

"I don't have blueprints," the writer replied.

"Well, get some, even if *you* have to make them," her friend advised.

So, the writer tried drawing up blueprints before she started writing. It took some time, which worried the writer at first. However, she eventually found that her writing went much faster, she knew exactly where to start, and she wasn't as stressed out.

The next time she had a beer with the plumber, she thanked her friend for the advice and told him, "The blueprints were a great idea. But I call them outlines and formats."

If you outline your work first, you'll find it much easier to master the different formats you need to have in your publicist's tool bag. The format you will probably use most frequently is the standard press release that announces news about your organization's activities. The release is sometimes accompanied by a supplementary fact sheet. The feature article, which is longer and not necessarily geared to a particular event, is another good publicity tool. In addition, you should learn how to prepare fillers and community calendar listings and to write effective letters to the editor on behalf of your organization.

Press Releases

Press releases are the cornerstone of any publicity program. Write them well, and your business or organization will get its share of coverage. If releases are poorly written, with cute leads instead of solid information, and misspelled words and inaccurate data instead of precise information, they'll end up in the circular file.

Editors across the country, at large metropolitan dailies and small suburban weeklies, all complain that they get too many poorly written releases, that they are engulfed in useless material, and that they have to spend too much time sorting out the few good releases from the mountain of drivel.

Yet, press releases are relied on by journalists. A survey mentioned in *Public Relations Journal* found that more than 200 travel editors rely on press releases almost as much as they count on material from their staff writers. To round out its coverage, even the *Wall Street Journal* uses press releases from businesses.

The press release isn't the only vehicle available, however. With the explosion of press releases coming at journalists by E-mail, fax, and snail mail, you can stand out by writing a brief, 250- to 300-word pitch letter instead. This approach can be stronger because you're not writing a story—you're presenting ideas for how journalists can write their own stories. Start by explaining your story idea in 50 words or less. Then discuss how you will help the reporter write the story, the possible news angles, the resource material you can provide, and the experts you can make available for interviews.

Press Release Format

Try to put yourself in the editor's seat for a moment. If she works at a large daily paper, she gets hundreds of press releases each day. She may have only an hour to read all of them, so she'll be able to spend a few seconds on each one—or even less. She'll have to make quick judgments based on a skim of the first paragraph or two, but she'll also judge your release by its format. If it doesn't look like news, she may not even read it. There are plenty of other releases that fit her format, will need less editing, and will create fewer potential problems.

You may be tempted to run a release on flashy pink paper with purple ink to grab attention. Don't do it. Says S. Griffin Singer of the *San Antonio Light*, "We had some stuff come through here not too long ago on fuchsia and chartreuse paper. It really looked awful. And that turned me off. Sure, it got my attention, but it had a negative impact."

Most publicists do use flashy letterhead for press releases, but you shouldn't, for the following reasons:

- Journalists prefer plain 8½-by-11-inch paper, and that's reason enough.
- If you use a letterhead, you won't be able to fit as much copy on the page as you would if you used a heading, because a heading takes up less space than a typical letterhead. A letterhead could make a one-page release flow over onto a second sheet.
- If you use plain paper, your release will stand out—it will be one of the few on simple white paper.

"Using plain white paper on news releases is important from a physical point of view," says Brian Youmatz of the *Framingham Middlesex News*. "If the press release is on a letterhead, we usually tear it off and glue the release to another sheet of paper, which is time-consuming."

Here are basic press release format guidelines for print publications. Broadcasters and Web-based journalists have somewhat different requirements which are covered in Chapters 6 and 8.

- Keep typed lines 50 to 60 characters long, including punctuation marks and spaces. This length is easy to read and allows margins wide enough for editing.
- Double-space the entire release. Some less experienced publicists double-space the first few paragraphs—or "graphs," as journalists call them—and single-space the rest of the release. Not only does this look awkward, but also it doesn't allow the editor space to edit. That's what goes between the lines, and you can't assume that your material won't need editing.
- Indent graphs 10 spaces rather than the standard 5. That makes your copy easier to scan and edit, and editors will appreciate your thoughtfulness.
- To prevent typesetting errors, avoid using hyphens at the ends of lines.
- If your release spills over to a second sheet, try to end the first page with a completed graph, or at least a completed sentence. Type "MORE" across the bottom of the first page at least three times. Start the second page with a brief heading that includes the name of your organization, the date, and the topic of the release.
- Mark the end of your release with "-30-," or the pound sign repeated several times "###"; these are two versions of journalese for "That's all, folks"!

Headings

Your release should start with a heading that includes the name, address, and telephone number of your business or organization and the name of a contact person. Believe it or not, one of the most common problems with press releases is the absence of a telephone number.

"It drives me nuts when I don't know whom to call. And please include a home phone number because I generally work until 7:00 or 8:00 at night," says Randy McCarthy of the *Boise Statesman*. That home number is especially important if your organization expects to be involved in hard, breaking news or controversy.

The inclusion of a home phone number on your release means that you will have to be ready to respond to reporters' questions at any time. Yes, that means during dinner, in the middle of a shower, or at 3:00 in the morning. A reporter working against a tight deadline needs the information now. So, to keep your credibility with the media, you need to have the information at your fingertips. And even if it's the most inconvenient time imaginable, keep that fact a secret; it's your job to sound cheerful, organized, and intelligent.

Publicists who work with hard, breaking news stories should include cell phone and pager numbers, as well.

If you are doing regional or national publicity and your firm or organization has a toll-free number, list it at the top of the release, just below your regular telephone number. If you have a website, include the URL in your heading. Many journalists read background material on websites first, before they call publicists. That way, the journalists are better prepared, and you can focus on developing a story, rather than answering basic questions.

Next in your heading is the date. You should guess at the date you expect the release to arrive on the editor's desk and date your release a day or two after that. The news in the release may be fresh and hot, but if it carries yesterday's date, an editor may assume it's stale and throw it away without reading it. So, lean toward the future.

The next words in your heading will usually be "For immediate release." Never write "For immediate publication." That looks as if you're commanding the newspaper to run your release.

The only time you would use a different wording in a news release heading is when you have a good reason for asking the editor to hold the story. You may be alerting him to a major story ahead of time so that he can do some preparatory work. Or you've mailed the release to different types of papers, and you don't want the dailies to run it ahead of the weeklies. In either case, your heading could read "For release after 10 A.M., May 17, 2002."

If there are pictures with your release, use the phrase "With art," and add a word or two to identify each shot. Also let journalists know if the photos are posted on your website. "It helps to put the Web address for the image on the release. Sounds obvious, but it doesn't always happen. And when you post your release to your Web site, include a link to the on-line image so journalists don't have to go hunting for the photo," says C. J. Martin, the Aerospace Communications director at NASA.

Exhibit 4.1 on page 108 shows an example of how your press release heading should look:

Exhibit 4.1

September 30, 2002   Plains City Robotics, Inc.

For Immediate Release   11011 Arkansas Avenue NE

                                                 Plains City 00001

With art: Contact: Linda Ramirez

1. Serving robot in tuxedo   Day: (123) 456-7890

2. Robot parts look human   Night: (098) 765-4321

                                                 Pager: (123) 555-5555

                                                 Cell phone: (123) 999-9999

                                                 Background information:

                                                 www.plainscityrobot.chl

---

Contributing Your Own Headline

Should you write a headline for your release? Some editors object to headlines, believing that press releases should be judged by their leads, and headlines only get in the way.

On the other hand, there are some compelling arguments for using headlines. According to Dan Schlesinger, associate promotion director of the Family Circle Press Service in New York: "Even if a newspaper picks up every word of your release, it probably won't use your headline. Even so, it still pays to use a headline on your release, unless you're positive the editor you're contacting hates headlines on news releases. The editor is conditioned to judge if something is worth reading by glancing at a headline. Much of what he or she reads on and off the job—including most news releases, newspaper articles, advertisements, magazine stories, direct mail pieces, newsletters, and posters—contains headlines. So chances are that if your headline doesn't immediately communicate that your release contains news or information appropriate for his readership, he won't read any further."

Bill Howard of *PC Magazine* confirms this: "In sending out press releases, it's important to include a brief headline that tells the whole story, since most press releases are read and acted upon (which typically means thrown out) within ten seconds. Make the editor realize instantly that this press release is worth reading."

Howard even goes a step further. "Announce the announcement on the envelope," he advises. "Editors often scan envelopes to see which of the day's mail looks most promising." Since direct mail specialists have proved that the right headline on an envelope can increase response, Howard's suggestion is on target.

In summary, if you're customizing your releases for each reporter, you're wise to take their preferences into account; if you're not customizing, it's smart to use a headline, since most press releases have them. And if your material has a strong news peg and is well written, any editor worth his salt will judge it on its merits, no matter how much he dislikes publicist-supplied headlines.

Leave at least two inches between the heading (or your headline) and the start of your text. "We need the top third of the page left blank so we have room to edit and write in headlines," says Brian Youmatz.

Organizing the Copy

To make sure the important information stands out clearly, press releases are written in inverted-pyramid form. Imagine an upside-down pyramid, its base in the air, its point in the sand. The most important information is up in the air, at the base of the pyramid, in the first one or two paragraphs. Even if you take away the rest of the story, those initial graphs still include all of the important information. Each subsequent graph contains less-important information, until you reach the least significant material at the end of the story. News releases do not have strong concluding paragraphs.

A release written in this form helps reporters and editors spot the vital information. It is also easy to edit; if there's not enough space in the paper for the whole story, it can be cut at any point, and the surviving graphs will still give the reader the basic information. Furthermore, since most readers skim through the newspaper, reading only a paragraph or two of most stories, this format lets them find the most important information quickly.

The inverted-pyramid format works for E-mailed releases, as well. "Structure press releases so the most important information is in the first screen," says Tina Koenig of Xpress Press, "because you do not know if reporters are going to scroll down. If you take that approach, it does not matter how long your message is."

The purpose of the lead paragraph is to present the essential facts that make your story newsworthy. It is not the place to position your company by quoting a tag line. Positioning statements belong in marketing communications and promotional material. In press releases they get in the way of your essential task: getting to the point immediately, so journalists and their readers can get the picture fast.

Following is a typical news release lead, hurt by a trademarked positioning statement and omission of the specific facts that would make it news. Unfortunately, many high-tech and dot-com publicists write this way. If you *don't*, you'll have a powerful competitive advantage!

> *Chelm Software Inc. (Nasdaq: CHLM), the leader in supplying solutions that implement operational service continuity™, today announced that The Acme Company has purchased several of Chelm Software's Revive® Restoration Programs for increased availability and reliability of their business-critical applications. With these products, Acme is able to automatically and promptly bounce back from database outages and get its databases on-line again immediately and rationally.*

The best way to draft a press release is to first list all the information you want to include. Then arrange it in order of importance. Your first graph or two, called the lead, will contain the most important material, usually the who, when, where, why, what, and how. Stress the points that are most newsworthy.

If it is important that readers call you, include your phone number in the lead; the most common place for this is at the end of the second graph. Don't assume that a busy editor will see your number in the last graph and keep it in when he performs drastic surgery on your story. He probably won't. As you write each paragraph, double-check to make sure it really is less important than the one before it. And make sure that you are covering only one topic, one concept, and one story in your release. Too many angles make a maze.

When you get to the end of the page: Stop! Even if you have more material, you should stop writing—unless you have a major announcement that you are sure will be page-one news. Then, and only then, should you write an additional page.

"I would never send out a press release longer than two pages," says Nancy Karen of United Way of Tri-State in New York City. "I always give a number to call for further information; if they're at all interested, they do call. You can add a fact sheet, but keep the press release, itself, short."

Using Newspaper Style

In addition to following the inverted-pyramid format, limit the length of your sentences and paragraphs. Long lines of typewritten copy get squashed into shorter lines in newspaper columns, so long paragraphs seem longer. With no paragraph breaks, copy becomes hard to read. So, limit your graphs to four or five lines, which make about one column inch of newspaper copy. Short sentences (10 to 12 words) are easier to read. Rarely make them longer than 20 words. Many of your graphs will contain only one sentence.

It is most important that a press release communicates efficiently. Every word counts. Review your copy to see how many words you can cut out. You may be surprised to realize that whole phrases can be blue-penciled, yet the meaning will become clearer. Be suspicious of the word *that*. It often isn't needed. And cross out as many adjectives as you can; they don't communicate, and they can alienate journalists. "I tend to disregard immediately any PR pitches for Internet and E-biz stuff that include the words *first*, *pioneering*, *leading*, and *largest*," said Bruno Giussani, the Computer/High-Tech columnist at the *New York Times*, as quoted in *Soft•letter*.

Always use the active voice. Say "Mayor Fernandez announced" instead of "It was announced by Mayor Fernandez." The active voice is a stronger statement, and it takes fewer words.

Make your copy lean. Instead of writing, "Additional topics that will be discussed in depth during the course include futures, options and the bond market," you should write, "The course will also cover futures, options and the bond market."

The most important part of a press release is the information. Sure, clear writing helps, but fancy phrases and verbal fireworks turn reporters off. Save them for public service announcements and feature stories. "I don't need cute, catchy writing. I just need the straight poop," says the *Boise Statesman*'s Randy McCarthy.

When you use a quote in the second paragraph of a press release, don't repeat the material you covered in the lead. Your quote should add material, it should have substance, facts and figures, and it should be interesting. Many press releases journalists receive sound the same and use the same type of repetitive quotes. They're predictably boring. Benny Evangelista, a staff writer at the *San Francisco Chronicle*, as quoted in *Soft•letter*, put his finger on the problem: "There are more boilerplate press releases that sound basically the same . . . something like:

XYZ Co. Inc., a leading supplier of the world's integrated real-time advanced software-aided microchips, announced today the availability of its latest product, the XYZ 4.2, version 3, which will revolutionize the software-aided micro-technology chip industry.

"This will revolutionize the software-aided micro-technology chip industry," said Joe Blow, XYZ Co. Chief Executive Officer and Founder.

Avoiding Jargon and Double-Talk

Many people think that long words and technical jargon make their news releases more official. If you listen to radio news shows, you'll often hear government officials and corporate executives make statements that sound eloquent—until you stop to consider exactly what they've said. More often than not, you can't tell. They've probably used such words and phrases as *instructional day, integral remediations, noncompliance, discontinuance of service*—or even *discontinuity in the integrity of the epithelial tissue*; believe it or not, that means "cut," "sore," or "pimple"!

There are even fad phrases, such as *impact upon*, that are replaced in a few months or years by other equally unclear but popular buzzwords.

When you're writing a press release, say what you mean. Avoid jargon. Try to use short, ordinary words. As author Rudolf Flesch points out, the more syllables there are per hundred words, the more difficult the writing is to understand. If you write as if you were actually talking to someone and you say what you mean, your press releases will be more direct and forceful.

If you absolutely must use a technical term or two, explain them in your release. One or two specialized words, clearly defined, can add color to your material.

Here are several examples and rewrites of double-talk and jargon from press releases:

According to Sandy Schlepper, supervisor, this profile will include vocational interests and aptitudes as well as an interpretation of these data in terms of specific jobs. In addition, core staff will pinpoint behavioral and attitudinal deficiencies that impact upon vocational feasibility and develop remediation procedures.

This can be more clearly written:

Job-training supervisor Sandy Schlepper says, "We find out what each person's work interests are. We test each of them to see what usable skills they have. Then we figure out what kinds of jobs each person would do best. If people in our program have behavior problems that get in the way of finding and keeping a job, we can help them change."

The following graph is long-winded and confusing:

"An overflow crowd is anticipated," says Hometown Hardware's marketing director, Ivor Gorodnikov, "because our expectation is that these home repair convocations zero in on problem areas that impact upon participants and generate enormous emotional involvement."

While the publicist can't edit a direct quote, she can go back to the marketing director and coach him on speaking plain English. This rewrite is more direct and has punch:

"We expect an overflow crowd," says Ivor Gorodnikov, who planned this home repair how-to series for Hometown Hardware. "These sessions zero in on problem areas. People get excited and involved because we show them simple techniques they can actually use. There's always a lot of enthusiasm."

Try this exercise: Translate the next two examples into plain English. If you have difficulty, read Rudolf Flesch's book *How to Write, Speak, and Think More Effectively*, listed in Chapter 13.

(1) Generally we first identify whether the complaint is legally cognizable under existing consumer law and advise the inquirer of the rights and protections so accorded. An attorney assigned to the complainant may identify relevant cases, statutory and regulatory provisions, and suggest alternative strategies for dispute resolution.

(2) An examination of the cases processed this year indicates that the average time between the receipt of a request for a fugitive's return and the issuance of a warrant is approximately three weeks. However, to ensure that fugitives are returned to the jurisdiction from which they absconded at the earliest possible time, I have directed that all extradition matters be processed by my office within 30 days of the receipt of an extradition request, unless additional time is required

to ensure protection of individual rights. Inordinate delays in extradition cases result in the unnecessary expenditure of funds by Chelm State and its localities for the housing and maintenance of fugitives from other states.

Writing the Lead

A lead paragraph may look like the following:

Six members (who) *of the Plains City Rotary Club received blue ribbons* (what) *for the best pies and cakes* (why) *at the County Fair in Marigold Heights* (where) *today* (when).

Another way to write this lead, using the same information but more in keeping with newspaper style, is:

County Fair judges awarded blue ribbons for the best pies and cakes to six members of the Plains City Rotary Club at the fairgounds in Marigold Heights today.

Be certain you don't include irrelevant material in your lead. In the example that follows, it's hard to tell what the news is. It's certainly not the cyclone of gatherings and parties; that's simply boasting.

Amid a whirlwind of high-level meetings and champagne receptions to formalize an agreement to exchange information on Codson's disease in Brussels, Mrs. Wentworth Mason was presented with the Platinum Medallion, the country's highest honor, at the Villiers Hotel. Recently elected as the first woman president of the Chelm Codson's Disease Foundation, Mrs. Mason has been instrumental in establishing working relationships with European organizations seeking a cure for the disease.

This lead could be rewritten as follows, to stress the news:

The Chelm Codson's Disease Foundation presented the Platinum Medallion to its first female president, Mrs. Wentworth Mason, in Brussels yesterday.
The award, the highest recognition the Belgian government gives foreigners, is for Mason's role in establishing working relations with European organizations seeking a cure for the disease. Codson's disease societies from seven

countries signed agreements to exchange clinical information at a meeting just
before the presentation.

Now let's look at a longer lead and its rewrite. The first two paragraphs sound more like rambling concert program notes than journalese:

Amanda Anderson, the exciting young sitarist and first American to be
invited to perform on the Classic Sitar at the Circular Club series, the unique set
of concerts featuring that enthralling Indian instrument, will play a wonderful
program of traditional Indian classical music. It will include a premiere of
Chester U. Corfu's incredible Ganges Suite which is based on an Indian classi-
cal theme and was written especially for Ms. Anderson.

The concert will take place on March 1 at 5:30 P.M. in the Louisa Harding
Holly Auditorium, named for the late patron of the arts, at 1055 River Avenue
in Chelm. The sitar series is presented by the Center for Indian and American
Exchange in cooperation with the Circular Club and Far East Instruments.

The rewrite is more effective, better organized, and written in journalistic style:

Sitarist Amanda Anderson will play a program of traditional Indian clas-
sical music at the Louisa Harding Holly Auditorium of the Circular Club, 1055
River Avenue, Chelm, on Sunday, March 1, at 5:30 P.M. For ticket information
call (123) 456-7890.

The program includes the Chelm premiere of Chester U. Corfu's Ganges Suite,
based on Indian classical themes. The piece was written especially for Anderson.

Anderson is the first American to perform in the Classic Sitar series at the
Circular Club since it started in 1997. The sitar, a stringed Indian instrument
dating back to the period before Christ, has a sound like a cross between a lute
and a guitar.

The concerts are sponsored by the Center for Indian and American Ex-
change and Far East Instruments in cooperation with the Circular Club.

The following lead is indeed confusing:

Hearing-impaired employees are not being overlooked in the state's coor-
dinated effort to alleviate problems for workers and others affected by the loss of
an estimated 3,500 jobs in the closing of the Cord Rotor Plant in Chelm.

Are there hearing-impaired workers at the Cord Rotor Plant? Is that because the plant causes hearing loss, or do they just happen to work there? Why do hearing-impaired workers need special attention? There may be good reasons, but they're not in this paragraph.

The lead paragraphs below, on the other hand, immediately tell us the news:

> *After several years of intensive research, Saab-Scania AB of Sweden has developed a new and revolutionary system, APC—Automatic Performance Control—that can offer a fuel saving of up to 8 percent while at the same time boosting acceleration up to 20 percent.*
>
> *The system also allows an engine to be run on fuels of different octane ratings without special adjustments.*
>
> *Volume production of Saab Turbo engines with the APC system is expected to start in about a year.*

Including Contact Information

It may seem like a straightforward request to ask that contact information in your press release appear in the finished story, but now that many media outlets have their own websites, they often want to direct requests for follow-up information *their* way. As Jed Nitzberg, APR, vice president of interactive communications for the Arthritis Foundation, explains, "Reporters and the media do not want to include your 800 number in their coverage. They do not even want to include your Web site's URL, because they want to push their own Web sites. We still push for a mention of our 800 number and Web site. But we also try to get links on their Web sites, as well. So if the "Today Show" is reporting an arthritis story, and the reporter mentions the show's Web site as a source of more information, I ask them to link their Web site to ours." The bottom line is that once journalists have agreed to give you coverage, you have to negotiate for mention of your contact information in the stories and on their websites.

Analyzing a Press Release

Exhibit 4.2 is an example of a complete, detailed news release that attempts to present the information, but it's not clear enough. It would be easy for a busy editor to miss some major points.

Exhibit 4.2

The Highway 138 asphalt recycling project completed in 2001 has been termed highly successful, with significant savings in much-needed highway funds and benefits in energy conservation and reduction of air and ground pollution, according to Waste Reduction Systems, Inc. and the Chelm State Highway Bureau.

Instead of discarding 120 miles of deteriorated pavement, the CSHB reused it. The old asphalt was milled or planed off Highway 138, hauled to an asphalt plant where it was mixed with fresh stone and asphalt, and used again to repave inside and outside shoulders of a 16-mile stretch of the Highway. The finished product was a hot asphalt shoulder mixture.

"If milling was compared to placement of conventional leveling course methods on Highway 138, the savings for the entire project would have amounted to 22 billion British Thermal Units (BTU) or 165,000 gallons of gasoline," reports G. C. Hobday, coordinator of the CSHB Engineering Staff.

"Approximately 14,000 tons of milled material from the old pavement was extended to 27,000 tons through recycling and was used to repave the shoulders," says Hobday. "In conservation of material resources, the combined savings were 2,900 tons of asphalt, or 712,000 gallons of gasoline and 55,700 tons of stone aggregates. Waste Reduction Systems, Inc. can be proud of its role here."

This type of project, according to CSHB officials, permitted the recovery of all of the asphalt and stone from the old pavement and produced a substantial saving because the cost of asphalt cementing material has risen dramatically. Bituminous concrete contains from 4.5 to 7 percent asphalt, a product of the crude-oil distillation process, so a high percentage of fuel also was conserved by recycling.

The project was environmentally significant because the entire removal and recycling process is smoke-free and does not pollute the atmosphere. It is also difficult to dispose of old road material due to the shortage of landfill space.

The Bureau, according to Hobday, is recommending that the recycling program be continued on other maintenance and reconstruction projects because of the success of the Highway 138 project.

The important news is buried in this release, under a lot of repetition, some unclear information, dull quotes, and confusing statistics. And the release is longer than it should be. Let's examine it graph by graph:

Graph 1: The release starts with some vague statements. *Who* has termed this project "highly successful": the Chelm State Highway Bureau, Waste Reduction Systems, Inc., or both? How are the two organizations related? What are "significant savings"? With such dramatic statistics available, this graph could be more forceful.

Graph 2: There are three problems here. First, the reader has to stop and figure out what CSHB means. An acronym or abbreviation should be introduced immediately after the full name and set in parentheses. Second, the words *milled* and *planed* don't tell most readers what was done to the highway. And finally, an alert editor will wonder why the old asphalt had to be mixed with new asphalt.

Graphs 3 and 4: The quotes here are hardly lively. There's actually no reason to have quotes at all, except that Mr. Hobday wants his name in the paper. The use of undefined technical language such as "conventional leveling course" obscures the main point: the project saved an enormous amount of money and materials. Also, we don't understand why Waste Reduction Systems, Inc., should be proud of itself. The role it played in this project needs to be explained.

Graph 5: This presents a puzzle. We were talking about asphalt, weren't we? Now, all of a sudden, we're talking about bituminous concrete. Perhaps they are related, but few reporters, editors, or readers will know that.

Graph 6: The copy here assumes the reader knows that regular repaving methods pollute the air, and the relationship between the difficulty of disposing of old road material and the shortage of landfill sites.

Graph 7: There's not enough information here. The release needs to be specific about the success of the Highway 138 project by providing facts or figures.

Let's fix this release so that it presents the important information clearly and forcefully. First we'll list the major points, in order of importance. Unlike the original release, which discussed what was done first, we'll start with the results, because the results *are* the news:

1. The project saved 2,900 tons of asphalt and 55,700 tons of stone.
2. Asphalt is a petroleum product.
3. The project saved enough petroleum to refine 712,000 gallons of gasoline.
4. The process was smoke-free and did not pollute the air.
5. There was no need to dump old road material.
6. There are only two dump sites in the southern part of the state.
7. The recycled material would have filled one of the dumps to capacity and thus forced its closing.
8. Twenty miles of cracked and pitted pavement was scraped off Highway 138.
9. Fourteen thousand tons of old asphalt pavement was mixed with new asphalt and stone to give it added resiliency and strength.
10. The new mixture was used to repave the shoulders of Highway 138.
11. As a result of the $3 million savings, CSHB will recycle all its old asphalt pavement.

Assuming that it is issued by the Highway Bureau and that Waste Reduction Systems, Inc., was the contractor who handled the project, the rewritten release may look as shown in Exhibit 4.3 on page 120. Notice that it now has a heading, as well.

A Model Press Release

The release copy shown below and continued on page 121 reads like a news story, which is exactly the point. A good release will sound as if it's been lifted from the newspaper. The copy is in proper inverted-pyramid form, so you can make sense of the part you're reading here even though most of the original has been cut. It was written for the Permanent Citizens Advisory Committee to the Metropolitan Transit Authority of New York by attorney Michael Gerrard, a former newspaperman.

> *Fires in the New York City subway system have more than doubled in the past three years, and escape is being hindered by locked car doors, the Permanent Citizens Advisory Committee (PCAC) to the Metropolitan Transportation Authority revealed today.*

Exhibit 4.3

February 18, 2002   Chelm State Highway Bureau

FOR IMMEDIATE RELEASE   675 Euclid Highway

With art: Chelm 00002

1. Pile of old asphalt   Contact: Samuel Driver

2. Asphalt scraping machine   Day: (800) 123-4567

3. Graph of savings   Night: (123) 456-7890

                                           Pager: (123) 555-5555

                                           Background information:

                                           www.chelmstatehwy.chl

The Chelm State Highway Bureau (CSHB) saved 2,900 tons of asphalt and 55,700 tons of stone by recycling old pavement that would previously have been dumped, according to G. C. Hobday, coordinator of the CSHB engineering staff.

Since asphalt is a petroleum product, the Highway 138 Asphalt Recycling Project saved the equivalent of 712,000 gallons of gasoline. And, unlike traditional repaving methods, recycling asphalt doesn't produce any air pollution.

Had the old pavement been discarded, it would have filled the Martinsville Dump to capacity, thereby closing one of the last two remaining dump sites in southern Chelm.

"Waste Reduction Systems, Inc., the contractor for this project, scraped 20 miles of cracked and pitted asphalt pavement off the surface of Highway 138. This old pavement was mixed with stone and new asphalt to give it body and resilience. The new mixture was used to repave 16 miles of shoulders on the highway. The traffic lanes of the highway were repaved with concrete, which stands up to heavy use better than asphalt," according to Hobday.

"We're extremely pleased with the results of the Waste Reduction Systems, Inc. technology. Because this is a new process, we're still trying to figure out exactly how much money we saved. But it's more than $3 million. From now on, we'll recycle all our old asphalt pavement. It's just plain good sense," says Hobday.

###

There were 653 subway fires in June, or an average of 22 a day, up 218 percent over the 300 fires in June three years ago, the transit watchdogs reported.

"This growing peril to subway riders is caused chiefly by the cumulative effect of years of too little maintenance," said PCAC Chairman Michael Gerrard, an attorney and daily subway commuter.

At the same time, the Transit Authority (TA) is making it harder to escape fires. The front and back doors on the new R-44 and R-46 subway cars have long been locked, but riders could use the emergency door switches to escape. The TA just disconnected these switches, claiming maintenance problems.

The switches and the signs labeling them are still there, however, so passengers may flip them in vain, trapped inside smoke-filled cars until help arrives. Several such instances have already occurred. The locks also prevent passengers between stations from fleeing muggers or telling train crews of seriously ill riders.

Editing Your Release

Whenever you can, let your draft sit overnight before you try to rewrite it. You will be able to see the rough spots better the next day, and your editing task will be easier when you are 24 hours removed from writing the first draft.

As you rewrite, aim to vary your use of words. Watch out for excessive use of the same word, and pay attention to the beginnings of your graphs. If two or more of them start the same way, change them. There's nothing more boring than reading four paragraphs that begin, "Mr. Olsen said."

Cross out as many adjectives as you can, and blue-pencil the word *that.* Think of yourself as a sculptor; the first draft is a nice hunk of stone, but you have to carve away extra material to create the smooth, flowing lines of a statue.

Look at all the names in your release. Are there any unusual spellings? If you're writing about Melissa Briwn, for example, most editors will assume you've misspelled *Brian* or *Brown.* Write a small "OK" above any name or word that appears to be wrong even though it's correct:

OK
Briwn.

At a certain stage in your rewriting efforts, you reach the point of diminishing returns. If you find yourself trying to rewrite the rewrite of a rewrite, you've probably gone as far as you can. So, if a small voice inside you says, "Hey! You're really finished," listen to it.

Checking for Accuracy

"Accuracy is the lifeblood of a newspaper," says Brian Youmatz of the *Framingham Middlesex News*. "If a publicist gets the facts wrong, and we use those wrong facts, it's our responsibility. If a publicist makes enough mistakes like that, I'll consider him unreliable, and I won't use his material."

Imagine what could happen if you misspell someone's name in your release. The journalist, working under pressure, doesn't have time to check. The story appears with the name spelled wrong, and the victim makes an angry call to the publication. The call is routed to the journalist, who squirms while he makes an apology. All the while he is wishing evil fates on your head, and when he sees another release from you, he may well tear it to bits.

At some of the smaller newspapers, your material will not be edited at all. According to Harry Cohn of the American Red Cross, "If it's a service story, if you're just telling people they can enroll in a first aid course or what they can do to avoid boating accidents, most weeklies will use those stories without any changes."

So, if you're tempted to be sloppy about your proofreading, don't be! A busy editor may just use your copy verbatim, and the spelling errors and grammatical mistakes in your release will grace the front page.

After your release is duplicated, proofread it once again before you mail it. If you find an error or two, all is not lost. You can make clear, handwritten corrections, and as long as you have no more than three corrected errors per page, your material is considered clean copy. Of course, your aim is to have no errors at all.

Correcting Errors

Despite all precautions, you may discover an error in a press release you've already sent out. You'll probably sit there feeling as if someone is practicing macramé on your insides. Snap out of it! It's happened to all of us at least once. Get on the phone and call every reporter or editor you've sent the release to. Do not offer profuse apologies; a quick, matter-of-fact "sorry about that" is all that's in order. Then do the following:

- Indicate what the error was.
- Give the correct information.

- Send out a corrected version of the press release by the quickest means possible. Fax it or E-mail it if you already know the journalist doesn't mind. Or send it by messenger or overnight courier. Sure, the costs can add up, particularly if you have to contact many media outlets, but protecting your organization's reputation with the media is worth money, too.

"Don't try to correct if the story has appeared—it's too late at that point," advises Harry Cohn. "When it's in, it's in."

Fact Sheets

Suppose your solar energy resource center is about to issue a press release on a new program to help home owners install solar water heaters. You have a mound of marvelous material to give to the press. You know that press releases should be limited to one page, but what about all that wonderful information? The answer is to use a fact sheet to round out your news release.

A fact sheet can run for several pages and include historical perspectives, anecdotes, and data. You get the best of both: a short press release that quickly gives reporters and editors the essence of your story, and material to do an in-depth article. Fact sheets should be well written, with short sentences and paragraphs, and wide margins. The name and telephone number of a contact person should always be at the top of the front page, along with your E-mail and Web page addresses and your beeper and cell phone numbers. Each page should end with a completed paragraph, and "MORE" typed several times across the bottom of the page. The last page should end with the numerals "-30-" or "###" typed several times across the bottom.

Exhibit 4.4 on pages 124 and 125 shows a shortened version of a fact sheet produced for the Northeast Solar Energy Center by Joel Strasser, former director of Hill & Knowlton's Industrial and Scientific Communications Services. Notice the historical, anecdotal, and factual information a journalist could use for an in-depth story, as well as the tight writing style, with short sentences and paragraphs.

Exhibit 4.4

Historical Perspectives on Solar Energy

The current need to expand solar energy applications and save oil is the latest manifestation of man's historical use of the sun's energy as a natural and abundant resource. Here's a thumbnail sketch of some of the efforts over the years to harness the power of the sun:

- In prehistorical times, cavemen sought south-facing caves as dwellings to take advantage of the sun's heat and light, as well as to protect themselves from northerly winds.
- In warfare, King Solomon's vastly outnumbered troops blinded the eyes of an attacking Egyptian army by reflecting the sun off burnished shields, causing the Egyptians to destroy themselves by falling into a hidden abyss.
- Later, legend describes how Archimedes successfully defended Syracuse by incinerating an attacking Roman fleet with a solar reflector which concentrated the sun's rays with polished brass onto the sails of the Roman galleys.
- During the French Revolution, the great French chemist, Antoine Lavoisier, used the sun for research purposes, and developed solar furnaces. Curved glass discs were fastened together at their rims, with wine filling the space between to focus the sun's rays enough to attain temperatures of about 3,000°F. These high temperatures were used to discover the nature of carbon and platinum. He also developed the science of the solar furnace by heating samples in a vacuum and in controlled atmospheres, using quartz containers.
- Solar pioneers also capitalized on one of the oldest uses of the sun— food preparation. August Mouchot demonstrated a solar cooker at the World Exhibition in Paris in 1878. His units were simple ones with glass lids to let in sunlight and trap heat inside.
- Distillation of water became another practical way to use the sun. In 1871, a huge solar still was built by an American engineer,

MORE   MORE   MORE

Charles Wilson, to convert locally available salt water into potable form at a Chilean copper mine high in the Andes. Covering nearly an acre in size, the still could produce over 4,000 gallons of water daily. And like today's solar stills, it consisted of a shallow basin painted with waterproof black compound covered with a glass roof and shaped like an inverted and flattened "V."

- At the turn of the century, solar experimenters in the United States focused on the sun for pumping water. The most spectacular solar engines were those built in Arizona by an English inventor, A. G. Eneas. He obtained backing from Boston financiers to build a giant solar concentrator to generate steam at pressures up to 150 psi [pounds per square inch], to pump water at the rate of 1,400 gallons per minute.

- Solar water heaters also interested many inventors, and their research resulted in the technology existing today. Previously, these heaters were developed mainly for use in hot baths, and during World War I many large installments were made in Army cantonments. Thousands of these thermosyphon water heaters are currently being used in Australia, Israel and Japan with a few in California and Florida.

###

Feature Stories

A news release is straightforward, with no fancy writing. It contains the who, when, where, why, what, and how. A few days after issuance it is no longer newsworthy.

On the other hand, a feature story, though it must also be newsworthy in the broad sense of the word, is relatively timeless. It can run in today's paper, or it can be used next week. That's why feature material is sometimes called "evergreen"—it won't fade.

Unlike a news story, a feature can have a point of view. And it usually isn't written in inverted-pyramid format. You can write news stories and features about the same material, increasing your chances of successful placement. The feature story is a valuable publicity tool and an ideal vehicle for helping people understand how to choose, buy, and use your product or service.

The "angle" is the most important attribute of a feature story, which usually highlights an intriguing or unknown facet of the organization, product, cause, service, or individual. While a feature may be related to breaking news, its appeal comes from its interesting perspective or unusual point of view, and it often helps bring dull facts and dry statistics to life. Unlike a hard news story, it doesn't have to be objective, and a feature story is often longer than a hard news story on the same subject.

Some Examples of Excellent Feature Stories

Drawing on a copyrighted article by Dr. Albert R. Milan in *Family Circle* magazine, Dan Schlesinger wrote the feature in Exhibit 4.5 for Family Circle Press Service. You may ask why a magazine would want to "give away" its material. The goal is to get potential subscribers to associate the magazine with interesting information, so they are more responsive when they receive a subscription promotion or see the publication for sale. A woman

---

Exhibit 4.5

A woman can feel the difference between harmless and possibly cancerous lumps in her breast as easily as she can feel the difference between the skin over her eyeball and the skin on her nose. That's the basis of a simple "eye-and-nose" test featured in a current *Family Circle* magazine how-to article, "The Best Breast Self-Examination."

Developed by Dr. Albert Milan, attending obstetrician and gynecologist at Union Memorial Hospital in Baltimore, this test is part of a comprehensive breast self-examination, described step-by-step in *Family Circle*,

MORE   MORE   MORE

that only takes 10 minutes per month. The *Family Circle* feature is excerpted from the *Breast Self-Examination Book* published by Workman Publishing Co.

Women should examine their breasts once a month by using a "palpation" (examine by touch) technique, insists *Family Circle*. Palpate by using the flat surfaces of two or more fingers and gently press them downward so the skin is moved along with the fingertips over the underlying structures.

Studies have shown that women who examine their breasts once a month greatly increase their chances of detecting a cancerous growth early enough to effect a cure. The chances of a complete recovery are 85 percent to 90 percent if a malignant lump is discovered while it is still localized in the breast tissue itself. The cure rate plummets to 40 percent if the cancer has spread to other organs.

Here's how to give yourself the "eye-and-nose" test to determine if you have harmless lumps, or attached, possibly harmful ones:

Gently move the eyelid over the eyeball's surface, and you'll feel how slippery the eyeball is and how the eyelid glides smoothly over it. Then pinch your eyelid to lift it away from the eyeball's surface. Notice how it lifts freely and easily. These are similar sensations to the ones you'll feel from touching normal milk glands and ducts of the breast and harmless, slippery breast cysts as well.

Now place the ball of your fingertip on the end of your nose, and try to move the nasal skin with your finger without moving the tip of your nose. It won't go, notes the article. It is fixed, and the tip of the nose moves with the skin. The next step is to try to lift the skin on the tip of your nose. Pinch it between your fingertips—the same way you did with your eyelid. It can't be lifted. This is a very important differentiating feature, says *Family Circle*. If you feel any lump in your breast that doesn't move, that is attached to the skin or underlying structures and above which you can't lift the skin, it should be examined by your physician immediately.

Not all fixed lumps are malignant, so don't panic if you find one. But don't put off seeing your doctor. Also see your doctor about lumps situated deep in the breast tissue. These are difficult for you to differentiate by self-examination.

###

concerned about her health who reads an article based on this release in her daily paper may turn to *Family Circle* for health advice in the future.

The business feature story in Exhibit 4.6 was written and released by John Guiniven for International Paper Company. It was picked up by about 50 editors across the United States.

Public relations executive Ravelle Brickman prepared the feature story in Exhibit 4.7 for the Neighborhood Cleaners Association.

Exhibit 4.6

A Good Business Letter Can Mean Money in the Bank

NEW YORK, N.Y.—The business letter, a basic and important form of communication, is in trouble.

That's the opinion of Malcolm Forbes. And he should know. As president and editor-in-chief of the respected *Forbes Magazine*, he receives over 10,000 business letters a year. Most of them are "mundane," he says, and many others are "stultifying if not stupid."

Declining reading and writing skills have hurt all forms of correspondence. But bad business letters are more than literary outrages—they can have a dollar-and-cents impact.

In an effort to improve them, Mr. Forbes has added his expertise to an ambitious communication program sponsored by International Paper Company [IP]. The program, titled "The Power of the Printed Word," is aimed at improving the overall reading and writing skills of young Americans through a series of "how-to" ads and supporting classroom materials.

The ads will run in magazines reaching the youth market, and will include comedian Bill Cosby, who holds a doctorate in education, on "How to Read Faster"; *Reader's Digest* editor-in-chief Edward Thompson, "How to Write Clearly"; actor-lexicologist Tony Randall, "How to Improve Your Vocabulary"; and Mr. Forbes, "How to Write a Business Letter."

In his ad kicking off the program, Mr. Forbes notes that "a good business letter can get you a job interview, get you off the hook, or get you money."

MORE   MORE   MORE

He says the most important step is taken "before you write your letter. Know what you want, and write it down. List the major points you want to get across. If answering a letter, keep it in front of you while you write and check the points that need answering." Among his other suggestions are:

- Be brief. Keep the letter to one page, if possible, with the first paragraph telling precisely what your letter is about.
- Be natural. Imagine the reader sitting across the desk from you. Write the way you talk, and avoid business jargon.
- Lean heavier on nouns and verbs, lighter on adjectives.
- Make it perfect. No typos, no misspellings, no factual errors.

In explaining why IP is spending $1 million on "The Power of the Printed Word" this year, chairman and chief executive officer J. Stanford Smith says, "Inadequate reading and writing skills among young people are a concern to all Americans.

"As a company with an historic commitment to the printed word and a significant stake in the future of printing and publishing, International Paper decided to act on that concern," he added.

Exhibit 4.7

New Pamphlet Points Out Perils of Poorly Made Spring Clothing—
Drycleaners Urge Consumers to Buy Carefully, Know and Exercise Their
Legal Rights

With the cost of clothing zooming out of sight, it pays to know what you're buying—and to buy clothes that will not only look good on the rack, but will continue looking good, on you, after being washed or drycleaned.

Sounds obvious, doesn't it?

MORE   MORE   MORE

But for the average consumer—the John or Jane Doe without a Ph.D. in fabric technology—figuring out what will last and what won't is not as simple as it sounds.

Reading the labels helps. But not always. According to Bill Seitz, Executive Director of the Neighborhood Cleaners Association, a group representing 3,200 drycleaners in nine eastern states, "A lot of garments are mislabeled. They'll say 'hand wash only,' when the garment really should be drycleaned. Or they'll say 'dryclean only,' when, in fact, the garment can't be cleaned at all."

One solution is to be armed with the new edition of "HOW TO BUY AND CARE FOR YOUR CLOTHES," a pamphlet published twice yearly and available free from the NCA as part of its consumer education program.

Judging by the NCA booklet, this spring's fashions present more problems than ever before. Here are some of the things a smart shopper should beware of:

Shrinking Violets—Cotton Jersey and Cotton Knits

100% cotton knit dresses and tops are very popular today. They're cool, they're comfortable, and they're nearly always labeled "washable." Trouble is, cotton knit shrinks. And unless the fabric has undergone proper preshrinkage treatment (rare in the case of imports), your brand-new T-shirt dress or top will come out of the wash at least two sizes smaller, and so tight that even a beanpole would be embarrassed.

Passing Prints

You've heard the expression "color fast." It applies to prints as well as solids. If a dye isn't "fast," it will run, bleed, travel all over the place or just plain disappear. This is a particularly serious problem with prints, since the pattern may be precisely what attracted you to the garment in the first place. Check the reverse side of the fabric to see if the print goes all the way through. A surface print (such as a flocked or painted design) is one that is literally pasted on, and it is bound to fade away—along with your hopes, dreams and clothing dollars—in the course of washing, cleaning or normal everyday wear.

MORE   MORE   MORE

Impermanent Pleats

Pleated skirts are the rage—in more ways than one. Many pleats are so transient that even a single washing or cleaning will banish them forever—leaving you in a rage and your skirt outrageously pleatless. If you want pleats, make sure they're permanent: the fiber content must be at least 55 percent nylon, acetate or polyester. Avoid rayon blends and intricate Origami-style fluting.

Fading Glories

Designer jeans (even though they shouldn't) are designed to fade—especially if, as is often the case, they come in deep solid colors. That is because they're often made of denim or duck cloth, and most dyes cannot penetrate those tight weaves. Faded jeans are fine, but not if you wanted—and paid for—designer colors.

Sequins, Beads and Glued-on Glitter

All that glitters is not gold. Some of it is poorly dyed plastic. And a lot of it isn't even sewn on. That's why most of the trimmings that brighten "Disco" outfits are bound to lose color, melt, curl or fall off in water or drycleaning solvent. Anything, in fact, that's glued-on will come unglued in cleaning. Make sure those sequins and beads are sewn (by hand) and confirm that they're colorfast.

Silk—Pure but Perishable

If you've ever wondered why synthetics were invented, it's because silk, while pretty, is highly perishable.

The dyes bleed easily and almost anything—water, perfume, deodorant—will cause color loss or a ringlike stain. Worst of all, perspiration causes the fabric to rot.

The solution? Buy silk only for "special" occasions.

Buy loose-fitting styles (tight-fitting silk tends to split). Avoid the very thin fabrics (look for something with weight and body), use underarm pads—and don't cry if, after normal wear and drycleaning, it shreds or fades away. Glamour costs.

MORE   MORE   MORE

Know Your Rights

Okay. You've read the warnings, studied the labels, bought carefully and followed the care instructions exactly. What happens if the garment still proceeds to fade, pill, melt, shrink, stretch or just plain fall apart?

The answer, according to the NCA, is, "Take it back."

As a consumer, you have a right, by law, to expect every garment you buy to be serviceable. If it isn't, you're entitled to a refund.

Too few consumers, the organization feels, are aware of their rights. And fewer still bother to exercise them.

"If more people took the trouble to demand a refund, the problems would disappear. The stores would stop carrying poorly made clothes, and manufacturers," Seitz predicts, "would shape up fast."

To help turn that prediction into a reality, the NCA has included the "Consumer's Bill of Rights" in the spring-summer edition of "HOW TO BUY AND CARE FOR YOUR CLOTHES." Also included in the pamphlet are helpful hints on home stain removal, do's and don'ts for wardrobe care and a guide to garment life expectancy.

For a free copy of the pamphlet, drop in at your local NCA cleaner or send a stamped, self-addressed envelope to NCA, 116 East 27th Street, New York, NY 10016.

###

Fillers

If you've toured your local newspaper's offices and plant and watched the makeup people assembling pages from copy and advertisements, you may have wondered where they get the material they use to fill in empty spaces at the last minute. Some newspapers and magazines use syndicates that provide filler, or their own reporters and editors write brief blurbs that are kept ready to plug news holes. But some of that filler material also comes from publicity people.

There are large publications that almost never use filler. They edit carefully, and their makeup people are precision artisans who take a great deal of care and time to make sure there is no need for filler. Other papers, small and large, may not have enough staff or resources to do that, and their editors may welcome a sheet of one- and two-paragraph items from you.

Before you spend any time writing a sheet of fillers, ask your target publications if this sort of material is of interest to them. If they are at all interested, it's time for a brainstorming session. Gather a group of your staffers, members, employees, or colleagues and make a list of brief items about your business, industry, cause, organization, club, product, service, association, or committee that will amuse, interest, or help the newspaper's readers. Let the list sit overnight. Then take your blue pencil and mercilessly cut out any dull idea. Try to imagine a reader coming across the information for the first time. Will he say, "Wow, I didn't know that!" or, "That's good to know!" or, "I think I'll try that little trick next time"? If you're not sure, drop the item.

Each filler should be 100 words or fewer, and 50 words is probably the best length. Several 25-word items may also be useful. Fillers should be in paragraph form, double-spaced, with wide margins. You can type several on a page. Following are three examples of interesting filler items. The first comes from the National Multiple Sclerosis Society, and the last two were written by Dan Schlesinger for Family Circle Press Service.

An estimated 500,000 people in this country alone suffer from multiple sclerosis and closely related disorders. That is more people than live in the city of Seattle, or Denver, or Pittsburgh, or Atlanta, or Cincinnati.

To prevent the tell-tale shine and crease from a previous hem when you're lengthening a garment, try this technique from the "Reader's Idea Exchange" in Family Circle *magazine. Apply white vinegar to the wrong side of the fabric and steam press. Both shine and crease will disappear.*

Within a year after having an abortion, most women have few regrets or guilts, according to the "Here's News in Medicine" column in the current Family Circle *magazine. The magazine cites a recent follow-up study of 63 women who had abortions. Twelve months afterward, more than 75 percent had positive attitudes towards themselves and the event. More than one-third noted that having an abortion had been a positive learning experience that helped them to cope better with other problems in life.*

Letters to the Editor

"Letters to the editor sections of newspapers are highly read. They are not used by publicists as much as they could or should be," says public relations executive Richard Weiner.

Although editors get dozens of letters daily, many papers make it a point to publish as many of them as possible. According to a *Masthead* survey, the *Detroit Free Press* runs about 20 percent of the letters it receives, the *Syracuse Post-Standard* and the *Fresno Bee* each run about half of theirs, and the *News-Journal* in Wilmington, Delaware, tries to run them all. In other words, newspapers take these letters seriously.

Always address your letter to "Dear Editor." If you start with "Dear Sir," and the editor is a woman, she may decide you're not really writing to her.

Letters to the editor should be short—a maximum of three to five paragraphs. Sentences should be concise. Make only one point per letter.

If your letter is about a controversial situation, start with the name of your organization and the purpose of the message. Your next paragraph should convey some brief background material. Your opinion should come in the third paragraph, and the concluding paragraph tells your readers what you want them to do.

Exhibit 4.8 shows a typical letter to the editor.

Exhibit 4.8

Dear Editor:

    I am writing for the Plains City Library Council. We are concerned about the effects of inflation on our public library's budget.

    During the past three years, the budget for the Plains City Public Library has been held to a bare-bones minimum of $750,000 per year, but book prices have increased an average of 3.3 percent yearly. That means our library can buy 10 percent fewer books that it could three years ago.

    That's a disaster for Plains City. Businesspeople can't find the information they need, students can't complete assignments, and do-it-yourselfers can no longer count on the library for the latest how-to books, at the very time when there is an unprecedented demand for them at the library.

There is a possible solution, however. If the city council adds a $400,000 yearly library tax to the cable television proposal now being considered, the library could have a generous budget. The tax could not be passed on to subscribers, and the franchise holder would still earn a generous return on investment. I urge Plains City residents to tell your councilman to vote for Measure 19 and provide this much-needed help for our library.

Sincerely yours,

Urhan Artebedian

President, Plains City Library Council

It is also possible to write letters to the editor to clarify misconceptions about or inaccurate coverage of your business or product. In fact, journalists expect you to do this.

For example, Jim Stott, the *Calgary Herald's* ombudsman, said in the *Masthead* article, "The main avenue of rebuttal for readers who disagree with *Herald* editorials or columns is the letters page. The paper employs a full-time letters editor."

Briefly mention the misconception or inaccuracy, then spend the bulk of the letter presenting the correct information. Your last paragraph should draw a conclusion or ask for an action. Once again, limit yourself to three to five paragraphs. Exhibit 4.9 on page 136 is an example.

Under special circumstances, you can also use letters to the editor to get your product mentioned. A letter like the one in Exhibit 4.10 on page 136 would never appear on the editorial page of a daily newspaper, but the paper's home improvements editor might run it. And it would stand a good chance in a special interest magazine for the home handyperson. Notice how carefully the product message is mixed in. Take away the product name, and the information won't be complete, since most editors and readers won't know how to find a soap with no moisture content.

Exhibit 4.9

Dear Editor:

I'd like to allay a common fear, expressed in these pages last week, that the noise from widgets can cause hearing loss.

In an evaluation last year by the Industrial Safety Research Center of Plains City University, 95 types of electric widgets were rated for noise output. Sound levels were measured with state-of-the-art electronic instruments.

All of them, including our complete line of six models, tested at under 70 decibels, even when running at high speed. A thunderstorm is louder than that! That's why our state's industrial safety code lists electric widgets in the totally safe category, with no protective devices needed by users.

Please let your readers know that electric widgets can sound raucous—so can teenagers—but they're not dangerously loud. They're real time-savers. And they're totally safe. Thank you.

Sincerely yours,

J. Maria Abogado, CEO

Arizona Electric Widget Corporation

Exhibit 4.10

Dear Editor:

I'd like to share a tip that will help home handypeople drive screws quickly by hand, even in hardwood such as oak.

Simply take a bar of bath soap, make sure it's absolutely dry, and rub the threads of each screw on it. The coating of soap will lubricate the threads—and the screws will be much easier to turn.

Use a high-grade soap with no moisture content, such as Brandex, because even a tiny amount of moisture will swell the wood fibers and rust steel screws, causing possible problems later on.

Jason T. MacSweeney, Product Manager

Brandex Soap Division

Conglomerate Household Products, Inc.

Checklist—Writing for the Press

1. Is your press release neatly typed on 8½-by-11-inch plain white bond?
2. Does your release header include the name, address, E-mail address, and Web page URL of your business or organization, the name of the contact person, telephone numbers with area code, the date, the words "For immediate release," and a brief description of any photos?
3. Have you included a nighttime telephone number, cell phone number, or pager number? Will you have someone ready to respond to calls and answer questions?
4. Have you dated the release a day or two ahead of the estimated arrival at the editor's desk?
5. If you are asking editors to hold the release, have you included the words "For release after . . ." and a date?
6. Have you decided whether to include a headline on the release?
7. If you do include a headline, does it summarize the story *and* generate interest?
8. Have you decided if you want to include a headline on the envelope?
9. Have you left at least two inches blank at the top of your text?
10. Are the lines in your release between 50 and 60 characters long?
11. Is your entire release double-spaced?
12. Are your graphs indented 10 spaces?
13. Do your lines end with complete words?
14. Have you made a list of all the points you want to cover?
15. Have you listed the items in priority order?
16. Have you included all the *w*s and the *h*?
17. Are the most important points covered first, and the least important last?
18. If your release runs more than one page, can you cut it, or cover some material in a fact sheet or backgrounder instead?
19. If you have a two-page release, does the first page end with a complete graph? Have you typed "MORE" across the bottom of the first page at least three times?
20. Does the second page have a heading to identify it?
21. Have you ended your release with "-30-" or "###"?
22. Are you using more short words than long words?
23. Do you let drafts of your releases sit overnight before you start editing them?
24. Have you cut out as many words as possible from your release, especially adjectives and the word *that*?

25. Have you avoided the passive voice?
26. Have you translated jargon and technical words into everyday language?
27. If you have to use one or two technical terms, have you defined them?
28. Have you cut out fancy phrases and verbal fireworks?
29. Are most of your sentences fewer than 20 words?
30. Are your paragraphs short, with an average of four to five lines?
31. Have you checked to make sure you don't have two or more graphs that start with the same words?
32. Have you avoided repeating words or phrases?
33. Have you double-checked all the information in your release to make sure it's accurate?
34. Have you written in a small "OK" above any unusual spellings?
35. Have you used your word processor's spell-checker, *and* have you checked spelling manually?
36. If it is important for readers of the published article to call you, is your telephone number in the first or second graph of the release?
37. Have you considered hiring a telemarketing firm to handle responses if you think they'll overwhelm your phone system?
38. Did you proofread the release again after it was duplicated?
39. Do you understand the difference between hard news on the one hand, and human interest, feature, or evergreen material on the other?
40. If you discovered an error after the release was sent out, have you issued a correction to every journalist it was sent to?
41. Are your filler items fewer than 100 words and preferably around 50? Are they in paragraph form, double-spaced with a wide margin, and typed on one side of the page only?
42. Does your letter to the editor pertain to only one issue?
43. Have you addressed your letter to "Dear Editor"?
44. Is it limited to three to five paragraphs?
45. If your letter concerns a controversial situation, have you identified your organization, stated your purpose, included brief background material, given your opinion, and asked for action, in that order?
46. If you're writing to clarify misconceptions, have you focused on the correct information and then drawn a conclusion?
47. If you're trying to get your product mentioned in a letter to the editor, have you entwined your product's name in really useful information?

5

Getting Newspaper and Magazine Publicity

D espite the rumors of the triumph of television over the printed word, and the explosion of websites, American newspapers are alive and kicking daily in more than 1,500 American cities. In addition, more than 9,400 weekly papers and at least 13,000 consumer, trade, and business magazines are published in the United States. The magazine industry in America is booming. According to the *Guide to New Consumer Magazines*, 360 new consumer magazines were launched in 1999.

American newspapers range from weeklies with one staff member and a few thousand readers to the *Los Angeles Times*, bought by more than a million people each day. There are national newspapers read from coast to coast, such as the *Wall Street Journal*, the *Christian Science Monitor*, and *USA Today*. Since many newspapers now have websites, local papers are gaining audiences around the world. This is especially true for papers such as the *San Jose Mercury News*, located in the heart of Silicon Valley, with six people of its large staff dedicated to covering high-tech news stories.

Some papers, such as the *Minneapolis Star-Tribune*, read in Minnesota and parts of Wisconsin, Iowa, and the Dakotas, serve as regional publications. Others, such as the *Arkansas Democrat-Gazette*, are read in most parts of the state of publication. And of course, there are the neighborhood, small-town, ethnic, foreign language, college, and special interest newspapers.

Each kind of newspaper appeals to a different audience, and each approaches stories differently. The large metropolitan daily, with circulation in the suburbs as well as the inner city, may not carry much information about topics of limited interest to their large audience, such as your scuba equipment store's new schedule of diving classes. But neighborhood weeklies will probably print your entire press release, and they may ask for additional material about instructors from their community. Each type of paper has a different focus, looks for a different angle, and reaches a different readership.

There are instances, however, in which a small business, such as a dive shop, could receive much broader coverage. Let's suppose that your shop discovered and encouraged a couple of budding young inventors. With your backing, they have developed a surprisingly simple tankless diving system that uses artificial gills to gather dissolved oxygen directly from the water. The system has been tested and tried, and you've been granted a patent for it. Both of the inventors, a Hispanic girl and a white boy, are still in high school.

This is national news, and a *Big City Morning Star* science reporter will be most receptive to your announcement. He'll want to interview the inventors and get the complete story from a scientific and technical point of view. The *Star*'s education writer, on the other hand, will probably want to write a story about how the youngsters mastered advanced biophysical engineering principles at a time when so many students can't handle basic math and science.

The neighborhood newspaper may want to run a feature article profiling the youngsters, their families, and their ties to the area. And a Hispanic paper in your region could do a story about the intercultural friendship involved. This is just one example of how an organization that *seems* to have limited appeal could get coverage in large-circulation publications. We'll explore other options and methods in this chapter.

Knowing Your Newspapers

If you've never done newspaper publicity before, you may think that you have to get your material in a big-city daily. Sure, that's nice, but it's hard to do. And it's not the only way to go. Don't underestimate the power of small community-oriented papers. "If we want reader response," says Harry Cohn of the American Red Cross, "those community newspapers are much more valuable than the large dailies. People trust the credibility of their local editor. If we are looking for funds or volunteers or we're trying to promote courses, we find we get much greater response from community newspapers."

When you do want to submit your publicity to a daily paper, you need to know exactly which editor or reporter to approach—either by name or by job title. A release about your business's financial outlook will be wasted on the theater and film reporter. And, although the business editor may be personally interested in your diving classes, he will not write a story about them unless there's a business angle.

Compiling a Press List

As you learn how to work with the press, your first step is to make a list of publications that will be interested in your business or organization. See Chapter 13 for an extensive list of media directories. You should also consult your local yellow pages to see if there are any new publications that haven't yet been listed in the directories.

Putting together a list of newspapers is just the start. "So many people who are new to publicity, especially in the high tech and Internet industries, rely on voluminous amounts of press releases," says Kimberly McCall, Sell columnist for *Entrepreneur*'s *Business Start-Ups*. "The irony is that the old fashioned approach works so much better. You still have to read a publication first, understand the publication's audience and then design news that is appropriate for the audience. You can't build relationships with journalists by just blanketing the world with your news."

Analyzing Newspapers

Newspaper policies vary widely, so you should try to read all the newspapers on your list for several weeks—or even months—and observe the kind of news they print. Are all the releases from community groups put on the family living page? Which papers have Community Events Calendars? Is there a reporter at the *Evening Moon* who specializes in feature stories about local people? Which reporter's byline usually appears on stories about small businesses? What kinds of businesses get short blurbs, and which organizations have two-column spreads with pictures? What types of products are featured in the mome and family living sections? Asking yourself questions such as these and writing down your observations will help you understand which papers will be most likely to use your material.

Don't be unwilling to send your release to the *Morning Star*, even if they've previously printed news only from the competition, or the "other side of the tracks." Some papers will be eager for news from businesses and organizations they haven't covered, and some won't. But you'll never know unless you give it a try.

"Most newspapers have policies on what they'll print, and a call to the city editor could probably get you a copy if it's in written form, or a brief description if it's not. While I don't see anything wrong with sending material that doesn't conform to that policy, don't expect that it will be printed," says Sylvia Smith of the *Fort Wayne Journal-Gazette*.

Taking a Newspaper Tour

If your local daily offers guided tours of its plant and offices, pull out your notepad and be guided. You'll begin to understand how the paper works and who is responsible for what. Ask the promotion director about tours. He can also tell you if the paper has free publicity seminars for nonprofit and community organizations.

On the tour, you'll probably meet the city editor first. She is the most important person you'll work with, since she is responsible for all local news in the city where the paper is published. If your organization or business is in a suburb or another city, you may work with the local bureau of the newspaper instead of the city editor.

As your tour continues, make a list of all the editors and beat reporters. You will want to know the names of the reporters and editors handling areas important to your business, industry, organization, or special interest group, since you will usually work directly with them. Make sure you're clear about which reporters handle what stories. For example, "The *Journal* drug store reporter covers Drugstore.com, not a tech [reporter]," explains Don Clark, the *Wall Street Journal*'s deputy bureau chief, San Francisco Bureau, in *Soft•letter*.

Keep in mind that some stories don't belong in the newspaper. This lead from a news release may be of interest to editors at trucking, shipping, and logistics trade magazines, but it's not appropriate for a newspaper:

Acme Freight System Website Now More User-Friendly
CHELM, Dec. 7—Chelm PRwire—Acme Freight System website users have spoken, and the company has responded with a redesigned website that makes it easier than ever for customers to access relevant information and manage multi-carload shipping activity.

Here is a list of some typical specialty areas at a large metropolitan daily:

Art	Internet
Books	Movies
Business	Music
Computers and High Tech	News
Dance	Real Estate
Editorial	Science
Education	Society
Entertainment (Criticism)	Sports
Entertainment (News)	Suburban Affairs
Events Calendar	Sunday Editor
Fashion	Television
Features	Theater
Food	Travel
Foreign Affairs	Women's Page
Home and Garden	

Ask if you can observe the makeup people at work. These are the folks with jigsaw-puzzle minds who build completed pages from articles and advertisements. Although many of them now work with computers, the basic process involves trimming articles to fit tight space or calling for filler for that empty space on page four, top left. Watch them at work, and you will understand why your release may get cut in the middle. Once you see that process, you'll be more able to write material that communicates the essentials despite drastic surgery. This will endear you to the newspaper staff. Ask your tour guide if the newspaper has a style sheet. This is a manual, ranging from a single page to a pamphlet, that sets standards for style and usage. If you can get your own copy of the style sheet, it will help you write more professional news releases.

If the paper does not have a style sheet or won't give you a copy, ask if it is a member of Associated Press (AP) or subscribes to United Press International (UPI). Both wire services issue stylebooks. Use the stylebook of the wire service your local daily is associated with. Find out if the paper has a handbook for community groups and small businesses; this explains exactly what publicity material the newspaper wants.

If you're involved with a nonprofit or community organization, inquire about public service advertising. At many newspapers, you will get a blank look, shrugged shoulders, and a "Nope, never heard of it," but some papers add a small surcharge to commercial advertising to create a fund for public service advertising by nonprofit groups.

Approaching Reporters and Editors

You've completed your survey of newspapers and magazines that you think will make good outlets for your publicity, and you're surprised that there are so many. Now all you have to do is get acquainted with all those reporters and editors and tell them about your fantastic products, superior services, or worthy causes, and they'll immediately beat a path to your door in search of stories. Right? Well, not quite.

In addition to the general advice in Chapter 2 about approaching the media, you should know some things about the likes and dislikes of newspaper and magazine people. We'll start our discussion with newspapers, then move on to magazines.

In some smaller towns and rural areas, reporters *will* seek you out, and your relationship may be quite casual and informal. But in larger urban and suburban areas, most reporters will not want to talk with you until you have a concrete story for them. "Have something in hand when you approach an editor," says Mary Jane O'Neill of the New York Association for the Blind.

Many reporters prefer that you approach them in writing first. "That way I can make some judgments about the validity of the material and decide how much time to spend talking with her when she calls me," says journalist Nancy Dunn. If reporters have had a chance to look at your written material before you call, they will be more familiar with your story, and the discussion will be more fruitful and to the point.

Even at the smaller newspapers, and even if you know reporters well, be careful about dropping in without an appointment. If you show up unexpectedly to deliver a press release, be brief and don't try to make a special case for your material; let it stand on its merits.

"There are many people who simply take the opportunity to drop it off, say 'Hi,' and leave, without trying to initiate a discussion about it or taking too much of my time. What is annoying is when a publicist brings in a press release and makes an obvious effort to get more favorable play for the story," says Sylvia Smith.

Journalist Leslie O'Bergin concurs: "I personally detest having people drop in on me out of nowhere, unless something amazing has happened to them. It interrupts me. Just because I happen to be sitting at my desk does not mean that I am waiting for someone to come by and talk with me, especially if it could take place by mail or phone. Phone gives me the alternative of saying I'll call back. Or I can ask for written material. I really believe in the phone.

"On the other hand," she continues, "if the publicist stops by with a well-written press release, makes a brief pitch, waits while I eyeball it, and then leaves when I'm finished, that's OK, except at deadline time. And I don't like people who attempt to intimidate or guilt trip me into writing an article. It hurts their chances immeasurably."

Meeting Journalists Through Networking

A good way to build better working relationships with journalists without disturbing them at their desks is to join professional organizations for communicators. Says Sylvia Smith, "One thing that improves my relationship with PR people is to be involved with them in Women in Communications." Through this group, Smith gets to know publicists whom she wouldn't otherwise meet, she says, and can gain a sense of how straightforward and trustworthy they are.

Sharon Haver, account executive at Public Relations Aids in New York, echoes Smith: "Women in Communications not only has given me the opportunity to make valuable contacts on a personal level, but also provides insight from media professionals through lectures, round tables, and general open discussions. This networking builds vital personal working relationships."

You can also network with journalists on-line. There are on-line news-groups designed for journalists that allow the public to participate. Don't be too quick to jump into the discussion, however. Observe first. Get a feeling for what's being discussed. Make it your goal to understand as much as you can about each journalist participating. And then ask yourself this critical question: What can I contribute that will be of genuine interest to the journalists in this forum? Is there any way I can help these journalists do their jobs—even if I don't get coverage? As with any other newsgroup, if you make interesting, valuable contributions, you'll make friends.

But beware! If you try to pitch publicity to journalists in newsgroups, you'll anger and alienate them. A newsgroup is not the time or place for pitching. Once you know who's who, and what each person's interests are, you can approach them individually to make your pitches.

You can also network with journalists at some newspaper and maga-zine websites where they have discussion groups. Journalists from the pub-lication often jump into the discussions.

The names and addresses of several professional organizations and newsgroups are listed in Chapter 13.

Contacting News Bureaus

Larger daily newspapers and many large magazines have news bureaus in major cities, where staff reporters cover news of interest to the readership back home. According to public relations executive Richard Weiner, news bureaus have also sprung up in the suburbs as the big-city dailies strive to cover suburban stories and develop a broader readership. These bureaus often have specialists in such fields as business, fashion, restaurants, and cultural activities.

Contacting news bureaus directly has several advantages. If an out-of-town paper is involved, you'll save money on telephone calls, and you'll be able to get your material to the bureau more quickly than if you mailed it to the main office. You'll also have a better chance to develop a working relationship with a staff member at a small bureau than you would at a dis-tant main office.

So, if you're working with out-of-town or suburban newspapers, find out if they have bureaus, where the bureaus are located, and what their policies are. Simply call them and ask. *Bacon's Newspaper Directory* and

Bacon's Magazine Directory, which are listed under "Media Directories" in Chapter 13, include information on news bureaus.

Working with Reporters and Editors

If you are going to have a major event that will interest several reporters at a large paper, ask if the city editor or your favorite reporter will serve as the newspaper's coordinator for coverage. Emphasize that this will avoid duplicate coverage. If, for example, you supply publicity material to both the science and education reporters, and they do similar spreads on your Lions Club science fair for high school students, the reporters will be furious, and you will have a hard time getting any further publicity from that paper. "It's a bad move," says Larry Kramer of the *Trenton Times.* "I think if any publicist is going to do that, he ought to let each reporter know that someone else is being clued on it. Because if both stories actually ran in the paper, it would be an embarrassment. And the last thing a publicist wants to do is put an editor in a spot where he's embarrassed. If a publicist did that and both stories ran, it would be bad times."

Even if you have two entirely different stories, with different angles and information, if they concern the same event, product, or service, you must let each reporter know that another journalist at that publication is working on that material. Suppose that there has been a sudden surge in shoplifting in your community, and your merchants association has decided to work with two angles. You've written a press release with information from your study of the typical shoplifter, pointing to the need for more parental responsibility. And you've written another story about the economic effects of shoplifting on neighborhood merchants. The editor of the family living page is interested in the first approach, while the business writer is open to the second. Even though they are different stories, with different news pegs, you'd better tell both reporters exactly what you're doing. They will then compare notes, and if they think that both stories stand on their own merits as separate articles, they will write and run both of them.

If you're sending a release to a reporter and a duplicate copy to the editor of an events calendar, label each release, indicating who else has gotten it. By the same token, do not send the same release to more than one bureau of a publication unless you have a *very* good reason for doing so—

and you inform everyone involved. Otherwise, you may arouse suspicions that you're trying to put one past the editors.

Timing and Deadlines

This section discusses general rules about deadlines. You should also get specific deadline times from every publication you work with.

For weeklies appearing on Wednesdays or Thursdays, the previous Friday at noon is often the cutoff point. Morning papers usually need their material by 2:00 the previous afternoon. Fewer evening papers are published each year, but if you are working with one of them, you should know that evening papers often have morning deadlines. For special sections of the Sunday paper, the deadline can be as early as the previous Wednesday.

If your area still has both morning and evening papers, consider that an early-morning release time will meet the deadlines for both papers, as well as the evening TV news broadcasts. Or, you may want to rotate, with alternate releases timed for the morning and evening papers' deadlines.

For hard news stories of major importance appearing first in the morning papers, some publicists rewrite their releases to give the evening editors a new angle or additional information. While there aren't many evening newspapers left, this strategy is still important because it encourages evening TV news coverage as well.

You could even plan a special event schedule that maximizes your press coverage. If you know that the *Evening Moon* runs color on the front page and your Rotary Club Midsummer Family Carnival includes launching three dozen hot-air balloons that will fill the sky with patches of pastel, make sure you launch those balloons early in the day, so you meet the *Moon*'s deadline.

Perhaps you're sponsoring a conference for utility executives on techniques for neutralizing citizen opposition to nuclear power plants. The science writer at the morning paper has been consistently against atomic power, but the *Evening Moon* reporter on the science beat is undecided. If your material is persuasive, he may write a favorable story. In such a case, you could arrange for a prestigious nuclear engineer to reveal the findings of his latest research on nuclear accidents early enough in the day to meet the evening paper's deadline. If the evening paper comes out with a fair or favorable story first, the morning paper is more likely to give your story adequate coverage, even if its writer is opposed to your organization's position.

When you are working with weekly papers, you may have to send your release to them before you send it to the dailies. "I send out the same press release to the weekly papers first, so they have it in time for next week. Then I send it out to the dailies a few days later, so they run it about the same time the weeklies do," says Harry Cohn of the American Red Cross.

Whenever possible, the best policy is to make sure your press releases are received several days before the deadline. Remember that you're asking for free space, and the editor may not have any room to juggle at the last minute. Yesterday there was a gaping news hole he had to fill with boilerplate copy from the wire services and the syndicates. If your release had been in his hands then, he would have used it and been grateful.

Don't go to the opposite extreme. Although most large papers and some small ones maintain files of upcoming events, your release may get lost if you send it more than 10 days ahead. "Don't send it too far in advance, or I'll forget all about it and blow it," says the *Norfolk Ledger-Star*'s Fred Kirsch.

When you send out press releases about an event, make it clear whether you are asking for advance publicity or inviting the press to cover the event. Of course, you can do both, but, says Harry Cohn, "If you send out a press release ten days before the event, even if the newspaper runs that story, it doesn't mean they're going to cover the event. They've probably thrown the press release away by then. So, you have to send a request for coverage a few days before and follow up with a call the day before the event."

Following Up on Press Releases

You wrote a fine press release and mailed it five days ago, but your phone seems to have lost its voice, and you've seen nothing at all in the newspaper. Should you call the editor or the reporter to ask if he's going to run your story? Yes. No. Maybe. This is a delicate area, and even seasoned publicists don't agree about how it should be handled. If you ask two veteran publicists for advice, you'll get three opinions.

Many publicists would never inquire about whether a press release will be used. Mary Jane O'Neill of the New York Association for the Blind says she "wouldn't call to ask if they're going to use a press release. Having been on the other side of the desk, I know the reaction of reporters who say, 'My God, I'm too busy to tell. I don't know whether I'm going to use it. I mean I sent it through. The editor is the one who decides whether to use it. I don't know.'"

Your story might have been edited, rewritten, typeset, and fitted into place, but at the last minute there was a spectacular 20-car crash on the freeway, and it preempted your write-up just before the presses started rolling. That sort of thing is hard to predict, and many reporters and editors do not like to make promises they may not be able to honor. Don't pressure them.

"I have been extremely annoyed by people who call up to tell me they want to make sure their press release 'gets in,'" says journalist Leslie O'Bergin. "They don't seem to realize that there is limited space, and there is some editorial discretion involved in what gets printed and what doesn't. I tell such callers that they're taking their chances with everyone else, and I ask them what makes them different. I can't think of a time when anyone has convinced me that they were, in fact, different. And I have been known to take their item, already typeset, and rip it up. Now that's not laudable, but I'm not the only person who has done that." However, if the topic interests her, and the caller makes a polite offer of more material and information, O'Bergin will accept.

On the other hand, public relations executive Richard Weiner contends that it is not necessarily considered impolite or overly aggressive to inquire about the status of a press release: "Public relations people tend to be shy about calling up; they don't quite know what to say. They're reluctant to say, 'Did you get my news release? Do you plan to use it?' So it's advantageous to figure out something better than that. Find some significant detail that wasn't covered in your release. Then you can hold your head up high and not feel embarrassed about making that call.

"Sometimes," Weiner continues, "the editor may have thrown away the release, or forgotten about it, and he can be sold by the phone conversation. Sometimes he will ask you to send it again. Send it again!"

From the other side of the desk, Randy McCarthy of the *Boise Statesman* concedes, "I'd just as soon they didn't call to ask about press releases, even though a lot of times it saves my life if somebody does call up and say, 'Hey, I sent this in and it hasn't shown up yet.' Then I will make an effort to find out what happened to the thing. If I've never heard anything about it, or if it's one of those I looked at, didn't see anything too interesting, and canned, if they can sell it to me on the phone, I'll ask them to send it again."

And journalist Nancy Dunn asserts, "It is useful to follow up your press release with a phone call, but keep it brief. Have the details ready: it is annoying to have to pull details out of a publicist. Be articulate. If you can't come to the point quickly, you're not going to be taken seriously."

The best approach for the beginning publicist is to call only after the journalist has had time to receive and read the release. Ask if it has been received. If it hasn't, briefly resell the story and offer to send another copy. If the reporter or editor has received it, ask if he needs more information and have some specific, brief material you can offer on the phone that was not in the release. Perhaps most important is to keep the anxiety out of your voice. Try to be warm and friendly. It's hard at first, but after you've played the role for a while, you'll find that you actually are relaxed.

Asking for Clippings

It is unwise to ask journalists for clippings of articles that their publication has run about your group. Publicists who make such requests will try the patience of the reporter. "We have a clipping service," says Brian Youmatz of the *Framingham Middlesex News*, "and I would send them to that department. I wouldn't have any of my people waste their time getting them." Fred Kirsch of the *Ledger-Star* says, "If they are outside the circulation area, I find their request legitimate. If they can obtain the paper, I feel they're just being lazy."

Says public relations executive Ravelle Brickman, "Stop and think for a moment how insulting it is to the editor of your local paper to imply that you don't buy or even read it."

Get those clippings yourself!

Keeping Advertising and Publicity Separate

Never discuss your advertising program with journalists. It's too easy for such a discussion to be misunderstood as a particularly nasty form of persuasion. At most large publications, your status as advertiser will have no bearing on your status as publicist. Although some small newspapers and magazines give better coverage to advertisers, that isn't always the case. Furthermore, even if a particular publication does cater to its advertisers with expanded coverage of their activities, you will win friends among the reporters if you always approach them with solid copy, newsworthy material, and an interesting angle. They'll feel that you're treating them as professionals, and you'll quickly gain a reputation as more than a mere advertiser demanding his "due."

Thanking Reporters

Be careful about thanking journalists; never imply that someone has done you a favor instead of using good journalistic judgment. Some reporters even take pride in completely avoiding public relations people, or at least not admitting any contact. Don't thank reporters.

There are even journalists, such as Larry Kramer of the *Trenton Times*, who like to hear occasional criticism: "Sometimes I get worried when people thank us for stories. A good crusty editor will tell you that he's only happy when both sides don't like the story. But I'm not that way. If people think we're covering them fairly, I think it's fine for them to say so."

Sylvia Smith of the *Fort Wayne Journal-Gazette* says, "Although everybody likes to be appreciated, that's a real fine line. If a publicist has a personal relationship with the reporter or the editor, I suppose it would be OK. But in general, I would shy away from it."

When you express your appreciation to a journalist, the important thing is to convey that the story was well written and perceptive and share the response you've had from the public. Ravelle Brickman takes this approach: "I'm a writer. Every journalist in America is a writer, too. When I call a journalist to say thank you, I'm not just saying the story was well written, but, 'one writer to another, you did a fabulous job.'"

The thanks, of course, should never be in tangible form. And it should never be elaborate. "I don't like a great army of people to march in with the president of the organization and the publicist to say thanks, nor do I like to be invited to a luncheon to say thank you. I just don't think that's necessary," says S. Griffin Singer of the *San Antonio Light*.

Working with Cartoonists and Editorial Writers

As you've read the editorial page of your large daily newspaper and looked at the cartoons and editorials, perhaps you've wondered why your organization couldn't persuade the cartoonist or editorial writer to take a stand on your cause. If you have great patience and tact, you may do just that.

Cartoonists

Editorial and political cartoonists range from the completely aloof, anonymous cartoonist who says, "I can't be approached. Period. You can't quote me," to David Norwood, political cartoonist at the *Baton Rouge Advocate* in Louisiana. "If they just came in the door and presented themselves in such a way that there was a gentlemanly exchange there, I would probably honor anybody," says Norwood. "Or they should call me up and make a suggestion. I would make a little rough of it and bring it to the editorial department. They decide if they can use it. The group I'm doing it for doesn't get to see the rough sketch unless they come down here and make a personal call. I'm actually interested in anything."

Norwood is unusually accessible and receptive. John Reidell, editorial cartoonist at the *Peoria Journal Star* in Illinois, speaks for most American cartoonists when he says, "I prefer to come up with my own ideas. I don't mind getting information, though. I'm open to hearing different views. But I wouldn't want to be expected to follow any particular line."

The following interview with Craig MacIntosh, political cartoonist for the *Minneapolis Star*, is a good indication of the point of view of most cartoonists.

> *Yale:* Are you ever approachable by special interest groups who want you to do a cartoon on their issues?
>
> *MacIntosh:* Most of the time I would shy away from that, unless it's such a gentle organization, so nonpolitical, that I could do it without any qualms.
>
> *Yale:* But let's say they wanted to approach you and take their chances. Would you prefer to be approached with facts, suggestions, or are you just not approachable at all?
>
> *MacIntosh:* I would probably just say no because I think I might somehow compromise my independence on the issues. Basically I'm unapproachable.
>
> *Yale:* Suppose they were to send you fact sheets and say, "This seems to us to be an interesting issue. Enclosed are some fact sheets. Do what you want with them"?

MacIntosh: Yes. I've had people do that. Everybody from air bag proponents to the United Way. I suppose getting those kinds of things in the mail is part of the job. But I've never had a suggestion about doing a cartoon.

Yale: So that, basically, the only way to approach you is with facts?

MacIntosh: Yes. I think I probably could speak for most cartoonists in the country. That's pretty standard.

Editorial Writers

Editorials are not the same as letters to the editor, although many people confuse them. Letters to the editor are written by the publication's *readers*. Editorials are usually statements of the *publication's* official position on an issue. They are written by the publication's editorial staff.

Similarly, not everyone understands that editorials, by their nature, have a strong point of view. Kerry W. Sipe, public editor of the *Ledger-Star* in Norfolk, Virginia, comments on this situation in an article in *Masthead*, the publication of the National Conference of Editorial Writers: "Readers say 'Your editorials are one-sided,' or 'Your editorial writer lets his bias show in his writing.' I often have to explain that criticizing an editorial for being biased is like criticizing water for being wet."

The major sources of topics for editorial writers are news stories and magazine articles. According to a survey conducted by *Masthead*, "Almost 80 percent of the respondents ranked the news as the number-one source of editorials. Book and magazine articles, reporters on their staffs, public officials, and experts outside their staffs are mentioned as important secondary sources by about a third of the writers."

Editorial writers usually do not like "duty" or "worthy-cause" editorials that merely endorse charitable organizations. They want to write about current issues, not fund-raising campaigns. In an article in *Masthead*, David B. Bowes, editorial-page editor of the *Cincinnati Post*, explains why:

> *Requests for "worthy cause" editorials are like phone calls at the dinner hour when the caller inquires after the condition of your storm windows. The first time you fidget but listen, the next time you invoke cloture, and the time after that you find yourself explaining to the children that yes, it's impolite to hang up on someone but life can come to that.*

Does the contemporary editorial page . . . attempting to reach new audiences, have the space to give each worthy cause "our annual editorial" as so many charity groups so airily put it? The quaint belief that a campaign will fail unless it is singled out . . . on the editorial page is a myth that all of us are loath to dispel, but something's got to give.

. . . We're finding less space for on-demand editorials of obviously praiseworthy causes. Their tidings may be news for news pages . . . but they aren't always candidates for commentary.

Approaching editorial writers is slightly less difficult than making overtures to cartoonists, but you still need the patience of a saint and the tact of several diplomats. Before you let those ice crystals start forming in your stomach, remember that many publicists have successfully approached editorial writers about topics important to their businesses, industries, or organizations.

Provide editorial writers with compelling facts, and *you* could become one of their "expert" sources. You will often find them more receptive if you provide them with fact sheets and all the information they need to fully consider your cause. And since editorial writers are news oriented, you may fare better if you approach them when your organization is making headlines.

"What you send to the editor of an editorial page is different from what you would send to a business-news writer," says public relations executive Richard Weiner. "It usually consists of background material and a letter which says that the enclosed material could be used as the basis for an editorial in the paper. Editorial writers, just like any other writers, are always looking for valid suggestions."

You may, or may not, want to send copies of your press releases to editorial writers. Your releases alone will not usually get editorial writers to write about your cause, but "It helps if we already know something about the organization before being directly approached," says Anthony Morley, editorial writer for the *Minneapolis Tribune.* "To the extent that being on a mailing list for press releases serves that goal, yes, it's helpful."

In any case, you should not submit suggested editorials that you have written yourself unless an editorial writer asks you for them. You may be asked to write one at some of the smaller newspapers, but most editorial writers pride themselves on their independence, and they will be offended if you imply that they don't write their own material.

In fact, the National Conference of Editorial Writers Statement of Principles specifically says, "The editorial writer should discourage publication of editorials prepared by an outside writing service and presented as the newspaper's own. Failure to disclose the source of such editorials is unethical, and particularly reprehensible when the service is in the employ of a special interest."

When you talk with editorial writers, show them that you are aware of other approaches to your topic. They may even ask you to tell them your opponent's point of view. You will have more credibility if they perceive that you take other viewpoints seriously, but don't be afraid to take a firm stand. "If somebody is an advocate, I expect advocacy," says Anthony Morley.

Since many editorial writers are more interested in your material if it has a local angle, and since it is easier for them to check out a local rather than a national organization, it is more productive for national organizations and businesses to approach editorial writers through their local chapters, distributors, dealers, or district offices.

Even if an editorial has been written that gives you solid support, keep your distance afterward. If you're tempted to ask the editorial writer for a contribution or invite him to sit on your board of directors, consider that a *Masthead* survey showed that 66.7 percent of editorialists agree that editorial writers should avoid involvement in partisan political organizations. "Management prohibition of political activity by writers has risen dramatically," *Masthead* concludes.

Approaching and Working with Feature Editors

Unlike editorial writers, most feature editors want written article suggestions. For example, Paul Neely of the *St. Petersburg Times* prefers to be approached "early and in writing." However, "I never want a complete article," he says. "I have people on my staff to write complete articles. If they send us a complete story, we're going to rewrite it anyway, so they might as well not waste their efforts. Some smaller newspapers prefer a complete article, though." So, it is best to find out the preference of each editor you will be working with.

You will often work personally with the feature editor, or a reporter, to develop a feature article. This means that you should have anecdotes, information, facts, and figures ready *before* you approach a feature editor.

A good way to approach feature writers is with a letter that pitches and summarizes your story. Letters to feature editors should cover the following eight points:

- Tell the editor that you are offering an idea for a feature story.
- Summarize the idea in one paragraph.
- Explain why the editor's audience would be interested.
- Emphasize the scope and importance of the story.
- Give a few interesting details.
- Suggest alternate approaches where possible.
- Describe picture possibilities.
- Enclose a prepaid return card along with your E-mail address, a toll-free number, or an offer to accept collect calls if the editor is interested.

Exhibit 5.1 and Exhibit 5.2 on page 158 present two excellent one-paragraph summaries of feature material. Both are examples of the typical summary prepared for feature writers. They were written by Hill & Knowlton's Industrial and Scientific Communication Services. The first generated 40 responses for the client, the American Iron and Steel Institute, while the second item produced 84 inquiries for client Frito-Lay.

Exhibit 5.1

Garbage Power

Thanks to a process called resource recovery, 20 American communities are now converting municipal garbage into energy. Ames, Iowa; Madison, Wisconsin; and Hempstead, New York burn garbage to generate electricity, while Baltimore, Maryland; Nashville, Tennessee; and Saugus, Massachusetts convert garbage to steam for heating and cooling buildings. According to a recent report from the U.S. General Accounting Office, if all the resource recovery plants under construction, or in planning, become operational by 1985, the U.S. will realize energy savings equivalent to 48 million barrels of oil a year. (Details, background information, interviews.)

Exhibit 5.2

Survey Says Educated Women Snacked More Over Past Decade

The passion for snacks—such as potato chips, and corn and tortilla chips—has increased dramatically among women over the past decade, according to a new study conducted by Barry Popkin, Ph.D., professor of nutrition at the University of North Carolina, Chapel Hill. In addition to a 26 percent increase in women with increased education that ate snacks, there was a 27 percent increase in the number who consumed green and leafy vegetables. These conflicting trends as well as others this survey discovered have resulted in changes by food manufacturers as they enter the next decade.

But there's more than one way to skin a cat. *The Publicist,* a former magazine with extensive coverage of the public relations field, described another innovative way to approach feature editors:

> *A public relations agency in Los Angeles placed substantial articles in daily newspapers across the country by arranging for the papers to interview its client by telephone.*
>
> *The client, a San Francisco doctor who had written two books for cancer patients and their families, was unable to tour the nation for interviews; thus the telephone technique. . . . A major side benefit . . . was the fact that the publicity cost far less than the usual book campaign.*
>
> *The Bruce Merrin Organization telephoned the largest circulation newspaper in each of the 100 largest cities in the United States. After locating the editor most likely to handle the story, it launched into a full scale pitch then and there.*
>
> *The agency then shipped him or her . . . copies of the books, a biographical sheet on the author, and a photograph of him. It was accompanied by a personalized letter expressing appreciation for the editor's interest, repeating the key points of the original pitch, and offering to arrange a telephone interview at the agency's expense.*
>
> *About 10 days after each kit was shipped, the agency followed up by telephone. Dr. Rosenbaum blocked out certain times when he could make himself available at the telephone in his office, and the agency scheduled the interviews accordingly. Some lasted as long as an hour.*

Why Features Are Exclusive

"If the newspapers in your area are engaged in a rather competitive situation with each other," says Sylvia Smith of the *Fort Wayne Journal-Gazette*, "it's important to know that it's bad form to take the same feature story idea to both newspapers."

Mark Shepherd of the *Columbia Daily Tribune* assesses the journalism scene in his area this way: "There's another paper in town, there are three television stations that have news programs within the market area, and there are some pretty aggressive radio news programs here. So it's a very competitive news situation. That's why I try to get exclusive news interviews, or at least set up interviews where I can deal with the source by myself, so I can ask my own questions."

Although journalists expect you to distribute news fairly, many of them assume that feature material is exclusive unless they agree otherwise. Even if you intend to send the material only to publications in other geographic areas, or to other special interest publications with different audiences, be sure the editor understands your intentions. If you fail to honor an exclusive commitment, you will badly damage your reputation in media circles. Reporters and editors talk about such foul misdeeds, and word about unreliable publicists can spread quickly in journalism circles.

"I wouldn't have much faith in what they bring me next time around," says the *Maine Sunday Telegram*'s Robert Cummings. "If we make an arrangement, I don't want it broken because then there's a complication with my editors. They like to run a fresh newspaper on Sunday. So if I start sending in stuff that's already been in the papers, it hurts both me and the group that wants publicity."

Instead of labeling your feature material "For immediate release," tag it "Special to the *Evening Moon*" or "Exclusive to the *Morning Star*." Then everyone involved knows exactly what the arrangement is.

Approaching Syndicated Columnists and Wire Services

Wouldn't it be great if your firm's new line of cosmetics could be mentioned by one of the beauty and fashion columnists? Or if your engineering firm's report on new techniques for containing chemical leaks from dump sites could be discussed in an ecology column appearing in hundreds of newspapers? Or if your trade association's position on defense spending could be explained in a syndicated political column? It can happen. And since syndicated columnists are widely read and highly influential, it would be quite a publicity coup.

Public relations executive Richard Weiner notes, "Syndicated columnists rarely use news releases and other mass-distributed material. A well-written letter to a columnist, offering an exclusive and demonstrating a familiarity with the type of column, is much preferred to a phone call or a news release."

One problem with offering an exclusive to a syndicated columnist is that she may not answer you if she isn't interested. Since you have offered the material on an exclusive basis, you are not free to take it elsewhere, and, without an answer, your material is tied up. Avoid that problem by indicating that the exclusive basis is for a limited time only. You could say, for example, that the material is available on an exclusive basis if it is used by September 15. It is a good idea to enclose a stamped, self-addressed postcard with boxes the columnist can check off to indicate interest or lack of it. It also is helpful to let the columnist know that you will accept collect calls from her if she needs more information, or provide her with your E-mail address or toll-free number.

How do you know where to send your material? Consult the list of syndicated columnists in *Bacon's Newspaper Directory*, listed under "Media Directories" in Chapter 13.

To interest wire service reporters, your material must really be of international, national, or regional importance. Wire services, such as the Associated Press (AP), United Press International (UPI), or Reuters, can help you place publicity material in dozens and even hundreds of papers. The wire services serve broadcasters as well, so the impact of material picked up by a wire service can be tremendous.

Both the AP and the UPI have scores of news bureaus in the United States. These are much like newspaper bureaus, and you should work with the bureau nearest to your town or city. A local bureau may have a city editor, science writer, business reporter, and feature editor, as well as other specialized reporters. Find out their names, and contact them directly. However, if you have specialized or technical information, ask the local bureau if the wire service has a specialist at headquarters who should get the material.

Some of the media directories listed in Chapter 13 include wire service bureaus as well. You can consult one of these sources if you're not sure where the nearest bureau is.

Getting into Magazines

There are four basic types of magazines, and each has a different focus. Some are harder to work with than others, but the results are often well worth your time.

General interest consumer magazines, with broad appeal and a vast audience, are not usually interested in specialized material. Although it therefore may be a challenge to get them to consider your material, their very large circulations can deliver a publicity message with stunning effectiveness. If you can possibly place material in them, your message will reach millions, but you will have worked exceedingly hard to accomplish your goal.

Examples of general interest magazines are *Reader's Digest* and *People*. The larger general interest magazines have local bureaus and specialized reporters, just like a big-city daily newspaper.

Because these magazines are "more selective," public relations executive Richard Weiner explains, "it is much more difficult to get publicity of any kind." He adds, "It's rarely possible to get articles simply by sending a news release. Many publicists ignore [general interest] magazines, figuring that they're too difficult and the batting average is too low." But there are techniques for approaching them that will work, if you have genuinely newsworthy material.

Special interest consumer magazines, the second category, always focus on a well-defined topic. If you approach one with newsworthy material on its subject, it is likely to be interested. The variety of topics covered is amazing, from *Art and Antiques* to *Bird Watcher's Digest* to *Classic Toy Trains*, some with circulations of a few thousand, and others that reach millions of readers.

The third category, *business magazines*, includes both national publications, such as *Fortune* and *Business Week*, and local magazines interested solely in business news in their local areas, such as *Business Atlanta* and the *Indianapolis Business Journal*. They often have reporters who cover special topics, and some of the national publications have local bureaus.

Finally, *trade publications* are written strictly for people in a particular industry, and the only news that interests them is material that will affect that industry. There are two basic types of trade magazines, those published by businesses and those published by trade associations.

Trade publications published by businesses accept advertising, and they are almost all listed in media directories. Examples are *PC Magazine* (the 16th largest American magazine), *Adhesives, Florida Grocer, Group Practice News* (a magazine for doctors), *Plastic Trends*, and *The Typographer.*

Journals published by trade associations are sometimes for their members only. This type of publication can be harder to find and is not always listed in media directories. If you're having trouble tracking down the trade magazine that would reach one of your target audiences, consult *The Encyclopedia of Associations*, available at any large library. It lists thousands of trade associations, and their publications.

Choosing the Right Magazines

As with any media outlet, you have to be familiar with the magazine before you try to get coverage. You may be tempted to use the information in one of the magazine directories listed in Chapter 13 as your only basis of information. Don't. You need to know firsthand how long articles are, what topics have been covered recently, and the general tone and style of the magazine. For special interest and trade magazines that run short product reviews, you must know their formats, so you can write to fit.

"Start by looking at the last three issues of the 10 most important magazines you're shooting for," advises Don Levin of Levin Public Relations Marketing. Read them carefully. Try to figure out which types of stories get full-length articles and which get mere blurbs or mentions.

As you examine a magazine, or "book" as we call it in journalese, it will help you to know that most of them are divided roughly into three sections: front of the book, middle of the book, and back of the book. More important announcements, blurbs, and columns usually appear in the front of the book. Feature articles usually start in the middle of the book and may continue into the back section. Less important material is usually relegated to the back of the book, and here is where the bulk of the advertising appears. Some ads are placed in the front of the book, with few or none in the middle.

A careful reading of your target magazines is worth the time. *PC Magazine* editor Bill Howard attests, "If PR people understand who we are and what we do, they will have a better chance of getting through to us." His colleague Gus Venditto, explains why: "There are three pages in the magazine, called the New and Improved section, where we use press releases as the basis for the articles." He emphasizes, "That's the only place where we use photos from publicists. For this section, a photo does give a story a bit of an edge. Black and white glossies are best." The only way to find specific editorial needs like this is to become familiar with your target magazines.

Other magazine journalists echo Howard and Venditto. "Few of the people who call me have made any effort to look at the magazine and see what kind of products and technologies we cover. And even fewer have investigated beat areas so as to approach the right editor," says Denny Arar, senior associate editor at *PC World,* quoted in *Soft•letter.* And Steve Hamm, associate editor at *Business Week,* told *Soft•letter,* "I get a lot of indiscriminate pitches. People don't seem to know what we're interested in. I guess they just want to tell their client they pitched us. It's a big waste of everybody's time."

Sometimes choosing the right magazines for your publicity is straightforward. Sometimes it's more complicated.

Let's say that your company markets equipment and supplies for cleaning up hazardous waste. If you send your publicity material to all the new publications in the environmental field, won't that get you enough coverage?

Probably not, according to Joel Strasser of Dorf & Stanton Technology Communications. "The companies affected by environmental problems often don't read or even know about the specialized environmental publications. A chemical company, for example, might look to *Chemical Week* or *Chemical and Engineering News* for information on environmental management," Strasser says. Furthermore, he points out that environmental problems are not always handled by the companies affected. "Who does an oil or chemical company turn to when they have a serious contamination situation on a piece of property they want to sell? Or suppose a company wants to finance a piece of property—that may be contaminated with industrial waste—for a new plant. They'll involve real estate brokers, lawyers, bankers, and insurers in the assessment of potential environmental problems. That's why there is a high degree of interest in stories with useful environmental information from real estate, legal, financial, and banking publications."

To reach the largest possible audience, you'll have to do some strategizing. Curl up with a media directory that lists magazines, and ask yourself whether there are additional publications that should be getting your releases and article queries. Sure, it's not exactly as gripping as a good whodunit, but as you read through the listings for magazines and ask yourself if their readers could have any possible interest in your stories, you'll probably make some intriguing, and highly fruitful, discoveries.

Using Editorial Calendars

For most magazine publicity, make your first contact at least three months in advance, and preferably six. Weekly news magazines, of course, have shorter lead times. But even in the dead of winter, many special interest and trade magazine editors will be planning their late-spring and summer issues. You'll be left out in the cold if you don't plan as far ahead as they do.

How do you know, in advance, what topics a magazine will be covering six months from now? It's not as hard as it sounds. Virtually every consumer special interest and trade magazine publishes an editorial calendar, usually for a year ahead. It lists the major topics, and sometimes even the article titles each issue will include.

Some editorial calendars are very detailed; others are not. Some magazines likewise are very helpful and go out of their way to provide information for publicists. *PC Magazine,* for example, even has a monthly update to the editorial calendar that lists changes and gives details as the topics become more specific.

Editor Bill Howard explains, "We set up our new editorial calendar around the end of August and publish it around the end of September. It's pretty much solid for the first half of the year. We might modify a quarter of our story items over the course of a year. The ones that do vary often slide by an issue or two, as opposed to being changed entirely."

Editorial calendars are usually yours for the asking. At most publications the receptionist will be happy to help you obtain one. In addition, several of the media directories listed in Chapter 13 include editorial calendars. You can also find them on-line at some magazines' websites.

Editorial calendars are used mainly by special interest and trade magazines, as well as some business books. But you won't find any at publications such as *Time* and *Business Week.* "Although there are certain seasonal and perennial topics, there's no such thing as an editorial calendar at the hard news books," says Bob Seltzer.

Approaching Magazine Editors

Once you've targeted the magazines you want to pitch to, your next step is to find the right reporter or editor. Journalists expect you to do this.

"I want publicists to approach the right person, rather than the top person," says Bill Howard. At large magazines, there may be dozens of possible contacts. At a smaller one, your task is easier: sometimes there are only two or three journalists working there.

To locate the right journalist for your story, call someone midway up the ladder who has a lot of experience at the magazine. An assistant to the editor or publisher can often steer you to the right writer or editor. No matter whom you talk with, be brief and to the point. You could ask, "Can you tell me who handles user stories on green-striped widgets?" or, "Can you tell me which editor covers new products in the gizmo industry?"

When you approach a trade magazine editor, never assume that you'll get favorable coverage just because your organization advertises in that book. "The trade magazines have often been accused of pandering to their advertisers," according to an article by Kim Foltz in the *New York Times,* but that is changing. There are more trade magazines, and they're competing with each other for readers. Foltz quotes John Emery, president of American Business Press, a trade organization for trade magazines, who predicts, "More magazines may turn to adversarial reporting as a way to enhance their reputations with readers [and] advertisers. When times get tough, advertisers naturally want to be in the book that everyone thinks is the only one to read."

This means that more and more frequently, journalists at trade books—and even special interest magazines—will be asking you tough questions. They'll be testing your products independently, and reporting the results to readers, even if they are unfavorable.

The policies at *Skiing* are a good example of the new breed of trade and special interest journalism. The late Al Greenberg, former editor at large, explained, "We decided that our magazine could not be objective if it simply took press releases from manufacturers, or even from industry-wide organizations. Realizing that public safety was at stake, we determined that the only way we could effectively judge equipment performance was to find out what made equipment safe or unsafe and then set up equipment tests based on this knowledge. And though it wasn't our primary intent, we did play a role in driving many inferior products from the marketplace."

Making the Pitch to Magazines

There are three basic ways to work with magazine editors, and each has advantages and drawbacks.

The first way to approach magazines is by sending a press release, with the hope that the journalist will write a story based on it. Although this takes the least amount of time, it is not always fruitful. However, if you're providing useful how-to information or addressing a hot issue in the industry, you're more likely to get coverage. And with some publications, it's the only way possible.

For example, Joel Strasser explains, "Most environmental publications usually don't want to talk with you or interview an expert; they prefer receiving written material, which they sometimes run unedited. The computer trades, on the other hand, like to talk to the people who make the news, and write their own stories."

If you're sending a release to magazines, it's a good idea to include supporting material. In a survey of editors cited in *Public Relations Journal*, 71 percent of respondents said they found backgrounders and white papers helpful.

The second approach involves persuading the editor to assign a writer to do the article, starting with your material, and building on interviews and perhaps other sources. This takes more time, but once an editor agrees, it's much more likely to produce results. You'll have more input as well.

When you want an editor to assign a writer to your story, first call the editor and make a brief pitch, or write a short query letter and then call to see if she's interested. Either way, be sure you understand exactly what commitment the editor has made to you, what her deadline will be, and what information, materials, product samples, and interviews with experts she'll need.

This approach works well with the consumer magazines, when you're trying to get them to interview your spokesperson. Bob Seltzer explains, "For Estraderm, which is a skin patch that delivers estrogen to menopausal women on a continual basis, we've created an educational campaign to help women cope with menopause. Our spokesperson is the actress Shirley Jones. We've done really well with getting reporters to interview her. It's her task to get our educational messages into the interview. Then we all hope it will make it through the writing and editing process."

With the last approach, you try to get the editor to agree to accept an article written by your organization's spokesperson, clients, experts, or you, the publicist. This takes the most time and effort, and some magazine editors won't agree to it, so you should make sure the editor will not find it offensive. Joel Strasser points out, "Publications like *Forbes*, the *Wall Street Journal*, and the *New York Times* always write everything themselves. They won't usually accept expert-authored articles." And Gus Venditto at *PC Magazine* warns, "It would not be fruitful for a publicist to send us an article or a query for an article. We would never run anything like that."

However, when this method is acceptable, it gives you more control than the other two approaches, as well as the most input. Bob Seltzer explains, "We've found that a lot of publications will accept an article with Shirley Jones' byline, in which we structure the message. This gives us a much better chance that our message will survive the editorial process. And that's because of Shirley's stature."

If you will be writing the article yourself, ask for a copy of the publication's guidelines for writers. This will give you valuable insight to the magazine's approach. Most magazines will be glad to send them. Once you have done that, you will want to find out which editor handles your topic, and call or write with a brief pitch.

A query letter to an editor may read like the one in Exhibit 5.3 on page 168.

Once you have an editor's interest, you'll want to get his tentative acceptance. At that point, it's a good idea to offer to send a detailed outline of the article, discuss the outline over the phone, ask for suggestions, and see if you can get him to commit to a tentative publication date.

You'll need to know how long he wants the article to be, and if he prefers it in manuscript or electronic form. Whenever an editor asks for an article in electronic form, ask whether he wants it delivered by E-mail or on disk. When an editor has requested an on-disk article, ask these questions:

Exhibit 5.3

Dear Mr. Edwards:

With the widespread concern about the harmful effects of poisonous chemical sprays on the environment, consumers are looking for options. And the nurseries that can provide alternatives will stand to make above-average profits—if they know where to find these products and how to promote them. From our contacts with nursery operators, we know that *National Nurseryman and Grower*'s readers are eager for more information on this subject.

I'd like to propose a two-part article written by Dr. Linda H. Coming, the research director of Ecolo-Grow, and Lucy Czaloski, our marketing director.

Dr. Coming, who has conducted research for the Plains State University on pesticide-free farming techniques, is the author of six books on the subject. Ms. Czaloski teaches advertising at the Plains City College Evening School. Her 2000 coop advertising campaign for Ecolo-Grow, which helped nurseries promote alternatives to poisonous spraying, won a gold medal at the Plains State Advertising Club Convention.

Part one of the proposed article will cover types of biological insect controls, insect- and disease-resistant plant varieties, and nonpoisonous sprays. In the second part, we'll include complete information about buying these products wholesale from a variety of suppliers, as well as how to promote and advertise them.

Since most of your middle-of-the-book articles seem to run about 3,000 words, we propose a 6,000-word article in two equal parts.

We can provide you with finished copy in WordPerfect for Windows 6.0, Word for Windows 7.0, or as a text file. Delivery can be on disk or by E-mail.

I will call you next week to learn of your interest. I look forward to talking with you.

Sincerely yours,

Robert K. Dajminnish

Publicity Director, Ecolo-Grow

- Does the editor use an IBM-compatible or Mac-based PC?
- What word processing software does the editor use?
- Does the editor prefer to have your article formatted by that software?

If you don't have access to that software, check the Save options in your word processing software. Many programs, such as newer versions of Microsoft Word, let you convert files to other formats when you save them.

If your software won't convert files to the desired software, ask the editor if his software will convert a file from the program you use. If not, ask if he'll accept the article as a text file. When you submit an article as a text file, all formatting, such as underlining, boldface, and italics, disappears. Be certain to include a formatted copy of the manuscript along with your disk. Mark the manuscript "formatted copy" on the top of the first page.

Using Freelancers, Experts, and Clients as Writers

If you've approached a magazine and been asked to supply an article, you should know about working with freelance writers, as well as using experts, customers, and clients as writers.

Always set two deadlines for your articles: the deadline you give your writers, and the real deadline, perhaps two or three weeks later—which you never reveal. If there's a problem or delay, you can still have the article finished and delivered by the real deadline.

What happens if you promise to deliver material and you miss the deadline? Gus Venditto of *PC Magazine* says that when publicists fail to deliver to his publication at the last minute, they don't get covered; the space gets filled with other material. Your organization or business may get covered later, but you'll get less space because your news is not fresh anymore. Venditto is unusually easygoing. At smaller publications, with fewer journalists on staff, a missed deadline can be more serious. You may leave them with a news hole and no time to fill it. They may never trust you again.

What do you do if the article by one of your customers (or an outside expert or the company president) arrives on your desk at the last minute and it's not usable? One publicist for a software company, who prefers to remain unnamed, tells this deadline story:

I was extremely disappointed. I had asked the most important user of our software to write an article. When it arrived, it was vague, badly written, and dull. Now I had talked with this client many times, and I knew the article did not reflect her experience with our product and her insight into her industry. I also knew that I'd never have another chance at that trade book again if I blew this deadline—and it's the most important publication for our industry. The deadline was only two days off. It was a tight spot for sure!

I took a deep breath and called her. "The article is great," I said, "but it needs just a little bit of fleshing out. Can I put you on speaker phone and start my tape?"

Once she started talking, I knew there would be no problem with the material. She knew her stuff, but she just couldn't write. I taped her for two hours, and when we were finished, she was even more enthusiastic about her article.

I called my wife to say I wouldn't be home at all that night, ordered Kung-Pao Chicken delivered from my favorite Chinese restaurant, loosened my tie, took off my shoes, and started transcribing the tape. I polished our client's words until they sparkled, took her best quotes, and used them to rewrite the piece. At 4 A.M. I faxed it to our client for approval, and went to sleep on the office couch.

The client loved the rewrite. I emailed it to the editor. It ran in the center of the book, as he had promised—under our client's byline, of course.

Was it worth it? You bet it was! The reprint of that article became our company's most important promotion piece. And it led to a nice promotion for me, too.

There are some important ethical considerations in working with a freelancer. Richard Weiner notes, "When we work with a professional freelance writer . . . being paid solely by the magazine, there is no ethical problem. Sometimes we commission a writer to do an article, and then the writer sells the article to a magazine and gets paid from both ends. If the magazine knows about it, there is no breach of ethics. But if the magazine is not aware of the double payment, then there is an ethical problem. It can be questioned whether the writer or the public relations source breached the ethics, and this is one reason it is a gray area."

The best way to avoid such problems is to have a clearly written agreement with a freelance writer. Good writers prefer that arrangement; many will not work without a written contract. Make sure your contract specifies how much the writer will be paid and whether the writer is barred from accepting payment from the magazine involved. Specify that you're buying *all* rights to the article and any other material the writer develops during the course of the assignment. Otherwise, the freelancer owns all rights to the material, and all you've bought is the right to use it once, in that particular magazine. If that's the case, he is free to resell and reuse the article anywhere and anytime—and you've lost control of the material you paid for.

A serious professional writer should be able to explain several possible angles or pegs for his story and discuss why this subject interests him. He should thoroughly understand your product, service, industry, or cause and be able to explain—in his own words—the technical material he will use when he writes that article for you.

You should also ask if the writer is a member of a professional organization, such as the International Association of Business Communicators or the American Society of Journalists and Authors. Not all professionals belong to such organizations, but membership is a sign of a serious writer.

Finally, ask a freelance writer for some clips. Read through the samples. Does he write well? Is his style alive? Will he likely be able to capture the essence of your business or organization? If you're not sure he's up to the task after reading the clips, you probably shouldn't work with him.

Sometimes a freelance writer may approach you, explain that he is interested in an aspect of your business or organization, and ask your cooperation so he can write an article which he will then sell to a magazine. Caution is in order here.

Keep in mind that many would-be writers can't produce the goods, let alone get them accepted by a magazine. Before you make a commitment in such a situation, ask whether he has a firm written assignment from a magazine. If the writer does not, he is working on speculation, and there is no guarantee the piece will ever be used. Moreover, an amateurish writer who has no working relationship with the publication can make *you* look bad—and hurt your reputation with the publication.

Seminars for Editors

In some industries, editors at the trade books are experts in their fields. In others, particularly new industries such as environmental management, many editors are good journalists, but they're not experts on the subject matter. The computer industry was like that in its early days. If you're involved in an emerging industry, or your discussions with trade editors convince you that their knowledge is limited, you could offer your company's expertise to them in a seminar.

If you run a seminar for journalists, be absolutely sure your speakers are experts in their fields and polished presenters as well. Talk with journalists and ask what topics they need to know more about—or send out a survey to find out—and use this information to determine your program. Make sure that no industry events such as trade shows conflict with the date and time of your seminar. Invite journalists six to eight weeks ahead of the seminar date, so they have plenty of time to work it into their schedules. It's also a good idea to give every participant an evaluation form, and speak with as many attendees as you can. That will help you make the next seminar even more useful.

Joel Strasser of Dorf & Stanton Technology Communications set up an annual seminar for his client Hart Environmental Management Corporation. Strasser explains why: "In an emerging business like the environmental management industry, the laws and the techniques are changing fast. A lot of editors recognize that they don't have the full background and up-to-date information on everything that is going on. We've been holding seminars for editors for the past three years. We take a look at industry events during the past year and our client's experts project what will happen during the year ahead. We hold them in November because it's a good time for publications doing year-end wrap-ups as well as projections for the upcoming year."

In an editorial seminar for Hart called "Outlook for 1990: Environmental Issues and Prospects in a More Demanding Decade," topics included what New York City's new administration faced environmentally during 1990, the 10-year timetable for upgrading millions of underground storage tanks, and the EPA's aggressive program for corrective action at active hazardous waste sites. Seminar speakers included Fred C. Hart, president of Hart Environmental Management and a former commissioner of air resources for New York City, and vice president Lawrence B. Cahill, both leading experts in their field. Hart is the author of numerous technical papers on environmental management issues, a speaker at national conferences, and a Registered Professional Engineer in New York state. Cahill, the principal author of the book *Environmental Audits* and a national lecturer on that topic, is trained as a mechanical engineer. With speakers like these, it's not hard to see why journalists are eager to attend the Hart seminars.

Checklist—Getting into Print

1. Do you understand the different editorial needs and focuses of daily, weekly, neighborhood, and ethnic newspapers?
2. Have you checked several media directories, as well as the yellow pages, to compile a press list?
3. Are you balancing your media list with neighborhood, ethnic, and suburban papers and not limiting yourself to just the big-city dailies?
4. Have you familiarized yourself with the newspapers that you'll be supplying with material by reading them for at least several weeks?
5. Have you requested a copy of the editorial policies for each newspaper?
6. Do any local papers offer tours of their plants? Have you taken one?
7. Have you made a list of the specialized reporters and editors at the larger publications?
8. Have you requested a style sheet from a large daily paper? If not, have you bought the AP or UPI stylebook?
9. Do any of the papers in your area have a handbook for community groups and small businesses that want publicity?
10. Have you asked about public service advertising at your local papers?
11. Have you decided the best way to approach reporters and editors in your situation?
12. Did you check out the on-line forums and newsgroups for journalists? Can you find a way to network in these forums without overtly pitching stories?
13. Have you thought about joining a professional communicators organization?
14. Have you checked to see if there are any local news bureaus you should be working with?
15. Have you determined which publications want you to approach their local bureaus, and which ones want you to direct publicity material to their main offices?
16. Have you asked the large newspapers to name a staff coordinator for major events?

17. Have you avoided sending duplicate releases or pitching the same story to more than one reporter at the same publication? Have you labeled duplicates where they are necessary?

18. Do you understand why you need to send separate requests for advance publicity and coverage of an event?

19. Are you delivering your releases several days before the deadline whenever possible?

20. Have you made a list of the deadlines faced by all the reporters and editors you'll be working with?

21. Have you planned events or release timing to take strategic advantage of media deadlines?

22. Have you decided whether you want to make follow-up calls about press releases? Do you know how you'll handle the calls before you make them?

23. Do you have information you can offer during your follow-up call that wasn't in the release?

24. Are you avoiding any mention of your advertising program when you talk with journalists?

25. Have you considered sending fact sheets on your special interest or cause to editorial writers and cartoonists?

26. Have you decided whether to include editorial writers on your release list?

27. Have you thought about asking for a conference with editorial writers about your cause or special interest?

28. Have you considered whether and how you want to thank journalists? Do you think this through each time?

29. Have you found out which feature editors want summaries and which ones prefer complete articles?

30. Have you written a letter that includes your feature summary? Does it cover all eight essential points?

31. Have you considered using the telephone interview method to place features in out-of-town papers?

32. Have you made a clear arrangement with the editor about exclusive rights to your feature story?

33. Have you considered approaching syndicated columnists with exclusive offers of material?

34. Have you put a time limit on the exclusive material you've sent to a columnist? Did you include a stamped, self-addressed postcard?

35. Before you send publicity material to a wire service, are you sure it involves a *national* story?

36. Do you know which wire service bureau and reporter should receive your story?

37. Do you understand the differences among general interest, special interest, business, and trade magazines?

38. Have you realistically evaluated the possibility of getting publicity in the general interest consumer magazines and the large-circulation business publications?

39. Have you read several issues of each magazine in which you're interested in placing publicity and *written down* your observations about the types of articles they print?

40. Have you thought about which publications in related areas of interest may be reaching your target audience?

41. Have you reviewed the editorial calendars of the magazines you're interested in to see where your article ideas may fit in?

42. Have you determined if the editors at your target magazines want press releases, phone pitches, or tip sheets?

43. If you're sending a press release, are you including a backgrounder and supporting material?

44. Before you offer a completed article, have you determined whether the editor uses outside writers?

45. If you'll be supplying the article, have you requested a copy of the magazine's guidelines for writers? If you made your request by mail, did you enclose a self-addressed, stamped, business-size envelope?

46. Have you reached a clear understanding with an editor before spending time writing an article?

47. Do you know how long the article should be and the editor's preferences for manuscript or electronic formats?

48. Has the editor approved a detailed outline?

49. Do you know if the editor uses an IBM-compatible or Mac-based PC?

50. Do you know what word processing software the editor uses?

51. Does the editor prefer to have your article formatted by that software?

52. Do you have access to that software?

53. If you don't have access to that software, will the editor accept the article in ASCII text file format?

54. Did you get a tentative publication date?

55. If you're working with a freelance writer, do you have a written contract?

56. Does your contract specify that you are buying all rights to the article and any other materials the writer develops while working on this assignment?

57. Have you set two deadlines, one for you and one for your writers, whether they're freelancers, clients, organizational spokespeople, executives, or staff members?

58. If a freelance writer has approached you, does he have a written assignment from the magazine? Have you looked at his clips? Is he a member of a professional organization?

59. Have you worked out any questions about double payment of freelancers? Do both the writer and the editor understand the arrangement?

60. Does the writer fully understand your product, point of view, or cause? Are the news pegs he suggests really interesting? Does his approach excite you?

61. If you're planning a seminar for editors, have you used a survey to determine what information the journalists in your field need?

62. Have you chosen expert speakers who are also good presenters?

63. Have you checked to make sure there are no industrywide events that could conflict with your seminar?

64. Have you mailed your invitations so that editors get them six to eight weeks ahead of the seminar date?

6

The Internet:
New Publicity Tools
and New Audiences

T he Internet offers a wealth of new tools publicists can use to expand their publicity efforts. You can reach more journalists, with more information, more quickly than you could just a few years ago.

On-line tools can help publicists target new audiences through specialized Web pages, E-zines, and on-line discussion groups. It's easier to reach specialized print publications and radio shows that might have gone untapped in the past with E-mail pitches and invitations to your website's pressroom. You can communicate your messages with more clarity and impact by sending digital photos as well as audio and video clips to journalists by E-mail. You can also post them on your website, where surfing journalists can find them. And instead of an expensive press conference, you can reach more journalists with Webcasting, in which you present your announcement, answer questions, and display visual material—all on the Web.

Moreover, since the Web has spawned an incredible flowering of highly specialized publications, you can reach audiences that weren't accessible in the past.

However, while some of the tools and audiences may be new, many of the old-fashioned rules still apply. You still need a solid news peg. You must still be familiar with the needs of journalists on your distribution list. As always, you have to write clearly. You need solid, verifiable facts. And you still have to meet deadlines.

"The journalistic process is the journalistic process; it doesn't change just because we're on the Net," states Wendy Sexsmith, chief Web producer for Globe Interactive, the electronic affiliate of the Toronto-based *Globe and Mail* newspaper. The site is the busiest Canadian Web destination, with more than 100 million page views as of March 2000. "We have to get information, evaluate and verify it, and then publish it. We go through the same process to determine the news value of a story as offline publications," says Sexsmith.

But unlike traditional media, when you foul up, it's not just a local affair anymore. The Web has wired journalists into a worldwide community. When you get embroiled in a controversy, you could well get calls and E-mail messages from journalists who are nine time zones away. For them, it will be the middle of their workday—even if it's the middle of the night for you. And since they're citizens of the new, wired world, they'll expect answers from you in Internet time—which means right now.

New Rules for Journalists

Not only that, but the Web has also changed how journalists work. Traditional, brick-and-mortar media are opening new, Web-based outlets, and there's a new breed of Internet-only media. Conventional broadcast and print journalists are not just turning to the Internet to get story ideas and gather information; they are also using the Web as a medium through which they communicate with their sources.

If you want to keep your competitive position as a valued news source, you will have to keep up with all the changes the Web is bringing to journalism. "Those public relations professionals who do understand and take advantage of the rapid changes taking place in media communications, without losing respect for the impact and value of journalism, are the clear winners. It is they who are shaping the future of public relations," says Don Middleberg, chairman and CEO of Middleberg + Associates, in New York.

And that future looks bright. "For the public relations practitioner, the Internet is one of the greatest innovations of all time. Its spreading popularity opens up myriad opportunities for improving our ability to practice our profession," says Robin M. Mayhall, APR, of Hieran Publishing, in Austin, Texas.

Already, more than 75 percent of journalists go on-line daily, according to the latest Middleberg/Ross PRINT Media in Cyberspace Study. More and more, journalists are using the Internet for "story ideas and pitches, article research, and gathering of reference materials." It's not just computer magazine editors who use the Internet on a daily basis. According to the study, "Journalists at non-computer publications have matched the attitudes and behaviors of their computer-focused counterparts." Reporters from "old-fashioned" beats such as gardening, lifestyles, real estate, and sports are using the Internet as an integral part of their work.

"Journalists are playing by new rules—developing story ideas from the digital world, reporting online rumors, and tapping corporate and association databases—especially when news breaks," says Middleberg. "New techniques include article research, reading online publications, use of digital images, and most interestingly, finding sources."

Content Is King

A compelling story with accurate information is even more important when you're communicating on-line. Just launching a new website or starting a new Internet venture won't get you coverage anymore. New sites and Internet ventures are a dime a dozen—so they're not news!

To make matters more complicated, the level of competition for journalists' attention has increased as distributing press releases to thousands of journalists worldwide has got less expensive and easier. Anyone can (and does) distribute publicity materials on the Web, so journalists contend with a lot of useless E-mail clutter in their in-boxes. This is one of the reasons journalists are so impatient with publicists.

At the same time, the Internet also creates opportunities for publicists who develop a reputation with editors for delivering solid story ideas with strong news pegs. By following the old-fashioned rules, along with applying the Internet's new tools, you can lift your publicity program above the competition in both traditional print and new on-line media.

Understanding the differences between on-line and off-line stories is essential if you want to be a successful on-line publicist. Stories published on-line offer more information than their print or broadcast counterparts, but at the same time, they're shorter.

While that sounds like a paradox, it's not. The basic story, which is short, gives the essential facts and includes links to in-depth information, video and audio clips, photos, interactive calculators, work sheets, and web-sites that offer readers the chance to buy your product now. Strong Web stories include multimedia.

Remember that, unlike print, the Web isn't a text-only medium. And unlike television and radio, the Web isn't limited to video and sound. On-line journalists want to provide story elements that their off-line counterparts cannot. When you're pitching Web-based journalists, offer links right in your pitch that journalists can click on to take them directly to:

- Background information.
- Anecdotes that could be used in the story or as sidebars.
- Stories about how customers use your product.
- Your organization's home page.
- Photos, charts, and other illustrations.
- Video and/or audio clips, perhaps to give the website's audience a chance to hear the full interview of someone you've quoted in your story.
- The websites for sources used in the story, such as industry analysts.
- Websites or E-mail addresses for other sources the journalist can use to develop a balanced story, such as trade associations and industry experts.

A great way to win friends in on-line journalism, and perhaps land a placement you may otherwise not get, is to offer experts willing to host a chat on the site to which you're pitching. "Last year I received a press release about a book covering bicycling in Ontario," says Mike Simpson, vice president of content and an executive producer for CANOE, one of Canada's leading news and information portals. "What helped sell the placement was that the author was willing to come in and participate in a chat."

Chats are the on-line equivalent of broadcast listener call-in shows, except your audience can participate from all over the world and never has to wait on hold. Websites like chats because they draw visitors—known as "eyeballs"—to the site. More eyeballs means higher advertising rates. In addition, "Chats are a great value to online sites because they develop content. The bicycling author's chat generated three pages worth of content," says Simpson.

Chat sessions offer your organization or client greater exposure. The website hosting your chat will take care of all the technical issues. All you need to host a chat is a computer hooked to the Internet with a high-speed connection. The website will promote your chat session and archive it after the live chat ends. All this, in addition to the story you were trying to place originally!

On-line stories and broadcasts are often archived by the media outlet that publishes or broadcasts them, so they can be found by using search engines. As a result, people can find and refer to them indefinitely. This is just one more way that the Internet helps you reach a wider audience.

Speed Is Queen

On the Internet, news deadlines are immediate and continuous. Content is king, and speed is queen. "The manner and pace of communication online is fundamentally different than offline," says Mitchell Friedman, San Francisco–based Internet public relations teacher, trainer, and consultant. "Think in terms of minutes instead of hours, and multiple editions rather than just daily updates." You need to be ready to act fast and deliver background information and executives for interviews now, not tomorrow.

Because Web culture emphasizes up-to-the-minute content, Web-based journalists are under tremendous deadline pressure. In addition, even though their deadlines are tighter, many on-line journalists have less help and heavier loads than their traditional counterparts. "If our site's not refreshed, we will lose readers to [the] competition with one mouse click," observes Wendy Sexsmith. "Online journalism doesn't have a lot of full time people working full time to create content." As a result, she says, "PR people can give a lot of help here."

At *People* magazine's on-line version, for example, on-line writers may grind out two or even three stories a day, while their traditional counterparts write just one story a week.

New Audiences

The Value of Reaching On-Line Audiences

As more and more homes and offices get wired, the Web is fast becoming a major source for news and information. According to the Pew Research Center Biennial News Consumption Survey, the percentage of Americans getting news from the Internet at least once a week has more than tripled in two years—going from 11 million to 36 million news users. The biggest draws on-line are news about science, health, finance, and technology. Moreover, those who go on-line for news are disproportionately younger, better educated, and affluent—just the type of audience that organizations usually covet.

Internet users are a news-hungry group. Fully 66 percent of those who go on-line for news say they follow national news most of the time, compared with just 47 percent of those who do not use a computer. Consequently, the Internet is emerging as a supplement to—not a substitute for—other traditional news sources, offering opportunities for delivering your message to a highly receptive audience. Significantly, 80 percent of consumers believe on-line news is just as reliable as traditional news sources, according to a Jupiter Communications Digital News Survey.

Equally important, the on-line audience segments itself according to which special interest sites users visit. No other medium offers publicists the ability to reach a mass, international audience with such highly targeted interests.

E-Zines and Websites

There are two main types of Web-based media you should target for your publicity. The first is E-zines and E-letters—electronic magazines and newsletters, such as *ClickZ* and *Slate*. They may have large circulations approaching several hundred thousand, or reach just a handful of readers, but their hallmark is that they're highly specialized. There are thousands of them; some are well established, while others appear for a few issues and then disappear forever.

Although all E-zines and E-letters are delivered by E-mail, that's often where the similarity between any two E-publications ends. Some charge a subscription fee, but most are free. Many carry advertising; some do not. Some are plain vanilla, text-based and black-and-white. Others are full-color and include graphics, photos, and even multimedia attachments. These are called HTML-based or "rich" media publications.

Put E-zines and E-letters in the same category as news and information websites for purposes of publicity, but know that they are slightly different. Often, an E-zine operates as both a website, from which content is "pulled" by visitors, and a subscription service through which content is "pushed" to subscribers by regular E-mail (usually daily or weekly). E-letters use only the "push" approach.

The editors of E-zines and E-letters, just like the journalists at conventional publications, are most concerned about running stories that will be of interest to their subscriber bases. Since so many of these publications are free, it's easy for publicists to subscribe to them, read them, and figure out how to develop news pegs and stories that will appeal to their readerships.

When you plan publicity pitches for E-zines and E-letters, you should ask yourself these questions. Some of them you can answer for yourself after you read a few issues. A short E-mail message to the editor should take care of the rest:

- Does the E-publication use outside material?
- Does it run bylines from outsiders, or are all stories staff-written?
- How long are the stories?
- Does the E-publication include links in the stories?
- Is the publication text-based, with black type and no color?
- If the publication is rich-text, or HTML-based, does it use photos, charts, illustrations, and audio and video clips? If it does, what are the technical requirements for these items?
- How much lead time does the editor need?

Several directories of E-zines are listed in Chapter 13.

The second main type of Web-based media you should target for your publicity is sites that carry news. Some, such as MSNBC, are general interest sites with broad appeal. MSNBC has more than 8.9 million viewers and a huge news staff. Others are one-man or one-woman bands, with limited but highly specialized audiences—and there's everything else in between.

Some websites that carry news exist strictly in cyberspace. But more and more brick-and-mortar newspapers, magazines, and broadcasters are also starting sites. The Middleburg/Ross study found that 83 percent of print journalists surveyed work for a publication that has a website.

Twenty-five percent of local television broadcast stations have sites, and this number is growing daily.

The top news and information sites in terms of visitor traffic are CNET.com, NYTimes.com, MSNBC.com, MarketWatch.com, and CNN .com, according to NetRatings, Inc.

Local websites, usually on-line versions of local newspapers and magazines, can also be very popular, as can audio and video feeds from local broadcast stations. SFGate.com, for example, home to both the *San Francisco Chronicle* and *San Francisco Examiner*, attracts San Francisco Bay Area residents eager for expanded content as well as tourists planning vacations and former Bay Area residents hungering for hometown news.

You'll also find a slew of special interest sites. The most popular of these include Salon.com, offering news and commentary on politics and society; TheStreet.com, providing financial information; iVillage.com, a collection of sites geared toward women; and ZDNet.com, all technology all the time. While these sites appeal to very large audiences, the smaller sites, with tighter focuses, are important as well.

Targeting Your On-Line Publicity Efforts

Knowing how to find the appropriate websites, E-publications, and Webcasters is a key to publicity success. While the equivalent is true when planning off-line publicity efforts, the on-line universe is several times larger. Because the majority of on-line media outlets are smaller and more highly specialized than their off-line counterparts, most Web-based publicity opportunities are less well known and harder to find.

Publicists can search for appropriate websites by using keywords on search engines and directories such as Yahoo!, AltaVista, and Lycos. Such searches can be time-consuming, and they yield only links to websites. That still leaves hours of research to determine if those sites' demographics match the audience you're interested in, and whether the sites' content is totally or partially original to the Web or a duplicate of the outlet's print version. Beyond that, you'll still want to know more specifics for pitching: editorial contact information; what type of content is used; use of audio, video, and images; and other details.

To meet the growing need for detailed website information, media directory publishers have added on-line media to their directories. Bacon's, MediaMap, and Press Access, among others, offer directories that profile thousands of news and information websites and E-zines. The information is organized by media type, geography, and subject matter for fast and easy research. There are also media directories on the Internet. See Chapter 13 for more information about both on-line and off-line media directories.

When you're using a media directory, keep in mind that no directory includes all placement opportunities. That simply isn't possible for a medium that's adding thousands of sites daily, and where even well-established sites can suddenly shut down because of funding problems. Thus, you have to use more than one directory, as well as your own contin-ual research, to find all the on-line media outlets that are important for you.

The process of pitching on-line sites is more complex than in the off-line world. "The Internet challenges many of the basic assumptions common to the PR process of trying to influence coverage in print and broadcast media," according to MediaMap, a service that profiles on-line and off-line media placement opportunities. MediaMap emphasizes these differences:

- Some sites do not have original content. All their information comes from feeds from other sites and sources, such as the wire services. They don't accept press releases. "Their staff may be totally pro-duction-oriented with no editorial responsibilities. Attempting to influence coverage is pointless." When you find a site that does not use original content, find out where the content originates. Then go to the originating sites, and ask if *they* will accept press releases and original content.
- For sites that *do* have original content and accept press releases, the publicist must "identify the appropriate editorial contacts, and approach them through their preferred channels, be it by fax, mail, e-mail, or telephone."
- Then there are the sites that are in-between. Some areas of the site have original content; other areas get the content from elsewhere. "You have to determine which areas are original," the service advises, since "without that information, you risk wasting resources and energy pitching your story to the wrong person."

Often, the story that is printed or broadcast off-line differs from the on-line version. Think of off-line and on-line as two partially overlapping circles: some of the content is shared, but some of the on-line content is created only for the Web version. Perhaps the on-line and off-line versions share some editorial staff, while each also has its own editorial resources. Also, the on-line version may get some of its content from third-party sources.

For example, *Architectural Record* is a leading trade publication for architects. The print version is published monthly by McGraw-Hill. The website carries content from the print version as well as original, Web-only articles such as product reviews. Some editors write for both the off-line and the on-line editions, but writers who are not on the print staff provide some of the on-line content.

AltaVista is another good example. According to MediaMap, "Alta-Vista, like most search engines, takes its editorial content from other sources. Content providers for AltaVista include the Associated Press, Reuters, the *New York Times*, ZDNet, the *Industry Standard*, the *Washington Post*, PR Newswire, and Business Wire." If you want to influence AltaVista's content, you have to work with its content providers.

Embargoes and NDAs

As more and more off-line publications start Web versions, we'll see more and more instances of publicists' entering into embargoes and nondisclosure agreements (NDAs) with print publications, only to see them broken by the Web operation. That's because the print and on-line entities may have different policies toward embargoes and NDAs. Even if the policies are the same, the left hand doesn't always know what the right hand is doing. Therefore, you should always check the policy of the on-line version before offering embargoed news to the print version. The safest practice is to get signed agreements from both sides of the house.

Ten Steps to Better Web Publicity

To get the most coverage for your publicity efforts, you have to know how to approach your target on-line outlets. Since that's more complex than approaching traditional print and broadcast outlets, MediaMap suggests you follow this 10-step process:

1. **Find the websites your target audience visits most often.** Your goal is to locate as many sites that compete for your audience as you

can. Start with the most popular off-line publications for your audience, as many of them will have on-line versions. (The URL, or website address, will often be included with the off-line masthead—the list of the publication's editorial staff.) Then do keyword searches on the major search engines, as well as any specialized search engines that serve your target audience. At each site you find, look for links to other sites. Determine each site's popularity by researching how many "unique visitors" it receives—how many different visitors came to the site during a specific period, usually monthly. The unique visitor statistics can be found through the advertising sales department, which usually has a link on the site's Web page.

2. **Use websites' visitor statistics to target on-line media outlets.** Usage statistics can differ significantly, so you have to understand what each type of statistic actually means. For example, the number of unique visitors is more relevant than the number of "hits," which tells you only how many files were accessed. One unique visitor can register several hits just by clicking on different parts of a Web page. Every story, graphic, or link is a different file, so each time you click on one, you are registering a hit. What you want to know is how many unique visitors the site gets. You'll also be interested in the number of repeat visitors. If visitors repeatedly visit the site, you can assume it is a valuable resource for your target audience. Sites that get a lot of repeat visitors are called "sticky."

3. **Understand the editorial structure of each site on your list.** Figure out what types of content each site uses and where your topic will fit in. Does it publish product reviews? Industry analysis? Company news? Headlines only? Do the stories include links, photos, and multimedia?

4. **Determine whether a site uses original content.** If it doesn't, find out where the content does originate. This requires a careful reading of the site. Look for story attributions and bylines. You can also ask the site administrator or Webmaster, whose E-mail address can usually be found under the "About Us" or "Contact Us" section.

5. **If a site has an off-line component, find out whether the two share stories and information.** You need to know if the off-line and on-line journalists have different needs and requirements, and whether their stories will differ. How do you figure this out? Again, read the site carefully and compare it with the off-line version. The site administrator or Webmaster also may be able to help you.

6. **Learn each site's deadlines and lead times.** "Some sites cover breaking news, others don't. Some have a mix of non-breaking and breaking news, with different deadlines for each," says MediaMap. How do you analyze this? Most news-oriented sites change their content at least daily. Sites covering frequently updated news areas, such as politics, business, and technology, often update their pages several times a day. Often, trade-specific sites, especially on-line versions of print publications, update the news portion of their site weekly but mirror the print version's weekly or monthly news cycle for most content. Research your target sites by checking in periodically and watching for fresh content. The site administrator and on-line editors may be willing to offer advice.

7. **Make a list of editorial contacts for each site.** Just as with off-line publications, assume that your story will be considered only if it goes directly to the journalist covering that beat. Maintain a list of journalists' names, E-mail addresses, phone numbers, and fax numbers. You'll have to compile this information from directories, the sites themselves, and questions to the site administrators or Webmasters. This information can—and will—change fast, so you'll have to update it continually.

8. **Determine how each journalist wants to be contacted.** "Your chances of influencing coverage are greatly improved when you approach the appropriate person by the means he or she prefers, whether it's electronic or otherwise. Knowing the preferences of the person you're dealing with enables you to design a press kit or release that's more likely to be noticed," says MediaMap. How do you learn these preferences? Start your dialogue through E-mail unless otherwise directed on the site, and ask each journalist how she likes to be contacted. Many sites list E-mail addresses under the "Contact Us" section. If a site doesn't list E-mail addresses, send an E-mail message to the site administrator or Webmaster.

9. **Find out if the website feeds stories to other sites.** Even if a site has a small audience, it may be worthwhile if it feeds your stories to a larger audience. The site administrator is your best source for this information.

10. **Determine if the site archives stories.** Archived stories will have a bigger impact, because search engines can find them. And since your audience can read them for a much longer period, the stories will have

more influence. How do you know whether a site archives its stories? Look for an "archive" link, or search the site using the keyword *archive*. If you find an archive, send an E-mail message to the site administrator or Webmaster asking how long archived stories are retained.

Finally, you should search the site to see if it uses chats, since these can be another source of placements for your organization's experts and spokespeople.

Internet Broadcast Outlets

The early technology for listening to audio and viewing video was not ready for prime time on the Web. Connections dropped like early cell phone calls, and the video was as herky-jerky as a dime-store flip book. But the technology has improved tremendously. Audio on the Net has advanced to the point where music artists are premiering new songs on the Web before making them available to off-line radio stations. Video still has a way to go before it transmits as smoothly as television, but it's getting there fast. Some experts predict that by the year 2003, home entertainment systems will receive television from the Web, with the computers connected to a big-screen TV.

Like other on-line outlets, Internet broadcast outlets offer several benefits to publicists. The listening audience is computer literate, a key demographic characteristic for many organizations. The reach is worldwide, 24 hours a day, seven days a week. And unlike traditional broadcast media, an interested listener or viewer can get to your organization's home page with the click of a mouse.

Internet broadcast outlets can serve as a proving ground, a place where interviewees can cut their teeth. "Clients who are having a hard time getting coverage on large, mainstream [offline] shows may get a good start on Internet radio shows," says Richard Strauss, president of Strauss Radio Strategies in Washington, D.C., and a former White House radio director. Publicists can then list archives of their spokesperson's interviews in their pitches to traditional broadcasters; talent bookers can "audition" your spokesperson by going to the archived interviews. It's a great way to prove that your spokesperson is a top-notch professional.

Because "most stations archive their shows on their Web sites," continues Strauss, "a show that aired weeks or even months ago can still get hundreds of listeners a week. And you can link your Web site to the archived show, so your prospects and customers can hear it anytime they want to."

Internet radio offers another important advantage over off-line radio: access to listeners in office buildings. "Particularly in major markets, AM radio reception in office buildings is very poor. But Internet radio can penetrate this market," says Strauss.

Pitch your guests to on-line broadcast outlets much the same way you would an off-line station:

- Listen to the station first, to hear what kinds of stories it runs.
- Find out whether the station runs original content or just replays feeds from other sources.
- Contact the producer via E-mail and let him know you have a guest of interest to his target audience. Your pitch should be similar to the pitches for off-line stations.
- Ask the producer what kind of Internet link is acceptable. Some stations won't use interviews done with modem connections because the quality is lower.
- Find out if the show will be archived and, if so, whether the archive can include links to your website and other material, as well as photos, charts, and graphics.

Where Are the Journalists?

The Internet is the new water cooler. Increasingly, people are more likely to log on to the Internet to learn what's new and discuss topics of interest than to walk down the hall and chat with a coworker. Journalists are not immune. They're changing their habits along with the rest of us.

Journalists are on-line, even if you don't know they are there, gathering information, often without identifying themselves or participating. Write this rule down on your thumb: Anytime you participate in a newsgroup or discussion group on-line, *assume* that there is a journalist in the audience. Don't say anything you wouldn't want to see on the home page of Microsoft Network or the *Los Angeles Times*.

Half of the journalists surveyed in the Middleberg/Ross survey used the Internet to develop story ideas and pitches in 1999, a significant increase over previous years. Related to that, a recent Tsantes & Associates study found that 20 percent of journalists monitor some form of Usenet newsgroup to follow industry trends, gauge the pulse of the marketplace, and search for sources.

Journalists participate in journalism-specific communities as well as communities devoted to the professions or industries that they cover.

On-Line Communities

An on-line community is simply a group of people who share a common sense of purpose. The community offers members the opportunity for social and professional networking. Just as in off-line communities, members can openly exchange information, ideas, concerns, and questions. After a while, members begin to develop bonds with other members, even though they may never have met in person. In fact, it's not uncommon for community members to form off-line meetings, either at trade shows or at local coffee shops. It's important to realize that members can exhibit intense interest in their subjects, especially when a community's topic is very specific.

Like everyone else, journalists lurk in newsgroups and read electronic newsletters, mailing lists, and other "push" information sources they have requested. That presents an opportunity. "Leading (PR) firms are also fishing where the fish are," comments Don Middleburg. "That is, they are tapping newsgroups, E-mail discussion groups, moderated forums, and message boards where journalists can be found lurking." That sounds easy enough, until you realize there are more than 40,000 newsgroups with 300,000 postings per day, 80,000 mail lists, and 90,000 chat rooms. And new ones are continually being created!

Journalists in the Middleberg/Ross study expressed "a clear willingness to use posted information, especially if it is confirmed by other sources." That's pretty startling when you consider that there is very little filtering of information on the Internet. Nobody has the job of checking the validity of sources or verifying the accuracy of posts. Even so, a "lack of credibility would not keep most journalists from using Web forums or Usenet group postings as sources for an article," according to the study. "Seventeen percent say they would consider doing so in the future, even if not confirmed by a source." Finally, 60 percent of respondents say they would consider reporting an Internet rumor if confirmed by an independent source.

If journalists are reading unfiltered information about your company and industry, don't you think you'd better know what they're reading? Here is your chance to stop inaccurate statements from gaining steam and ending up in the broader media. Likewise, if unflattering comments have merit, it's better to learn about them early and respond, rather than be on the receiving end of an investigative reporter's unexpected phone call.

Intel learned this the hard way when it ignored complaints of its flawed Pentium chips—complaints that ultimately worked their way into countless media stories, and forced the company to recall the faulty chips and write off millions of dollars.

More proactively, you can contribute information that may catch the eye of journalists. When you participate in on-line communities, you have an opportunity to prove yourself as a knowledgeable, balanced source of information to all who read your postings—including journalists.

Usenet Newsgroups

Usenet newsgroups are discussion groups focused on specific topics. Technically, newsgroups are not part of the Internet, but the point is academic, as they are widely picked up by Internet service providers. The word *Usenet* refers to the fact that the discussion groups are essentially a collection of tens of thousands of electronic bulletin boards that are connected by a network of Unix computers. These computers, in universities and organizations around the world, "serve" access to newsgroups to various clients, such as you. Since there are so many newsgroups, servers can't provide access to every one of them. Therefore, the server administrator chooses which newsgroups to connect to and offer to users.

Individuals connect to a newsgroup in much the same way as they connect to a website. Find a newsgroup of interest by connecting to a newsgroup directory such as Dejanews (www.deja.com/usenet). There you can search the universe of newsgroups by topic. Once you find one of interest, click on the link the directory provides. You'll be automatically connected to that newsgroup, which will include every message, or "posting," that has been made. You can read what other people have to say, comment on their messages, or create a new one for everyone to see. Messages that follow up on earlier postings are grouped together to make it easy to follow the conversation. That group is called a "message thread."

Along with Dejanews, other newsgroup search services include Tile.net (www.tile.net), Remarq (www.remarq.com), and AltaVista (www.altavista .com). Microsoft Internet Explorer and Netscape Communicator also include newsgroup search capabilities. Intellinews.com (www.intellinews .com) lets you filter the postings to all of the Usenet newsgroups by keywords you choose. Intellinews will scan all of the newsgroups and notify you by E-mail whenever a post is made to a newsgroup that covers a topic or issue you're interested in.

"I've bookmarked a couple of Internet discussion groups," says Jed Nitzberg, APR, vice president of interactive communications for the Arthritis Foundation. "I just pop in every month or so, read through the list of subject lines and get a sense of what is going on, what topics related to arthritis are hot, and which messages I want to respond to."

The most valuable newsgroups for public relations practitioners will likely be industry specific. That's where your marketplace is most likely meeting and therefore where journalists covering your industry are most likely to be found.

Mailing Lists

Mailing lists are similar to newsgroups in that they are on-line communities focused on specific topics. The key difference is that postings to mailing lists are automatically "pushed" to members via E-mail, as opposed to Usenet newsgroups, which are based on a "pull" paradigm. You have to choose a newsgroup, open it, and then open each message you wish to read.

Some mailing lists send each posting to every member as the posting is made. Other lists compile the postings into digests, sent at regularly scheduled intervals—daily or weekly.

Both newsgroups and mailing lists can be moderated, where someone ensures that messages are appropriate prior to posting them to the list or newsgroup. Some newsgroups are "retro-moderated," so that messages deemed to be off-topic or otherwise inappropriate can be removed after they are already posted.

Anyone with an individual E-mail address has the ability to subscribe to a newsgroup or list. Although some mailing lists are closed, most are open to any interested person. Mailing lists have a simple structure: subscribers to a list send E-mail messages to a central address, which then distributes the message to all the other subscribers.

One of the best places to find relevant mailing lists and learn more about how they operate is Liszt (www.liszt.com), a directory of 90,095 mailing lists. It can help you find mailing lists that may interest you and tells you how to get more information about the lists, including how to join. You can also search for lists at Tile.net (www.tile.net), The DartList (www.dartlist.com), Meta-List.net (www.meta-list.net), and Publicly Accessible Mailing Lists (http://paml.alastra.com).

As with newsgroups, subscribing to industry-specific mailing lists is recommended. A list of especially useful mailing lists related to public relations and journalism is provided in Chapter 13.

Participating in On-Line Forums

Just as in off-line communities, manners and etiquette are important on-line. Begin by watching, to learn the community's norms and to get a feel for the types of topics covered. Before you jump in, read two weeks' worth of the conversation to get a sense of the tone of the group and to make sure you don't repeat something another member contributed recently.

Many newsgroups post a list of frequently asked questions (called an FAQ) which explains the group's purpose and the procedures for joining in the discussion.

For people new to on-line communities, there's a complete introduction to the Usenet and newsgroups at news.announce.questions, a Usenet newsgroup whose purpose is the dissemination of questions and answers about Usenet and the Internet. You can read all about it at the group's official home page: http://www.geocities.com/nnqweb.

One way to participate in on-line communities is to start a conversation on a topic you want to explore in front of journalists. (Remember, they're lurking even if they don't post.) You can then follow the discussion and find friendly sources.

Subtlety is key here. Any overzealous commercialism will create ill will. Take a nonpromotional approach; your role is to add useful information to the discourse. The most low-key approach is to actively participate in the group, offering advice in response to other members' requests for information. Coauthor Andrew Carothers has been interviewed several times by journalists who learned of his expertise from on-line posts he made and who wanted to include his comments in stories they were writing.

A slightly more proactive approach is to ask the group for comment on your redesigned website or other item you're trying to get journalists' attention with, and include the URL in your post. You could also discuss a trend or customer success in the context of a post, hoping to pique an editor's interest. However you do it, make your subject header snappy. Most group members will decide if they want to read your post based solely on the header.

If you have a product or service that you are sure people want to know about, it may be all right to post a discreet announcement. Keep it short, though, and not too promotional.

And here's an important caveat for publicists who are newsgroup newbies: Don't post a given article to more than one newsgroup or mailing list. Doing so creates "pollution" on the Net, a close relative of spam. Pollution, like spam, makes enemies, and enemies won't be receptive to your messages.

The concept of pollution is similar to being careful to send an E-mail pitch to an editor just once, rather than annoying him with multiple E-mails about the same news peg. So, choose the most appropriate newsgroup, and post your message there. The people you want to reach will probably see it, since most people monitor more than one newsgroup on topics that interest them.

Monitoring On-Line Activities

Publicists need to know what's being said in on-line publications and communities just as much as in off-line publications. Find and subscribe to key on-line publications for your industry. Monitor relevant discussion groups weekly. To manage your time, focus on the principal groups. Watch to see if your messages are reaching the group members or if a moderator is removing them, and intervene to clear up misinformation. Track the various discussion topics and threads over time to identify industry trends and outside sources that you may be able to leverage in your publicity efforts.

New Tools for Publicists

When is E-mail better than a Webcast? How do I manage a virtual media tour? What is the most effective way to track on-line publicity efforts?

What do journalists want from my website? Even veteran publicists are asking these questions.

The Internet has brought a new set of tools that publicists can use to deliver information with greater speed and impact. In effect, your bag of tricks has expanded significantly. Of course, that means you need to know when and how to use them.

Effective Use of E-Mail

E-mail is a quick, inexpensive way to communicate with journalists. That's both good news and bad news. The potential for expanding your reach and building a network of relationships is at your fingertips. On the other hand, with one ill-timed mouse click you can make a fool of yourself and your organization, across the world.

Some editors become livid if you send them E-mail without permission. Other journalists prefer to receive story pitches and press releases via E-mail because they feel it puts them in the driver's seat. They (and you) don't have to worry about phone calls interrupting their work. If they like what you've sent, they can copy and paste it directly into their word processing programs for editing—a great time-saver.

When journalists are receptive to E-mailed pitches and releases, you benefit from what Tina Koenig of Xpress Press calls the "huge pass along factor." She explains, "If journalists don't cover an interesting story, they may forward it to a colleague, especially if they know the colleague is working on a related story." Of course, if you've already established yourself as a trusted resource, you're much more likely to have journalists forward your E-mail to their colleagues.

You must follow the same rules for electronic press releases as for traditional print pitches: They must have strong news pegs, newsworthy content, and solid facts and research. Lead with the most important news, explain the who, when, where, why, how, and what up front, and write in inverted-pyramid style, in which the most important information comes first.

Since journalists are inundated with E-mailed publicity pitches, much of which is a waste of their time, you have to follow some basic guidelines when sending editors electronic press releases and story ideas—if you want to get results. Here are the 10 Commandments for sending E-mail to journalists.

1. **Get permission first.** Call your targeted journalists and ask them if you can send them publicity materials by E-mail. It's best to do this with an actual story in mind, so you can quickly establish that you are a bona fide news source by pitching them something they can't resist. If they agree to E-mailed pitches, find out their E-mail addresses.

2. **Keep your headers short.** Take the time to write a short, compelling subject header, for two reasons. The first is that many E-mail systems can't display long headers, so they cut headers short at about 50 characters. For example, a firm in Chelm wrote this header for an E-mail press release:

   > *Acme Introduces Rapid Implementation Methodology for Building B2B E-Portals; Customers Achieve Functional Portal Implementation Within Six Weeks*

   Many E-mail systems displayed just the first few words, which didn't communicate anything at all:

   > *Acme Introduces Rapid Implementation Methodology for*

   Here's a better solution, which communicates the real news in the story:

   > *New Method Gets B2B Portals Running in 6 Weeks*

   I know, I know, the header doesn't include the company's name. But in most cases, it shouldn't! The company's name is not news. The new, time-saving portal development system is the news peg that will grab journalists' attention.

   The second reason for writing short, newsworthy headers is impact. Many journalists get hundreds of E-mailed pitches and releases every day. If it takes 15 seconds to open and scan each release, it will take an hour and 15 minutes to scan 300 releases. With today's tight deadline pressures, no journalist has that kind of time for screening. If the header doesn't sell them, your release will get zapped into cyber-oblivion.

3. **Tailor your pitch to individual reporters.** Even when sending essentially the same pitch to multiple recipients, personalize each one with the reporter's name. And make slight modifications to the content to better suit each reporter's beat and interests.

4. **Never list multiple recipients.** If you list dozens or hundreds of recipients in the "To" or "CC" fields of your E-mailed release or pitch, you've accomplished two things, neither of them good. First, you've let all these journalists know that they're just one of dozens or hundreds of reporters who were pitched that story. News doesn't seem as much like news when every Tom, Dick, and Harry with a press card in his wallet has the same lead. Reporters know that you are probably sending a press release or pitch to multiple media outlets, but you don't have to rub it in their faces. Doing so is annoying and will only prove to reporters that you are more concerned with broadcasting your message than developing relationships with them.

    Second, your message will begin with a list of recipients, instead of the news. Reporters will have to scroll through a sea of names to get to the lead paragraph. After several screens of names, they are likely to delete your pitch without even reading it.

    Send releases and pitches one at a time—or at least list multiple recipients in the blind copy (BCC) field. Sure, reporters can tell if they've gotten blind copies, but that annoying list of names isn't standing between them and the news when they open your release.

5. **Place your contact information at the bottom of the message.** Remember, you've already identified yourself through your E-mail address in the "From" field. List your name, E-mail address, and phone number, and the URL of your organization's on-line pressroom. When giving URLs, always use the "http://" beginning to ensure automatically created hyperlinks. Journalists can click directly on these hyperlinks and jump right to the Web page without having to key in the URL. Some E-mail applications don't recognize "www." as the beginning of a URL and thus don't create a hyperlink.

6. **Don't attach documents.** Unless a reporter asks you to attach a file, don't do it. Reporters travel, and they may work from home. Slow modem speeds from home or hotel rooms make downloading documents a slow process, and a costly one when the user is paying for hotel phone lines. Journalists become annoyed at having their E-mail download jammed up by an attachment that they didn't request. Also, many computer viruses spread through attachments. Many journalists will automatically delete unsolicited E-mail that contains attachments.

7. **Make your E-release just a summary.** Think of your electronic press release as a summary of the complete document. Keep it short

and to the point: no more than 500 words of tight copy. Some E-mail programs will cut off long messages, with the same effect as a long voice mail getting cut off—reduced placement opportunities. Most journalists "want to understand your story by the time they get through the first screen, and have enough information to run with it or decide to assign a writer by the time they get to the end of the release," observes G. Armour Van Horn, editor of *Digital Eyes*, an Internet publication focusing on scanners, digital cameras, and related software.

8. **Create virtual press releases.** Instead of trying to cram every bit of information into your E-mail, think of it as a teaser to get reporters interested. In the body of the text and at the bottom, provide URL links to additional information, such as a more detailed version of the press release ("the full story"), photographs, charts, supporting customer and/or analyst quotes, product demos, streaming audio or video, white papers, and your corporate website's newsroom. A virtual press release takes advantage of the user-driven nature and linking capability that sets the Web apart from other media. Reporters can quickly scan your message to determine which additional information is most relevant to them. Even if they don't respond to your pitch, they'll appreciate your approach. So, while journalists expect a very short E-mailed release with a link to an extensive website, they also insist on one-stop shopping for photos and any important content they need to write the story.

9. **Avoid fancy formats.** Remember that not everyone uses the same E-mail software. Avoid sending HTML-formatted (rich text) E-mails. It may look nice on your screen, but it can't be read by some widely used E-mail programs. Even journalists at high-tech and computer publications may end up with screen garbage instead of your carefully designed, four-color release.

    Stick to plain, unformatted text. Also, send a test version to to yourself before sending the release to journalists. Check to make sure no strange formatting errors crop up, such as unintended line breaks.

10. **Make it easy to revoke permission.** Give journalists the opportunity to be removed from your E-mail distribution list without a lot of hassle, and honor their requests. If you follow the rules for writing newsworthy press releases and pitches, you will get few, if any, requests for removal.

Exhibit 6.1 exemplifies a virtual press release that follows the 10 Commandments. Autodesk is a leading supplier of PC and Web design software and digital content creation tools, and is one of the largest software companies in the world. To reinforce its message that effective website design can be a competitive advantage, the company made liberal use of multimedia to build a website illustrating an international, high-profile boat race.

The website helped the company garner significant media coverage for its message (including stories about the site itself) in regional daily newspapers such as the *San Francisco Chronicle*, and *Computer Graphics World* ran the story on its cover.

Most of the communication with journalists was by E-mail. Each pitch was personalized with the journalist's name and included additional customized notes tying the pitch to other stories the journalist had covered. When the publicist knew of a journalist's interest in either sailing or the delivery channel (Webcasting), he included a note about that, as well. The pitch was short and concise, and it enticed editors to click on links to the boat race website, so they could learn more about the competitive advantages of strong website design.

Webcasting

Webcasting is rapidly becoming a major publicity tool, even though it's a relatively new process. Taking advantage of the Web's multimedia capabilities, publicists are combining audio, video, slides, product demos, charts, and more into virtual press tours, interactive news conferences, and trade show presentations, all broadcast over the Web.

Webcasts can be live events. Or they can be archived, available on demand anytime, from anywhere in the wired world. Webcasts are a cost-effective, instantaneous method to communicate with media all around the world, in a compelling, interactive manner that meets journalists' needs. In addition, Webcasting can ensure that an organization's message is communicated consistently across the world and all its audiences.

When the *San Antonio Express-News* wanted to take the mystery out of editorial board decisions and open up the news process to the public, it used a Webcast. The paper's website carried a live audio and video feed of

---

Exhibit 6.1

To: Jason L. Journalist

Subject: America's Cup Challenger Builds World's Fastest Sailboat with Autodesk Software

Every minute counts in the race for the America's Cup, the world's most prestigious boating event. But for many contenders, the race will be won or lost months before they reach the starting buoy. That's because the real race against time is in the planning and building of the world's fastest sailboats, when an efficient design process, not wind or waves, determines who will cross the finish line first. The stakes in this design cycle are sky high.

A leading challenger for the America's Cup, *AmericaOne*, knows it needs to out-design the competition, because on the water, even a skilled crew can't make up for a boat that is slower than the competition's.

"A good sailor in a slow boat will rarely beat a bad sailor in a fast boat," said Bob Billingham, chief operating officer of the *AmericaOne* team, from his offices in San Francisco. "There's no question that the fastest boat will win this race. And you'll be talking about time differences of seconds between teams."

For the complete story, visit

http://www.autodesk.com/pressrm/industry/quote/gdstory/aone.htm

For background information, including video, photos, fact sheets and daily journals during the America's Cup trials, visit

http://www.autodesk. com/aboutus/americaone/index.htm

For more information about design as a competitive advantage in the America's Cup races, contact: Andrew Carothers, Autodesk public relations, pr@autodesk.com or (000) 000-0000.

---

a meeting among the editorial board, representatives of the community, and city transportation officials. It was as if the public were invited to sit in on the meeting.

How Hewlett-Packard Used Webcasting to Increase Coverage

When the Aberdeen Group, a computer industry analysis firm, examined Hewlett-Packard's (HP) use of Webcasting, Aberdeen found that HP could streamline product introductions, increase the effectiveness and reach of its communications, and significantly reduce the costs of key communications, such as product launches.

Instead of having HP staff travel to dozens of cities, or set up expensive audio bridges for telephone conference calls or satellite links for video conferences, they switched to Webcasting.

HP's initial investment was for the infrastructure needed to manage Webcasting in-house, including a dedicated studio with video production cameras and lights, and all the hardware and software needed to convert audio and video into Web-ready signals.

The cost savings were impressive: approximately $1.2 million in the first year, which generated a return on investment of more than 1,800 percent, and a one-month payback.

According to the Aberdeen Group's report, HP estimates that the streaming Webcast for one major product launch reached twice as many reporters and analysts as other methods, resulting in 25 percent more press coverage. In addition, the Web events are archived and are available on demand to Web journalists—at their convenience. This approach increases press coverage and helps reporters understand the material even better, because they can pause, rewind, and review the presentation and the question-and-answer sessions.

Advantages of Webcasting

Webcasting can help public relations professionals reach more journalists than traditional methods such as press conferences and product demonstrations. How many times have you missed meeting with a journalist because he was unavailable when you were coming into town with a spokesperson? With on-demand access to information, journalists who may be unavailable for a conventional media tour can view your presentation anytime, anywhere—even if they can't attend a live event.

For product launches, trend story pitches, news announcements, and corporate positioning, Webcasting offers many benefits over traditional publicity methods. Using this tool, you can:

- **Extend the reach of your PR efforts:** You can schedule many more interviews if you don't have to travel from city to city and match your schedule to journalists' availability. So, when you use Webcasting, you can meet with a higher percentage of your A-list media and extend your efforts to B- and C-list publications you might not have had time for in the past.

- **Help ensure the success of on-site news conferences:** "We did one press conference where almost nobody showed up, but we did a live stream onto the Web and we had 240 reporters watching it," says Marc Wein, president of Murray Hill Studios in New York.

- **Reduce your budget for spokespeople:** While Webcasting can't replace all media tours, it can reduce the need for physical travel and dramatically decrease travel, lodging, and salary costs. In addition, since your spokespeople will be focusing completely on speaking, without being diverted by the demands of travel, they can do a better job.

- **Better serve journalists:** Not only can you better fit into journalists' schedules, but also you can tailor each presentation to the reporter's or publication's interests. Since a Webcast allows you to vary the contents for each media outlet, you can profile different customers, or different aspects of a product, for each publication.

- **Provide more compelling supporting elements:** A Webcast lets you combine live presentations from experts, executives, and customers around the world into one powerful presentation. Busy executives and customers who don't have time to travel to a press conference may well be willing to record a presentation right in their offices. Combine a series of first-rate presentations with video product demonstrations, and the old-fashioned slide shows that have been the mainstay of news conferences look pale by comparison.

How Webcasting Works

Until recently, it was difficult to deliver audio and other multimedia over the Web, because users had to wait while the content was downloaded to their hard disks, and that content took up a lot of disk space. The breakthrough came with the development of "streaming media," where content is fed to the Internet user as it is viewed, like television or the radio.

You don't need to know a whole lot about that technology to arrange Webcasts, but you do need to understand the six basic steps involved:

1. Content, including audio, video, text, photos, graphics, and interactive screens, is created and edited.
2. The content is "translated" for use on the Web, which involves compressing each file to make it small enough to travel across the Net quickly.
3. As part of the "translation," the files are also encoded into the formats required by the streaming media software. There are three major streaming media formats: Microsoft's Windows Media and RealNetworks' RealPlayer dominate the market, with Apple's Apple QuickTime in third place and growing. You should provide Webcasts in at least two of the formats, as journalists with a RealPlayer player won't be able to view a Webcast in Microsoft's format.
4. Files are then placed on streaming servers (high-capacity PCs designed for this purpose) at the host website. The host site may be your site or your Webcasting vendor's site. A separate streaming server is required for each format (Microsoft, RealPlayer, and Apple).
5. The encoded files are streamed out over the Web.
6. Journalists access your Webcast using their players. The players for each technology are free, and most journalists have one or more of them.

Planning Your Webcasts

The keys to a successful Webcast are fundamentally the same as for any publicity activities: planning, execution, and attracting an audience.

To begin with, you have to know your audience. Here are the questions you must ask about your audience before you invest time and money in your first Webcast:

1. Do their computers have the external speakers required to listen to the audio portion of a Webcast?

    Most newer computers do, but some journalists, particularly freelancers, as well as staffers at smaller publications and trade magazines, may have older, speakerless machines.
2. What type of Internet access do they have?

    Many freelancers connect from standard phone lines using 28.8 K or 56 K modems. Journalists from large organizations probably connect using dedicated, high-speed lines such as a T1 or DSL line at 100 K or higher—but even here, there are surprises. Thirteen percent of *on-line* journalists still use a 56 K connection, according to a Delahaye Media Link Communications survey cited in *Ragan's Interactive Public Relations*. Although better quality comes with higher speeds, if you stream at 100 K, you will exclude reporters with lower connection speeds. You may want to stream at two different speeds if your budget allows you that option. For those dialing in from home or while traveling, offer a 30 K to 35 K option. This will allow you to reach both 28 K modems and 56 K modems. Also offer a high-speed connection at 100 K for those with DSL, cable, T1, or T3 connections.

3. Do the journalists on your list prefer the Microsoft, RealPlayer, or Apple QuickTime format?

You'll probably end up with no consensus, and you may have to encode your Webcast in all three formats.

The next thing to consider is that your objective is to communicate your message, not to display the most dazzling technology. It's easy to lose sight of the fact that technology is your slave, not the other way around. Extra bells and whistles may sound appealing, but they add complexity, time, and cost to your project. And they may even make your message more difficult to understand. If you focus on technology instead of your message, don't be surprised if journalists miss your point.

> The publicist for Kebibble Technologies, in Chelm, decided to show the world all the fancy formats on the new video title-screen generator he had just bought. His Webcast included curly type, exploding type, dancing type, and even singing type that looked like his favorite pop star. Journalists were entranced with his presentation and wrote great stories about the title-screen generator. But they never mentioned Kebibble's new software release, because the fancy bells and whistles eclipsed the content of the new product announcement.

Another consideration when you're planning a Webcast is that complex messages need more than screen after screen of text to make a compelling presentation. The integration of text, sound, and visuals, when done well, will increase comprehension.

But don't think you have to shoot new videos, record new audios, and bust your budget every time you create a new Webcast. The trick is to leverage content you already have. Make use of existing audiotapes, videotapes, PowerPoint slides, logos, animations, and photos. All of this material can be digitized and encoded for streaming.

Another decision you'll have to make is whether your Webcast will be live or on-demand. Live events involve a lot more time and planning. They also cost at least twice as much to produce. Make sure you really need a live broadcast, in which everyone sees the same thing at the same time. Live broadcasts are more critical for breaking news, financial announcements that could affect your stock's price, and crisis situations. They're probably not needed for most product introductions and routine publicity situations.

On-demand events also have some significant advantages besides lower cost. Users can choose to view your Webcast when it is convenient and can *control* the experience. The ability to fast-forward, pause, rewind, and search by keyword, topic, or speaker makes your presentation much easier to use and understand.

Finally, make your Webcast interactive in every way you can. This both keeps your audience engaged and helps you learn more about them. Chat sessions work well, because you can provide editors the option to ask questions. If you're going to do this, ask yourself if the journalists you work with are highly competitive. If they are, they may not want competing journalists to see their questions. In that case, you can structure your chats so the questions—and perhaps even the answers—are not displayed publicly.

"I've asked some reporters about on-line press conferences, and a number of them have told me that they do not want to divulge their questions in front of other reporters," says Jed Nitzberg.

To get some useful information about the journalists in your audience, you can also use polling, in which you ask the audience questions, and they key in answers. If, for example, you think journalists tuning in to a Webcast have misconceptions about your product or industry, you could poll them, and then include facts and figures that will counter these erroneous beliefs right in your presentation.

You can also use interactivity to demonstrate product benefits. If you're introducing a new carburetor, for example, that increases engine efficiency in cold weather, you could include an interactive calculator that lets journalists enter data such as miles driven, outdoor temperature, truck speed, and loads carried; in an instant they could see for themselves exactly what kinds of savings fleet owners could expect under varying conditions.

The bottom line: The more situations you can set up where journalists can "see for themselves," by taking part in an interactive experience, the more effective your presentation will be.

Execution

How Much to Outsource.   Your first question, when you plan the execution of your Webcast, is how much you can handle in-house and how much you should outsource. This decision will be determined in large part by the expertise of your in-house technical support staff. If you don't have a support staff, or they don't have time to give you wholehearted assistance, you'll need to hire outside vendors to help you.

If you're new to Webcasting, outsource the project to an experienced vendor that can hold your hand. It's best to walk before you run, and a good vendor can teach you how to walk. If you plan on using Webcasting as an ongoing tool, you may want to bring capabilities in-house *after* you've cut your teeth with an outside vendor. Even then, you will probably want to consider outsourcing some elements, especially the servers for your streaming content.

"I often suggest outsourcing the streaming, because it involves specialized server hardware that needs a lot of bandwidth and attention," says Cory Smith, general manager of StarMedia Broadband, which produces streaming content for Latin American portal StarMedia. "Streaming is not a core competency for most organizations." You probably don't want to tackle hardware and software concerns, Smith advises, when it's critical to concentrate on the messages you want to communicate to the media, and on developing the content that will convey them.

Another important benefit of outsourcing the streaming servers is that you don't have to worry about keeping up with new technologies, or sinking money into outdated hardware. This can be a wise strategy when working with streaming media. The industry is relatively young, and the technology is advancing rapidly—which means that equipment and skills become obsolete faster than you can say "Jack Robinson."

If the audiovisual vendors you've built relationships with have some experience in creating output for the Web, great! Use them! But you should consider bringing some encoding expertise in-house as soon as possible to create the HTML pages you'll need for Web conferencing. When you use in-house staff for integrating the streaming media into a Web page, you can keep the look and feel consistent with the rest of your organization's website.

You need a page dedicated to your Webcast to allow you to integrate all of the elements of your presentation—text, audio, video, photos, logos—in one organized spot, so journalists can quickly get the whole picture and find the resources they need to write stories.

The page can be part of your organization's current website, or it can reside on a vendor's site. You'll need your information technology department's full support for hosting and serving the website and streams, as well as its project management skills. If your IT department can't provide that type of support and expertise, you'll have to outsource this function.

Unless you have a staff that's solely dedicated to Webcasting, you should outsource for live events. You can't make errors with a live broadcast if you want to keep your credibility with journalists. Live Webcasts are complicated, and unless your staff does them regularly, errors are likely.

When choosing a vendor, be sure to find one that understands what you are trying to accomplish and is familiar with Webcasting. Ask lots of questions about prospective vendors' track records—how many Webcasts have they done, how often do they do them, what kinds of equipment do they have, and how do they handle technical problems. Then check references. "Do not judge on price alone!" cautions Don Rhodes, owner of WBC Imaging in Oro Valley, Arizona, a company specializing in website enhancement utilizing streaming media technology. "Turnaround time, hosting capabilities, and technical knowledge have associated costs that are often overlooked," he adds. In other words, you don't get what you don't pay for.

The publicist for Kebibble Technologies, in Chelm, used the cheapest vendor to set up an international chat with the company's chief technology officer. Kebibble spent a small fortune lining up journalists for this high-profile chat. And since its chief rival, Chaim Shmendrick & Company, was about to release a highly competitive software package, a lot was riding on it. But the Web hookup for the chat crashed after just a few minutes, because the vendor decided to save money by using his laptop as a server.

Laptops are not streaming media servers, which are totally different from ordinary PCs and even Web servers. You, or your vendor, will need a streaming Web server specific to the format(s) in which you're streaming, such as RealPlayer, Microsoft, or Apple's QuickTime. These streaming servers require much more technical knowledge to operate than standard, HTML Web page servers. Be sure your in-house or vendor's staff has proper computing power and training to support your efforts—or your event may crash like Kebibble's.

Delivering your streaming content is the area of most concern to network managers. Streaming media requires significantly more of the network's bandwidth than simple HTML Web pages. If your network can't handle the load created by your audience viewing your Webcast, or if you're not sure how great that load may be, outsourcing is a better option. The load is a function of how many people will access your content at a time. Live events create peak usage all at once, so the load tends to be higher than for archived content, which people access on a random basis.

How much bandwidth you need is a function of audience size multiplied by the average connection speed for your audience. A typical modem hookup these days is 56 K, but you'll need to estimate the average, realizing that some of your audience will dial in over 28 K modems from home, and some may have 384 K DSL hookups. (This is where experienced network managers earn their pay.)

For example, if you stream the audio and video of a press conference to 100 people who all access it live, at the same time, and you estimate that the average connection will be 100 K, then you'll need 10 megabits (10,000 K) of network bandwidth. That's a lot, and it will probably require outsourcing of the streaming. Essentially, you're renting network bandwidth and server capacity on an as-you-need-it basis.

Web Conferencing: The Low-Budget Alternative to Webcasting.   If you don't need video to communicate your message, and your visuals are limited to slides, charts, graphs, and documents, Web conferencing may be a lower-cost alternative to Webcasting. You can still communicate with a worldwide audience, and you can still do it live, in real time, if you need to, but since Web conferencing doesn't include video, it's technically much less complicated and is also less expensive. Several vendors that handle Web transmission of your visual elements are listed in Chapter 13.

The audio for a Web conference can be delivered over the Web or on standard phone lines. It's basically a souped-up conference call.

Web conferencing is ideal for many press conferences and product launch meetings that rely more on PowerPoint presentations. Web conferencing vendors offer easy-to-use tools that make the technology invisible to both you and your audience. You concentrate on the words, the graphics, and the message; the vendors concentrate on putting it all together on the Web. You can have multiple presenters in multiple locations, and all they need is an Internet connection.

The downside is that the Web conferencing software may use lower bandwidths and slower connection speeds, which can result in a noticeable lag time as you shift from one slide to the next. If you know that your audience is connecting to the Internet at high speeds, make sure the Web conferencing vendor you choose offers high-speed transmissions. Since some vendors charge a per-month license fee, you'll want to clarify all costs and charges, and compare them carefully.

Production Quality.   Many of the principles of off-line audio-video production, which are discussed in Chapter 8, transfer to the on-line world. However, there are some special considerations for Web production.

One main difference is the amount of time viewers will spend watching streaming video. Watching video on your computer is not the same as watching TV. The screen is much smaller, the image is not as crisp, and people will watch long items only if there is a particularly compelling reason to do so. Keep your clips short, or you'll end up losing your audience. Two minutes is a good ceiling to go by. You also run the risk of losing the audio-video synchronization with longer clips.

Since the compression required to stream videos lowers their quality, try to capture content at the highest-quality level and work from there. This means you must use broadcast-quality equipment.

Avoid moving the camera from side to side; zooming out is better than panning. The technology can't support fast-paced action at this point, so spokespeople have to be trained to avoid rapid movements. Capturing clean audio is also important, so minimize outside noise and the rustling of papers. Invest in a high-quality microphone.

Ray Harris, president of PRWebcast.com, a Webcasting services firm in Cleveland, offers the following tips to get the best-quality video:

- ■ **Focus:** Have your subject in focus and the background slightly out of focus. This is accomplished by filming your subject with the background 15 to 20 feet in the distance. The background should be either a solid color or a soft, diffused mix of colors. The soft background compresses more easily and leaves more room in the video file to make your subject crisper.

- **Clothes:** Avoid high-contrast fabrics, such as plaids, checks, and red-blue mixtures. A light blue shirt is better than a white shirt. Since the compression process removes a lot of the contrast, blacks and whites end up more like gray.
- **Lighting:** Avoid harsh lights. Place a light in front of the subject and on both sides. Fluorescent lights give off a hum that may be picked up by the audio capture.

Provide Context. Whether you're launching a product or discussing a trend, streaming live or on demand, using Web conferencing or Webcasting, place the presentation in context. Create a Web page specific to the Webcast that includes other pieces of the puzzle that journalists may need for writing a story. Include bios and photos of speakers and how to contact them for interviews. Add market research data, white papers, product images, and demonstrations as additional resources. Include quotes, in text format or as audio or video clips, from customers and industry analysts, with contact information so journalists can do in-depth interviews as they develop their stories. Add links to any players—Microsoft, RealPlayer, Apple—that journalists may need to view the Webcast. The developers of all three major players encourage this.

If you're offering a live event, make it the centerpiece of the site, and provide clear instructions for accessing it. In essence, create a one-stop-shopping environment where journalists can get everything they need to write their stories.

Attracting an Audience

It's easy to concentrate on developing the message and the Webcasting vehicle, but the fact that you build it doesn't mean they will come. Spend sufficient time informing the media, just as you would with a traditional media event. Notify them of all the resources you've provided to help them prepare stories, and encourage them to visit the site's URL in advance of the live event.

When contacting the media, alert them using the channel each journalist prefers. If your event is for journalists and analysts only, make sure any alert or press release you send over the wires goes only to newsrooms and is not made available to the general public. You'll have to request this special distribution from your wire service, as the standard distribution includes databases and other outlets available to the general public over the Internet.

Tell the journalists you've invited what players they can use to access the audio-video, and provide a link for downloading these players in advance. If you are password-protecting the Webcast, be sure to issue passwords confidentially.

When the event is over, follow up with journalists who attended to get feedback on the event, answer any last-minute questions, and perhaps offer a brief update. But don't ignore the reporters who didn't attend. Contact them, recap the Webcast in 15 seconds or less, and let them know how to find the archive. You can archive the full event, or just post the highlights. You may want to offer a transcript, any PowerPoint presentations, a storyboard summary, and/or sound bites from the event, as well as links to other resources and information.

Multiple Spokespeople, One Message

Webcasting also provides an effective means of disseminating information to an organization's spokespeople. Too many times a publicist toils to create compelling messages, only to see them get blurred when multiple spokespeople speak with the media. Organizations with lots of local offices, each of which use a different local PR agency, risk facing this problem, especially when dealing internationally across different time zones and languages.

Simply distributing a printout of the slides used in a media presentation may explain what is to be communicated, but it doesn't teach local spokespeople how to communicate the message effectively. With a streaming interview training session, all remote publicity staff, and their agencies and spokespeople, can watch to see how the information is presented, including subtle nuances and inflections. Even better, the trainees can ask questions—and see as well as hear the answers.

Archiving the training session allows communicators to review it again before conducting media interviews, even from a hotel room during a media tour. It also allows for all spokespeople to view the training at their own pace.

Autodesk Case Study

Autodesk, cited earlier in the chapter, began Webcasting in 1998 as part of a major launch of its next generation of software. Since then, the company has incorporated Webcasting as a way to gain credibility with journalists in new market sectors and to position itself as the thought leader in its key markets.

One of the company's more innovative Internet-based publicity applications has been its Executive Roundtables. These live panel discussions bring together senior executives from leading companies to discuss trends shaping their industries. The Roundtables are conducted solely on the Web, for an exclusive audience of journalists and industry analysts using Web conferencing. The one-hour events are streamed live, with the audience receiving the visuals on the Web and the audio over the phone. Each live event is built into a larger website that provides background information on the trend and the panelists, along with contact information for arranging interviews.

Coauthor Andrew Carothers and his team developed the Executive Roundtables as a way to attract the interest of the business, Internet, and IT press. When Autodesk began communicating its Internet strategy, it had little credibility as an Internet-savvy company. It was viewed as a computer-aided design (CAD) company, not as a source of information that IT, Internet, and business press readers considered relevant. In a nutshell, the company had limited success getting the attention of these journalists who were critical to its strategy.

The Autodesk publicity team made a strategic decision to reposition the company in the minds of those journalists by developing trend stories their readers really care about. The Autodesk strategy linked the company with the major business, Internet, and IT trends, as well as with other companies their target journalists typically covered.

To attract media interest, Autodesk produced an Executive Roundtable discussing how manufacturers are taking advantage of new Internet technologies to change their business models and thrive in the new economy. The Internet technology was an integral feature of one of Autodesk's products, but a straight product pitch wouldn't have garnered much ink with these journalists, because the company didn't yet have much credibility as an Internet player.

Instead of having company representatives alone talking about the trend, Autodesk added credibility and interest by involving leading companies the media often cover. By using the Web, instead of physical travel, the team was able to bring together high-ranking executives from across the world who wouldn't have been able to coordinate their schedules for a traditional media tour. Their commitment was limited to preparing their presentations, dialing in a few minutes early, and making themselves available for follow-up interviews. The speakers at this virtual Roundtable were located in Los Angeles, San Francisco, Ohio, Michigan, and Germany.

The panelists' presentations consisted mostly of PowerPoint slides. Autodesk also gave a three-minute demonstration of the Internet technology in action, so that reporters unfamiliar with it could easily understand it. It was pretty dramatic stuff: Trendsetting manufacturers are using new Autodesk software to enable the designers and architects who specify their products to drag and drop smart-content libraries from the manufacturers' websites directly into building designs on their desktop. That saves designers and architects a lot of time, because they don't have to draw the items on their blueprints. They just go to the manufacturers' websites, click on the machinery, furniture, building materials, or fixtures they want, and drag them into the blueprints or plans—that's it. The result: more accurate renderings, hours of time saved, and drastically reduced drafting costs.

The panel presentations were followed by a question-and-answer session.

The event attracted journalists from the business, Internet, and IT press, as well as Autodesk's usual journalists from the architecture and CAD trade press. They came because the company had a good story to tell, and because they wouldn't usually have the opportunity to speak with such a high-powered group of executives in a small, controlled environment. They usually get to talk with a group of executives from different companies only at trade shows, where they're competing with hundreds of non-journalists in the audience to get questions answered.

Many journalists viewed the archived event as well as the live Webcast. The archive included a searchable replay of the event, scrolling text, and the complete transcript in a downloadable Word document. Autodesk staff monitoring attendance after the event found that some journalists returned two weeks later.

The Roundtable's website includes background facts and figures on the E-business marketplace; panelist photos, bios, and contact information;

an audiovisual demonstration of the technology under discussion; a backgrounder on Autodesk's product and the technology behind it; and a customer case study.

Autodesk decided not to password-protect the site, so as not to erect any obstacles for journalists. But the publicity team did want to know who attended: for the live event, attendees had to provide their names to the phone conference operator. Visitors to the archived event have to complete a short registration page. The publicity staff is automatically E-mailed when a journalist registers.

Autodesk built the website internally, with its creative services team developing the graphics and its Web team handling the coding. A producer from the Web team acted as project manager. For the live event, the PR team used PlaceWare's Web conferencing technology. The audio portion was a simple telephone conference call handled through MCI.

Exhibit 6.2 shows the media alert that Autodesk used for its E-business Executive Roundtable. It was sent both electronically and on paper.

Exhibit 6.2

MEDIA ALERT

Trends in E-Commerce Executive Roundtable
Changing Business Models with New Internet Technologies

Manufacturers are taking advantage of new Internet technologies to fundamentally change their business models. In the $672 billion architecture, engineering and construction (AEC) industry alone, E-commerce is expected to grow to $28.6 billion in the next three years. Trend-setting manufacturers are using new software to enable the designers and architects who specify their products to drag and drop smart content libraries from the manufacturers' Web sites directly into building designs on their desktop.

MORE   MORE   MORE

Exclusively for media and industry analysts, leading AEC executives will discuss how their segment of the industry will address the new e-commerce market and leverage the new technology.

WHAT: Journalist/analyst only online Executive Roundtable with industry leaders discussing how their business will be affected by the new economy and the key Web technology enabling the AEC industry to develop a true business to business environment.

WHEN: Tuesday, February 15, 9:00–10:00 A.M. (PST).

WHERE: The Roundtable will be conducted live over the Internet from www.autodesk.com/ebusinessroundtable.

WHO: The panel will include leading industry executives from:

- Autodesk (Carol Bartz, CEO), the leader in PC- and Web-based design solutions
- Gensler (Ed Friedrichs, President), one of the world's largest architecture firms
- Herman-Miller (David Mitchell, Director), the world's leading designer and manufacturer of office furniture
- ERCO Lighting (Klaus Maack, CEO), the leading provider of architectural lighting in Europe
- Owens Corning (Chuck Stein, Vice President), the global leader in building materials systems
- Deloitte & Touche (Steve Riordan, head of e-Business Practice), will serve as moderator and provide insight into global trends

In addition to the live event, we will offer interviews with the panelists and provide other information.

CONTACT: For more information, contact Andrew Carothers, Autodesk Public Relations, at (000) 000-0000 or pr@autodesk.com.

On-Line Clippings

You've launched your on-line publicity effort, and so far you have several press releases, a handful of pitches, and even a Web conference out there in cyberspace. You know you've had a few stories on-line, but your boss is asking you questions: "What are we actually getting for our money? How do you measure the return on those on-line PR dollars?" Those are good questions, and your boss is right on target. If he hasn't asked them, you should anticipate that he will.

One way to demonstrate the value of on-line publicity programs is to collect "clippings" of the electronic stories your publicity generates. On-line clipping, or "cyberclipping," can be a labor-intensive effort, because tracking placements on-line is even harder than off-line. Some websites update their news daily, others hourly. Some get their content from other websites. You could spend your whole day just tracking clips.

PR veteran Howard Schulman, writing in the Xpress Press newsletter, *i-PR*, points out, "The web is sectioned. Searching in one area will not always yield complete results." In addition, "Not all web-clipping services search Usenet newsgroups, often the site of early news before more traditional media publish a story."

Also, according to Schulman, "Some areas that need to be searched have restricted access through paid subscriptions or special arrangements. In these cases it helps to understand if a clipping service is able to provide full text and graphics, or merely a reference listing."

Finally, the article you see on your Web browser's screen is not always the same as the one in the publication's print edition. "Sometimes print is expanded or carries more graphics, while at other times the opposite situation occurs." To complicate matters even more, Schulman says, "Several editions of a story may appear on the web. As new information becomes available some web publishers will update their copy, while others will post one version and then not make a revision until the next day. It is important to know if your clipping service will continually search for updates. And, details of the story [supplied by your service] should tell you if it is an original or an updated article."

You can choose from a variety of methods to track electronic placements. To know where to begin, you must decide what you need. Here are some questions to ask as you work toward clarifying your cyberclipping needs:

- Do you want to know which sites and E-zines ran your press release?
- Do you want to know about placements that result from an on-line publication's reuse at its off-line sister publications, and vice versa?

- Do you need to see all variants of your stories, or will just one version suffice?
- Do you want to track usage on all websites, or just those sites that are on your A-list?
- Are you interested in international stories or just placements and mentions on sites based in your country?
- Do you need to track mentions in newsgroups?

Once you know what you're looking for, you're in a better position to decide if you want to try to manage cyberclipping internally or hire a service. Of course, it costs less to handle the function internally, but you may spend too much time doing it.

If you decide to do it on your own, you can search by keyword on the directories and search engines. Most newspapers also allow you to search their websites for the previous one to five days for free, but after that you often have to pay to view the archives. This approach is manageable if you're interested only in a few key sites.

You'll probably get more comprehensive coverage on a regular basis by using one of the cyberclipping services listed in Chapter 13. The cost depends on what level of service you choose. You can pay a few hundred dollars per month for basic services that track the top 100 news sites, or several thousand dollars per month for services that search thousands of on-line publications, news sites, discussion groups, and listservs, which automatically forward E-mails from members to everyone on the list.

"It usually requires a combination of two or more approaches to create a truly effective monitoring program," advises Ellen Sharon, president and founder of CompetitivEdge Electronic Clipping in Bloomfield, Connecticut. "Don't be shy about asking questions or requesting samples, trial periods, references, or discounts."

On-Line Publicity at Trade Shows

Trade show participation, that most brick-and-mortar activity, requires a lot of effort from an organization's marketing and public relations teams. For publicists, the trick is to arrange interviews and background meetings with as many journalists as possible. The problem is that every attending organization is attempting the same feat, leaving journalists with jammed schedules.

Also, there are the journalists you want to reach with announcements you make at the show but who don't attend. Organizations often prefer to announce news of acquisitions and other important developments at industry-specific trade shows, but hometown papers and the business press usually don't go to trade shows. The Internet offers a couple of cost-effective ways to generate interest among the reporters attending, while also reaching many journalists who don't make the trip.

Press conferences are staples of publicity programs at trade shows. You can broadcast your press conference over the Internet using either Webcasting or Web conferencing. This same approach can be used for broadcasting special company and customer presentations at your booth. In both cases, media attending in person and virtual attendees who couldn't come to the show watch the same presentations in real time. On-line attendees can participate in the questions and answers in a chat format or through a phone hookup to the booth's sound system, so that other on-line participants and the on-site journalists can hear the questions and comments.

The combined on-line/off-line interaction can be attractive to journalists. Of course, the entire event can be archived, with a transcript posted for future reference, so even journalists who can't attend and can't log on during the show can access the press conference later, at their convenience.

Another option for integrating the Web into trade show publicity efforts is to create a virtual trade show in your on-line pressroom. The goal is to give journalists a peek into the show and the excitement your organization creates there. Much of the content can be created in advance and supplemented with "from-the-show" updates and other collateral, such as:

- Interviews with key executives, industry analysts, and customers. The easiest way to handle interviews is to audiotape them and post them to your website's newsroom, accompanied by digital photos of the subjects. You can send the audio and photo files to an in-house Web manager by E-mail, or a vendor can handle quick turnaround for posting sound bites that the media can use. You can even edit the files on your PC first, using tools that come with Microsoft and Apple operating systems, or pay a professional to do the work.

- Digital photos of the show and your booth filled with interested visitors.
- Daily text updates reporting on the major news of the conference, panelist presentations, and keynote speeches. Include news that isn't "yours" to add credibility to your site and attract visitors who want more than a vendor-only commercial.
- News releases.
- Links to background information on your website.
- The show's schedule of keynote addresses, your organization's booth presentations, and media activities.
- Videos of product demonstrations.
- A list of partner organizations with exhibits at the show, and a map of the exhibit hall showing their booth locations and yours.
- An easy way for journalists to request interviews during the show via E-mail.
- An E-mail feedback mechanism, so journalists can let you know what's on their minds.

To get the most mileage from your website's coverage of the show, you have to promote the coverage ahead of time. Your promotion efforts to journalists should be conducted both on-line and off-line, and you should position your site as a media resource. Let the media know that they can check the site daily for news highlights, third-party quotes, show news, and other content that make their hectic job of covering the conference a bit easier.

After the show, check your log files to see who attended the virtual show, to help you target your publicity efforts for the next big event.

On-Line Pressrooms

How would you like to have a staff of assistants answering media requests 24 hours a day? Too expensive? Not if your "staff" is an on-line pressroom. On-line pressrooms—or newsrooms—have moved beyond the experimental to an expected practice. If you don't have one, you're operating at a disadvantage when it comes to meeting journalists' needs.

Many journalists these days will search for an organization's website first when they want information. According to a survey by Ameritech cited in *Ragan's Interactive Public Relations,* "Reporters tap the Web frequently—more than a dozen times a week on average—to look for information on various corporate sites. [Those] who have access from their primary work desk also have access at multiple locations: 93 percent at work, 48 percent at home, and 18 percent while traveling. These reporters access the Web 50 times a month."

The benefits to the working press are numerous. A well-designed pressroom offers an easy-to-use, "always-on" news and information tool that journalists can reach no matter when they're working on a deadline story—even if they're 12 time zones away. Reporters can work more efficiently, by cutting and pasting text and graphics directly into their stories for editing. They never have to rummage through old files for information; if your site is searchable by keyword, the information is always at their fingertips.

Publicity professionals can benefit because they will spend less time fulfilling routine information requests and will save money in postage and other administrative costs. At the same time, organizations can reach a larger number of publications and serve publications they normally wouldn't have time to work with.

In addition, your tech staff or your Web hosting service can collect site statistics that help you continually analyze and refine your site to better meet journalists' needs. You can see which areas and information types are frequently or rarely accessed.

What to Include

The vastness of the Web allows you to put everything a journalist could possibly want in your site's pressroom. If you're including only press releases, or (worse) linking to an external site that lists your press releases, you're not giving journalists what they need and ask for. Why should they come to your site if Yahoo! has the same list of press releases in its archives? The fact is that many reporters pay scant attention to press releases, says Jed Nitzberg. "They just want facts and figures they can use immediately, and contacts who can answer questions now."

"A website designed for journalists has to be super content rich. There is nothing worse then going to a site and finding it is really just promotional, with no information of real value. That's a waste of my time," says Kimberly McCall, columnist for *Entrepreneur's Business Start-Ups.*

To get started, first think of the types of information you already have in your organization, both inside the public relations department and outside. Then look at the types of information your organization creates on a daily basis. Use this as your base. Here are some of the types of information you should consider adding to your website's pressroom:

- **Breaking news:** According to an Ameritech survey cited in *Ragan's Interactive Public Relations,* "Breaking news is overwhelmingly the most important content for journalists," with 75 percent of the journalists surveyed ranking it as a critical website newsroom feature. "Financial, regulatory and background information, executives, and industry news also ranked highly."

- **Publicity contact information:** Phone, fax, E-mail, and pager numbers, as well as areas of responsibility. Staff photos are a nice touch.

- **Press releases:** List the most recent headlines in one place, for quick access to your latest announcements. Archive old ones by date, and build in the ability to search them by keywords. Be sure to post press releases on-line at the same time they're distributed to news wires, and include publicity contact information with hyperlinks for sending E-mail to the publicity staff.

- **Corporate/organizational information:** Executive bios, frequently asked questions, fact sheets, links to coverage in the major media, annual reports and other financial information, acquisitions and strategic partnerships, community involvement, awards, company structure, major milestones.

- **Executive speeches.**

- **Product information:** Spec sheets, brochures, on-line demonstrations, pricing and availability, product photos, short customer case studies and customer testimonials.

- **Industry information:** Market research; white papers; industry glossary, history, and background; relevant newsgroups; industry and financial analysts' reports.

- **Images:** Eighty-four percent of the journalists Ameritech surveyed, according to *Ragan's Interactive Public Relations,* said they are able to download photos and graphics. *Ragan's* concluded: "So, your newsroom should include product photographs, executive photos, logos, and corporate culture shots. Show thumbnails that can be expanded for easier viewing, and provide a mechanism for downloading or requesting hard copies of high-resolution versions." Photos must be a minimum of 300 dots per inch (DPI), according to Tina Koenig of Xpress Press. Have photos in different sizes and formats, including the two most common file formats for photos, .gif and JPEG, as well as compressed files. Include optimized versions of photos, in which you have simplified the file to make it smaller, using software such as Photoshop to reduce the number of colors, so journalists can download them quickly. And keep photos smaller than three by five inches to cut download times. But let journalists know you can customize the specs on any photo to meet their needs, and that you can overnight hard copies to them.

- **Events:** Create ad hoc press kits for announcements, trade shows, press conferences, or other events by compiling links to information from across your site, such as photos, press releases, backgrounders, marketing collateral, and contact information for appropriate PR staff and organizational spokespeople. Once the information is posted on your site, you can easily add a button that displays a well-organized press kit with all the information journalists need to cover the event.

- **E-mail queries:** Give journalists the chance to ask questions of the publicity staff, and even your executive team. But be absolutely sure that incoming E-mail is monitored continually and answered immediately.

- **Feedback:** Give journalists an E-mail mechanism to easily provide feedback on the pressroom or on your organization and its publicity efforts in general.

- **Customized opt-in E-mail:** If you have the resources to manage a mailing list, offer journalists the opportunity to register to receive information based on their areas of interest. You can automatically send E-mail to journalists with relevant news and information as it's posted to your site, based on a profile they fill out. Journalists can know that they will receive relevant information in a timely manner without having to make needless trips to your site to search for new material. This also automates your news distribution activities. Just be certain to ask journalists for permission to add them to this list!

Keep your newsroom simple; journalists aren't looking for bells and whistles for their own sake. For example, after Ameritech "flattened" its website newsroom, "to tailor to the immediacy journalists require," it got twice as much traffic from journalists. While other design improvements also helped improve traffic, "flat" Web newsrooms, where it takes just a click or two to get to information, make it easier for journalists to find facts fast. "Previously, it took up to six clicks to access some content, including downloadable graphics. The redesign allows users to get to most of the information in three clicks or less," according to *Ragan's Interactive Public Relations.*

However, if audio and video will help you communicate your message, use them. Traditional and on-line radio reporters can use audio and scripts. Television producers can view video news releases (VNRs) on your site and decide if they want to request broadcast-quality versions that meet the higher standards required for TV.

Determine what you have the time and expertise to manage internally, and outsource the rest. You can outsource all the development and maintenance of your site, or just certain aspects. Outside photo database services can manage digital images, and others can manage any streaming media. Still other vendors can manage your E-mail databases and services. And while you're considering which functions to bring in-house, ask your IT staff about adding software that will let nontechnical publicity staff "paste" new content into the site, so you can update your content in a hurry.

Ease of Access

Just making the information available isn't enough. Your press room has to be easy to find and easy to use. Remember, journalists require fast and easy access to your newsroom's material. In the Ameritech survey, cited by *Ragan's Interactive Public Relations,* journalists made it clear that "the most important reason for using . . . a site [regularly] was the short time frame required to receive information. Efficient use of resources and increased competitiveness were also rated as important reasons."

Have a direct link to your pressroom on your home page, as this is where most journalists will come to begin their research. You have to organize your pressroom well, with quick and easy navigation features, including a search capability for the content. Make it easy to find names and phone numbers for publicity contacts, the company's full name and address, and basic product or service information.

Ask yourself, and journalists, "How would you like information organized." You may choose to organize information by industry if your company serves multiple markets, by product line, or by format, or all of the above. The beauty of the Internet is that you can easily organize information in multiple ways once it's on your site. Do not include promotional gimmicks such as gifts or contests. They may be appropriate for other marketing purposes but are not for working with the media.

Password Protection

Some organizations password-protect their sites, believing that journalists want information not readily available to the public. Others shun passwords, arguing that keeping the site easily accessible to the media is more important.

"I think it should be password-protected just so that journalists have the assurance that they're getting real news," says Kimberly McCall. "If a journalist is not getting the news [first], why would it be a story? Why would I want to write something that everybody in the world may have seen already?"

Other journalists disagree. "I'm not a fan of passwords. I want the easiest way to get a lot of information quickly," says Dan Fost, technology writer for the *San Francisco Chronicle*.

"If reporters have to take extra time to register for a Web site press room, and they have to remember another password, that's going to turn them off," says Dennis Bowman at the Arthritis Foundation. "Reporters ask me to make it quick and easy for them to get in, get what they want, and get out. We have no problem with the public's seeing our press releases at the same time as the press. Reporters put the press releases into a larger context, flesh them out with interviews, or use the information in a story with a different angle."

Some companies, such as Autodesk and Bell Atlantic, have chosen middle ground. They don't password-protect most of their pressroom, but they keep some information exclusive to journalists. Embargoed news or exclusive content can be password-protected or posted on a nonpublic, or "blind," URL that is distributed only to journalists.

Clearly, the trend at many large corporate websites is to drop password protection altogether. Ameritech, for example, found that 44 percent of the journalists surveyed did not find password-protected areas usable. Reporters didn't even know about the existence of downloadable graphics in a password-protected area of Ameritech's pressroom. So, staffers at Ameritech "compared their site to other top telecom Web sites to see how they stacked up. The research revealed a common trend: Web sites are doing away with password-protected areas," according to *Ragan's Interactive Public Relations.*

Finally, be sure to publicize your site to the media. Notify everyone on your media list when the site's ready. Provide the specific pressroom URL on all your press releases, and consider putting it on your business cards. Guide journalists to the site when responding to inquiries, and demonstrate it at press events.

How do well-designed website newsrooms help publicists get their jobs done? "Often, reporters have already gone through the basics of an issue on our Web site before they contact us. So they already have some general basic knowledge before contacting us. What they need from us is answers to their questions. This is very beneficial for us because we don't have to spend time on the basics," says Dennis Bowman. "During a telephone interview," Bowman continues, "I can refer reporters to documents on our Web site that have the information they need." In a nutshell, a first-rate newsroom can make it easier for both journalists and publicists to do their jobs, and free everyone up to think about the content of the story, instead of the mechanics of getting the material.

The Direct Publicity Trend

According to *Ragan's Interactive Public Relations,* "Direct PR—bypassing the media to reach consumers—is a key emerging online trend." As more of the general public go on-line and receive immediate access to press releases and other information, what will be the impact on journalists and journalism? Understanding the effect of direct publicity on the press is important for publicity professionals trying to build stronger relationships with journalists by understanding how they work.

The phenomenon of communicating directly with consumers started in the mid-1990s, with national political candidates frustrated by what they believed was too much filtering and distortion of their messages by the print and broadcast news media. Candidates responded by reserving important announcements for television talk shows, such as "Larry King Live," and public town hall meetings, which they used as an unfiltered platform.

Pharmaceutical companies picked up the idea at the end of the decade by advertising prescription medications to the general public, rather than to physicians, and encouraging people to contact their doctors to learn more. The companies were attempting to create demand for their products among end users, who might then pressure their doctors—the traditional filter for such information—to prescribe them.

Now publicists are flooding the publicity news wires with press releases, knowing that consumers, employees, and potential investors will see them via news tracking systems, on AOL, Yahoo!, and other leading portals, and on news and information websites.

Why Direct Publicity?

With the use of direct publicity increasing, many companies, particularly high-tech and Internet-based ventures, think they have to pump out a steady stream of press releases, even if they don't have anything newsworthy to say. They're concerned that if they don't flood the world with press releases, and their competitors do, customers, prospective employees, and venture capitalists will think they have disappeared. Many small companies use direct PR to gain exposure they wouldn't otherwise receive.

Press releases are the most prevalent example of direct publicity, but Internet radio and video broadcasts are also being used. Large brokerage companies such as Merrill Lynch are Webcasting what amount to self-produced financial information shows featuring their analysts discussing the economy and stock recommendations.

Impact on Journalists

With the news-consuming public getting immediate access to company and organization announcements, journalists have to change the way they report the news. More than ever before, journalists have to synthesize information from multiple sources into interpretive and analytical reporting that helps readers understand the big picture.

"Publications must do more analysis to add value. Journalists need to flesh out a story with reactions from competitors, analysts, and customers," notes Bob Henkel, who covers the semiconductor and electronics industry for several CMP Media Inc. publications. That's why journalists increasingly need to write stories based on information from multiple sources, not just your press releases.

If you include other sources in your pitches, sources that help reporters write about the big picture beyond your own organization, you will help journalists do an important part of their jobs in an increasingly difficult news environment. The new economy has created many more companies to cover, new legions of publicists are phoning, faxing, and E-mailing information, and intense competition between on-line and off-line publications steps up the pressure even more. All of this has squeezed many journalists, who don't have the time to do as much fact checking as they once did.

Looking at it from another perspective, a lot of the information found on the Internet is raw material. Some of it is accurate—and some is not. "With so much raw information on the Internet, adding context and filtering is growing in importance," says Associated Press workplace writer Maggie Jackson. "The public needs journalists to interpret the news, explain why something happened and what might happen next. People will increasingly depend on sources with a track record. It's another reason why newspapers aren't folding in the face of the Internet."

"News organizations must build their brand as a trusted source," agrees technology reporter Dan Fost, who has reported for the *San Francisco Chronicle* on what he calls "press releases masquerading as news." Trusted news organizations, with name recognition and a track record, help guide people through the explosion of information. If you, as a publicist, build a reputation for providing accurate, verifiable information, journalists will come to count on you, just as their readers count on them.

Checklist—the Internet: New Publicity Tools and New Audiences

1. Do your E-mail pitches include links to additional information and your organization's home page?
2. Are you or your spokespeople willing to host chats?

3. Have you volunteered to do chats in conjunction with the publicity you target to websites?

4. Have you checked with the chat's producer to see if your on-line access is fast enough?

5. Will the chat session be archived? Can you link your site to the archive?

6. Are you set up to respond immediately to the pressing deadline needs of on-line journalists?

7. Have you added E-zines and E-letters to your publicity distribution list?

8. Have you invited E-zine and E-letter editors to your website's newsroom?

9. Do you know which E-publications use outside material?

10. Do you know the format and length requirements for all of the E-publications you're pitching to?

11. If the E-publication is rich-text, or HTML-based, does it use photos, charts, illustrations, and audio and video clips? If it does, do you know the technical requirements for these items?

12. Do you know how much lead time E-publication editors need?

13. Have you determined which Web-based news media and radio broadcasters have original content?

14. Do you know the contact preferences for journalists at Web-based news media that carry original content?

15. Have you arranged for any news embargoes or nondisclosure agreements with *both* the on-line and off-line versions of the publications you're working with?

16. Have you made a list of the websites your target audiences visit most often?

17. Are you taking advantage of usage statistics to help you find key websites for your publicity program?

18. Do you know which websites feed stories to other sites?

19. Have you reviewed the key websites on your list, so you understand their editorial structures?

20. Do you know each site's deadline and lead times?

21. Have you identified media websites that have archived stories or broadcasts about your organization?

22. Did you set up links from your website to archived media stories or broadcasts about your organization?

23. Are you checking these links regularly to make sure they're still working?

24. Do you include a brief list of links to archived talk show appearances when you're pitching to talent bookers from radio and TV talk shows?

25. Did you ask what kind of Internet link is acceptable for your on-line radio talk show appearance?

26. Have you checked the on-line directories of newsgroups, discussion groups, and mailing lists to build your list of key on-line communities?

27. Are you monitoring mentions of your organization in newsgroups, discussion groups, and mailing lists?

28. Have you spent a week or two studying the postings to a newsgroup or mailing list before you jump in and start posting?

29. Did you read the frequently asked questions for each new newsgroup or mailing list?

30. Have you made sure that your newsgroup or mailing list posts are made to only *one* group?

31. Do you always make the assumption that journalists are lurking when you participate in newsgroups or discussion groups?

32. Have you been extra careful to avoid shameless self-promotion in your newsgroup and mailing list posts, and to provide genuinely useful information?

33. Do your electronic press releases have strong news pegs, newsworthy content, and solid facts and research?

34. Do they lead with the most important news and explain the who, when, where, why, how, and what up front?

35. Are they written in inverted-pyramid style, with the most important information first?

36. Have you got permission from each journalist to send them publicity materials by E-mail?

37. Do your E-mail headers include the news peg? Are they no longer than 50 characters?

38. Are you tailoring your E-mail pitches to individual reporters?

39. Are you using the "BCC" field on your E-mail software to avoid lists of multiple recipients on your publicity materials?

40. Is your contact information at the *bottom* of your E-mail releases?

41. Have you gotten permission to E-mail attached documents to a journalist before doing so?

42. Is your E-release a short summary? Does it include links to additional material, your organization's home page, and your website's newsroom?

43. Have you avoided fancy, formatted E-mail which some journalists can't read on their software?

44. Do you have an easy way for journalists to revoke permission to receive publicity materials?

45. Have you evaluated whether Webcasts or Web conferencing are better alternatives than on-site news conferences?

46. Are you making this evaluation on a case-by-case basis?

47. Have you considered extending the reach of your on-site news conferences with the addition of a Webcast?

48. Have you considered extending the reach of your on-site news conferences by archiving them at your website's newsroom?

49. Do the journalists on your press list have the external PC speakers needed to receive a Webcast or Web conference?

50. What type of Internet access do they have?

51. Will you need to stream your Webcast content at two different speeds?

52. Do the journalists on your list prefer the Microsoft, RealPlayer, or Apple QuickTime format?

53. How are you going to use sound and visuals to support your text?

54. What content do you already have that you can use for this support?

55. Will your Webcast be live or on demand?

56. How will you make your Webcast interactive?

57. Do you need to structure your question-and-answer or chat sessions so that journalists' questions are kept private?

58. How much of the Webcasting workload can be handled by your in-house IT staff?

59. Do you have staff people who really understand the technology behind streaming media?

60. Is it worthwhile for your organization to invest in streaming media servers?

61. Can you bring some encoding capability in-house, so you can keep the look and feel of your Webcast consistent with your organization's Web page?

62. Will your Webcast's Web page be hosted as part of your existing website, as a separate website on your current Web server, or by a vendor?

63. Have you asked prospective Webcast vendors how many Webcasts they have done and how often they do them?

64. Do you know what kinds of equipment each vendor on your short list has and how each handles technical problems?

65. Did you check each vendor's references?

66. Has your IT staff calculated the projected bandwidth load for your Webcast and figured out if your organization's network can handle it?

67. Do you really need a Webcast with video to communicate your message, or will a less expensive Web conference that can include slides, charts, graphs, and documents do the job just as well?

68. Have you checked whether your Web conference vendor's connection speeds are fast enough for your audience's connections?

69. Did you get a written statement of all costs and charges from each Webcasting or Web conference vendor you're considering?

70. Have you limited video segments of your Webcast to two minutes or less each?

71. Have you made sure that your Webcast video will be filmed using broadcast-quality equipment?

72. Have you instructed your camera operators to avoid panned shots, where the camera moves from side to side?

73. Has your video crew arranged for a background that's a solid color and slightly out of focus?

74. Will your lighting be soft and even, with no harsh shadows?

75. Did you train your spokespeople to avoid rapid movements?

76. Do your spokespeople know which clothes will look best on compressed videos?

77. Does your Webcast's Web page help journalists find all the information and content they need to do strong stories?

78. Does it include links to all the streaming players that can be used to view your Webcast?

79. Have you included step-by-step instructions for accessing your live event, as well as the archived version of it?

80. Have you sent the media an alert for your Webcast or Web conference?

81. If your event is for journalists and analysts only, have you told your wire service that this transmission goes only into newsrooms and is not made available to the general public?

82. Have you told the journalists you've invited what players they can use to access the audio-video and provided a link for downloading them in advance?

83. If you are password-protecting the Webcast, have you issued passwords confidentially?

84. Have you repitched the Webcast to journalists who couldn't attend the live session?

85. Are you using internal-training Webcasts to make sure all of your organization's spokespeople know how to communicate your publicity messages?

86. Will you get clippings yourself for stories you place on websites and in E-zines and E-letters, or will you hire a vendor?

87. Do you want your Web clipping service to include Usenet newsgroup mentions?

88. Will your Web clipping service search the paid-subscription areas of Web-based news media?

89. Will clips from paid areas include full text and graphics, or just a citation?

90. Will you get clips of all versions of your story?

91. Do you want to know about placements that result from an on-line publication's reuse at its off-line sister publications, and vice versa?

92. Do you want to track usage on all websites or just sites that are on your A-list?

93. Does the Web clipping service you're considering search for stories in E-zines and E-letters?

94. Can you try out the prospective Web clipping service on a trial basis?

95. Have you asked prospective vendors for references?

96. Did you get a statement of all the charges and fees from the service you're considering?

97. Have you considered a simultaneous Webcast of your trade show press conference and booth activities?

98. Will you offer a separate newsroom on your corporate website?

99. Do you have an easy-to-find link to your newsroom on your organization's home page?

100. Will your newsroom be keyword searchable?

101. Have you considered using site statistics from your newsroom to better understand journalists' needs?

102. Will your newsroom include breaking news?

103. Is the publicity contact information easy to find in your newsroom?
104. Will your old press releases be archived and searchable by keyword?
105. Do you plan to include organizational information, executive speeches, product data, industry facts, and financial information at your newsroom?
106. Can journalists download photos and images from your newsroom?
107. Will your photos be in a variety of file formats and optimized versions?
108. Will you use your newsroom to create ad hoc press kits for each new publicity event?
109. Do you have a procedure that lets you answer journalists' E-mail queries immediately?
110. Have you considered offering opt-in E-mail news bulletins based on journalists' areas of interest?
111. Is your newsroom design "flat," so it takes just two or three clicks to get to all the information you have there?
112. If your newsroom is password-protected, have you reexamined this policy, given that most journalists don't like passwords?
113. Have you promoted your on-line newsroom to the journalism community?
114. Can journalists still call you to clarify information about stories they're working on and to request hard copies of photos in the formats they need?

7

The Art of the
Publicity Photograph

Maybe your bakery has just put the last touch of frosting on the world's largest cookie, or your company is celebrating the 50th anniversary of your founder's invention of the widget. Perhaps your Elks Club chapter is presenting a Citizen of the Year Award, or your E-business has an exclusive new line of grunge clothing. You know that when a newspaper, magazine, or website story has pictures along with it, there's a better chance people will read it—so you'd like to snap a few shots and send them along with your press release, query, or feature article. Not so fast: before you load that film cartridge in your handy-dandy instant camera, there are more than a few things you need to know.

Some publications use publicity photos more often than others. Large dailies, general interest magazines, and business and trade publications that can afford their own photography staffs generally prefer to cover an event themselves, but many smaller publications and websites do accept publicity photos. You have to find out the policies of the publications you'll be working with.

PC Magazine, for example, "almost invariably takes its own photographs, with the exception of three of our 200 editorial pages each issue. We want to have a consistent look," explains editor Bill Howard, "especially since we primarily do comparative reviews. It would be almost impossible to get 12 publicity photos that would look the same."

There are two ways to get that prospective photo published. For magazines, you would work directly with the editor who covers your type of story, letting him know in your first or second contact exactly what the photo possibilities are. At the larger newspapers, you can try to interest either the photo editor or a reporter in your story. How do you know which to approach? Standard practice is to call the reporter who covers that beat if the photo is for a specialized story; if it's really a photo essay—more visual than verbal—pitch it to the photo editor.

You can also submit really first-class photos directly to news wires such as the Associated Press, United Press International, or Reuters. "At the wire services," advises Bob Seltzer of Porter Novelli, "you absolutely have to go through the photo editors" with a photo story.

Once you've decided whom you are going to approach, call him and make a brief pitch on the phone, with a description of the photographic possibilities of your event. Even better, send him a photo tip sheet, including the good old who, when, where, why, and how, along with a description of the visual possibilities. Then, after you're sure the journalist has had a chance to read your tip sheet, you can make a follow-up call. Your goal is to find out two things: if the publication is interested and, if so, do they prefer to shoot their own photos.

The second way to get that photo published is to shoot it yourself. Smaller publications frequently depend on outside sources for photographs, but there also may be occasions when even a sophisticated large daily with a big staff will use your publicity shot. "In some cases publicity photos are useful because there's no way we can get a picture quickly ourselves," says one newspaper's photo editor. But, he goes on to say, "I think the rules for pictures we accept from publicists should be the same as the rules we impose on our own staff photographers." In other words, your publicity picture has to be as good as the shots taken by the publication's regular photographers.

There is a third way to get pictures published that will work if you have a very expensive—and photogenic—product. "We offered to loan Audi cars to photo editors," says Bob Seltzer. "Some of the travel magazines which do a lot of outdoor shots accepted our offer, so an Audi is shown at sightseeing attractions in *Alaskan Highways,* for example."

You may also be able to use this technique with houses, home furnishings, jewelry, boats, and other high-ticket or luxury items.

Here is an example of good visual planning for an event that press photographers and television cameramen were invited to cover:

> *The popular director of a neighborhood recreation center in Plains City was leaving after five years on the job. The children were having a hard time accepting his coming departure. He felt that a ceremony would help the kids cope with their feelings and understand what was happening. So he developed a plan that would let the children see him becoming a "new man."*
>
> *On his last evening at the center, the staff hung a large sheet of paper on the wall and asked the children to help make him a giant good-bye card. With the card in the background, the director sat in a chair while two staff members shaved off his long, curly beard. As the children watched, a new man emerged from beneath the beard, and while a band played farewell songs, he walked slowly to his car. The children held a purple ribbon across the hood. The ribbon was cut, the drummer rolled the drums, and the director drove off into the sunset.*
>
> *Because it was so photogenic, the ceremony was covered by almost every newspaper and TV station in town.*

Here are some tips that can be drawn from the example. If you invite the press, plan your ceremony so that it will be visually stimulating. Spend time talking with photographers to explain what is going on, and let them know of any unusual visual angles. Tell them what to expect and at what points in the ceremony you think the best photo possibilities will occur. Sometimes a photographer will ask you to rearrange your program so that he can get the best shots at the outset. If that's possible, do it, because he may be on a tight schedule. If you can bend to meet his needs, you have a better chance of getting optimal photo coverage.

Photos of Events

Journalists call news pictures *art*—not art in the sense of museum pieces, but communication art. Good news photographers think through their pictures before they shoot, and they take their work seriously. Publicists, unfortunately, usually give pictures short shrift.

As Larry Kramer of the *Trenton Times* points out, "Art from businesses is notoriously bad. So a good business item with an interesting handout picture stands a better chance of making it. And there are stories that make page one because there was art with them."

The same is true for art from nonprofit organizations, trade associations, and government agencies. The newspaper photo editor quoted at the beginning of the chapter amplifies on this: "Publicity photos we get are staid and unimaginative. That's why they seldom get in the paper. Ninety-nine percent of the photographers who take publicity photos have not had newspaper experience and don't know what we want. We want good action photos. Since publicity photos are often advance shots of things happening in the future, there's nothing going on in them. They're posed pictures of people doing nothing."

There are five standard pictures that most publications won't touch because they have become clichés:

- The check pass.
- The shovel dig.
- The handshake.
- The ribbon cutting.
- The plaque pass.

All of the listed shots usually share the same problem: lack of context. You can't tell what the ceremony is about. If you don't know the people, it could be any ceremony, anywhere, anytime.

"Instead of shooting an award ceremony," suggests Phil Douglis, director of the Douglis Visual Workshops, publicists should ask themselves, "Who will benefit from the award or check or medal?" Once this is determined, "Then go shoot the benefits. Instead of taking a picture of a man who set up a therapy center for mentally ill people getting a medal for his efforts, good public relations people will go to the therapy center, shoot real people involved in real benefits, and sell the idea to the press. This is the ultimate value of publicity pictures—to sell news, features, benefits—instead of superficial awards and ceremonies."

If you must take pictures of a ceremony, try to have your photos capture the feelings of the people taking part. Aim to show why the ceremony is important: what it *means*. Ask yourself why this ceremony is different from every other ceremony and how you can show that difference on film. Another question to ask yourself is why you want these pictures. What message are you trying to convey to your audience? How will these pictures carry that message?

A good technique for ensuring that your photos get your message across is called *photo illustration*. "You go out and construct a picture to illustrate a concept or situation," explains Andrew Yale, a freelance editorial photographer based in New Hampshire. "Although most publicists don't use this technique, it's a good bet because it's dramatic and unusual. And since it's a recognizable, familiar style, most editors will use it."

Here are several examples of powerful photos created with the technique of photo illustration:

- In the middle of a long corridor, the publicist for a hospital lined up all the paperwork required to admit one patient. Along both sides were all the people who had a part in doing that paperwork. The lens used gave the maximum depth to the picture, so the lineup looked longer than life.
- A piece of art for an organization concerned with overpopulation showed a standard highway sign that read "Los Angeles City Limits." Hanging from that was a hand-lettered cardboard sign reading "No Vacancy."
- A photo by James Visser, photojournalist for Six Flags over Mid-America, showed a woman touching a static-electric generator. Her hair, standing straight up and lighted by an electronic flash, looked like a giant dandelion gone to seed. It's an unusual image, and it rivets the reader's attention.
- Daniel E. Dahlberg, editor of the house publication for Allstate Insurance Company's agents, wanted to remind agents forcefully that their customers might need million-dollar liability insurance, even if they don't sit on the board of directors of a large corporation. Dahlberg stacked a million bucks in bundled bills on the front of a boardroom table and had photographer Chris Kattson shoot a photo

with the loot looming large in the foreground. In the far background, slightly out of focus, two executives confer. The almost empty boardroom with the two men strongly suggests a crisis or unusual situation. Combine that with more money staring the reader in the face than he's likely to make in a lifetime, and his curiosity is piqued.

For the best effect, the pros advise that you weigh and balance several important elements when you compose photos of events and people. Most important is to make your photos exciting and interesting.

Include action in your photos of people and events whenever possible. Good stop-action shots can be dramatic if they are done well. (They are almost never used by publicists.) Capture the spirit of the occasion. What is most important in an ideal publicity photo, according to George Waldman, assistant graphics director for the *Detroit News*, is "a unique viewpoint." Waldman means more than choosing a unique camera angle or special lens. What he's looking for are photos that tell you something interesting about the people involved.

Natural poses make the best photos. As you arrange the people in the photograph, talk with them. Laugh, joke, frown, stamp your foot, and do whatever you must to get them relaxed and looking natural. If they're too aware of the camera, try telling a story, and as soon as they've forgotten about the camera, snap a shot without breaking your narrative. This technique works with all but the most self-conscious people. If, however, you're not a ham, or if you're photographing an activity in which your song and dance would distract people from their tasks, an alternative is to be as quiet and unobtrusive as possible. You hope that people are so involved in what they're doing that they'll forget about you.

As you shoot, ask yourself what the focal point of the photo will be. Every publicity photo should have one, and only one, point of interest. That's the spot in the photo that draws your eye first. From there your attention travels to the less dominant parts of the picture. If you have two, three, or more competing points of interest, the shot will seem confusing because people won't know where to look first.

The way you arrange the people in your art will have an effect on the point of interest, so position people carefully. "If you've got a line of people, that detracts from having a strong point of interest," says Robert Asbille of the *Des Moines Register and Tribune*. That lineup of people can look like a picket fence.

Phil Douglis attests: "Boring picket-fence pictures . . . do nothing for anybody—the subjects are wooden, ritualized objects lined up in rigid horizontal rows. It is relatively easy to improve on this kind of cliché. The easiest way to do it is to simply relax the subjects, group them informally and in depth, vary body size via vantage point, and get much, much closer to the subject."

Douglis, writing in *IABC News*, published by the International Association of Business Communicators, advocates that you arrange the people in your photos so some are in the foreground and some farther back in the picture. A person in the foreground appears larger and gives the picture a focal point. The eye moves back from that image into the picture.

Many publications have rules of thumb that encourage pictures with fewer than five people in them. "The more people there are in a shot, the more difficult it is to compose a good photo," says photographer Andrew Yale. So, unless you or your photographer understand how to photograph large groups, avoid them in your publicity shots.

In general, the people in your art must not have their backs to the camera, and they must be identifiable. But if you're taking pictures of people in a confidential situation, such as a clinic or a hospital, it is OK if you can't see their faces.

Choosing an interesting angle can help make your art more compelling. "To the beginning photographer . . . all 'news' takes place at a distance of six to ten feet from the camera and is always viewed from shoulder height. Because such photographers always assume the same position in relationship to their subject matter, all their pictures look the same," Phil Douglis says. To fight such redundancy," he advises, "photographers must seek variety in vantage points." His solution: "The key to winning the battle against visual redundancy is to forcefully and emphatically shift camera position."

Shoot from a balcony or stand on a ladder. Group your subjects on a stairway and shoot from below or above. Take a shot from the side, crouch down, or even lie on the floor. If you're working with a hired photographer, suggest these viewpoints to him.

If you can't change your vantage point, change your lens. For example, you or your photographer should know the difference in effect between a 28 mm lens and a 135 mm lens. The resulting photos can be stunningly different. "Take many shots; film is cheap. Try different cameras, lenses, f-stops, depth of field, lighting, poses," advises Donald M. Levin in an article in *pr reporter*.

Consider the background. If your pictures must be shot against a busy background, use the depth-of-field adjustment to blur that backdrop to make it less distracting. "The background should not distract from the main action in the picture," says Andrew Yale. "You should especially avoid a strongly patterned background or repetitive architectural elements which can pull the eye away from the people and the action. Don't shoot in front of a window. If you really can't move, then draw the drapes or the blinds."

Whenever possible, include a banner, a poster, or some other item that identifies your firm or organization in the shot. But don't let it compete with your main action.

People in publicity photos must be presentable. Make sure everyone looks his or her best.

Ensuring that subjects look picture perfect may sound obvious, but to one publicist in Chelm it wasn't. The Chelm publicist sent out 8-by-10 glossies of the president of the Circular Club making an important announcement. There was a large, clearly visible stain on the prexy's shirt, and the pictures weren't used. The publicist still hasn't figured out why.

If you're not sure about the quality of your publicity photo, show it to someone who is unfamiliar with your organization or business and knows nothing regarding the event. Ask the person to tell you what the photo is about. The more the viewer can tell you, the better the photo.

Don't forget that photos need editing, too! Sometimes, by cropping, you can save a piece of art. Although you can edit photos on your PC screen, try this old-fashioned manual process first so you get more involved with the photos. Ask your camera shop to print four-by-five proofs for you. Then use pieces of plain white paper to blank out parts of the photo that are dull or not relevant or that compete with the focal point. As you move these "cropping sheets" around, you may suddenly see an ordinary shot take on impact. Once you've decided which parts of the photo you want to crop out, you can use a waterproof marker or a grease pencil to make marks right on the proofs so the film laboratory knows exactly how to print the enlargements. If you're not familiar with the process, ask your camera store for advice.

What Makes a Good Product Shot

While the technical requirements for product shots are similar to those for photos of events and people, the visual approach is quite different.

Freelance photographer Jerry Pozniak explains, "It's important to hire the right photographer for product shots. A newspaper or publicity photographer will probably not have the right skills or equipment. A photographer who specializes in product shots, on the other hand, will know how to make your product look its best."

The quality of your product shots is less important in newspapers, more important in magazines, and most important when the photograph will be enlarged. Especially if you send the same shot to many publications, you should shoot in both color and black-and-white. Some publications want product shots with people in them; others do not. So, shoot your product art both ways, and either find out the editorial preferences or send both types of shots.

A camera that uses large sheets of film, called a view camera, is essential for product shots, advises Pozniak. "You need large format (4-by-5 or 8-by-10) transparencies to hold more detail and give better reproduction. A view camera also allows you to correct for distortions, which won't be apparent in photos of people but will be magnified in product shots."

Even if you're working with a top-notch pro, you'll have to be involved in the shoot. The photographer will need to ask you about lighting, positioning, angles, and all the other considerations that go into creating the photograph you want. Some photographers will shoot test photos with a Polaroid camera after each shot is set up and ready to go. That gives you a chance to see what the finished art will look like and do last-minute fine tuning.

Product photos should have simple, plain backgrounds in neutral colors. Seamless photographer's paper gives you a continuous background that doesn't distract from the product. The background should contrast sharply with your product, so the item seems to pop right off the page. "Grays, off-whites, and pastels work better than bright colors. You can't go wrong with a gray. Black, on the other hand, does not work as well. And a very bright background may overwhelm your product. If you use an off-white background, you can make the product seem to float in space. Off-white also minimizes shadows, makes the shot easier for an editor to crop, and lets her run type across it," says Pozniak.

Good lighting is also critical for product shots, since deep shadows will distract from your product. "Make sure the lighting is even and diffused so there's no glare. And keep lighting simple," cautions Pozniak. "Use a single main light source and perhaps a background light to keep the background from fading into darkness."

It's sometimes difficult to judge the size of products shot against a plain background, since there's no reference. If it's important for readers to know the size of your product, you may have to include a recognizable item in the shot, such as a coin.

Photographers use special techniques to make products look their best in photos. For instance, sometimes it's to your advantage to have a model made of your product, rather than shooting the actual item. "Mass produced merchandise often has small flaws that you don't want reproduced and magnified," explains Pozniak. "For example, many items are not quite square, especially cardboard product containers. It's often cheaper to make a model than to retouch the photo."

If you have a shiny product, such as a cardboard box printed on glossy stock, be especially careful about glare. You may want to make a nonshiny model or spray your product with a matte lacquer spray to cut the glare. In such cases, your product photographer must be an expert.

When you photograph food, use a food stylist who knows how to prepare and arrange each dish so it looks appealing on camera. Since the photographer's lights generate heat, the stylist will have to continually replace food as it wilts or dries out. Good food photography is expensive, but the results are worth it.

Technical Requirements for Photos

You may have the publicity shot of the century, with great content, a strong point of interest, and an arresting image, but if it's not well done technically, it will find a home in the wastebasket instead of on page one. Your publicity photographs should be shot with a professional camera. Instant cameras often have plastic lenses, and the images are not crisp enough to reproduce well on newsprint. Polaroid shots likewise are generally frowned on by photo editors. "Most of the time we don't like to handle them because they don't reproduce well," says Robert Asbille of the *Register and Tribune*. "They're always a hair out of focus. We have used them now and then for somebody who has been killed, when that's the only picture available."

The standard for newspaper publicity is the 8-by-10 black-and-white glossy. Don't send out color pictures to newspapers unless you check with your contact there first. If you have a color transparency, such as a 35 mm slide, include a brief note with your black-and-white shot, letting the editor know that a color transparency is available.

"If you're speaking generally about magazines, I would say that it never hurts to include two or three black and whites and maybe even one color transparency, with an offer of more photos by overnight courier," says Bill Howard.

At most newspapers that use color photos, the photos can be run only on selected pages. The editor may have a news hole on a black-and-white page, which he'd love to fill with your story. If you've sent only a color shot, he can't.

Your publicity art for newspapers should have strong contrast, since a lot of its sharpness will be lost when it is transferred to newsprint. And since newspaper columns are narrow, your pictures should be shot in a vertical format so they can be reduced to fit one column, if necessary. You can include some horizontal shots as well, in case the editor really likes your art and decides to run a shot across several columns, but the vertical shot is the basic one.

If you're submitting photos to magazines, ask the editors you work with whether they prefer vertical or horizontal shots.

Your photos must have a white margin. This is the space where the photo editor at the newspaper puts crop marks to let the printers know exactly which part of the photo to use.

Don't write on the back of a photo. The pressure of your pencil or pen can cause indentations in the surface of the shot that will show up in reproduction. Write or type any necessary information on a label, and attach it to the back of the art. Never use paper clips on photos because they, too, can cause indentations. And always handle photos by the edges. That fingerprint you can hardly see, right across the president's face, may show up vividly when the picture is reproduced in the newspaper.

If you're going to submit the same shot to a number of newspapers, use machine-made "copy prints" instead of individually made enlargements, since they are less expensive in large lots. A few phone calls to photo laboratories will get you exact prices, so you can make your own comparison.

The requirements for magazine photos are more exacting, particularly if they are printed on slick paper. Because this paper has a special coating, photos reproduce better than on newsprint, and they show more detail.

This means that the photos you submit have to be larger and even clearer than photos for newspapers. For slick magazines, handmade enlargements are necessary because too much detail is lost when copy prints are made by machine.

Since the quality of pictures for most shots reproduced in major, mass circulation magazines is very high, these publications must have an 8-by-10 photo to work with; a smaller photo will not reproduce well enough to meet their standards. Besides, groups of people as well as scenery and location shots look their best in an 8-by-10 format. If your photo includes only one or two people, or a simple object, you can submit a 5-by-7. And you can drop the size of the photo down to 4-by-5 for head shots.

Some publications will accept publicity art in electronic form, but you must make sure your photos are in a format they can use by asking these questions:

- What format do you need: JPEG, TIF, or something else? Most publications can't use .gif images because the resolution isn't good enough.
- Do you need color or black-and-white?
- What density, in dots per inch, do you need?
- What size do you need, in inches?
- Do you have any other format requirements?
- Is it OK to send the photo to you by E-mail in a compressed file? Files containing digital photos are large. Don't send them to journalists by E-mail unless you have their permission. Large files can jam E-mail systems, and some media outlets automatically refuse to accept them. Let the journalist know how large the file is when you're asking permission.

Although many publications will accept photos in electronic format, even in this electronic era, you can't rely completely on electronic photos, for two reasons.

"Posting an image to the Web does not mean that you never have to produce a print again," says C. J. Martin, Aerospace Communications director at NASA. "What looks good on your desktop monitor may not have enough resolution for a publication to use. Really high quality images mean really huge digital image files. Be prepared to offer a transparency or 8 x 10 glossy." That way, the publication can get the quality it needs. Otherwise, the outlet may not be willing to use your photo, even if it's great art.

Martin also explains the second reason why you'll still need old-fashioned, printed photos. "Many editors still use hard copy prints to screen for what they want to use, and then go to a digital product afterwards," he says. If you don't include photos with your pitch, some editors won't be interested—even if your publicity material lists links to photos on your website. They're used to looking at something they can hold in their hands, and they're not comfortable with viewing art on a screen.

Photos are cheap. Publicity is valuable. Send the photos!

Posting Photos on Your Website

Many journalists surf through websites, looking for story ideas—and good art, as well. You can help them find your best publicity photos by grouping them together in your pressroom. Make it easy to find them, by having them searchable by subject matter. And make it easy to sort through large numbers of photos quickly. C. J. Martin suggests, "A 'contact sheet' of small thumbnail images that load quickly can help journalists screen photos quickly." Each thumbnail should be clickable to produce a full-size photo.

Include different file formats, densities, and sizes for each photo in your website's pressroom so journalists can find exactly what they need. Let them know that you are willing to send them original photos or transparencies by overnight courier, if that's what they need. And be sure to include complete captions for each photo you post.

Hiring Your Own Photographer

If you don't want to take on the job of photographer, and no one else in your organization is qualified, consider hiring a moonlighting press photographer. This is a good way to get publicity shots of events and people that will interest the press.

Call a newspaper, ask for the darkroom, and briefly tell the person who answers what you want. Even if he says he's not interested or he doesn't know anybody who can help you, ask him to take your name and number just in case he hears of somebody. He may call you back after he's finished work. Bear in mind that if the darkroom is dark at the moment, he won't be able to write down your number. Ask if he's developing, and find out when you should call back.

If your photographer does not have press experience, be sure that he can work fast enough to meet newspaper deadlines. It is good policy to specify in writing that the photographer is an independent contractor. In that case you probably won't be liable for social security, unemployment, and workers' compensation taxes.

Unless you specify otherwise, in writing, the photographer owns the negatives. You buy only the actual physical photographs he provides you, and even those can be used only for limited purposes. You cannot, for example, use a publicity shot in advertising without the photographer's permission. And if you plan to post your photos on your website, be sure your contract with your photographer permits you to do this. "Posting a high resolution digital version of copyrighted material may interfere with a photographer's or illustrator's sale of 'residuals.' Make sure that your use of an image is consistent with the terms of sale. No one likes surprises," says C. J. Martin.

If your photographer is any sort of businessperson, he will charge you an additional fee for advertising, website, and other specialized uses. If you want to buy all rights and the negatives, be sure you have a specific written agreement.

Tell your photographer when you hire him that he will not be able to have credit lines with his work. "Most publications don't like to give credit lines to outside photographers," says the American Red Cross's Harry Cohn. "Usually the only credit lines they give are to their own staff photographers. Why even imply you want a credit line when you know the policy of the paper is against it anyhow?"

Photo Captions

When you send out those publicity pictures, be certain to include captions. Otherwise, how will the photo editor know who is in the photo, what's taking place, or what the story behind the product is? Assume that your press release will not be used at all—that only the picture and the caption will be run. That's why it's a good idea to make your caption a summary of your story, with all the important information included. Repeat the obvious, rather than leaving potential questions unanswered. Identify everyone from left to right, with first and last names, or at least first initials and last names.

Include the name, address, contact person, phone number, and release date on your caption. You can type your captions when you view the proofs, send them to the lab when you order your full-size shots, and have the lab shoot them so they actually become part of the photograph. If you handle your captions this way, they won't get lost, and the editor can see both the picture and the caption at the same time. Or, you can tape typed captions to the back of the photo.

Exhibit 7.1 and Exhibit 7.2 on page 250 are examples of good picture captions.

Model Releases

You should have a signed model release from everyone in each of your publicity photos. This standard form, available at most camera stores, says that the person in the picture gives you permission to use that shot for any and all purposes.

Exhibit 7.1

2,000 Heads Are Better than One. XYZ Food-O-Rama manager Dale Johnson (left) presents a week's supply of lettuce to Red Cross Disaster Relief coordinator Kcaj Nodrog. The 2,000 heads of lettuce will help make a mountain of sandwiches for people left homeless by the recent tornado in West Plains.

XYZ Food-O-Rama
385 Rock Street East
Plains City 00001
Contact: Marie Tinaka, (123) 456-7890
June 26, 2001

Exhibit 7.2

Contact:

Diana Tedesco

Suzanne Jones

Porter/Novelli

(212) 315-8000

OR

Bruce Cleverly

Gillette North Atlantic Shaving Group

(617) 421-8492

A patented, easy-loading system makes blade changing with the new Gillette Sensor shaving system virtually foolproof, and its convenient organizer fits comfortably in the hand. The cartridges feature ultra-narrow chromium platinum-hardened blades, individually mounted on highly responsive springs, and an open-backed, flow-through design which allows for easy rinsing and cleaning.

Why do you need written permission? Someone in a shot may decide the photo is unflattering or may change his mind about appearing on page one. It's not possible to have people sign all their rights away, but chances are if they have signed a model release, you won't have any problem. This is especially important if you are involved in a controversy, but in any case, you and your lawyer should discuss model releases for your publicity photos. Although model releases still don't make you 100 percent legally secure, they will help if somebody in one of your pictures tries to sue you.

"If you're doing publicity on a Hadassah dinner, for example, and you get a shot of the chairman and the woman who is doing the cooking," says Robert Asbille of the *Des Moines Register and Tribune,* it's clear that "they've agreed to the picture." However, he notes, "If it gets into a controversial area, or if somebody is being photographed in an institution, then we do want a model release. There have been lawsuits on invasion of privacy, and these are real tricky areas now." Also, if there's a child in the picture, it's a good idea to make sure you see the actual release, signed by the parent. Even if you are using paid, professional models, you still need model releases from them.

Permits

If you schedule a special event—or even just a quick publicity picture with two or three people—in a public place, you may think you don't need a permit. Find out first; you don't want your work or photo session interrupted by the police. In many cities you will need one or more permits to hold special events or just to shoot pictures in public places.

Submitting Photographs to the Press

Your photographs should be sent with sturdy cardboard stiffeners inside the envelope so the art won't be bent in the mail. If you bend a photograph, the surface may crack, and then it can't be reproduced well. Don't skimp on cardboard or postage. After all, you've put a lot of time and money into those shots, and you want them to arrive safely. They should, of course, be sent by only first-class mail, messenger, or overnight courier.

If you are submitting photographs to a publication unfamiliar with your organization, be prepared for questions. "Of course we don't accept photos from new organizations until after we have checked them out," says one photo editor. "Otherwise it can get very sticky."

Some small newspapers charge an "engraving" fee when you submit a publicity photo. You should call and ask prospective outlets about their policies for publicity art. Don't mention the possibility of a fee; wait to see if they bring it up. If the fee is minimal, it will be worth paying because it's probably a great deal less than the cost for the same amount of advertising space.

Don't expect your photos to be returned. Editors are flooded with photos, and they will either file them for future use or, more likely, toss them into the trash if they can't use them. They do not have the time to return them to you, and you'll only annoy them if you request it.

Finally, find out if the journalist expects exclusive rights to use the shots you have submitted. "Some organizations expect print media to use the same images posted to the web for publication," says C. J. Martin. "I have spoken to editors who are understandably reluctant to run the same photo anyone can get from the web site. They would like to have a fresh image to better serve their readership. Be prepared to help them get an image that has not been broadcast."

Be certain you honor your commitment if a journalist is asking for exclusive photos. This is especially important at magazines, although it is a good idea to ask newspaper and Web-based reporters if they expect exclusive use of photos as well.

Checklist—Getting Pictures Published

1. When you approach an editor with a story idea, are you ready to suggest photo possibilities?
2. Have you found out the policies about using publicist-supplied photographs at the publications you'll be working with?
3. Have you prepared a photo tip sheet for your event and sent it along with your request for coverage?
4. Have you tried to get the larger publications to assign a photographer to your story?
5. Have you planned your event so that it's visually interesting?
6. If you make or sell luxury products, such as boats, houses, or cars, have you offered to make them available to photo editors at magazines?
7. If you are shooting your own publicity art, have you avoided the five standard clichés in publicity pictures?
8. Do your photos of people show something about the relationship between them?
9. Do your photos of events and people show some action taking place whenever possible?
10. Have you captured the meaning of the ceremony to the participants?
11. Have you considered showing the benefit rather than the ceremony?
12. Have you considered using photo illustration to construct a picture that illustrates a concept?
13. Can someone who knows nothing about your organization and the event shown in your photo tell you what's going on without a caption?

14. Are you avoiding "picket-fence" shots by grouping your subjects imaginatively? Are you keeping your groups small?

15. Do your pictures have only one point of interest?

16. Unless you know how to photograph large groups, do your photos have fewer than five people in them?

17. Have you included an object that identifies your organization in the shot?

18. Are you getting variety in your vantage points by shifting your camera position?

19. Are you using different lenses, f-stops, depth-of-field settings, and lighting arrangements to get shots with a range of effects?

20. Unless the shot is of patients in a clinic or similar situation, are all the people in the art identifiable?

21. Are you avoiding backgrounds that detract from the important part of the picture? Have you avoided taking photos in front of windows?

22. Are you editing and cropping the proofs before you have your final art printed?

23. Have you hired a photographer with product shot experience who knows how to make your merchandise look its best?

24. If you're sending product photos to a variety of publications, are you shooting in color as well as black-and-white?

25. Are you shooting your product both with and without people?

26. Is your photographer using a large-format view camera?

27. Do you get to choose the models for your photo shoot? Will you be able to see them in person before you make your choice?

28. Do you attend the photographic shoots so that your photographer can have your input?

29. Have you asked your photographer how long your photo shoot will take?

30. Does your photographer shoot sketch shots for products with a Polaroid or digital camera so you can see what the final shot will look like?

31. Are you using simple, neutral backgrounds such as gray and off-white for your product shots?

32. When you look at your sketch shots, do you check to make sure there's no glare and the background is well lit?

33. Have you talked with your photographer about whether you'll get better results by shooting a model of your product rather than the product itself?

34. Have you checked with your photographer to make sure that your product doesn't need antiglare treatment?

35. If you're shooting photos of food, have you hired an experienced food stylist?

36. Are you using a professional 35 mm camera rather than an instant camera?

37. Are the pictures you send out to newspapers black-and-white glossies? Are they at least five-by-seven inches, or four-by-five for head shots?

38. Have you checked what file format, density, and size journalists need for electronic photos?

39. If you're working with newspapers that run color, do you know which pages the color runs on? Have you checked with an editor to see if there's any possibility your story can run on a color page?

40. Does your art have strong contrast?

41. Are most of your photos for newspapers vertical rather than horizontal?

42. Have you asked the magazine editors you work with if they prefer vertical or horizontal art?

43. Do your shots have white margins?

44. Have you avoided getting fingerprints on photos, writing on the back of photos, or using paper clips on them?

45. Have you determined if you can use less expensive copy prints, or are handmade enlargements necessary?

46. Are you posting publicity photos in your website's pressroom?

47. Are they searchable by subject matter?

48. Have you included thumbnails so journalists can screen a lot of photos fast?

49. Are your thumbnails clickable, so a journalist can quickly see a larger version of the photo?

50. Have you included different file formats, sizes, and densities for each photo in your pressroom?

51. Did you post a caption for each photo?

52. Have you let journalists know that you're willing to send them original photos or transparencies by overnight courier?

53. Have you considered hiring a moonlighting press photographer to shoot your art for newspapers?

54. Can your photographer meet tight media deadlines?

55. Have you specified in writing that your photographer is an independent contractor? Have you made a written agreement concerning both print and electronic rights, ownership of negatives and electronic files, and credit lines?

56. Have you included captions that tell the whole story, identify everyone in the shot, and have your organization's name, address, and telephone number as well as the date?

57. Do you have model releases from everyone in all your photos, including paid, professional models?

58. Have you checked to see if you need permits to shoot photos or hold special events in public places?

59. Have you sent out your art by first-class mail, messenger, or overnight courier and packed it in sturdy envelopes with stiff cardboard to protect it?

60. Do you have a clear understanding with the editor about exclusivity?

8

Preparing Broadcast Publicity

In this chapter you will learn some of the tricks for preparing material designed to be heard rather than read: news releases for broadcasters in written form, video and audio news releases recorded on tape, public service announcements and short features for television, as well as community calendar listings. You will also find out how to assemble visual materials to accompany your TV spots or to add impact to your special programs.

When you are writing material for print media, you do not have to worry about how it will sound. "Trade your two left feet for a matched set at the Fifth Street Dance School" will look fine on paper, but "matched set" is difficult to say, and the announcer may stumble. So, test all copy you write for broadcasters by reading it aloud. If it reads easily, fine. If you stumble, rewrite your piece to eliminate the problem words.

Try to use short sentences when writing spoken material. Long, involved syntax with dependent clauses will be difficult to follow when it's heard. Unless you're selling snakes, avoid too many "s" sounds because microphones exaggerate them and make them hiss on the air. Be careful when you use the words *he, she,* and *they.* Will your listener know to whom these words refer, beyond any possibility of confusion?

If your copy contains a homonym (one of two or more words that are spelled differently but sound alike, such as *night* and *knight*), be sure the meaning is clear. You don't want your listeners to wonder whether you are referring to a dashing fellow in iron clothing on a white horse—or the period just after sunset.

Writing Effective Broadcast News Releases

The most important thing about a broadcast news release is that it must be short. Many broadcasters like stories that are 60, 30, or even 15 seconds long, sprinkled with a few 90-second "in-depth" items. So, don't send the same news release to broadcasters and newspapers. Write a different version of the story for broadcast media, and limit yourself to 90 seconds of reading time at the maximum. The best approach is to write 15-, 30-, 60-, and 90-second versions. That lets a harried news director pick the length that fits a particular news hole exactly. You can tell how long a release will be by reading it aloud and timing it.

You can either write a brief but pithy release, just as you would like to hear it read on the air, or provide the information in outline form and let the news director draft the actual words. In either case, each news item should be on a separate sheet of 8½-by-11-inch plain, white paper. At the top, list your organization's name and address, the date, the name and telephone number of the contact person, and the reading time in seconds. If the release is for immediate use, it should say "For immediate release." If you are getting it to the station early, but you don't want it released until later on, you should write "For release at 6:00 P.M. on Monday, February 29," or "For release after 12:00 noon on Friday, August 13."

Your release must be typed, double-spaced, and on one side of the page only. Be sure to leave wide margins both on the sides and at the top and bottom. This is space the assignment editor and news director need to write instructions and make changes. A 55-character line will leave plenty of room on the sides. If you limit yourself to 12 to 15 lines of copy per page, your top and bottom margins will be deep enough. Following are some guidelines for writing good news release copy for broadcast:

- Use the present tense whenever possible. News is happening now.
- Unless you have a reason to be specific, round out your figures. If the sixth-grade class at the local school donated 365 books to your library, you could say, "Almost 400 books are being given to the library." But if the kids made a point of contributing one book for every day of the year, and that point is central to the story, give the exact number.
- If any names in your release are difficult to pronounce, spell them out in phonetics enclosed in parentheses directly after the names. For example, "Writer Ken McEldowney (mack-ihl-down-ee) says . . ." will make it clear to the announcer exactly how the name should be pronounced.
- Keep background material to a minimum. If you consider supplementary information necessary, add a separate background sheet or include the exact addresses on your website where the journalist can find more information.
- Test your release by reading it aloud. How long does it take to read? Is it conversational? Easy to understand? Interesting?

Written out completely, a good broadcast news release might look like the sample in Exhibit 8.1 on page 260.

Some news directors prefer an outlined release. "Don't write the story for me," says KGW-TV news director Larry Badger. "I'm not going to use it the way you write it. But give me the information." KTVU-TV's Fred Zehnder expands on this point of view: "The best press release enables the assignment editor to get an idea of what you're all about in five or six sentences and then to look down and see the important information set off. If all that information is in the text of the release, the editor has to go through and underline it, and it takes more time."

The news release in Exhibit 8.1 is shown in outline form in Exhibit 8.2 on page 261.

Public Service Announcements

Public service announcements (PSAs) are among the most common kinds of publicity. Since they are short, broadcasters run a lot of them, and they are easier to get than specials, interviews, features, or news coverage. Even though they are only 60, 30, 20, or 10 seconds long, don't underestimate

---

Exhibit 8.1 (full-text format)

Citizens for Rapid Transit
1980 Strauss Street
Plains City 00003
Contact: Anand Gupta, (123) 456-7890

FOR IMMEDIATE RELEASE
September 15, 2003
Reading Time: 0:30

A rapid transit system in Plains City could save a million barrels of oil a year, cut air pollution by 45 percent and decrease average commuting time by one-fifth, according to a study released today by Citizens for Rapid Transit, or CRT for short.

The study, conducted by Ellington and Sczobosc (show-boss) Engineering, suggests that a $13 billion light rail system could be built in three phases during the next 12 years.

Gretchen K. Panaanen (pan-ah-ah-nen), president of CRT, says, "We'll be mailing a copy of the study's highlights to every household in the metro area." She adds, "The rapid transit bond issue will be on the ballot this fall, and we want everyone to have the information in this study before the election."

###

---

them. You can say a lot in 20 seconds. And since your PSA will almost certainly be repeated several times, your message will have multiple impact. For example, MG Productions, a video production house in New York, found that one of its client's spots went to 400 TV stations and aired 13,470 times, according to the company's president, Margie Goldsmith, in an article in *Public Relations Journal.*

The Federal Communications Commission (FCC) defines a PSA as "... any announcement ... for which no charge is made and which promotes programs, activities, or services of federal, state or local governments ... or the programs, activities or services of non-profit organizations ... *and other announcements regarded as serving community interests*" (emphasis added).

Exhibit 8.2 (outline format)

Citizens for Rapid Transit
1980 Strauss Street
Plains City 00003
Contact: Anand Gupta, (123) 456-7890

FOR IMMEDIATE RELEASE
September 15, 2003

A rapid transit system in Plains City could have economic benefits for the entire metro area, according to a study done by Ellington and Sczobosc (show-boss) Engineering. The study was released today by Citizens for Rapid Transit.

Savings:
A million barrels of oil a year.
A reduction of air pollution by 45%.
A decrease of commuting time by one-fifth.

Suggested System:
A light rail system.
At a cost of $13 billion.
Built in 3 phases during 12-year period.

More Information:
Complete study with details, statistics.
Mailed to all metro-area households before fall election.
Includes rapid transit bond issue.

###

That may sound bland, but PSAs these days are often controversial. James Wexler, vice president of West Glen, a New York video production and distribution house, comments, "Today, the issues are . . . hard-hitting and cover a wide range of topics. AIDS and drug abuse dominate the scene, followed closely by the homeless, concern for the environment, and missing children. Indeed, PSAs very much reflect the changing face of American society. Who would have thought even two years ago that the word *condom* would have been allowed on the air? Or that networks would actually consent to air a PSA about kids who watch too much TV? The fact is they *did* and 'Couch Potato,' distributed by West Glen for the American Academy of Pediatrics, received a flurry of publicity about its content, and was one of the 'hottest' PSAs on the air." (The script is shown in Exhibit 8.5 on pgae 277.)

What do you do if you are not part of the government and you're not a nonprofit organization? You have two choices:

- You can take the "service" approach and provide material that will benefit your audience. If your business or trade association presents information that can be regarded as serving community interests, you have a good chance your PSAs will be used.
- You can underwrite a PSA for a nonprofit organization and have the group include a sponsor's credit so that your organization's name is mentioned. Since this practice is becoming more common, many television stations don't object to it.

If you ask them in theory, public service directors will often tell you that they don't ever use PSAs produced by businesses and trade associations. But when a public service director sees an interesting PSA, chock-full of useful information about the safe use of lawn mowers, for example, she will probably be inclined to use it because it does serve community interests, even if it was produced for the Power Tool Association.

For example, PCS Broadcast Services, an audio-video production house in Ridgewood, New Jersey, produced and distributed a TV PSA for the Aluminum Association. Called "Recycle and Save," the spot ran on 244 stations covering 364 cities in 46 states. Viewers were asked to call a toll-free number for the address of their nearest recycling center. Before the spot aired, there had been about 400 calls a month. During the peak month of response to the PSA, 9,500 people called! The total exposure for the spot was 164 hours. The same amount of commercial time would have cost a whopping $4 million.

PCS Broadcast Services has also done PSAs on safe winter driving for senior citizens (Colonial Penn Life Insurance); Halloween safety (National Confectioner's Association); recycling your tires (Tire Retread Information Bureau); and the safe storage of detergent in households with children (Soap & Detergent Association).

The second approach is to sponsor a PSA produced by a nonprofit organization. In addition to the good feeling that comes from helping a worthy cause, your corporation can benefit by being identified with social responsibility in the view of the public. That's why credit to the business backing the effort is so important on sponsored PSAs. It is also possible, with careful planning, to weave your product into the finished spot in such a way that it is part of the fabric and seems to belong right there. If you're planning to do that, choose a production house with some experience in producing sponsored PSAs that include product mention. Ask to see some successful spots they've produced, and be sure to look at the usage reports, showing how many stations ran the spots. Find out how the production house knows that the product mentions weren't edited out of the spots. Finally, ask to speak to references at several sponsoring companies.

Many stations prefer to use local spots, written or produced by organizations in their own towns or cities. But they'll also air national spots for either of two reasons:

- They know that the national organization has a local chapter or affiliate in their area.
- The spot will serve the public interest of the community.

Large national organizations often have a lot of media production money, and their spots can be quite polished. However, that doesn't mean that your organization's PSA, written at your kitchen table, doesn't have a chance.

There are a number of formats for PSAs, and it is important to find out in advance what formats are preferred by each broadcaster you will be approaching. At the same time, you should find out if they have other requirements, such as transcripts of recorded spots or certain information about the sponsoring organization. In addition, every broadcaster has specific technical requirements for recorded PSAs. "Minor technical errors, like making a PSA a few seconds too long or too short, can cause unnecessary problems and even rejection of a PSA in which great effort and expense was invested," says Andrew McGowan, president of PCS Broadcast Services.

Keep in mind that your PSA is competing with commercials for viewers' attention and interest. A single commercial can cost a million dollars to produce and air on TV. That can be awesome competition, and you may find that you need production help with your spots.

If you're working with a nonprofit or community organization, your first step is to ask the stations in your area if they will help you produce PSAs in their studios. Although many stations offer PSA production help to nonprofit and community organizations and government agencies, studio time is tight, and only a few spots are produced each month. If the station does offer this service, ask how far in advance you will have to make arrangements.

If you can't find help at the stations, try approaching advertising agencies in your area. Many advertising people are willing to help nonprofit organizations produce PSAs. But even if they offer their services, the donation is usually limited to creative work only. Production costs may still be sizable, and *you* will have to pay for them. Ask at the start of any discussions with volunteer advertising personnel just what size they expect the production budget to be.

If you decide to have your PSAs produced commercially, you may want to check the list of PSA production houses in Chapter 13. Or ask the program directors at local radio and TV stations for their recommendations. If a local production studio is mentioned by several program directors, it's a good bet that the studio does a nice job.

Technical Requirements for Radio PSAs

The least expensive kind of PSA is "live" copy, in which you write out your material and the announcer or disc jockey reads it live, on the air. The advantage of live copy is that it is cheap and can be produced quickly. While businesses and trade associations typically use prerecorded PSAs, many nonprofit groups rely on live PSAs. If yours are clear, focused, and imaginative, they'll serve you well. But remember, when you submit your PSA as live copy, there is always the chance that the public service director or even the announcer will edit or change it—for better or for worse.

If you are lucky enough to have a production budget, you can submit prerecorded radio PSAs. But don't reach for your hundred-dollar discount-store cassette recorder. Prerecorded spots must be professionally produced. You may not be able to tell the difference, but to the trained ears of radio people, your amateur production will sound terrible. If you cannot afford to hire a sound studio, ask the broadcasting department at your local college for help.

"Radio stations accept PSAs in various tape, disk and perhaps newer formats. Some formats that don't require expensive set-up are less expensive in small quantities, but others that may require set-up but then can be duplicated quickly in a manufacturing process are much less expensive in large quantities," says Andrew McGowan. Ask your PSA producer which broadcast-quality format will be most cost effective for the quantity you plan to distribute.

Once you have decided to have your PSAs professionally produced, take advantage of every opportunity to create memorable, attention-arresting spots. Some people can remember the words and the music to advertisements from more than 30 years ago. Your PSA is really an advertisement, and you should try to make it as effective as the best ads.

Use sound effects, music, dialogue, and drama, not simply a voice. Even if you have not dramatized your spot, consider using two voices. It will sound less monotonous, and your spot will be easier to understand and require slightly less of a pause between sentences, allowing you to get in a few extra words.

If you use any music or sound effects in your PSA, you must get permission from the copyright owner or buy material from a sound-effects house. Even a nonprofit organization could face a lawsuit if it uses copyrighted music or sound effects without permission.

When you submit a prerecorded radio PSA, send a script along with it. This makes the public service director's job much easier, and she will be more likely to use your spot. And whether you send "live" copy or tape, always include several different lengths. You may have a wonderful 30-second spot that the public service director simply adores, but she has only 10- and 20-second spots available. Send the four most common lengths: 10, 15, 20, and 30 seconds, and if you want to cover all the bases, you can also include a 60-second version.

Technical Requirements for Television PSAs

When you send "live" copy to TV stations, you should include visual material. Otherwise, while the announcer reads the material, the station may bore its viewers by showing a slide that reads "A public service announcement from Chelm United Charities." No matter how interesting the announcement is, that slide will brand you as dull.

Standard 35 mm color slides are the visual material for live-copy television PSAs. But, before you spend money shooting and duplicating them, find out if the television stations you'll be approaching still use live copy for public service announcements. Some do—others don't. Live, script-slide PSAs will work for spots of 10, 20, and 30 seconds, but 60-second PSAs really require videotape to keep viewers engaged.

If you find stations that will use live spots, write this rule down on your thumb: You usually need one slide for each five seconds in your spot. That way the station can change images fairly rapidly, and your PSA will have the illusion of motion. That illusion is essential if you want to keep a TV audience tuned in.

Many stations will not even consider using slides that are not mounted in glass. If the public service director tells you that her station will accept plastic or cardboard mounts, you can save some money, so it is worthwhile to ask.

When a 35 mm slide is televised, part of the image is cut off by the camera, and you lose about 10 percent of the height and 20 percent of the width. To gauge the effect, you can cut out a piece of $\frac{5}{8}$-by-$\frac{23}{32}$-inch paper. Place it behind the slide and center it; whatever part of the image is not over the paper will be lost in transmission.

Also, since TV screens are horizontal, your slides must be horizontal. Otherwise, that great shot of the mayor showing off one of the city's new police horses may end up as the headless horseman.

If you want to record your own TV PSAs, your spots *must* be professionally produced, with expert lighting, camera work, and editing. Few TV stations will use tape from home camcorders—unless you have *exclusive* footage of a major news event such as a volcano eruption or an airplane crash.

When you create PSAs, you have to take three steps into account. Each can be executed in a different tape format:

- Shooting or producing the raw footage.
- Editing the footage into finished spots on a master tape.
- Distributing the spots to stations in several formats to meet the needs of each.

Some productions may be shot on film, to achieve a rich, big-screen look, and then transferred to tape, a process that is as high in cost as it is in quality, according to Andrew McGowan. And some facets of the production process may be "tapeless," such as editing that involves "digitizing" the material into a computer for better manipulation.

No matter what medium they use, PSAs have standard format requirements. "The spots should be edited *exactly* to standard length: 60, 30, 20, 15 and 10 seconds. And there should be no sound in the first and last half second of a TV spot, since this is how stations ease the transition between adjacent commercials," says McGowan. Also, "The name of the organization must appear somewhere in each spot, usually as a title at the end."

Once you have your master tape, you need to produce copies, or "dubs," to send out to television stations, cable systems, and/or regional and national networks—in the proper format. As broadcasters update their equipment, their needs change, so you have to keep up-to-date with each outlet on your list, or hire a production or distribution house that tracks changes in broadcasters' requirements.

Some of the larger PSA production houses listed in Chapter 13 have continuously updated databases that track station format preferences. If you use such a house to produce or distribute your PSAs, it will take care of matching the correct format to each station.

Taped PSAs should always be accompanied by either a script or a storyboard. A storyboard is a sequence of pictures, in black-and-white or color, showing highlights of your spot. The audio portion is written under each picture. This helps the public service director get a concrete idea of just how good the PSA is, and it may persuade him to preview your tape.

A typical script for a television public service announcement will look like the one in Exhibit 8.3 on page 268, which was produced by MRA Communicators, Inc., for the American Foundation for the Blind. Joel Saltzman was scriptwriter. For this 60-second spot, there are two scripts, side by side, one for sight and the other for sound. "CU" means a close-up shot.

What length PSA should you send to television stations? There's no one correct length, according to Andrew McGowan. "As in radio, length preferences for PSAs vary among television outlets. Almost all use 30-second spots, but some may prefer 60s or one of the shorter lengths. Rather than trying to determine the 'ideal' length, consider this: most stations will air more than one length of the same message, so producing and distributing a couple of lengths is probably the ideal." It makes a lot of sense to provide several lengths, according to McGowan, because

Exhibit 8.3

Video	*Audio*
Slow zoom-in on woman removing mixing bowl from kitchen cabinet.	(Sound under, ticking of timer)
Places it on counter with baking utensils, flour, eggs, sugar, etc.	In the next 60 seconds, this woman is going to bake a cake—without looking once.
Medium shot, moving mixing bowl to center of table.	How does she do it?
CU, dispensing shortening with shortening measure KC 108.	Watch closely, because something she does . . .
CU, adding pre-sifted flour to mixing bowl.	. . . is going to give her away.
Medium shot, reaching for milk container.	
CU, measuring 1 cup of milk, pouring it into mixing bowl.	
CU, stirs batter by hand.	
Zoom-in on breaking egg. CU, overhead view of separating egg with egg separator, KC 807.	
Medium shot, reaches for bottle of vanilla; zoom-in on feeling for label.	There's the clue. A label printed in braille.
Medium shot, pours out 1 teaspoon of vanilla.	She isn't looking at what she's doing because she can't; she's blind.
Medium shot, pours egg whites into large mixing bowl.	. . . But she can bake a cake—and cook anything else she wants.
CU, placing mixer into bowl and mixing.	She uses aids and appliances made available by the American Foundation for the Blind—things like:
CU, shortening measure in use.	This shortening measure.
CU, egg separator in use.	The egg separator.

CU, bottle of vanilla with braille label in hand.	Labels made in braille.
CU, CM 20 timer on table.	(Timer rings) . . . Even the timer.
Zoom-out from timer to woman removing cake from oven.	For a free catalog listing these and 200 other aids and appliances write:
CU, overhead view of cake with address information superimposed, letter-by-letter, as if being written by hand.	Aids for the Blind Box 111 New York, NY 10011

"each additional length usually can be produced and added to the distribution package for less than half the cost of the first spot."

This is important if you're aiming for prime time in large metro areas, where the competition for airtime can be brisk. "Ten-second spots are likely to get the most exposure in heavy viewing time periods, particularly in major cities," according to an article by Margie Goldsmith in *Public Relations Journal.* "Sixty-second spots will get 15 to 25 percent less airplay." Goldsmith adds, "PSA directors specifically request that you don't submit a 15-second PSA alone; they prefer two for a 'split 30.'"

Special Requirements for Television Network PSAs

The television networks also run PSAs. The spots must, of course, be of national interest. And the competition for network airtime is stiff. "The broadcast networks and some of the national cable networks may require a 'viewing copy' in a non-broadcast-quality format, to be sent first, along with background information. If they accept the campaign, they will request multiple copies in the broadcast quality format they use," says Andrew McGowan.

The names and addresses of the network public service directors can be found in some of the media directories listed in Chapter 13. If you will be submitting preview PSAs to the networks, contact them ahead of time and ask for their specific requirements.

Format for Live Public Service Announcements

Since you have to establish your organization's credibility, particularly at first, it is a good practice to send your live PSAs on letterhead. Even though businesses can get PSAs, you may have to document your status as a non-profit organization. In many larger cities, public service directors require a copy of your IRS tax-exempt-status letter. Organizations raising funds should give the permit number from the city, county, or state agency that certifies that they are legally entitled to collect money. You may send PSAs for months and never know that the reason they weren't being used is because you didn't provide this information. Ask a sampling of public service directors in your town whether they require documentation before they run PSAs.

"Because stations are much less likely to air PSAs that ask for money than ones that give information, the most effective 'fund-raising' spot may be one that has only an oblique reference to contributions," according to Andrew McGowan.

If you are sending different lengths of the same PSA, each spot should be on a separate 8½-by-11-inch sheet of paper, since this is the way stations handle them. Use one side of the sheet only, and do not staple them together because that makes them harder to handle.

At the top of the sheet, list the following:

- Your organization's name.
- A contact person and telephone number with area code.
- The date you expect the spot will arrive at the station.
- The reading time, followed by the words "Public service spot."
- The word count.
- The words "Use until," followed by the last date on which you would want your spot to run.
- A website address to provide background information about your organization.

It's important to include an expiration date on PSAs. Don't assume that public service directors will carefully monitor a spot. If an event or program ends on a definite date, put that expiration date at the top of the script, or on the label of the cassette, and highlight it.

A heading on a public service spot sent out on letterhead may look like the following:

Relapsing Polychondritis Foundation, www.relpoly.chl
Contact: Sam Berg, (123) 456-7890
January 20, 2003
Use until: March 3, 2003
20-second public service spot
43 words

Public service spots should never say "News release" or "For immediate release." If you are sending them in ahead of the time you want them used, combine lines two and three of the heading so that they read, for example, "Use between January 20 and March 3, 2003."

Your live PSA copy should be double- or triple-spaced and typed in a narrow, 35-character column because it is easier to read aloud than lines that are typed all across the page. Although PSAs are often typed in all capital letters, you should use upper- and lowercase because that, too, reads more easily.

Words to be emphasized should be underlined, but don't overdo it. Having all emphasis is, after all, no emphasis. And just as in a broadcast news release, difficult names should be spelled phonetically in parentheses following the first occurrence.

Think about who will hear and see your PSAs and what such information as phone numbers and locations will mean to them. "If you put a local spot on a New York TV station telling people to go to the Mayor's Office on the Aging, the spot is going to be seen in White Plains, Hackensack, and Garden City—places that may not have such an office or it may not be a participant in the promoted program," says Andrew McGowan. Be sure to include the area code with phone numbers, as well as specific locations that name the city or town for the program you're promoting.

You may not even give your telephone number at all, if it will be easier to find a telephone directory than to memorize the number or write it down. This is especially true if you work for a national organization with chapters in most cities, listed similarly in phone directories. You could say something like, "Find your local Help-A-Kid chapter in the telephone directory under 'youth services,'" McGowan suggests.

Last of all, if you are sending out a script-slide PSA for TV, you'll need a video column and an audio column in your script (the same format as shown previously in Exhibit 8.3). Each slide should be numbered on its mount. In the video column of the script, write the number for each slide and a brief description opposite the audio part of the narrative it illustrates.

Writing Public Service Announcements

When you write a PSA, remember who your audience is and what people are likely to be doing while the spot is airing. During a radio spot, there's a good chance your listener is cooking dinner, talking with neighbors, or driving home through a horrendous traffic jam after a long day at work. You have to compete for your listener's attention, and you have to keep it once you've got it.

If your spot is for TV, consider that the picture comes half a second before the sound starts. "I think you need to start with the most arresting visual you can do, so that you are not saying, 'Here comes another commercial,'" says ad executive John Rand of Reva Korda & Associates.

"There's a natural tendency to break," Rand continues. "Viewers have just seen a very exciting drama, and it's the end of the scene. The impulse is to talk, go to the bathroom, get a drink, or do something during that commercial break so that they can be back when the quarter starts, or the next scene opens, or the interviewer introduces the next guest. This is a natural time not to listen. People are not sitting there waiting for your PSA."

It will be easier to rivet the viewer's or listener's attention if you start by telling him why he should pay attention to you. Don't say, "You should listen to me because . . ." Think, instead, of how your message will benefit your listener. Start it with a strong statement of that benefit—a short sentence or two that appeals directly to the listener's self-interest. Then follow that with the good old who, when, where, why, how, and what. Conclude by telling the audience what you want them to do: call you, write to you, come to an event, or change their thinking on an issue.

"You've got to make sure that your most important point of interest is done right away," Rand stresses. "So you might say, 'Your son may not go to college. That's right. If you don't help our library now, we may have to close. There will be no other place for him to get the books he needs.' But you wouldn't say, 'Don't forget the library. It's a really marvelous place. We have so many books. And, you know, we may have to shut down if we can't raise more money, and your son . . .' You should make sure the viewer is riveted before he can leave," says Rand.

Be sure you grab people's interest by finding a way to make *your* message fascinating. Never try to get attention by talking about something more interesting and then switching to your message; that implies your message is dull. Yes, borrowed interest is often used in advertising, but that's bad advertising, since you are not talking about *your* product or service.

For example, it's not effective to open your PSA by saying, "Just as Nero, the Roman emperor, played the violin while the city burned to the ground, so too could you be letting things burn right now if you haven't developed a fire safety plan for your home." In that case you've delayed the message. You've taken valuable time and cluttered the scene, instead.

"You've got to establish your identity right from the start," Rand asserts. "And you've got to mean something to that person right off, so that he is involved. Your story should come from within your product, your institution, your business. It should come from your own strength."

According to Rand, "The viewer feels cheated when you start with something that has nothing to do with your message, and suddenly you start selling. What you're doing is putting your sell in the middle of some entertainment. It's already in the middle of some entertainment. So you've diluted your appeal with this borrowed interest, and you've taken the person's mind off your message."

This PSA uses borrowed interest:

> *Before you buy a new household appliance, I'm sure you look at several makes and models. When it comes to buying life insurance, you should use every tool available to help in your selection. The Chelm County Insurance Agent's Association has a booklet to help you buy the right kind of insurance. For your free copy call (999) 121-3700.*

A typical radio listener will probably ask himself what life insurance has to do with appliances and ignore the rest of this announcement. If he does get past the confusion, he may miss part of the message while he puzzles it out. Even if he gets the whole message, the spot hasn't told him that there *are* different kinds of life insurance. Many listeners don't know this, and rather than talk about appliances, the spot should explain why all life insurance is not the same.

A common problem with PSAs is that they try to say too much. Choose one main point in a spot that is 30 seconds or shorter, and make sure that everything else supports, clarifies, and elaborates on that main thrust. In a 60-second PSA, you can sometimes manage to include two points, but they should be related.

The following spot includes too much information; the listener would have a hard time figuring out what is important:

> *The distinguished Chelm Dramatic Arts Ensemble and the Chelm A Capella Chorus will present alternating programs of drama and choral works which probe man's inhumanity to man among other philosophical issues. Featured in program number one will be Richard Smith's two classics:* Miss Marie *and* The Wonderful Washerwoman, *as well as the contemporary choral piece* Interstate 98, *by Wiggins-Starbank. Program number two, a tantalizing selection of contemporary dramas, will include* The Night They Closed the Disco Down *by M. T. Head,* Lance's Promise *by Jean Spear, and the poignant* DDT *and* Old Denim *by Marsha Costello, as well as art songs by the little-known German Romantic composer Werner Rosenkopff. Both programs will be performed on weekends, except Friday nights, from April 17 through May 12 at either the Downtowner Theater or the Highway Playhouse. For information, dial (999) 131-1826. Or write Box 15662, Chelm Main Post Office, Chelm 00009.*

Your PSA must contain solid information about your organization's services or cause. A spot announcement that says "Don't forget your recreation center" is hardly interesting. "People feel they know a lot about you," says John Rand. "If you start off with a general story, either they will have heard it before, or it can apply to anyone else who has the same kind of service or institution. So you're not helping yourself. If people haven't helped you before, there's no new incentive to help you now, just because your name pops up. When your announcement is finished, you want them to say, 'Boy, that recreation center (library, store, political group) gives me a lot more than I thought!'"

Tell people what you do, specifically. Just mentioning your organization's name is not enough. Your name is important only to you.

Verify all information. Be sure that you can back up the facts, figures, and statements in your PSA. "If you make statements, you should be able to substantiate them; otherwise they don't go on the air. It's truth in advertising, even though it's free," says WCBS-AM community affairs director Teresa DiTore.

End on a forceful note. "Keep the end of your spot focused and simple. If you have a lot of clutter at the end, you're taking away from the telegraphic impact. Be single-minded. Be strong. And make only one point. The last line should be a call to action. You should end as strongly as you began. You can't get your audience all excited in the first line and then leave them in a morass of generalities," says John Rand.

Editing Your PSAs

Always review your copy for conciseness. "There's no formula or trick," says John Rand. "It's just economy of the greatest order. When you have that short a message, especially when you're not of primary interest to the person you're trying to reach, every word must count. You must eliminate all unnecessary words. And never let up your pace. Make it short, make it staccato, keep it going. No long, drawn-out sentences that people will bog down in. Your writing should be almost telegraphic. And your words should have rhythm."

Writing PSAs is like writing poetry: you have to get your word's worth. Every word has to carry meaning. Go through your copy and cross out as many words as you can. You'll find you can make your copy stronger by eliminating most of the adjectives. And the word *that* can often be dropped. Be merciless with your blue pencil.

As you edit, try to vary your sentence structure and length. Is it OK to break some "rules," such as starting a sentence with a preposition? "I think you can, in advertising," says John Rand. "I think you can have three words set off by periods: Wild. Wacky. Wonderful. That moves. It's quick. It's telegraphic. Those are not complete sentences. But I think they help you when you want people to hear you." Don't be afraid to edit more than once, or even more than twice. If you can let the draft sit overnight between those editing jobs, you'll have an easier time. Try to arrange your work schedule so there is always time for this important step.

Read your copy aloud, and time it. Try not to say too much in one spot; it's hard to understand even a professional announcer when he has to speak out of both sides of his mouth to cram all the copy into the time slot.

Finally, examine your organization's name. "Especially in radio spots, when you have to state the name, sometimes more than once, a long name can be a problem," says Andrew McGowan. "I've seen names that would fill a ten second spot, leaving no room for a message. Stations for the most part require that the full name of the sponsoring organization be in the spot. They won't take a shortened version unless the name can be simplified officially and legally. I've seen broadcasters reject spots that didn't have the full name of the organization." With that in mind, you may want to follow the example of the Extended Studies Program at California State University, Bakersfield. The program's official alternate name is CSB Plus.

Some Effective PSAs

The spot in Exhibit 8.4, prepared by Barbara Marshall and Kristyn Halbig, directors of public relations for the University of Wisconsin Extension, is a good example of a straightforward PSA. Notice that it immediately identifies its audience and tells them what the service benefit is.

Exhibit 8.5 is the script for the 20-second version of "Couch Potato," a spot distributed by West Glen for the American Academy of Pediatrics. It was released to 400 television stations nationally. The spot got excellent pickup by the big three networks, MTV, Nickelodeon, and more than 200 local stations for each of two versions. The intense discussion this spot generated in the media led to international airplay in Holland, Italy, Belgium, and England, as well.

Exhibit 8.4

Musicians, look at what the UW-Extension Indianhead Center in Shell Lake has for you this summer.

Trumpet and synthesizer symposiums will be offered at the Center August 4th through the 8th.

The trumpet symposium will be taught by three outstanding musicians—Dominic Spera, Renold Schilke, and Ray Crisara. Chris Swanson, founder of the New York Improvisation Ensemble, will be teaching the synthesizer courses.

College credits are available for these classes. For more information write: Darrell Aderman, Indianhead Center, Shell Lake, Wisconsin 54871.

Exhibit 8.5

Video	Audio
1. Boy and girl on couch watching television.	MUSIC: Up and under
2. Boy turns into potato.	CHORUS: "Couch potato."
3. GRAPHIC: Too Much T.V.!!	DEEP VOICE: "Too much T.V."
4. Boy potato holds television.	BOY: "Leave me alone; just let me groove on my tube!"
5. GRAPHIC: Don't just plop in front of the T.V.	HIGH VOICE: "Don't just plop in front of the T.V. 'cause you've got nothing else to do."
6. Girl potato on couch.	GIRL: "Gotta have that. . . . Mama, can I buy that?"
7. GRAPHIC: Watch out for overeating.	HIGH VOICE: "Watch out for overeating."
8. Family of potatoes turn back into humans.	"Don't be a . . ."
9. GRAPHIC: From the American Academy of Pediatrics.	CHORUS: "Couch potato. Couch potato." CHORUS: Out

When the New York Diabetes Association wanted to explain that contributions are still needed because there is not yet a cure for diabetes, the group decided to use a humorous approach. Although the tone of voice in the original is important, you can get a good deal of the flavor from Exhibit 8.6 on page 278, the script for the 30-second prerecorded radio PSA. Written by Howard Weinstein, the spot won an award from the Community Agencies Public Relations Association (CAPRA) in New York.

The National Society to Prevent Blindness approached PCS Broadcast Services about doing a PSA asking parents to write for a free home eye test for their preschool children, and the two organizations came up with an unusual approach. Folksinger Tom Glazer wrote a song, which he performed in a 60-second TV spot. The audio portion is reprinted in Exhibit 8.7 on pages 278 and 279.

Exhibit 8.6

Voice 1: An apple a day keeps diabetes away.

Voice 2: No, it doesn't.

Voice 1: A peach a day?

Voice 2: Nothing keeps diabetes away. There's no way to prevent it and no cure, either. It can be very serious, but it can be controlled with proper care.

Voice 1: A pomegranate?

Voice 2: Doctors and scientists are working very hard to find out what will.

Voice 1: A watermelon a day?

Voice 2: You can't eat a whole watermelon.

Voice 1: If it's a small one.

Voice 2: *Do* something to help. Call the American Diabetes Association today.

Voice 1: Avocados? Nectarines? Casaba melons? Cantaloupes?

FADE OUT

Exhibit 8.7

Tom Glazer sings:

Precious sight, precious sight,

Oh the lovely things I see,

The lovely things I see,

In my sight, in my precious sight.

Precious days, precious nights,

And a thousand precious sights,

A thousand precious sights,

That I see in my precious sight.

Glazer voice over:

Vision problems could limit a child's view of things forever. Age three or four is the prime time for the first vision test. Ask your Society to Prevent Blindness to send you a free home eye test for preschoolers.

Tom Glazer sings:

And the precious faces that I love so well,

Much more than mere words can say,

Precious love, precious love,

Precious gifts from above, gifts from above,

That I see in my precious sight every day.

Superimposed title:

Address to write for the free home eye test.

By Tom Glazer, © 1980, Songs Music, Inc., Scarborough, NY 10510. Used by permission.

The Advertising Council, which has done public service advertising for Smokey the Bear for decades, created a simple and effective script for a 30-second TV PSA that appeals to people who are concerned about ecology or interested in the chains of events that cause ecological problems. The audio portion of the script reads this way:

> *A fish died. Because it couldn't breathe. Because its gills got clogged with silt. Because mud ran into the river. Because there was nothing to trap the rain. Because all the trees were gone. Because someone got careless with fire. So please be careful with fire. Because.*

Video News Releases

Instead of sending your printed press release to television news directors, what if you shot some great video footage of people using your new instant wipe-on baldness remover—and added narration? Then you had it edited down to 90 seconds and offered that, instead of a press release. Would it work? It sure would! You've just created something called a video news release, or VNR for short. In only a short time, it's become a popular publicity tool for organizations that can afford the price tag of $15,000 to $30,000.

A video news release is just like a television news story: it must be objective as well as sound and look like a news report. Long television news stories run for a minute to 90 seconds, but more and more frequently, TV news stories are being squeezed into 15- and 30-second slots. Make sure your video news release is short, so it falls within common television time slots. You may even want to offer the story in several lengths. Package it in a format that's ready for on-the-air use but that also allows stations to edit the material. And remember, you can't focus on plugging your product or service—this has to be a *news* story.

Since VNRs look and sound like news stories, news directors have strong feelings about them. Medialink, a satellite distribution service for VNRs, sponsored a national survey of television news directors in which three-quarters of the responding journalists said that video news releases should be "clearly identified" as public relations releases. "Identification must include the source of production, and who is the ultimate sponsor of the VNR," according to Medialink's president, Laurence Moskowitz. This is actually a legal requirement when the VNR involves political or controversial issues, according to Section 317 of the Communications Act of 1934.

Since a VNR is a news report, you have to make any mention of your product an integral part of your story. As James Wexler of West Glen explains, "A good video news release should be structured so that your client's message is entwined with the newsworthy material, and can't be separated."

With VNRs, as with any other publicity material, you have to think like a journalist. "If you're in the business of packaging news for public relations purposes, you try to produce it as if you were on assignment for the individual station," says Paul Gourvitz, president of Gourvitz Communications, a video production house in New York.

A three-step formula works well for VNRs—whether they're about products, services, or causes. In an article in *O'Dwyer's PR Services Report,* West Glen president Stan Zeitlin explains, "First, *establish a problem,* which then becomes your news peg. Second, *tell how you or your product can solve the problem.* Third, *summarize with a wrap-up of problem and solution without getting too commercial.*" Although this is a workable approach, it's not cast in stone. Your creative team may develop a different angle that will serve you well.

But the subject of a VNR is only part of what makes it appealing to journalists. According to the Medialink survey, 83 percent of television news directors say that "a suggested local angle increase[s] the likelihood" that they will use a video news release. Andrew McGowan offers two solid tips for localizing VNRs:

- Suggest a news peg for local illustrations of the story. In one case a world-class hospital that had performed the first coronary bypass in the United States approached PCS Broadcast Services to create a VNR to gain national coverage for the anniversary of the event. "Our plan included suggesting to stations that they use the VNR as a news peg to do a story on how many such procedures are done by a hospital in their area," McGowan reports. PCS also suggested that the station could interview the longest surviving patient in the vicinity.

- Provide a list of local experts from your organization who can cap off the story with a local perspective. These experts can be dealers, wholesalers, distributors, members, staff, or perhaps even customers. PCS did a VNR for a national association of colleges that was "completed" by the station, which interviewed the president of a member institution in its area. "This combination should achieve more coverage than either the national office or the members could alone," McGowan points out.

Making Sure Your VNR Is Broadcast Quality

If you want broadcasters to run your video news release, it has to meet industry standards of *broadcast quality*. This term refers to both the technical format and the content.

From a technical point of view, broadcast quality refers to measurable standards. James Wexler explains, "You can actually measure the intensity of the signal on a tape. If the signal is too weak, you won't have broadcast quality. VHS [ordinary home videotape], for example, is not broadcast quality because the electronic data on the tape is not sufficient to create a picture that can be broadcast and received clearly." That's why your VNR must be produced and edited by professionals using broadcast-quality equipment.

"Broadcast quality in video news releases also has to do with style," Wexler continues. "A broadcast quality VNR has the look and feel of a local news story." For example, you wouldn't use fancy visual effects or music in a VNR, because that would make it look like an advertisement.

To capture and keep viewers' attention, the video should be visually stimulating, with signs of real life right there in the background. Since VNRs shot in the studio often look dull and artificial, shooting at the location of the actual story gives a more interesting, "newsier" result.

"It's better to have something more interesting to fill the frame than just a bare studio," says Wexler. "When we're doing an interview, we'd rather have someone in an office or at their work location."

Technical Requirements for VNRs

To produce VNRs of broadcast quality, you must meet certain standards.

All broadcast news stories are made up of basic building blocks called *sound bites*. A sound bite is a news maker speaking on camera, so you see him on the television screen. Sound-bite building blocks are tied together with narration by an announcer. As Paul Gourvitz explains, "A typical news story begins with a reporter putting it in perspective. Then there are one, two or three sound bites, each with a different newsmaker's voice." The narrator smoothes the transition from one sound bite to another, making logical connections between them and putting them in perspective. After the last sound bite, the reporter draws a brief conclusion and closes with a "tag"—for example, "This is Soanne Soh reporting."

To be acceptable to news directors, your VNR should fit within a 60- to 90-second time frame. "However there is no set rule" for how long a VNR should be, according to James Wexler. "The story must tell itself." So, your VNR may run for 66 seconds—or 87—as long as you keep it to no more than 90 seconds. (Sixty-four percent of the news directors responding to the Medialink survey said that 90 seconds is a good length for a VNR.)

Make sure your raw sound bites will work within this framework, so your video editor can shape them into a VNR without cutting your news makers and spokespeople off in midsentence. That's why you don't want someone in your video news release talking for 30 seconds. "That's just too long," says Wexler. "But they usually have to speak for longer than four seconds, just to make sense of what's being said. The best length for each sound bite is somewhere in between 10 and 20 seconds—and that's an artistic call." This need for very concise statements may mean you'll have to spend time training your spokespeople to talk in bursts of 10 to 20 seconds—well before the raw footage for your VNR is recorded.

The second technical requirement involves the sound tracks on the videotape. Broadcast-quality tape has two tracks for sound. All the sound bites should be on one track, but the narration should be on the other. James Wexler explains, "This lets a news director . . . air the story without your narration. Using the timed script you supplied . . . the station's announcer can read the audio portion and make the story sound like the station's own." Since many news directors will want to supply their own narration, having separate sound tracks is an important factor in getting your video news release aired.

For the same reason, Medialink's Laurence Moskowitz advises, "Never superimpose your own written information on the actual videotape," unless you also supply an alternate version of the finished story. Many TV news departments want to supply their own titles using the typefaces that match their station's style, and they can't do that easily if all you've given them is a version that already has titles.

Moskowitz adds that you should also never have your narrator or reporter on-screen. "Stations do not want a reporter appearing in their newscast who is not on their staff." (Sixty percent of the stations Medialink surveyed would not use a VNR in which the sponsor's reporter appears on-screen.)

Still another technical requirement for video news releases is the inclusion of additional raw material on the tape you provide to stations. This lets the news director produce his own story, with his own announcer and his station's look, feel, and point of view. This extra footage is called *B-roll*. In fact, 52 percent of the television newspeople responding to the Medialink survey were even willing to work with a B-roll alone—without any publicist-prepared story at all!

Of course, there's a contradiction here. Your organization spends thousands of dollars to produce a finished, videotaped news story from *your* viewpoint. Why should you let journalists edit it? That's a good question, and you should be prepared with an answer, because your organization's top executives may raise it. The explanation is simple: you have no choice. This is not advertising, and, just as with a printed press release, you have to *earn* coverage. You have to accept the fact that journalists may not see eye to eye with you—and that editors will edit. In fact, a West Glen survey of television stations found that 37 percent of their news staffs always edit VNRs, and 32 percent edit them frequently. Just 2 percent of the stations reported they never edit VNRs.

But, if your VNR has a good news peg and you have nothing to hide, it's likely that those editors preparing their own stories from your raw material will give you favorable coverage. Paul Gourvitz sums it up: "That's the beauty of B-roll; it gives News Directors options. If they like what you sent them, but it isn't exactly the way they would do it, they can edit the story to suit themselves."

B-roll can include several types of material, and you can even plan several types of useful shots, especially for your B-roll, that will help a news director create a better finished story. James Wexler describes one example: "Let's say you're doing a story on a hospital. You might give them a few extra shots of the medical procedure taking place, so if for some reason they want a longer story than your edited piece, they have the raw material."

Paul Gourvitz describes another case: "In an edited story about a nuclear plant, which you're trying to keep to 90 seconds, you might have a wide shot of the nuclear plant. And then you'd go inside and show one or two interior scenes. But in B-roll you might give them a zoom-in, a zoom-out, a static shot of the exterior, and a few more inside shots. That way they can pick what they want. What you're doing is trying to provide variety for them."

One of the problems with videotape editing is what's called a *jump cut*. This is a sudden, jerky movement of a person—or a head or hands—when a piece of the tape is removed during editing. Video editors use what's called a *cutaway* to avoid jump cuts. The camera switches to the cutaway at the point the tape is edited, and then back to the original scene, so there's no jump. When you plan your VNR, ask the video production house what types of material they recommend for *cover footage* to make it possible for the news director to do cutaways.

If your video news release is shot on location, you will also want to include the standard types of shots news directors rely on. An *establishing shot* is used at the start of a story. It's a wide-angle view, which puts the location into perspective and helps the viewer get an orientation. You should also include *zoom-in, zoom-out,* and *static* shots for both outside and inside locations. Zoom-in shots start in the distance and get closer, so you move from the broad view to the more specific, with the details emerging as you go. They are more likely to be used at the beginning of a story, or when the camera moves to a new scene. Zoom-out shots are the opposite; they start close in and move out, and are most likely used at the close of a story. Static shots keep the same perspective. The people in them can move, but the camera perspective stays the same.

Finally, you should provide news directors with an index for your VNR. This should be in two forms: a printed copy that goes with the support materials, and a copy that's on-screen right at the start of the tape.

Your index should tell the news director whether the tape includes titled and untitled versions of the finished story, describe additional sound bites, and list any cover footage, establishing shots, zoom-ins, and zoom-outs, as well as extra exterior and interior shots. Be sure your video production house includes exact tape locations for everything listed in the index.

Producing a VNR

Producing a broadcast-quality VNR, even an ultrabrief one, entails an astounding number of steps. Tempting as it may be to take shortcuts, particularly if you're working with a tight budget, you can't skip any steps. However, if you understand how the production process works, you *can* cut costs with careful planning.

Shrewd strategizing can make it possible to produce several VNRs from one shoot at a far lower cost than if they were produced individually. For example, you could create VNRs with different news pegs: one version could be hard news, but two others may be evergreen. You could produce one in English and another in Spanish. Or, you could produce longer minifeatures, running up to 10 minutes, from footage taken at the same shoot. But, you probably won't be able to do this unless you plan ahead to get the footage you need for each video version.

The first step in producing a video news release is to develop a concept. This is a rough outline that describes the news peg, the goal for your piece, who will speak, what points the speakers will make, where the tape will be shot, whether you'll be able to cut costs by using any "stock" footage from a film library, what props you'll need, and what types of shots are necessary both for the finished story and for the B-roll. Think of a concept as a starting point, not a blueprint. Your concept will change as you and the production house start work and discover what is possible, what could be done if you had unlimited funds, and what can't be done, even with all the gold in Fort Knox.

The next step is usually handled by the production house. These pros have to check each location indicated in your concept, in order to find or anticipate any problems that could make a shoot impossible. A good location scout will ask and answer questions like these:

- What kind of lighting is called for?
- Are there deep shadows at any time of the day?
- Is there a possible crowd-control or security problem?

- What props will be needed to make studio scenes look real and interesting?
- Are the locations available when you need them?
- Are permits needed?
- What are the user fees for the site, if any?

Once you and your creative team have developed a concept and secured the locations, you can build the concept into the script, including tight descriptions of each shot. The narrator's dialogue should be complete and polished; however, lines for the news makers will depend on each person's style. Some speakers need to be provided with the exact words they'll use on camera. Others do much better with a loose outline. You'll have to find out their preferences.

Be prepared for several meetings with your production house just for this phase of the project. It takes time to do it well, and if your creative team tries to do it without you, you probably won't be satisfied with the results.

Once the script is written, all locations have been arranged for, the props have been bought, rented, or borrowed, and the production house has secured camera and lighting crews, you're ready to shoot. You'll be shooting only the sound bites. The narration will be recorded later, in a sound studio, and added onto the tape.

You should be at the shooting. And don't be surprised if it takes hours and hours to get enough footage for a 90-second finished story plus B-roll. A professional producer will insist on shooting many *takes* for each scene, to make sure that one of them will be perfect. But the time you spend at the shoot will be well worth it. As Margie Goldsmith of MG Productions explains in an article in *Public Relations Business*, "Whenever I shoot, I insist that a company representative be present so the client can have final approval along the way."

Once the tape is shot and *in the can*, you and your producer should view it, before the editing session. Your task is to choose which *take*, or version, of each scene is the best one. As Goldsmith notes in an article in *O'Dwyer's PR Services Report*, editing studios charge by the hour. "It requires a great deal of time to roll back and forth looking for the perfect take . . . and you are paying for every minute of the search," if you do it at the editing studio rather than ahead of time.

When the editing is done, and you have approved the final result, the production house makes two master tapes: one for safekeeping and one to use for duplicating. Then the production house's station relations staff takes over, working with you to develop supporting materials such as backgrounder sheets, names of local contacts for interviews, facts about your story from each local area, and anything else you can think of that will help sell your story. They will also include in the support package a pitch letter that sells your VNR and a timed script.

Finally, you have to decide how you'll distribute your VNR. Unless you want the expense of sending cassettes and support packages to every television station that reaches your target audience, you have two basic choices:

- Have the production house's station relations staff send out an announcement offering the VNR, including all the supporting materials *and* a prepaid reply card the news director can fill out if she wants the cassette. If the production house has a toll-free number, include that, and its E-mail address, as well. When a station asks for the cassette, it's mailed out along with a *second* package of supporting materials, in case the news director has misplaced the first packet. You can also have the station relations staff at the production house call stations that don't respond, but you may want to limit the telephone follow-ups to the most important names on your list.

- You can have the station relations staff make the contacts but offer to send the VNR and B-roll by satellite. If the video production house doesn't have satellite facilities, the staff can work with a dedicated satellite transmission service (see Medialink, which is listed in Chapter 13). Compare costs carefully before you decide if you want to offer stations this option, and be sure to balance the increased cost of satellite transmission against the savings of eliminating multiple cassettes and delivery fees.

Satellite transmission of VNRs is still new enough that it's hard to say if news directors prefer it to traditional practice. One survey (conducted by a satellite transmission facility) shows that they do—overwhelmingly. Another study (conducted by a distributor of videocassettes) concludes that they don't—overwhelmingly. If you're a member of a professional organization for publicists, you may want to compare notes with colleagues who have had experience with each method of transmitting video news releases.

Questions to Ask a Video Production House

The care with which you choose a production house for your video news release can mean the difference between a newsworthy video and a pile of expensive cassettes accumulating dust.

According to an editorial in *Public Relations Journal,* "A growing number of distributors/producers themselves are concerned about suppliers who deal in poor quality VNRs lacking viable news or feature angles. . . . And many feel that there should be a code of ethics for the VNR industry."

If you ask your contact at a video production house the following questions *before* you sign a contract with them, you'll have a better sense of whether they can do an excellent job:

- How many seasoned television newspeople are on staff, and what are their qualifications? It's much more likely you'll get broadcast-quality stories from experienced journalists. With the spate of cutbacks of television news staff in recent years, many highly qualified journalists are now working for video production houses.
- Is all their equipment broadcast quality?
- Can they guarantee that they will meet media deadlines? This is especially important if you plan to use video news releases to announce or respond to breaking news; you may have to produce an entire VNR, from script to placement, in one day.
- Do they have a full-time station relations staff that places VNRs and other publicity material with broadcasters? It takes a lot of work and know-how to place video news releases effectively with television stations, so you should be working with experts. If you have found a really crackerjack production house that doesn't have this capability, you should arrange for one of the larger video news release distributors to place the story for you.
- How often do they update their media contact database? What types of specialized reporters does it include? Can they sort lists of stations geographically and by audience rating? Does their database include information about each station's technical needs?

- What, exactly, is included in their contract? What is extra? Can they guarantee they'll shoot this VNR in one day? Will there be overtime? Under what conditions? How much will it cost?
- Who have they worked for? Can they supply references? Can you see other video news releases they've done? What kind of airplay did their VNRs get, and do they have documentation to prove it?

Audio News Releases for Radio Stations

The radio equivalent to the video news release is the audio news release (ANR). They're not as popular as VNRs, and not all radio stations seem eager to air them. On the other hand, they're relatively inexpensive and quick to produce, and some radio stations, particularly in smaller cities and towns, will be interested in running a timely ANR. Your ANR should last 90 seconds or less and be professionally recorded on audiotape. Any competent sound studio can record it for you.

ANRs start with an announcer introducing the story. Next comes the voice of a news maker, in a sound bite that lasts between 10 and 20 seconds. If your ANR uses more than one sound bite, the announcer provides a transition between each of them. At the end, the announcer sums up the story and adds a tag line ("This is Soanne Soh reporting"). The result sounds just like the typical radio news story.

Broadcast Feature Programs

Video and audio news releases are not the only prerecorded publicity material you can successfully place with broadcasters. You can provide prerecorded programs that run for as long as an hour or as short as a minute or two. Producing them is similar to creating VNRs and ANRs.

"The secret," according to Andrew McGowan of PCS, "is finding a formula for content and format that satisfies your objectives, broadcasters' programming needs, and audience interests. It's easier than you may think: stations are often quite willing to 'barter' airtime for good programming they can get without charge."

McGowan strongly suggests that you offer feature programs on an exclusive basis to one—and only one—broadcaster in each TV or radio market. "What usually characterizes this kind of project, is that the commitment is to a continuing series, most often in one-season (13 week) units, that each station airs on a constant schedule," McGowan says. He gives two examples of successful broadcast feature programs developed by PCS:

- "Trends in Living," a weekly half-hour television show sponsored by the National Association of Realtors, presented studio interviews and stories filmed on location. Topics included urban renewal in Baltimore, high property values near national parklands, and home equity loans. It ran for 13 weeks on 75 stations.
- "A Minute for Health," a radio feature, has been sponsored by pharmaceutical, insurance, and other health care companies. The show covers subjects of concern to the sponsors and names the company in closing credits. It has been given airtime worth an estimated value of $4.6 million by 1,077 radio stations.

James Wexler suggests taking a "library" approach to distributing television feature programs. "Television library programs are made available to broadcast stations and cable systems throughout the country without charge," Wexler explains. Of course, this involves promotional mailings, but once they know about your titles, program directors request the cassettes for preview. If they like what they see, they can decide to use this free loan material in open time slots or as regularly scheduled shows. Once the programs have been aired, the videocassettes are returned to you.

If you choose this course, returned tapes must be inspected for damage and loss of broadcast quality before they are sent out again. You ask how that can happen? The images and sound on videotape are captured in magnetic fields stored in the tape's coating. If the coating is damaged during playback, or the tape is exposed to magnetic fields during shipping and handling, the picture and sound can lose quality—or even disappear in spots. Wexler figures it takes about 50 cassettes per title to make the basis of a library generating 600 showings per year for each program.

Broadcast television stations prefer 5- to 10-minute-long feature programs, whereas cable systems are more interested in 28-minute and 54-minute features that fill half-hour and hour-long slots but leave time for commercials, according to Wexler. "The most usable subjects for free programs are health, sports, entertainment, travel and recreation," he says. "Opening and closing credits are permitted as well as limited sponsor or product exposure during the program."

Since producing features can be expensive, it's a good idea to survey program directors at a sample of your target stations. Get their input after you create a rough concept but before you start scripting. You'll find out quickly if they're interested and whether some changes to your concept could mean your feature will get more airplay.

Community Calendar Listings

Community calendar listings are similar to PSAs except they are used for promoting events, rather than ideas, causes, and services. They usually air for 10 or 15 seconds, although some stations have different formats. In smaller towns and cities, public service directors will need them a week or two ahead of time. In a large metropolis, lead time may be as long as eight weeks.

The following is a 10-second community calendar listing:

> *Learn how to check your home for signs of termites in a free workshop spon-sored by Plains City Real Estate Board at a location near you. For information call (123) 456-7890.*

Television Specials

Some television stations are merely conduits for programs produced else-where and fed to them by the networks or independent producers. Others produce their own programs in their studios. If the station does its own programming, you can ask it to produce a special program about your product, service, cause, or industry. You just have to convince it that you have material that is interesting to its viewers. Pitch to it much the same way you'd pitch a feature story to an editor at a magazine, shifting the emphasis to the visual aspects of your material.

You will increase the impact of a special program if you provide the sta-tion with good visual material. TV people don't like "talking-head" situa-tions where there are no interesting images to relieve the monotony of endless speaking.

The National Association of Broadcasters (NAB) recommends that you check with the producer of the show well in advance of the production date to make sure that your material is the right size, shape, and format for the station and that the technicians will have equipment ready to handle it.

"Simple, uncluttered artwork and photographs televise best," says the NAB. "Care must be taken to assure good contrast. Otherwise, graphics may be lost against the background. Printing should be in bold, heavy lines, with a minimum of words." Black against white is fine; however, pink against yellow will probably look like mud on the screen because of the lack of contrast. Also, "Dull finishes are more satisfactory than glossies that reflect light."

If you're not sure how many words can fit on a TV visual, watch for an advertisement that flashes a telephone number on the screen. Does it fill the screen from side to side? Is it a simple 10-digit number with an area code? Can you see why each line must be limited to 12 letters, numbers, or spaces, and that three or four lines is the limit for each visual?

Television stations want professional-looking material from you. No station is going to jeopardize its technical reputation or risk losing its audience by using sloppy slides, tapes, or visuals. "We are inundated with so many promos for nonprofit organizations that we can be selective. Whether it's for a prime-time program or a PSA, the better it looks, the more chance of getting it on the air," says KSTP-TV's Linnea Crowe. Again, always check technical requirements with the producer or public service director well in advance. This gives your material the best odds for garnering airtime.

Always ask the producer or director whether your visual material can be returned to you. It almost always can be, but usually arrangements must be made ahead of time. Just to be on the safe side, *keep* the original slides, charts, photos, and videotapes. Send duplicates to the station.

When you work with cablecasters, ask if there is studio space and time available to record your programs on videotape. You may be pleasantly surprised. According to the *New York Times,* fledgling producers have increasingly been given access to professional training and facilities by cable operators. If cablecasters do not have studios but will let you provide programs on videotape for transmission over the public access channel, find out the technical requirements before you start the reels rolling. With technology changing so fast, it's not uncommon for cablecasters to have different types of equipment with different media and technical requirements.

What do you do if you need help producing videotapes? Nonprofit or community organizations have some options. First ask the broadcaster or cablecaster for suggestions. You could also contact the communications or broadcast department at your local college. Colleges may welcome the chance to give their students practical experience, and you'll get your program videotaped at little or no cost. You may even find that the school has unusually creative, capable students, and your program may be of professional caliber. If you're not sure whom to talk with, call the public relations department. People there should be glad to help you, especially if you offer to give the college credit for its contribution to your videotape.

If your organization is a business, you should hire a video production house or an advertising agency with television experience to conceptualize, script, and tape the program for you. Sure, that's expensive up front, but you want results. And the results will almost always be far better with a professionally produced television program.

Checklist—Preparing Materials for Broadcast

1. Have you read your material out loud and cut out anything that's difficult to say?
2. Are your sentences short?
3. Have you avoided having too many "s" sounds?
4. Is it clear what the words *she*, *he*, and *they* refer back to?
5. If you have any homonyms (words that sound alike but have different meanings), such as *night* versus *knight*, is the meaning clear from the context?
6. Is each broadcast news release on a separate piece of 8½-by-11-inch paper?
7. Does your news release heading include your organization's name and address; the date; the name, telephone number, pager number, cell phone number, and E-mail address of a contact person; and the reading time in seconds?
8. Is your release typed, double-spaced, on one side of the sheet only? Is it no longer than 90 seconds? Have you considered sending several shorter versions as well?
9. Have you used the present tense and rounded out numbers?
10. Have you spelled out in phonetics any names that are difficult to pronounce?
11. Have you found out which news directors prefer releases in outline form?

12. Have you asked if the station has policies about PSAs? Do you know what format and length stations prefer and if they use tapes, "live" copy, or both?

13. Have you thought about how your business or trade association can present information in PSAs that serves community interests and meets your goals at the same time?

14. Have you considered underwriting PSAs for a nonprofit organization that could help you meet your goals?

15. Can you come up with a creative way to work your product mention into the heart of a sponsored PSA?

16. Have you given the public service director a choice of two or three lengths for your PSA?

17. If you're producing prerecorded PSAs, are they exactly 10, 15, 20, 30, or 60 seconds long?

18. Have you made sure there is no sound in the first and last half-seconds?

19. Have you asked your local stations if they will help you produce your PSAs?

20. Have you checked with public service directors to find out the stations' technical requirements for PSAs?

21. If you are producing prerecorded PSAs, do you have rights to use the music and sound effects?

22. Have you sent a script or a storyboard with the spot?

23. Have you considered sending out a script and prepaid request card, rather than massive numbers of prerecorded PSAs?

24. Have you checked with the producer to see whether the spot will be shot on film, videotape, or videocassette?

25. Who will distribute your taped PSAs, and how will the distributor know which format each station prefers?

26. Does the distributor have an up-to-date station information database?

27. Do you know which stations use live copy for PSAs?

28. Do you know what stations' requirements are for visual material?

29. Have you timed your live-copy scripts to fit common time slots?

30. Have you included visual material with your live copy for TV PSAs?

31. Do you have one slide for each 5 to 10 seconds, and are the slides all horizontal?

32. Do you know whether your target stations insist on glass-mounted slides, or if they'll accept cardboard or plastic mounts?

33. Have you checked which parts of the images in your slides will be cut off around the edges?
34. If you are sending out a script-slide PSA, does the script describe each slide?
35. Have you numbered the slides and keyed them to the script?
36. If you're involved in a nonprofit organization, have you found out if public service directors in your area require copies of fund-raising permits and your IRS tax-status letter?
37. Have you thought about increasing station acceptance of your PSAs by not mentioning fund-raising directly?
38. Does your PSA heading include a contact person and telephone number with the area code, an E-mail address, the date, an expiration date, the reading time, and the number of words?
39. Did you list the *w*s and the *h* before you started writing your PSA spot?
40. Is your spot double- or triple-spaced and typed in upper- and lower-case with 35-character lines and wide margins?
41. Have you taken into account that your audience will probably be doing something else besides just listening and watching?
42. How will you grab audience interest immediately?
43. Have you limited your PSA to one main point?
44. Have you avoided borrowed interest in your PSA?
45. Have you closed by asking people to take an action?
46. Can you back up the facts, figures, and claims in your PSA?
47. If your organization's name is long, can you suggest an official alternative?
48. Do you let the draft of your PSA sit overnight before you edit it?
49. Have you cut out extra words, particularly adjectives?
50. Have you planned your video shoot so you can get as much use from the taped material as possible?
51. Is your video news release as objective as a news story?
52. Does it look and sound like a news report?
53. Is it 90 seconds or shorter?
54. Can you shorten it even more by putting some of the material into a backgrounder?
55. Have you identified your organization as the source of the news?
56. Have you entwined mention of your product or service with the news peg?

57. Have you established a problem, solved it with your product or service, and drawn a conclusion?
58. Have you provided suggestions for localizing your VNR?
59. Can you shoot all or part of your VNR on location?
60. If all or part of your VNR must be shot in a studio, can you use props and stage settings to make it look as if it's shot on location?
61. Have you trained your spokespeople to talk in 10- to 20-second units?
62. Has your production house kept the sound bites and narration on separate tracks?
63. Have you included one version of the edited story without any titles on it?
64. Have you made sure your narrator never appears on screen?
65. Have you planned your B-roll before you shoot?
66. Does your B-roll include extra sound bites; establishing, static, zoom-in, and zoom-out shots; as well as cover footage?
67. Have you included an index at the start of the tape and enclosed a printed copy with the support materials?
68. Have you developed a detailed concept and a script before you start shooting?
69. Do you know whether your spokespeople need tight scripts or prefer loose guidelines?
70. Have you rented or bought any props you'll need?
71. Have you scouted for locations?
72. Has your producer looked at lighting and crowd control considerations for each location?
73. Do you have permits and reservations for locations where they're needed?
74. Is there any "stock" footage you can use to cut your shooting costs?
75. Will you and any other executives from your organization who need to give approval be present at the shoot?
76. Have you arranged to view the raw footage to choose the best takes before the editing session?
77. Will you be at the editing session so you can give your approval at each stage and help cut costs by speeding up the process?
78. Has your production house made both a dubbing master for duplicating copies and a second master for safekeeping?
79. Does the support package sent out to news directors include a timed script, background material, and a pitch letter?

80. Have you decided whether you want to distribute your VNR by mailing cassettes or by satellite? Have you compared costs for these two distribution methods?

81. Have you asked each video production house you're considering how many seasoned television people are on staff?

82. Is the production house's equipment all of broadcast quality?

83. Can the producers guarantee they'll meet media deadlines, particularly with breaking news?

84. Do they have a full-time station relations staff? If they don't, will they be comfortable working with one of the larger video houses that also distribute VNRs and do have this staff?

85. How often do they update their media contact database?

86. What types of information does the database include?

87. What, exactly, is included in the contract? Under what conditions will there be extra or overtime charges?

88. Have you considered creating radio and television feature programs?

89. Do you understand the difference between PSAs and community calendar listings?

90. Have you asked about the technical requirements for visual aids for TV special programs?

91. Do you know if your visual materials can be returned to you?

92. Do you have duplicates just in case?

93. Do your visuals have good, sharp contrast? Are they bold and uncluttered?

94. Have you limited typeset visuals to four lines of 12 characters each?

95. Do your visuals have a dull, nonreflecting finish?

96. Does your local cablecaster have studios you can use? Technical help? Editing equipment? Are there fees involved?

9

How to Work Effectively with Broadcasters

O nce you have mastered the art of writing for broadcast and preparing good visuals for different types of TV formats, you will need to understand how to approach broadcasters most effectively.

Americans listen to an average of three hours of radio every day. And 98 percent of the homes in this country have at least one television set. The average household's TV viewing time has jumped to more than seven hours a day. There are 14,321 radio and television stations licensed by the Federal Communications Commission (FCC), as well as 2,194 low-power TV stations, 10,466 cablecasters, and 214 cable networks. That adds up to a huge potential audience for your organization's publicity. All you have to do is produce interesting, newsworthy, informative material and persuade journalists to air it.

Whether you are approaching your local radio or television station, cablecasters, or the networks, you need to consider what kinds of airtime are generally available and which formats will work best for you.

In the previous chapter you learned how to prepare material for the PSA format, as well as for community calendar listings, newscasts, and short features. This chapter discusses how to reach the right people with your material and how to obtain other types of airtime involving live appearances.

Seven general types of airtime are available to publicists:

- **News broadcasts.** Most radio and television stations have news programs, and broadcast news has become more influential. Station executives have found that while producing news reports is relatively low-cost, they increase listener and viewer ratings. "In some markets," according to *O'Dwyer's PR Services Report,* "local stations are now generating two and a half hours of news daily, in addition to carrying the network evening news. In many U.S. TV markets today, these local shows account for 40 to 50 percent or more of stations' profit." To place your publicity material on news programs, contact the news director or the assignment director at larger stations. If the station has morning talk shows that include news segments, find out who handles those. It may be someone on the talk show staff, rather than the station's news director. To supply publicity material to news directors, you can send written material, audiotapes, or videocassettes—or use the telephone to make "live" reports or transmit taped audio news releases to radio stations.
- **Short features running from 1 minute to 10 minutes.** Short features may be of interest to public service directors and program directors, as well as news departments at stations with longer newscasts. But be careful: if you send the same pitch to two or more journalists at the same station, and more than one is interested, you have an embarrassing problem. They can't all cover the story, so you'll have to take it away from one (or more) of them. That's not healthy for your working relationships. Approach one person at a time, and if he isn't interested, try another. You can also try to get a station to produce a short feature itself, or offer to supply a finished program on audio- or videotape.
- **Special programs.** Longer than features, entire shows devoted to your organization can run for 15, 30, or 60 minutes. Your material may fit into a series with a regular time slot and host, or the station may create a single program especially for your organization or cause. KGW-TV in Portland, Oregon, for example, has produced specials on preventive health care, myths about rape victims, and heating with woodstoves. Special programs may range from two-

or three-minute miniprograms repeated several times during the week, to full-fledged, hour-long, in-depth documentaries. Bear in mind that even half an hour is a lot of time to fill, and an hour can stretch from here to eternity. If you have never been on the air before, start small. Ask to be on one of the shorter programs, or see if you can share a special program with one or two other organizations. Always try to limit the length of special programs so that you end before the audience is satisfied. Then they'll be more interested in seeing your activity in person, getting more information, or listening to you next time you're on the air. Your pitch for a special program should be made to the station's program director.

- **Talk and interview shows.** Since talk shows are always looking for interesting guests, they are a great way to get your message to the world. It is much easier to arrange an appearance on a talk or interview show, whether live, by telephone, or by satellite, than it is to set up a special program or a short feature. Like specials, talk shows are effective when you want to present a long, detailed message. Arrange your appearance by calling the talent bookers for the shows that interest you. (Several of the media directories discussed in Chapter 13 include listings of talent bookers.) Your appearance can be in person, on videotape, or via satellite tour for television, or in person or by telephone for radio talk shows. Find out which methods are acceptable to each show's talent booker, and then figure out the best approach for you.

- **Free-speech messages or guest editorials.** Individuals or groups can offer broadcasters opinions on major public controversies. You will probably record the message at the station in your own voice. Many stations that run editorials encourage organizations with opposing viewpoints to record replies. These formats are useful to alert your community to a problem or to take a stand in an ongoing debate. You should contact the station's editorial director to make your request.

- **Public service announcements.** PSAs are the easiest kind of airtime to get. Your approach here should be through the station's public service director. Businesses, as well as nonprofit organizations and trade associations, have all successfully used PSAs to get their messages to the public. Specific hints for placing PSAs are discussed later in the chapter.

■ **Community calendar listings.** Calendar placements are handled in much the same way as public service announcements. They're generally available only to nonprofit and community organizations, but businesses can sometimes be listed if the event is free and serves the public interest. Unless you're contacting a very large station with a staff person assigned to handling community calendar announcements, you should send your listings to the public service director.

Compiling Broadcast Data

One of your first tasks as a publicist is to put together a list of broadcasters and cablecasters that serve your area. Your list should include the following:

■ Names of public service directors.
■ Names of talent bookers for talk shows.
■ Names of news directors.
■ Names and formats of locally originated programs.
■ Deadlines and lead times for these programs.
■ Lead times for PSAs and community calendar items.
■ Each station's format requirements for PSAs, video news releases, and audio news releases.

Drawing up this list will be a pretty easy job in rural areas and small towns, but if you live in a large city, it can be complicated. Remember, stations in other cities and even other states may serve your area, and programs run on network and cable television may originate in cities thousands of miles away. Check to see if the TV listings in your local paper include any helpful information, and supplement this by consulting *TV Guide* and the yellow pages. The media directories listed in Chapter 13 will help you round out the information for your local area, or plan a national campaign. Most large libraries have at least one of these directories.

Call the public service directors at the largest stations serving your area and ask for lists of locally originated programs the stations produce. Ask if the stations offer tours of their studios, and if they do, take one at the first opportunity. It will help you understand how broadcast journalists work.

If your organization is a nonprofit one, you could also call the local United Way office to see if the group sells a local media list. The information will be well worth the price if it's available.

You will have to update your list continually. Media people move from job to job at an astounding speed, and even radio stations have been known to suddenly change their formats and their call letters, or to disappear from the airwaves entirely. In cable TV, growth is so rapid and changes so frequent that you'll need a second set of toes, since you'll always be on them. A channel that was empty yesterday may be filled tomorrow with 24-hour satellite-beamed newscasts—or locally originated programs.

Selecting Suitable Stations

A publicist who wants to place material on a station he doesn't listen to or watch should become familiar with that station first. How do you become familiar with stations across the country when you're working on nationally oriented publicity? There are three ways.

One is to familiarize yourself with the program descriptions provided in some of the more complete media directories.

The second technique is more involved. Hire a clipping bureau to provide you with transcripts, audiotapes, or videotapes of programs that you absolutely *must* appear on. (The larger clipping bureaus listed in Chapter 13 offer this service.) When you're pitching your idea to a news or program director on the other coast, he should be impressed if you're familiar with the content and format of some recent programs on his station. If you work for an organization that doesn't have such a large budget, try to get volunteers, dealers, or distributors in your selected cities to tape the programs you're targeting.

The third method is to visit the station's website. The content of broadcaster websites varies widely. Some stations will have actual Webcasts of some of their programs. Others may have their shows archived, so you can download and view or listen to them. Even if you can't view or listen to shows on the station's website, you should still be able to get a good feeling for the station's approaches, interests, policies, and audience.

You have to decide whether you want to approach your audience via TV or radio. Your choice will depend on the particular message and the type of audience you want to reach. There are important differences between radio and television audiences. For instance, morning and evening "drive time," when people are commuting to and from work, is when most folks listen to the radio. After dinner, Americans switch their allegiance to TV, and radio's audience gets much smaller. Of course, broadcast TV reaches a broad audience, while radio stations and cablecasters are often more selective. By choosing a particular type of radio station or cablecaster, you can aim your publicity at teenagers, young adults, people over age 40, African Americans, people with a Hispanic background, opinion makers, and other defined groups.

The most popular commercial radio format is country music, with more than 2,300 stations playing it in the United States. There are 1,131 stations with a news/talk/business format, 844 devoted to adult contemporary music, 799 that play oldies, 561 where adult standards rule the airwaves, and 493 Spanish-language broadcasters. Religious and southern gospel stations are another large group, with 629 in that category. Although only a comparative handful of commercial stations play classical music (40) and jazz (88), many public radio stations also program these types of music.

You will improve your audience targeting results even further if you can get some of the demographic material that many stations prepare for potential advertisers. For example, it may tell you how many women listeners work outside the home, the average age of the audience, and how much the typical listener earns. Although you won't usually be able to specify the time of day your "live" copy will be used, you can select talk shows to target based on demographic information and the differences among audiences at various times of day. Ask public service directors if they can supply you with any demographic material for their stations. If they cannot, ask if there is somebody in the station's advertising department who can. Make your request as specific as possible.

Let's say you want to reach retired people with a PSA about your anti-crime program that provides escorts for older Americans who have to walk alone at night. Even if the station does not have a neat packet of demographic information, it will probably be able to tell you what portion of its audience is over age 65. You may be surprised when you find out which stations older people tune in to. Or suppose your company has just launched a line of products for new mothers. Although none of the stations in your target area may be able to tell you how many of their listeners are women with newborns, you will be able to eliminate stations with audiences that are too old.

Some stations try to reach a broad audience, but even they may be willing to use some PSAs that appeal to a segment of their listeners. "Because we air at least 230 spots per week, some of these spots are geared to specific communities," says WCBS-AM's Teresa DiTore. "We focus on smaller communities because I think people out there like to hear their communities mentioned. But we need a nice mix of things that appeal to everybody and things that appeal to one particular segment."

Working with Public Service Directors

Public service directors are sometimes more willing than reporters, editors, and news directors to talk with new publicists about the station's needs and preferences, and about where a particular organization fits in. Says Mary Jane O'Neill of the New York Association for the Blind, "It's important to know the public service directors on radio and television. The better you know them, and the better they know the organization you're promoting, the more apt you are to get your material aired."

Public service directors work in a pressured world surrounded by nonstop deadlines. A typical public service director may also double as the station's editorial director and speechwriter, as well as host and producer of a couple of talk shows. This same person may also assist with the overall direction of the public affairs department, all without any clerical assistance. Each day, a typical public service director receives piles of mail and dozens of telephone calls. Therefore, when you call a public service director, be brief and to the point. Always ask if it is a good time to talk; if it isn't, offer to call back at a better time. Never just drop in and expect the person to have time to chat with you.

The public service director, as the name implies, is your prime contact for public service material, particularly for PSAs and community calendar listings. But she doesn't run the news department. So, don't send your news releases to the public service director and assume that she will ease your way into the newsroom. She probably won't, because she doesn't have the time.

Determining a Station's PSA Policies

First of all, ask the public service director if the station has any special policies regarding PSAs. In addition to basic information about format, length, and lead time required, find out if the station prefers a particular angle or approach. Although many broadcasters will use taped copy and will read "live" copy as it is written, some stations handle PSAs differently. "We use fact sheets that the individual announcers play around with so they sound different each time they're read," says Ken Barlow, public service director for KOFM Radio in Oklahoma City.

"Our station is 'personality' oriented, and our [announcers] have more influence on people in this area than [the celebrities] they send out on tape. I rarely use the script that is sent in, preferring to adapt it to fit the individual personality's style," explains Harry O'Toole, public service director for KDKA-AM in Pittsburgh.

In some areas, stations will use PSAs for one-time events. In other cities, PSAs are reserved for ongoing programs and information efforts, while single events are covered in a community events calendar. At KGW-TV in Portland, Oregon, for example, PSAs usually run for three months. The length of PSA usage may even vary from station to station in your hometown, so when you talk with public service directors, ask about the policy for single events.

Be sure to find out how much lead time the station needs for PSAs. West Glen's James Wexler explains, "Public service directors usually need one or two weeks to screen a spot and another one to two weeks to schedule it. For example, a spot intended for airing the beginning of August should be in the mail by mid-June to allow time for shipping and previewing."

If your PSAs are going to use a public figure, make sure the person doesn't plan to run for public office during the life of the PSAs, because broadcasters will be reluctant to air them for fear of facing "equal-time" requirements. "PCS Broadcast Services was set to distribute a campaign on thyroid disease, featuring George and Barbara Bush when he was president and right after his thyroid disease was in the news," says Andrew McGowan. "Because of the President's busy schedule, shooting was delayed, and I warned the client that we were getting close to the time when Mr. Bush would run for re-election. But they had no choice but to wait for their important spokesperson, and the Presidential campaign was beginning when the spots were released. Many stations said they couldn't air the spots because of the 'equal time' requirement, but, surprisingly, some stations did air the spots."

If your organization is going to use a spokesperson, check and double-check to make sure he or she doesn't have secret political ambitions which could knock you out of the water. In addition to political candidates, "You should also beware of using TV, radio, and movie personalities in your spots. They could be linked, permanently or temporarily, with a particular TV or radio station. If that's the case, the other broadcasters will not use your spots," says public relations executive Ravelle Brickman.

Mailing PSAs

Mail delivery of PSAs is not as effective as working directly with public service directors, but the results can still be worthwhile. There will be times when you will not be able to use the personal approach to public service directors because you are sending out too many spots or mailing them to stations in other cities and states.

When you mail PSAs, be sure to include a brief cover letter. Explain why the event or service or campaign is important, how it meets the needs of people in the station's area, and when it is taking place. Mention the type of audience you're seeking and the time during which you would like the spots to air.

A cover letter to a public service director may look like the example in Exhibit 9.1 on page 308.

If you intend to use professionally prerecorded spots, you may not have a budget large enough to send cassettes to every station on your list. Instead, screen broadcasters to make sure they're interested before you send them the tape. Screening takes a lot of work, according to an article by Margie Goldsmith in *Public Relations Journal.* For a small national campaign, "The follow-up will probably need full-time attention: preferably two full-time people per spot, to telephone public service directors. You will average between three and eight telephone calls per station, and it will take one person two to three weeks, full-time, to contact 200 stations."

A more cost-effective alternative to screening is used by Andrew McGowan:

> *When an organization wants to get exposure on more television outlets than they can afford to send tape to, I often use a plan I call "tape to the best, query the rest." I select between 100 and 500 of the country's 1,000 plus television sta-*

Exhibit 9.1

Dear Public Service Director:

Many people are getting married later in life these days, and women are becoming mothers in their late 30s and early 40s. Although most older women have no problems with pregnancy, there is an increased risk their babies will have Down's syndrome. This disease, which causes mental retardation and other problems in the infant, can be detected by using a quick diagnostic test on pregnant women over the age of 35.

When the expectant mother knows the results of the test, she can make an informed decision about whether to continue the pregnancy. During the next six months, a grant from the Louise Jones Foundation will make it possible for the Plains City Women's Health Center to offer this test, at no cost, to any pregnant woman in her first trimester who is over age 35. There is no residency requirement.

Enclosed are 20-, 30-, and 60-second PSAs explaining this service. We would very much appreciate your running these spots until December 31. It would also be helpful to us if you could use the enclosed stamped and addressed reply card to let us know when and how often the spots are used.

We think we've covered the bases in this letter, the PSAs themselves, and the enclosed background sheets, but if you have questions, please call us or go to our website, www.ljf.chl. Many thanks for your help.

---

tions, based on the size of their audiences and their track record in using previous PSAs (as measured by electronic monitoring of campaigns I distributed and tracked previously). Those stations are sent tapes. All other appropriate stations are sent a "query," or offer mailing, consisting of a letter pitching the campaign, a photoboard of the spots, and a business-reply card for ordering the tape. (When a photoboard is printed for this purpose, it is included in the tape packages to the "best" as well.) If a photoboard, which is printed with frames captured from the PSA tape in full color, is too expensive for an organization, I may use a storyboard—with drawings instead of pictures and printed in black—or a typed script.

McGowan's "tape to the best, query the rest" method usually results in 15 percent to 20 percent of the queried stations asking for the spots. If your campaign is a small, local or regional one, but sending tape to all outlets is still not possible, McGowan suggests using the phone to screen, check format preferences and other requirements, and find out to whom the packages should be addressed.

Placing PSAs to Best Advantage

When deciding where to send your PSAs, you must differentiate between commercial and educational stations, and between local and national coverage.

PSAs are run on virtually every commercial radio and TV station, according to the National Association of Broadcasters. James Wexler notes that his firm's research shows PSAs are actually needed to fill these open slots because most stations simply can't sell all the commercial time they have scheduled.

Although a lot of unsold commercial time will be available during off-peak listening hours, PSAs are aired around the clock, including prime time. During January, February, and the summer months, when fewer paid commercials are running, there is more time for PSAs than during the rest of the year.

Since public radio and TV stations don't run advertising, they do not have unfilled advertising slots, and as a result, some of them don't run as many PSAs as the commercial stations.

Local PSAs often have an advantage over nationally oriented spots. Broadcasters know that their audience is interested in local community events, problems, issues, and information, so running local PSAs is good for the station's ratings. If you can localize a national PSA campaign, you'll almost certainly increase your total airtime. Andrew McGowan describes a way to do this: "We have at times arranged for sponsorship by local affiliates [of the national organization sponsoring the PSA], tagged the spots with their names and word-processed cover letters on their stationery to each public service director by name. Or we asked stations to add the local tag (space was left for it on the spots) from a list of affiliates we supplied."

Broadcasters in the smaller cities and towns desperately need PSAs, so this is where many national organizations will want to place their emphasis. "We get smaller stations writing to us all the time asking if we can send them spots," says McGowan. "They don't sell as much commercial time, and they have more time available, but the number of organizations looking for them is smaller."

On the other hand, broadcasters in large cities are swamped with requests to run PSAs, and even though the average commercial station runs more than 200 spots each week, many more are rejected. Jim Dressier, public service director at KEZX-FM in Seattle, estimates that he uses half of the 300 spots he gets each week. Some stations are able to use only one-fifth or one-tenth of the spots publicists send them. So, if your organization is trying to run PSAs in large cities, be prepared to compete for airtime with first-rate spots.

How many spots do you have to send out to blanket the nation with your message? For a national PSA campaign, plan on sending your spots to at least 200 stations to have an impact, according to Margie Goldsmith of MG Productions. If you send out fewer PSAs, your efforts will be spread too thin.

Monitoring PSA Coverage

How do you find out if and when your PSAs were used? One way is to listen to or watch the station, but you may not be tuned in when your spot graces the airwaves. And this won't work when you're handling a national PSA campaign.

If your PSA is a good one, of interest to the audience, you may notice that your telephone lines are jammed and sacks of mail crowd your office. In fact, offering free information, particularly if you include a toll-free number in your spot, is a very handy way to track PSA usage. But not all PSAs, even some fine ones, are designed to produce tidal waves of telephone calls and mammoth mail deliveries. Since there is no direct response to the spots, it is a challenge to track their usage.

Some of the larger stations will automatically let you know when and how often your spot was used. "I choose the PSAs, and they are entered in our records," says KNBR's Gimmy Park-Li. "I make certain they are used during different times of the day. Since we recognize that many nonprofit organizations can benefit by reporting them as in-kind contributions, we send them a letter telling them how many were run and what their approximate market value is."

Smaller broadcasters don't have the staff and computer facilities to keep track of PSAs, so don't expect every public service director to drop you a note telling you when your spots were used. Instead, you can use several other means to try to find out exactly who used your spot:

- The least expensive means to track PSA usage is to include a stamped, self-addressed postcard with each spot. Type the name of the spot and the call letters of the station on the card, so all the public service director has to do is check off a box or two. Most will take the time to fill out such a card and mail it to you. Using a word processor, creating personalized postcards is a snap.
- Have one of the larger video production houses distribute the spot for you. They have the staff to follow up on your campaign by telephone and mail, and a production house's report can tell you the number of stations using the spot, how many times it aired, the estimated audience size, and the approximate dollar value of the time donated by broadcasters.

Working with Newscasters

Many radio station news departments have one full-time person, and a part-time assistant, if they're lucky. Some stations have no full-time news staff at all. As a rule, the larger the city and the station, the larger the news staff, and in metropolitan areas where the population is more than one million, the usual radio news staff includes several full-timers.

Try to imagine what it is like to run a news operation all by yourself—while handling other duties as well—and you'll begin to understand what many radio newscasters are up against and why they need material that fits their format without rewriting.

Since news staffers move continually from job to job, you will have to keep your contact list updated and your ear to the ground. If you hear rumblings that your favorite newsperson is about to move on, be ready to greet his replacement, quickly let the new person know who you are, and tell him how you can help him. Offer to fill him in on the local scene, since he might have just arrived from out of town.

Remember that many radio news directors are interested only in local news. They use network and wire service material to cover the national scene.

Television news shows are usually longer than their radio counterparts, and the average TV news staff is bigger. The larger the city, the larger the news staff, with some stations in major metropolitan areas employing dozens of people in their newsrooms.

In some large cities, broadcasters want all the news in writing, and to them you should submit standard broadcast news releases as described in the previous chapter. But in many places, you can call the newsroom and read a statement over the telephone that will be taped for broadcast. (This is more common for radio, less usual for TV.) News directors will be more receptive to phoned-in news if they are familiar with your organization. However, the telephone approach may be fruitful anyway, if you have an interesting story, if you sound coherent and reliable, and if they can check the facts.

If you call after hours or on weekends, when the station's switchboard is closed, you will need the number for the direct line to the assignment editor. (Some of the media directories listed under Chapter 13 include these direct telephone numbers, but you can probably get them yourself simply by asking.)

Unless you have developed a working relationship with a particular reporter, calls and written material for broadcast news shows should be directed to the news assignment editor. At some larger stations, where reporters have specialty areas, such as consumer affairs, business, or environment, contact the specialists directly, rather than the assignment editor.

Whenever you call a broadcast newsroom, assume that you are being taped. "We let them know we're taping. And we don't tape unless we're going to use it on the air," says Ralph Graczak, news director for KRAE-AM in Cheyenne, Wyoming. Still, there may be newspeople who won't bother to tell you that the reels are already rolling.

You can help get the tape recorder started by sounding professional and authoritative. Introduce yourself, state the essence of your story in three dozen words or fewer, and then ask if the journalist wants to run a voice-level test. This test, based on a sample sentence or two of your speech, gives the journalist time to adjust the sound equipment to your voice, so you won't sound too soft and fuzzy or loud and harsh on the air.

It is a good idea to write out your story before you call it in. Even a practiced speaker can become tongue-tied or can repeat material when ad-libbing on the telephone. Try to state the essence of your story in no more than 20 seconds. Practice it out loud, using rising and falling inflections, so it sounds as though you are speaking instead of reading.

When you have finished reading your statement, be prepared for the editor or reporter to ask you questions. Try to anticipate these questions before you make the call, and write out your answers. If you notice that the reporter asks the same question more than once, he is probably trying to get a briefer, more interesting, more quotable statement from you. If you can come right to the point, you increase the chances that your story will include your own words on the air and that your statements won't be heavily edited.

You can even prepare a taped, audio news release ahead of time, call radio stations with your pitch, and feed it to interested news directors over the phone. Andrew McGowan says that audio news releases are especially helpful when, for example, your organization is sponsoring a conference at which newsworthy statements will be made, but obtaining broadcast coverage from distant broadcasters would be difficult. In that case, McGowan advises, "You arrange for key speakers to be interviewed early in the conference or a few days before. Their statements are recorded, edited, and, with an announcer's intro and bridges, turned into one or more complete radio stories under one minute in length. Then newsrooms at radio networks and individual stations are called and offered the story, which can be fed to their recorders in the same telephone connection." McGowan says that such stories cost about $4,500 to produce and place with newsrooms covering 2,000 to 3,000 or more stations.

In addition to symposia and conferences, McGowan suggests the following applications for audio news releases:

- New product announcements.
- Survey or study results.
- Tie-ins with holidays or events.
- Statements on controversial issues.

When you approach a TV news director or reporter, tell her if the story has visual possibilities. If your Lions Club picnic will feature a brightly colored hot-air balloon, be sure to mention it when you call. Visual potential is powerful bait for TV news staffers.

Whether you are calling radio or TV newsrooms, do not approach them near deadline time. For TV, avoid the hour just before a news show. If the radio station you're calling has an hourly news program, the best time to talk with the news director is immediately after the show.

Even though radio and TV are "instant" forms of communication, broadcasters need lead time. This is especially true with TV news. "Get the damn thing here early enough!" says KGW-TV's Larry Badger. "That's the number one priority. Even if you have to say 'Hold for release tomorrow.' But get it here so we can read it, and we can decide whether it's newsworthy, if we want to send a video crew to cover it on location, and how we're going to cover the story."

Pitching Video News Releases

When you pitch a video news release (VNR) to a television news director, always consider how journalists feel about this news vehicle. "VNRs are a sensitive topic at stations," according to *O'Dwyer's PR Services Report.* "They will usually admit to only the most guarded use of footage from outside suppliers and in some cases actually deny such usage even though they have done so." Yet, 73 percent of the television news directors responding to a Medialink survey said they use as many as 10 VNRs per month, while only 27 percent reported they never use them. And for B-roll usage, the figures are even more interesting. West Glen found that 93 percent of the stations it surveyed use B-roll materials from publicists to produce stories.

Why would news directors say they *never* use VNRs, when they actually air them? Because news production budgets are being cut as broadcasters seek to fatten their bottom lines, but news shows are increasingly important profit generators, so they are being expanded. This means news directors are caught between the proverbial rock and a hard place. Journalists want to maintain their independence and write their own stories, but they don't always have the resources they need.

Based on West Glen's findings, this trend should continue. Twenty-seven percent of stations responding predicted they will increase their use of VNRs in the future. Half of those said that they would use more VNRs because they had more news programming to fill, while 25 percent cited the high quality of the footage on VNRs.

Instead of reminding journalists of this dilemma, present your VNR in a way that makes it so newsworthy that they can't resist it. James Wexler points to four factors to stress when presenting your VNR to journalists:

- The information is of interest and importance to their local viewers.
- The desired footage exists only on the tape you are sending.

- The material can't be easily produced locally.
- It has a *real* news peg.

While the last point may sound obvious, it isn't. In West Glen's survey of news directors and assignment editors, 75 percent of respondents said they feel that "Most VNRs do not contain a good news angle."

What kind of airplay can you expect for your VNR? That depends on your news peg, the topic, and even the newsmakers on your tape (well-known celebrities and politicians will increase the usage). You're also competing with other breaking news events, which can't be predicted.

It seems that each person in the VNR field has a different estimate of how many viewers can be reached with a video release:

- "If you can reach an audience of three to four million viewers—that's Nielsen or Arbitron viewers, not some pipe dream of viewers, but numbers of people who actually watch local news and talk shows—you've done a good job," according to a major supplier quoted in *Public Relations Journal.*
- Based on her experience, Margie Goldsmith says, "On a two hundred station release, we anticipate at least 80 telecasts with an estimated reach of from 2,500,000 to 3,500,000 viewers."
- According to the Nielsen Research survey conducted for Medialink, "The average VNR is seen by more than one million viewers in 20 markets, with a large number reaching a far larger audience."

Getting accurate usage figures for video news releases is always a challenge. According to *Public Relations Journal,* "For the many suppliers who strive to produce accurate usage reports, definitive monitoring remains a major problem, largely because getting and verifying the information from stations is so difficult." So, if you're relying on usage figures supplied by a VNR distributor, be sure you understand exactly how they are calculated.

Also, not all stations will use your entire VNR. "If a station uses 30 seconds of your story . . . re-edits your story or cuts its own story from the B-roll . . . that means they thought your story was worth their time . . . That's quite a compliment," says James Wexler. They used as much material as they could in the available airtime.

Sixty-four percent of news directors surveyed by West Glen said they are inclined to edit their own stories from VNR footage, and almost half would substitute their own reporter's voice for the voice in the prepared video news story.

Unless your video news release is about breaking news, you have to give news directors enough lead time to schedule your story. Forty-four percent of the news directors responding to the West Glen survey said they prefer a two-week lead time; 20 percent need three weeks.

Before the VNR is even produced, you can start by mailing news directors a "warm-up" pitch. Here's what to include:

- A backgrounder.
- A letter selling the story.
- Biographical sketches of spokespeople or news makers who will appear in the story.
- Localization ideas.
- A description of the B-roll contents.
- A printed copy of an advance story that can be read as "live" copy on the air.

Plan to make extra copies of this support material to send out, *again*, with the cassettes. Busy news directors may, with even the best intentions, misplace or throw out the supporting material. Make it easy for them by sending a duplicate set.

Let journalists know that you'll follow up, but also include a prepaid reply card, an E-mail address, and a toll-free number, if possible. If the VNR will be an evergreen, say so. If it won't, let them know how long it will stay fresh.

If you will be transmitting your VNR by satellite, there are two steps your distributor should follow beforehand, according to Medialink's Laurence Moskowitz:

- Transmit an advisory note to news directors, preferably using a news wire service. "The advisory should contain the basics—the key elements of the story, background and description of the visuals, editorial and technical contacts, satellite coordinates, and date and time of transmission," says Moskowitz. It should also specify "the visual elements of the VNR, including . . . B-roll . . . graphics and how long the self-contained VNR runs. List the people featured in the VNR and why they are important."
- "A few hours before the satellite transmission, Medialink transmits the script [by] newswire, along with a suggested anchor lead. The

text of the VNR script is on the right hand side of the page, and the visual description on the left. This helps producers select elements from the VNR as they watch it being recorded at the station from the satellite [feed]."

Approaching the Networks

You've just come home from your Rotary Club's planning meeting for Flag Day. After your nighttime cup of tea, you don your pajamas, turn off the light, and climb into bed. You toss. You turn. But no matter which way you arrange yourself, you can't get the thought out of your mind: "Can't we get network radio and TV coverage? After all, we're going to make the biggest American flag ever sewn, and we're going to hang it from the Marigold River Bridge. Sure, they did that in New York, but our flag is going to be twice as large as the one they hung from the Verrazano Narrows Bridge. Gee! If I only knew how to get to the networks."

It's not hard. Yes, there will be more competition than at your local stations. Your material will have to be more interesting, newsworthy, and unusual. And it will have to be of interest to a national audience. But relax! Approaching the networks involves the same skills as approaching local stations.

Sometimes an organization gets network coverage without even trying. If your material is covered by a network affiliate, or by the local Associated Press or United Press International broadcast bureau, you may find that the story has gone out over the wires before you can say "Jack Robinson."

You can, of course, try to help the process along. Some of the media directories listed in Chapter 13 will supply the information you need. Once you have the name, address, and telephone number of the network public service director, news assignment editor, specialized reporter, or talent booker for a talk or interview show, write or call him and make your presentation.

Making Live Appearances

You've flipped through some media directories and discovered dozens of talk and interview shows bouncing through the airwaves in your town. It looks as though your organization will fit right in, and you can't imagine why you didn't think of this before. You're so excited, you wish you had two telephones and you could talk out of both sides of your mouth in order to contact twice as many producers. Your finger is poised over the telephone, ready to start. Cut! Hold it! You've left out part of the script.

Before you approach radio and TV stations, you have to figure out exactly what your objective is for this interview or talk show appearance. What main points do you want to get across? How can you make those points come alive for your listeners with examples, anecdotes, facts, and figures they'll never forget? Make lists of these ideas. You'll need them later.

The next task is to convince the producer, host, or talent booker that your speaker will be an asset to the show. If you want to be invited back, you can't fudge here. "We have publicists who call us on every occasion," reports By Napier, program director for WCCO-AM in Minneapolis. Based on his experience, he says, "We trust some and not others because some publicists will always say, 'I have a great interview for you!' And that person is not a good interviewee!"

Before you try to place a spokesperson on talk shows, temper your enthusiasm, stand back, and ask yourself these questions:

- Is the person you're trying to get on the air really polished?
- Will the person be able to hold the interest of the audience?
- Can some practice sessions help smooth the rough spots?

It's up to you to *make sure* that the spokesperson is really good and will be a credit to your organization. Publicists—even seasoned pros—can tell you horror stories about spokespeople who grabbed the limelight themselves and overshadowed the organization's message, or about "experienced" speakers who became tongue-tied and immobile in front of the cameras on live television.

Once you're absolutely positive your spokesperson is first-rate, write a tip sheet that summarizes the general topic to be discussed. Include five or six specific subtopics, a brief biographical sketch, and a backgrounder sheet on the issues, the topics, and your organization. Send that to the show's contact person, and let him know that you will call in a week or so to discuss the speaker with him.

Once you have made arrangements to provide an interviewee, you have made a solemn commitment. If you back out at the last minute, you'll wish your name were mud—because it will be far worse, at least at that particular radio or TV station. The American Red Cross's Harry Cohn has a suggestion to avoid last-minute problems. Sometimes a nonprofessional spokesperson can get so nervous about going on the air that he just can't face it; plan to take the interviewee to the station yourself to prevent a last-minute no-show, Cohn advises.

The interviewee is not the only person who gets the last-minute jitters. Broadcasters get worried, too. "When we get close to the appearance day and start promoting the fact that a particular celebrity will be on our 'Boone & Erickson' show, we get a little nervous that he may have missed the plane in Philadelphia. There's where we need a confirming telephone call, perhaps the day before," says By Napier. Even if your interviewee is not a celebrity, media people will appreciate that confirmation call.

Practicing for an Interview

The person to be interviewed should prepare for her appearance. She should practice answering questions, especially aggressive, rapid-fire questions.

She must make those lists of ideas, facts, figures, and anecdotes part of her thinking process so that she can discuss them easily and naturally, because memorized answers may sound as if she is reciting the material by rote.

If she has any hint of a monotone, make her practice raising and lowering the pitch of her voice. Get her to sing the material. Keep after her until your animation has rubbed off on her.

It's OK to use notes on a radio show, but they should be no more than guideposts to jog the memory. These notes must never be on onionskin, or any other paper that rustles and rattles as the leaves are turned. That soft and quiet sound of turning pages will get amplified by the microphones so that it resembles something like a thunderstorm. If your interviewee must use notes, have her write them on three-by-five-inch index cards; they are easy to handle, quiet, and unobtrusive, and the small size will prevent her from writing down too much material.

It can be helpful to your interviewee and the host if you provide a list of suggested topics and questions in advance. According to By Napier, talk show people appreciate publicists who provide background material and suggested questions. "There's no way our personalities have time to read as many books as we have authors on the air, even though they're very good at speed-reading," he says. Whether your spokesperson will be discussing her new book, your organization's services, or the company's new product, be sure to help the interviewer understand your material. And don't be upset if he is not familiar with it. Interviewers are trained to ask the right questions, not to become instant experts. If he does the job right, you'll have a good interview, even if he doesn't know a whole lot about your topic.

Although many talk show hosts will use questions you prepare, some will not. Or they may add questions of their own, particularly if the show has an adversarial atmosphere. Your spokesperson should always be prepared for difficult and even hostile questions, no matter how uncontroversial the topic may seem.

If you want a product credit, telephone number, or website address mentioned on the air, say so—in advance. If the show's producer doesn't agree, you want to know that up front. On the other hand, if you can get agreement, the show's host will often help lead your spokesperson directly into the mention.

Your spokesperson should practice answering questions in 10- to 20-second phrases. If a question calls for a longer answer, she should pause every 20 seconds. This will make it easier for the host or hostess to break in if it is necessary for a commercial interruption. She should also practice stopping the moment she is asked to, because the engineers will not hold the commercial break just for her. Or anyone. She will not make a graceful exit if she insists on talking right to the last second.

When there's a microphone or TV camera staring her in the face, she'll probably have a tendency to speak much too fast. Fast talk will make her sound unsure, hurried, and nervous. Teach her to slow down and make deliberate pauses between sentences. Those breaks may seem like six-year silences to her, but they last for a mere fraction of a second, and they'll make her sound witty, wise, and very much in control.

Remember, also, that she is there to inform and entertain the listening or viewing audience. She should give her audience plenty of concrete information and not worry about giving away her expertise or too much of her book. Whether she is an author, a consultant, a teacher, or a performer, she has to give her audience enough information so they'll know why they *have* to buy her book, engage her services, take her class, or watch her show.

"If an interview really doesn't offer anything beyond plugging a book, if there's nothing entertaining or informative, we feel we're wasting our listeners' time. Although this may be the author's fault and not the publicist's, I think publicists should train authors better," says Napier.

What to Wear for TV

While the clothing you choose for a television appearance can help you look stylish, cool, and collected, if you wear the wrong outfit, it can undermine your credibility. That's because the TV camera exaggerates some colors and patterns and tones down others.

The National Association of Broadcasters advises:

- "Wear medium tones of gray, brown, or blue in a style in which you feel most comfortable. Avoid distracting stripes, pronounced checks, or sharply contrasted patterns that compete for audience attention. Off-white or pastel shades for shirts and blouses are best. Avoid hats with wide brims since they cast sharp shadows on the face from overhead lights."
- "Avoid highly polished gold and silver jewelry or large diamonds or rhinestones, since they reflect studio lights and tend to 'flare' and distort the picture. Pearls or dull-finished metal jewelry are preferable."
- "If you wear glasses regularly, don't try to appear without them. Since your eyes are accustomed to glasses, they will react unnaturally if you do not wear them. The studio crew will arrange the light to avoid any glare or reflections." Also, don't wear glasses that turn dark in sunlight: the bright television lights will make them darken, and you will look sinister.
- "Women look their best in regular street makeup of natural tones. Eye shadow should be used sparingly. Makeup for men is necessary only for a shiny bald spot, a heavy beard, or exceptionally oily skin." Men with heavy beards should either ask for help from the makeup person or whip the problem with a shave just before going on the air.

Finally, men with short hair should wait a few days after a haircut before going on TV.

Tips for the Actual Interview

When your spokesperson finally does get into a TV studio, she should ask the producer whether the staff will be using hand signals. If so, she should find out which ones will be helpful for her to know. For both radio and TV interviews, she should take a moment to check out the type of microphone she will use. A tiny lapel clip-on presents no problem, but a large, old-fashioned mike that sits on a stand or is hidden in a table has a limited pickup range. The interviewee should keep within that range so that there is no fading if she moves too far away.

Any jingling jewelry must be removed! And remember to tell her that *b*, *p*, and *s* tend to pop, explode, and hiss over the air and should be minimized as she speaks. Of course, she should always assume that all microphones are live, even after the interview has ended, until her host tells her otherwise.

The engineer may make a test recording of her voice and play it back for her. If she is like most folks, the sound of her own voice will embarrass her when she hears it played back. She is not the one to judge how she sounds. The engineer will add a touch of treble or a bit more bass if he thinks it will make her sound better. If her throat feels tight, she can relax by stretching or yawning—before she goes on the air, of course!

The National Association of Broadcasters has several more suggestions to make a person's TV appearance more effective:

- Avoid unnecessary movements and gestures. They distract from what you say and do. Quick hand or body movements also are difficult for the camera to follow. So, move more slowly than you normally would.
- If you are being interviewed, look, listen, and speak to the person talking to you—unless you have something you wish to address directly to the television audience. In that case look directly at the camera with the red light on.
- Resist the temptation to look at yourself on the TV monitor in the studio. It is distracting to the viewer. And to you, as well.

Satellite Media Tours

Not so long ago the only way for a spokesperson to appear on local television talk and news shows across the United States was to physically travel to the TV studios in each target city. While that method allowed for interviews with local print media and radio stations as well as personal appearances in each city, it was expensive for the organization, and time-consuming and exhausting for the spokesperson.

Today a satellite media tour allows the celebrity or spokesperson to travel to a single television studio. The tour operator can prearrange as many as 25 interviews a day with talk show producers and news directors at television stations all over the country. The studio feeds a broadcast signal to a communications satellite, and one after another, the television stations use their satellite dishes to capture that signal. The stations can see and hear your guest, who will appear to be live, on camera, as far as their viewers are concerned. Your guest can hear the interviewer, even though she can't actually see him.

Satellite media tours open up all kinds of possibilities for publicists. Here are just three examples:

- When January storms pelted Hawaii, the Visitor's Bureau wanted to tell tourists on the mainland that flooding had not hit the popular resort areas. On The Scene Productions, a Los Angeles satellite media tour operator, arranged a tour from the beach at Waikiki—within 36 hours after being called. The Visitor's Bureau credits the satellite media tour for helping prevent a drop in tourism.
- After a disastrous forest fire in Yellowstone National Park, the Wyoming Travel Commission wanted potential tourists to see that the park was open again and Old Faithful was still stunning. Media-link brought a portable satellite "uplink" truck into the park. "The 'talent' and camera crew stood in front of the geyser," according to Medialink. "Stations were so pleased when they tuned in for their interviews, several timed their shots to Old Faithful's eruptions."
- Porter Novelli Public Relations, a New York agency, arranged a satellite media tour to "bring" New York journalists to a press conference in London. Bob Seltzer explains, "An article that was favorable to one of our client's products was going to be in . . . a very prestigious British medical journal. We had an exclusive question

and answer time for the American journalists. The Satellite Media Conference allowed us to get same-day coverage in the U.S., including a front-page story in the *New York Times*. With video satellite transmissions," Seltzer concludes, "you don't have to go there to reach there. Distance doesn't matter anymore."

Most television stations in the United States have satellite dishes to receive network programs. So it's no surprise that a survey of television stations by West Glen showed that 69 percent of television stations use satellite media tours as part of their news and talk show broadcasts.

Although satellite media tours offer immediacy, many television stations do not run them "live." A Medialink survey found that more than 60 percent of news directors will tape the material for broadcast later on, while about one in eight will run the interview live, as it is being transmitted.

Even though it takes some effort on the part of a station's staff to receive a satellite media tour, there's no guarantee that every station booking the interview will use it. Three out of four producers in an On The Scene Productions survey have not used satellite media tour interviews, for the following reasons:

- 39 percent thought the unused interviews were boring.
- 15 percent felt they were too commercial.
- 11 percent had technical problems with the tape that made it unusable.
- 8 percent said the interviews were bounced by more important, breaking news.

The lesson here is that when it comes to station usage, satellite media tours are no different from any other form of publicity material.

Arranging for a Satellite Media Tour

You will have to hire an outside satellite media tour operator, unless you work for a large corporation, with its own television studios, a *very* experienced technical crew, and a satellite uplink. The arrangements are complicated and highly technical, so look for a highly experienced tour operator.

"A successful tour requires continuity. Switching smoothly from station to station during the interviews is crucial," says Laurence Moskowitz.

"Unless you are fully experienced, once the tour is underway, stand clear." Moskowitz explains the importance of expertise: "The job of the coordinator is to make certain all goes smoothly—that your client does not overrun one station's window and thereby interfere with another station's window. A skilled coordinator can manage the windows effectively. If he sees that your talent is very engaged with one interview, he can alert the next station that the segment will be late."

Although a satellite media tour can be booked in a matter of hours in a crisis situation, you should plan routine tours at least two weeks ahead. A survey of TV stations by West Glen found that 39 percent want at least one week lead time, 43 percent need two weeks, and 14 percent need three weeks or more. Planning ahead is also important. Two-thirds of the stations in the West Glen survey reported that they can participate in only one satellite media tour a day, while 31 percent were limited to two a day.

You'll want to work closely with the tour operator to develop an overall concept, decide what material to include in your B-roll, book the talent, scout the locations, locate props and stage settings, and draw up the list of news and talk shows to pitch. Satellite media tours should be offered to one station in each metro area on an *exclusive* basis.

Since one or two stations may cancel at the last minute because of breaking news or technical problems, you should schedule an extra booking or two, advises Moskowitz.

Like any other publicity material, a strong local angle can make your tour more appealing to journalists. Of the TV reporters and producers responding to the On The Scene Productions survey, 82 percent pointed to a local angle as a major criterion for using a tour. The same survey showed that certain topics are most interesting to producers and reporters:

Topic	Percentage of Journalists Interested
Celebrities	35
Topical issues	30
Breaking news	30
Sports	21
Recording artists	17
New products	16
Medical/health	14
Authors	12
Food	10
Business news	2

There are some similarities between video news releases and satellite media tours. According to the On The Scene Productions survey, 8 out of 10 journalists prefer tours shot on location, rather than in a studio, and they want B-roll material to use for editing their own stories based on the tour interviews. The B-roll material is taped ahead of time. During the tour, "The taped material is usually 'fed,' or transmitted, prior to the interviews and again during an intermission," explains Laurence Moskowitz.

He also suggests that you have a press kit prepared for the news reporters or producers. "Include a brief biography of your spokesperson, a summary of the issues, a statement of the importance of the story or idea, and any news clippings that tell your story in a straightforward, desirable way." Suggest possibilities for local angles, and questions for the interviewer. This printed background material can be sent to the station ahead of time, or it can be transmitted by E-mail on the day of the tour.

When you are a satellite media tour participant, get to the studio early enough so you have a chance to get settled and make sure you have everything you need to be comfortable during your interviews. Check to see that your earphone fits securely and that you know what to do if it pops out. Remember that this is how you will hear what your interviewers are saying to you. Ask for a dry run, while you talk, so that you can handle instructions from the tour coordinator as well as questions from the interviewers naturally and easily.

Be certain there's a cue card or TelePrompTer to remind you of the name of the interviewer and the city. Otherwise, after several sessions, you may lose track.

Ask the crew to let you briefly practice looking straight at the camera while you talk. This technique will give the illusion that you are looking right at the interviewer—and practicing will help you get used to talking to someone you can't actually see.

Finally, ask your tour coordinator to introduce you to each interviewer before the actual session starts so you can banter for a moment or two. That helps set up a warm and friendly interview and also gives you a chance to make sure that the person is pronouncing your name correctly.

Promoting Special Programs

You've taped that special program, and it will be aired in three weeks. Can you go back to your office, put your feet up on the desk, lean back in your chair, and relax? No, you can't, at least not until you've spent some time publicizing your show. This is especially necessary with locally originated programs on cable TV, where you often have to create your own audience. Be certain that your organization's newsletter or promotional material will have information about your segment. Be sure to let your customers, dealers, and distributors know, too. And think about whether there are people who do not ordinarily get your promotional material who should know about the show. Can you reach them with a special mailing?

It is a good idea to send sample copies of newsletters and promotional material with information about the show to the station's public service director or producer. This lets them know that your organization values the airtime and takes itself seriously. You can also call the station's public relations director and ask if he plans to send out a news release about your special. If he is not planning to do so, ask him if it's OK for you to prepare one, and promise to send him a copy.

Your release should go to the television and radio editors at your local newspapers. Did you know that more people read the TV listings than any other part of the newspaper except the front page? Even people who buy the paper just for wrapping fish will look at that TV section.

Lee Winfrey, television writer for the *Philadelphia Inquirer* and president of the Television Critics Association, will accept a press release directly from an organization—if the station's publicist is not going to send one out. He likes at least one week of lead time. "Written material," he says, "is easier. It's also more reliable. And I might miss the phone call. The best packet includes material on when the show will air, what it's about, who is in it, who produced it, and an 8 x 10 black-and-white glossy or two." You should also send your news release to the editors of association, club, and specialized newsletters.

Finally, you could try to get the station to run 10-second spots, often called "bumpers," promoting your special program. Depending on the station's policies—and the amount of free airtime available—bumpers can run during the week before your special, or the day, the hour, or even a few minutes ahead of show time.

Thanking Broadcasters

By all means, write notes of thanks after your organization has received coverage on the air, but be careful how you word them. In the case of a newscast, be sure that you compliment the journalist for the good job she did when she covered your organization's story, and never imply that she did you a favor. It is probably best to send the thank-you note directly to the journalist, and not to her supervisor. According to KTVU-TV's Fred Zehnder, "Some publicists feel it's wise to write a letter to the general manager. That's a little intimidating to the news department. A letter of thanks usually indicates that you've given preferential treatment to somebody, and no news department wants to be accused of that."

Showing appreciation after a special program is also important, particularly if you want another show from that station in the future. Drop a brief thank-you note to the producer and the public service director. If you've been on an interview show, send a note to the host as well. Don't imply that a favor has been done; focus on what a first-rate job he did. Describe any public response or reaction to the show. If your telephone lines are jammed with callers and your letter carrier looks like a beast of burden bent over double under stacks of mailbags, be sure to mention that. Broadcasters, like everyone else, have the very human need to be praised for a job well done.

Approaching Cablecasters

Although cable TV has built an impressive audience, it is still a medium that is growing and changing rapidly. While new digital systems can have up to 130 channels according to the National Cable Television Association, older analog systems may have only 40 to 60. Any way you add that up, it spells opportunity for enterprising publicists. By 1999, there were more than 10,466 cable TV systems, and 65 million households (that's 70 percent of television households) subscribing to cable TV. Most cablecasters are equipped to receive network programming via satellite from 214 cable-only networks. Twenty-five of those cable-only networks reach more than 18 million viewers each. Three of them—Entertainment & Sports Programming Network, Cable News Network, and Superstation TBS— boast more than 50 million subscribers apiece.

If you want to place publicity material on a cable TV system, your first question is whether it has locally originated programs. Some cablecasters are merely pipelines; they can only bring in other stations or packaged programs produced in other cities or supplied by the cable networks.

Cablecasters who do originate their own programs can help you in two ways. First, and easiest, they may already have regular talk shows, newscasts, and public affairs programs that use material from publicists. Find out if this is the case, and ask who the contact people are.

Some cablecasters will not have readymade programs available for you to step into but may have public access channels. Public access channels are set aside by the cablecaster so that local organizations and businesses such as yours can have access to TV time. These access channels are often required as part of the contract with the city or county. About one-third of the cable systems that have locally originated programs have public access channels.

Although this is usually a free service, some cablecasters charge for the use of their public access channels. Always ask about this at the beginning of your conversation so there are no surprises later. If there is a fee, it may seem large at first, but if you compare the cost per person you reach with your message, you may find that cablecasting is no more expensive than your organization's other promotions.

Depending on your area, cable may well be worth the effort and cost. In parts of New Jersey, for example, where there are no local broadcast TV news shows, people have turned to cable TV for news of local happenings, and cable has started to build a substantial audience. In other areas, however, cable programming is still third-rate, and it is not at all clear whether your time and money would be well spent.

You will have to do some research in your community to find out who watches cable TV and the access channels. While you may be able to get solid information on audience demographics for regular cable channels, there is little data on the viewership for public access channels. "But the consensus is that the audience is expanding," according to the *New York Times*. Where audience studies of access channels have been done by universities, they reveal "a committed, desirable body of viewers, who boast high incomes, education levels and voting records and who watch access at least once per week . . . the ragtag 'amateurs' are moving into the mainstream," the *Times* concludes.

The cablecaster can supply you with some audience data, and the TV writer at your daily newspaper may have information he would be willing to share with you. You should also contact the broadcasting or journalism departments at nearby colleges to see if they have conducted viewership research for channels in their communities. A major clue will be the kinds of advertisements your cable system carries. If large, established firms and national businesses are running ads, it is probably worth your while to try to get your message on cable.

Even if you decide that cable TV is not worth your time now, keep an eye on it. The situation may change in a few months or a year.

Checklist—Getting on the Air

1. Do you know whom you should approach at radio, television and cable stations for the various types of airtime?
2. Are you familiar with the differences among the seven main types of airtime?
3. Do you know your target stations' policies on the various airtime types?
4. Have you compiled a media list?
5. Does your list include names of journalists as well as titles?
6. Are you aware of the various deadlines and lead times at each station you're pitching?
7. Do you know whether your target stations prefer live or prerecorded PSAs and news releases?
8. Do you update your information on station preferences and needs continually?
9. Do you have information on locally originated programs at your target stations?
10. If you work with a nonprofit organization, have you checked to see if an access guide for community organizations is published for your city?
11. Have you checked to see if any of your target stations offer tours?
12. Have you become familiar with the programs on your "must appear on" list?
13. Have you asked about the availability of demographic material on station listeners?
14. Have you checked broadcasters' websites to see if they have archived programs or live Webcasts that can help you become more familiar with program formats?

15. Do you understand the difference between radio and television audiences, and when you should use each medium?

16. Do you want to reach a broad, general audience or a specific, defined one?

17. How will that vary from one publicity campaign to another?

18. Have you learned about PSA policies at the most important stations on your list?

19. Do you know which stations will run PSAs for one-time events, and which limit events to community calendar listings?

20. Are you trying to get to know public service directors rather than simply sending out PSAs?

21. If you send PSAs by mail, have you included a cover letter that does a real selling job as well as a stamped, self-addressed reply card?

22. If you are sending out PSAs on a national or regional basis, can you get your local affiliates, branches, dealers, or distributors to submit them as localized material?

23. Can you include localized tag lines or localization suggestions with your PSAs?

24. If you're sending out professionally prerecorded PSAs, have you considered pitching to broadcasters by mail first?

25. For a national campaign, are you planning to send spots to at least 200 stations?

26. Have you made sure that no one appearing in your PSA will be on the ballot in an upcoming election?

27. If you're considering using a celebrity in your PSA, have you made sure the person is not identified with a particular station or network?

28. Have you timed the news stories on your local stations to see what length is preferred?

29. Do you have the telephone numbers for the direct lines to news assignment editors and news directors?

30. Do you know which stations have specialized reporters?

31. Do you always assume you'll be taped when you call a newsroom?

32. Do you write out your story or pitch before you call?

33. Are you prepared to answer questions?

34. Have you considered distributing taped radio stories by telephone?

35. Do you know when deadlines are so you can avoid disturbing journalists at those times unless you have breaking news?

36. Have you made a list of visual possibilities before pitching a television news story?

37. Have you made the pitch for your video news release so newsworthy that journalists can't resist it?

38. Does your pitch stress the importance of the material in your VNR to the station's audience?

39. Have you pointed out that your VNR is the exclusive source for this desirable footage and shown the news director exactly why it is so worthwhile?

40. Is your news peg highlighted in your pitch letter?

41. Have you discussed tracking your VNR's usage with your video production house or public relations agency?

42. Have you allowed at least a two-week lead between delivery to broadcasters and airtime for VNRs that don't involve breaking news?

43. Have you thought about starting to pitch a VNR even before you produce it?

44. Have you built a feedback mechanism into your preproduction pitch so you can draw on journalists' opinions to produce a more newsworthy story?

45. Can you include an advance story with your preproduction pitch for journalists to read "live" on the air?

46. Does your VNR's support material include a pitch letter, background information on the story, brief bio sketches of the speakers, localization ideas, and a description of the B-roll contents?

47. Are you sending the support material with advance pitches and again with the cassettes?

48. If you're transmitting your VNR by satellite, will you or your distributor use a news wire service to send an advisory to stations?

49. Will you or your distributor send the timed script to stations by news wire or E-mail before the VNR is transmitted by satellite? Have you asked each station how it prefers to receive the script?

50. Have you written down your objective for each talk show appearance before pitching to the talent booker?

51. Have you sent the talent booker a brief tip sheet and followed up with a telephone call?

52. Are you *positive* your speaker will be interesting and dynamic?

53. If your speaker's presentation has rough spots, can they be polished with practice?

54. Have you figured out how your speaker can use anecdotes, examples, figures, and facts to make the story come alive?

55. Have you made a list of main points you want your spokesperson to cover in an interview?

56. Can he handle aggressive, rapid-fire questions?

57. If the appearance is on radio, has he prepared brief notes in outline form if he feels he needs them?

58. Does he need "singing" exercises to help break a monotone?

59. If you want a product mention, telephone number for more information, or a website address on the show, have you discussed this with the station in advance?

60. Has your interviewee practiced giving short responses and speaking slowly?

61. Have you given the talk show host a list of suggested questions and topics, as well as background material?

62. Does your spokesperson know to wear medium tones and avoid clothing with stripes and bold checks for a television appearance?

63. Does your speaker know to avoid a white shirt or blouse in favor of ivory, ecru, or pastel?

64. Is all of the speaker's jewelry nonreflective?

65. Has she discussed hand signals with the studio crew?

66. Has she asked about the range of any fixed microphones and how she should position herself?

67. Have you taught her to assume that all mikes are live?

68. Has she learned to tone down gestures and move more slowly than usual?

69. Has she practiced looking at the interviewer unless she wants to address the audience directly?

70. Have you found a highly experienced satellite media tour operator and checked the service's references?

71. Can you trust the operator enough that you'll feel comfortable standing clear during the tour?

72. Have you allotted at least six weeks' lead time for tours that don't involve breaking news?

73. Will you develop an overall concept for your tour ahead of time?

74. Can you stage it on location, rather than in a studio?

75. Have all locations been checked and reserved?

76. Have you planned your B-roll material?

77. Have you selected stations in which to offer your tour on an exclusive basis in each metro area?

78. Have you signed contracts with any outside spokespeople?

79. Have you rented, made, or bought the props and stage settings you'll need?

80. Have you thought about how to add local angles?

81. Have you sent background material to stations in advance?

82. If your tour doesn't deal with a popular topic, have you surveyed several journalists to make sure there will be interest?

83. Will the tour operator feed your B-roll material to stations during the tour?

84. Have you made arrangements to get to the studio early?

85. Has your spokesperson checked the fit of the earphone and tried it out before the tour begins?

86. Have you checked to make sure there is either a teleprompter or cue cards for each station on the tour?

87. Has your spokesperson practiced looking straight at the camera while talking?

88. Have you arranged for the tour coordinator to introduce your spokesperson to each interviewer before the actual interview starts?

89. Have you made arrangements to promote your special?

90. Have you sent copies of your promotional material about the show to the public service director and the station's publicist?

91. Have you let your customers, dealers, distributors, staff, and board of directors know about the special?

92. Are there key people in your audience you can reach with a special mailing about your show?

93. Have you asked the station if it's sending out a press release about your special?

94. If it's not, will you?

95. Have you suggested that the station create and run bumpers for your special?

96. Have you written thank-you notes to newscasters, when appropriate, and to public service directors, producers, and hosts for special shows?

97. Are you sure you're thanking broadcasters for a job well done rather than implying they've done you a favor?

98. Have you made a list of locally originated programs on your target cable TV systems?
99. Can you get cable TV time on a public access channel?
100. Is there a charge?
101. Are video production facilities and training available?
102. Can you get solid information on the audience of your targeted cablecasters?

10

When the Media Come to Your Doorstep

The media are at your doorstep. You have 37 other top priorities, and you weren't looking for any press coverage this week. Now what? Do they really have to cover this fire, strike, accident, or scandal that brings them to your doorstep today? Well, yes! They do. And whether you've invited them or they've invited themselves, *you* play a major role in determining the kind of coverage your business or organization will get—even in an emergency. The fact is, you'll almost always get better coverage if you're prepared. Procedures for planning and running smooth press conferences and special events are so similar that they are covered as a unit in this chapter, followed by tips for coping with sudden visits from the press in times of crisis.

Press Conferences and Special Events

The most common way to get the media to visit you is by holding a press conference. No, it's not a major meeting called only by politicians with pronouncements: ordinary mortals such as you and I can arrange successful press conferences.

There is only one reason for calling a press conference rather than sending out a news release: the subject demands a question-and-answer format. If reporters want to meet and question your speaker, a press conference is in order.

Says Albert Feldman, public relations director of the New York Multiple Sclerosis Society, "It isn't how often you use a press conference, but why. A press conference should be called when there's a reason for two-way communication between the organization's spokesman and the media . . . to permit a forum. If a press conference doesn't have that purpose, it will result in a loss of credibility to the sponsor. If everything can be made clear in a press release, then a press conference becomes superfluous. You do not use a press conference to achieve greater publicity."

Reporters and editors rely on press conferences to supply them with news they wouldn't get otherwise. On the other hand, so few press conferences produce useful news that many reporters and editors view them generally with suspicion. As Cindy Loose of the *Staten Island Register* puts it, "There are a lot of press conferences that are obviously just ploys to get publicity." She adds, "I think phony press conferences are a bad mistake. You're going to defeat your purpose. People are going to get mad at you, and the next time they see something from you, they're not going to pay any attention."

When the Chelm Institute for People with Disabilities held a press conference to announce a new program to teach people with disabilities the skills they need to work on assembly lines at electronics plants, the group got a good crowd of reporters, but there was almost no coverage. R. E. Porter, business writer for the *Plains City Morning Star*, explains why:

"I couldn't understand why we were there. I got a press release about an innovative new program to train people with disabilities in electronics assembly skills. Even though the press conference announcement was not exactly clear, I drove all the way to Chelm because I thought there would be a good story.

"When I got there, I wasn't sure what the program was about. When I left, I still didn't know. Aside from a few clichés and generalizations, they didn't tell us anything about the program. They could have told us about placements of disabled workers on actual jobs, and there are probably some interesting things about how assembly-line equipment is adapted for workers with disabilities. But they didn't offer this information, and they were vague when I asked them about these areas.

"Not only that, but also they seemed confused about whether they were presenting this new program or all of their programs.

"I saw only 2 or 3 people participating in the program, but I saw 50 people running it. And I didn't get to see the trainees working. None of them seemed disabled, although their disabilities might not have been apparent. But that was never made clear.

"I couldn't tell if they were just inept or if they had something to hide. I had suspicions of both. There were so many staff people there, it was as if they were trying to overwhelm us, to keep us away from something."

When You Shouldn't Have a Press Conference

Before you set up a press conference, take a long, hard look at your plans and answer these questions:

- Is there a more effective way to handle this information?
- Do you really need a question-and-answer session with journalists?

If you answered no to the first question and yes to the second, your next step is to take a look at the press kit you have assembled for the conference. Can anything be added to this material? Does it cover all the bases from all angles? If it does, then send it to the press; you don't need a press conference! It maddens reporters to spend time at a press conference when they could have been given the same information in a press release or press kit.

If your material is not hard news, consider approaching a few carefully selected reporters and developing stories directly with them instead of calling a press conference or inviting the press to an event. The results can be better, particularly if you're introducing a complex new product journalists will want to examine.

This is particularly true in the computer industry, for example. A survey of 21 high-tech editors cited in *Public Relations Journal* concluded, "Press conferences are regarded as rarely useful; press tours or mailed releases are preferred."

PC Magazine's Bill Howard explains why the journalists at his publication find press conferences only minimally useful: "We very much prefer to see products before they are released, under a non-disclosure agreement. That's because we want to be able to cover them when they're new, which means we have to write about them as much as three months before they're available. If we wait for a press conference to learn about new products, our readers won't know about them until they're old news."

There's another reason press conferences don't cut the mustard, according to Howard: "We prefer one-on-one product demonstrations so we can cover the ground our readers want to know about. We're more technical than other magazines at the bits and bytes level."

Find out the preferences and needs of the journalists you work with. And if you determine that they don't like press conferences, don't worry! There's sure to be another, more effective way to work with them.

Where to Hold Your Press Conference or Event

If you work with a national or regional organization or a business, you have to decide which city is best for your press conference. You should consider the following factors when you choose a location:

- Sometimes the subject demands an on-the-scene location. A press conference about uranium mining in Utah would, most likely, be held in that state. You could also hold a simultaneous, auxiliary conference in a more accessible location, perhaps using a satellite media tour to bring the out-of-the-way site to big-city journalists.
- Some cities have specialized print and broadcast reporters who will be more likely than generalists to understand the subject of your conference and give you first-rate coverage. Washington, D.C., for example, has reporters and commentators who specialize in stories

relating to the federal government. New York has more journalists who specialize in financial stories than any other American city. Press conferences concerning show business work best in Los Angeles and New York. Journalists specializing in agriculture are concentrated in Chicago and Washington, D.C.

- Cities where the local press usually gives you favorable coverage are better places for your press conference than areas where the media are neutral or hostile to your business or organization. Local reporters often set the tone for the conference and influence the attitudes of national reporters. On the other hand, make sure it doesn't look as if you're avoiding an obvious problem by running away from areas where you have troubles.

- If you hope to get network TV and radio coverage, try to stage your press conference in a city with a network news staff. However, don't choose a location just because it has network-affiliated stations, since the networks often don't use material from their affiliates except for disasters and major crimes. Approach the local bureaus of the networks instead. Check the media directories mentioned in Chapter 13 for lists of network news bureaus, or contact the network headquarters and ask.

Once you have chosen your city, you will have to find a good setting for your press conference. Determine whether most major media offices are in the same area of the city. If that is the case, and it often is, you'll get better coverage if your conference is in that part of town.

Hotel and motel conference rooms are often used for press conferences, but private clubs and other centrally located meeting rooms are also possibilities. It is not a good idea to hold a press conference or special event in a building with restricted access. Reporters will not appreciate having to sign in and wait for security approval. If you must use such a facility, be sure you know in advance which reporters are coming. Give the list to the security guard, and have a publicity staff member or a volunteer from the publicity committee on duty with the guard to make sure that reporters are admitted instantaneously.

If you expect extensive radio and TV coverage, think about sound and lighting for your press conference. Some hotels have meeting rooms with complete built-in sound systems, which can make order out of chaos. Ask in advance. If you cannot find a meeting room with a sound system, take a quick look in the yellow pages to find and rent the sound equipment you need. Without a sound system, reporters converge on the speaker and poke microphones in his face. That can rattle even the best spokesperson and interfere with his effectiveness.

Check to see if the room you rent has suitable lighting for TV cameras. This has two important advantages. One, *you* decide how to light the scene so your speaker and props look best. And two, television crews can travel lighter, arrive later, and spend little or no time setting up. Given the tight schedules in most newsrooms, this could be a deciding factor.

Check each potential press conference or special event site to see if it is accessible to TV crews. Are the passageways, doorways, and elevators large enough to accommodate bulky equipment? If the crews will bring their own lights, are there enough heavy-duty circuits for them?

If the press conference concerns a highly visual topic that TV reporters and newspaper photographers will want to shoot, consider holding it on location instead of in a conference room. Betty M. White, chief of the Public Affairs Office, U.S. Army Corps of Engineers, Omaha District, writing in *Public Relations Journal*, explains why. White called a press conference and party to announce a grant for a floodplain park, a new concept. Instead of the traditional practice of channeling a stream, the new park allowed for periodic flooding, a more natural way of handling the environment. No media people came to the press conference and party, which was held in a hotel. When White canvassed them afterward, she discovered that several of the TV stations had used the release, but they had gone to the location of the new park and filmed there. The moral of the story is that this conference should have been held on location.

KGW-TV's Larry Badger confirms this. "We'll do anything to avoid having to cover a news conference because they seldom make news. We want to show the end product of the announcement as opposed to the announcement. We want visual possibilities. There's just not that much of an impact if somebody says, 'I'm going to build a dam on the Snake River.' I want to go up to the Snake River and say, 'The dam is going to be built here. It will cost $20 billion. And it's going to flood this and this,'" Badger concludes.

If your press conference will be outdoors, be sure to plan for the following:

- Shelter from bad weather.
- Adequate lighting.

- Crowd control.
- Noise control.

Scheduling Media Events

Be aware of media deadlines. If you schedule your press conference between 9:00 A.M. and 11:00 A.M. on Tuesday, Wednesday, or Thursday, reporters from almost all the media will be able to attend and still have time to digest the material before their deadlines. Avoid holding press conferences when major national events and holidays will make it harder for you to get coverage. "I wouldn't want to hold a press conference on Election Day, during the primaries, or around Christmas," says Nancy Karen of United Way of Tri-State. "There's too much competition."

Invitations

Invitations for press conferences and special events should always be typed with wide margins and limited to one page. Use a format that covers who, when, where, why, how, and what. Mention any photographic possibilities. If the conference or event is not in a well-known location, include travel directions.

Exhibits 10.1 and 10.2 on pages 344–346 are examples of good invitations to press conferences and special events.

Exhibit 10.3 on pages 347–348 reproduces a tip sheet inviting the press to a special event, prepared by publicist Joel Pomerantz for Rockaways' Playland, Inc.

Whether you're contacting newspapers or broadcasters, send your invitation to the reporter who actually writes about your subject. Even though the invitation could be sent to the city editor at the newspaper or the news assignment editor at a radio or TV station, and forwarded to the right reporter, it is better to direct it to a specific journalist. The city editor and the news assignment editor are generalists, and they may miss something that a specialist would know is important. The larger the newspaper or broadcaster, the more important it is to get your invitation directly to the right reporter.

For a large daily paper, if your event or press conference will offer unusual photo possibilities, send a duplicate invitation to the photo assign-

Exhibit 10.1

PRESS CONFERENCE   PRESS CONFERENCE   PRESS CONFERENCE

Plains City Bus Authority
1511 Industrial Avenue
Plains City 00003
January 31, 2003

Contact: Martha H. Einhorn
Business Hours: (123) 456-7890
E-mail: mhe@pcbus.chl
24-hour pager: (555) 000-0000
Background information: www.pcbus.chl

Major Focus

The recent 25 percent cutback in the Plains City Bus Authority's budget has caused major maintenance problems. Even though we have not increased wages and have cut back service by 25 percent, we do not have enough funds to purchase new buses or maintenance equipment. Almost half of the PCBA buses are out of service or in unsafe condition.

Speakers

PCBA chairwoman Marilyn Ilonescu will outline the problem and answer questions. State Senator E. L. Press will announce the revenue plan for PCBA that he will present to the state senate later this month, which would authorize a bond issue and revenue sharing to end the funding crisis. PCBA is the only transit system in the state that has not received state or federal aid.

Where

Conference Room, Plains City Bus Authority, 1511 Industrial Avenue, near Rider Road. Golden Road exit, south three blocks, right on Rider Road to Industrial Avenue. Or the #12 Industrial Avenue bus to Rider Road. Map and driving directions at www.pcbus.chl/map1511.

When

Thursday, February 6, 2003, at 10:30 A.M.

MORE   MORE   MORE

Picture Opportunities

- 337 buses, parked in formation, which are out of service because of mechanical problems.
- 122 buses with safety hazards, many of them highly photogenic.

###

Exhibit 10.2

MEDIA CONFERENCE   MEDIA CONFERENCE   MEDIA CONFERENCE

Plains City Solar Energy Company	Contact: Harry M. Kwan
6406 Industrial Avenue	(123) 456-7890
Plains City 00005	Cell Phone: (555) 000-0000
March 30, 2001	E-mail: harryk@plainscitysolar.chl
	Background information:
	www.plainscitysolar.chl/pressroom

Major Focus

The first Sunwater Brand solar water heater will come off the assembly line at the new Plains City Solar Energy Company factory on Tuesday, April 5, 2005. This compact water heater is easy to install and costs less than $200. Governor J. Kousoulas will present the Plains State Energy Award to Martin Kagawa, designer of the heater.

Speakers

- Governor Kousoulas will present the award and discuss the contribution the Plains City Solar Energy Company will make to the state's economy.
- Jane K. Manzelli, Plains state energy commissioner, will give figures and facts about the amount of energy that will be saved by the solar heaters produced in this factory during the next year.

MORE   MORE   MORE

■ Mayor Michael Olaffsson will take a solar-powered shower.

Where

Plains City Solar Energy Company, 6406 Industrial Avenue, Plains City. Marigold Heights Road exit, six blocks north to Industrial Avenue. Entrance to the plant is one block west on Industrial Avenue. Look for the huge yellow sun sign on the lawn.

When

Tuesday, April 5, 11:00 A.M.

Photo Possibilities

■ Mayor Olaffsson taking a solar-powered shower. (He will, of course, wear a bathing suit.)

■ The assembly line.

■ The presentation of the award by Governor Kousoulas.

■ The factory's sun garden, where gold and orange marigolds grow side by side with solar collectors.

-30-   -30-   -30-   -30-   -30-

ment editor. Be sure you let him—and the reporter—know who else has received the invitation.

Two important people on your invitation list are the Daybook editor at United Press International and the Daily Budget editor at Associated Press. They both compile lists of press conferences, conventions, meetings, product and political demonstrations, picket lines, and special events, which are sent out on the wires and arrive by Teletype in the newsrooms at broadcasters and newspapers. Not all press conferences will be listed by the Daybook and Daily Budget editors, but if yours is, your credibility is boosted substantially. A press conference seems more official when it is announced on the AP or UPI wires.

Reminder Calls

Once you have sent your press conference or special event invitation, you may think that reporters will appear without further prompting. Even with

---

Exhibit 10.3

TIP TO ASSIGNMENT DESK
Rockaways' Playland, Inc.
185 Beach 97th Street
Rockaway Beach, NY 11693
718-945-7000

Event
1,000 handicapped, homeless, and underprivileged children from 20 hospitals, shelters, and health and welfare agencies in the metropolitan New York area will be treated to a fun-filled afternoon at a Queens amusement park.

The youngsters, many in wheelchairs and on crutches, will come from Queens, Manhattan, Brooklyn, Staten Island, and Nassau.

When
Thursday, August 7, starting at 1:00 P.M.

Where
Rockaways' Playland Amusement Park, Beach 98th Street,
Rockaway Park, Queens

Background
Annual "Fun in the Sun" outing is sponsored by Walter Kaner, *New York Daily News* columnist, who has entertained 64,000 children at his parties in the past 27 years. Playland is donating free use of its rides; L.I. Lighting Co. is contributing refreshments.

Among groups participating: Cerebral Palsy of Queens and Nassau, Willowbrook State School, New York Foundling Home, Muscular Dystrophy Association, Queens Children's Shelter, Brooklyn Developmental Center.

Rain Date
Tuesday, August 12, 1:00 P.M.

MORE   MORE   MORE

Contact

Joel Pomerantz, (718) 689-2288

Ann Leichner, Playland, (718) 945-7000

interesting, newsworthy events, that's not usually the case. Early on the morning of your event, call each reporter, editor, or news assignment director to remind them. The best time is probably between 8:00 and 9:00 A.M. Larry Kramer of the *Trenton Times* explains why:

"A paper's assignment desk is flooded daily. We may have looked at some future event and said, 'We're not going to have time to cover that.' And sure enough, that day is the quietest news day of the year. But we don't remember the story we threw away. Then somebody calls up and says, 'We're having a press conference on this and this,' and we say, 'Whoops, that's not a bad one, let's do that.'"

However, some journalists do not like reminder calls. For example, David Morgan, news director for WOW-AM in Omaha, Nebraska, says that his office has a filing system to keep track of events. He feels it is his station's obligation to be there, without a reminder, if it has decided to cover the event.

If any of your media contacts express a strong wish not to be reminded, make a note of that and honor their preferences. But continue to remind everyone else.

Don't get carried away and call two, three, or four times, or have half a dozen people call to urge journalists to attend your event or conference. "That's a turnoff," says KTVU-TV's Fred Zehnder. "It creates such a negative attitude that the assignment editor (or reporter) isn't likely to cover an event even if it seems worthwhile. It smacks of real pressure tactics."

When you make those calls, be brief. Introduce yourself, tell the reporter or editor that you're having a press conference or special event, describe it in 15 words or fewer, and ask if she got the announcement. Be prepared for a negative answer; don't let it shake you up. You may have stumbled on an opportunity, since you can make the pitch one-on-one. Try to briefly convince her that your conference or event is newsworthy.

Before you ask her if she's coming, say, "Let me give you the time and location." You're trying to get her to write down the information because that helps involve her. If you feel that she really should have the information in the written invitation, or if she asks for background material, offer to send it by fax, E-mail or even messenger.

If she has received the invitation, ask her if she's planning to cover the event or conference. She may tell you that she will not be there. Don't argue. Don't try to persuade her. Ask her if you can provide her with a release and background material after the conference is over. Find out when she'll need it. Then make sure she gets that material with time to spare, even if that means using a messenger to deliver it. Ask her what delivery method she prefers: fax, E-mail, or old-fashioned messenger.

Getting Your Act Together

Whenever you can, prepare visual aids for a press conference or event. Charts and graphs help reporters understand facts, figures, and comparisons more quickly. Pictures, props, slides, and videotapes make your presentation more interesting. And of course, the TV reporters will be delighted if your visual material can be televised; it makes their stories more interesting to viewers. That helps them. And since your message will be more effective, it helps you, too.

Make sure your speakers are brief and to the point. The purpose of your press conference is for reporters to question your speakers. A 20-minute presentation is long for a press conference. Some publicists limit their speakers to five-minute opening statements. You needn't cover every detail; if things are not clear, reporters will ask questions. And that is what you want.

Since questions and answers are the essence of any press conference, your speaker should practice answering every possible question, fair and foul, that may be thrown at her. If you have a diabolical, cynical friend, he will be most useful. Ask him to think up the nastiest, most underhanded questions. Have your speaker practice answering them until she can counter every question with a convincing, positive answer.

Your speaker should be able to make her central point in 10 to 20 seconds. If she can do that, she has a better chance of getting her statement on the air uncut and unedited. It may well be all the time she is allowed.

Radio and TV people may ask for brief interviews after the conference presentation. Be prepared to schedule them on the spot, and have an area set aside to conduct them.

Anticipating Problems

The last thing you want at a press conference is your competition or opposition. If the conference is on private property, you can exclude them. If you expect a demonstration or heckling and harassment from your opposition, take steps in advance to quickly and quietly contain it.

List all the things that could go wrong, and figure out how you'll cope if they do. Murphy's law changes when you make contingency plans: If it can go wrong, it will, unless you've spent a lot of time preparing for problems; then it probably won't.

On the Big Day

"Always attend the events, conferences, and broadcast interviews you have arranged," says public relations executive Ravelle Brickman. "You, the publicist, are the host or hostess. You make journalists feel welcome when they are visiting your organization, and you help people from your organization feel at ease when they visit the media. But most important of all, when you are on the scene with the media, you will get to meet journalists. And that can and should be the start of your working relationship with them."

Don't invite many people from your organization to your press conference. Since they will probably not know any of the journalists, they will tend to talk with each other. That behavior is natural, but it gives the appearance of aloofness. The people from your organization or business who attend should greet journalists, make them comfortable, and answer their questions. With only a few people from your organization on hand, there will be less of a tendency to talk among yourselves.

As the reporters and editors arrive, give them each a press packet that includes the following:

- A basic one-page release.
- A longer, three- or four-page version.
- A copy of the speaker's statement.
- Background information on your business, organization, product, industry, or cause.
- A brief biography of the speaker.
- Copies of any relevant documents.
- Any other information you think will help a reporter write a good story.

- Small souvenir items, such as pennants, T-shirts, or imprinted balloons.
- Product samples, if they will help journalists write stories.
- Where to find in-depth information on your website, with URLs that take journalists to the exact information they seek, so they don't have to slog through your site, searching for it.

Many photographers get no briefing about the story they are covering. Take some time to fill them in, and offer them copies of the press release or backgrounder sheet, but unless they ask for advice (which is not likely), don't try to tell them how to shoot their pictures. It is a courtesy, however, to let them know if there will be photo opportunities, and what times these will occur.

Don't wait for latecomers. Start your press conference on time even if there is only one journalist there.

If you're demonstrating a product for journalists, practice ahead of time so that everything will move right along without a hitch. Bill Howard suggests, "Run through your demo quickly, and stay within the allotted time. Make sure you get to the point very quickly. Suppose the two principal editors are called out after 25 minutes for a deadline conference. And all you've shown them so far is your introductory flip chart. Well, you're out of luck!"

Record your press conference on audiotape—or videotape if you can afford it—using broadcast-quality equipment. The tape will help you write the news release to send to newspaper and TV reporters who didn't attend, and it can also be edited into video and audio news releases to be sent directly to broadcasters. Moreover, you will have a record of the information and of your organization's positions on the issues for later use, perhaps with your board of directors, shareholders, distributors, dealers, volunteers, members, or staff. You can easily make it available to them by archiving it on your website.

"We might send copies of the tape to our chapters," says Albert Feldman of the New York Multiple Sclerosis Society. "Sometimes we offer them to National Public Radio for the program 'All Things Considered.' We tape if the information we're presenting at the press conference is of importance and deserves to be preserved."

One final arrangement is often overlooked, particularly by organizations without full-time offices: have someone on hand at the telephone number listed on your press conference or special event invitation, so that media people who cannot attend can call for information and get an immediate response. And make sure that you have thoroughly briefed that telephone person.

Following Up After Your Conference or Event

What if you give a press conference and nobody comes? Should you slink off to the wilderness, find a hole, and crawl in, never to emerge into the world of publicity again? You don't need to do anything that drastic. Believe it or not, all is not lost. Even if no one arrives or only a few journalists join you, if you act quickly and confidently, you may still drum up coverage.

The journalists who did not come *will* want to hear from you. "They may have been busy with other assignments, and even if they did not honor you with their appearance, they are entitled to news," says Albert Feldman. "If you decline to give them news, the next time you run a press conference, you can be sure those people will not show."

Put your pride on the shelf, confidence in your voice, and your brain in high gear. And don't refer to the number of people who attended your press conference or event; that is not important. What matters is that you have newsworthy material. Period.

Your immediate first step is to call the number listed on your invitation. Ask your telephone monitor if there are any messages. (If there are, you'll begin to feel better immediately.) Make a list of journalists who called and asked for information. Add the names of reporters who said they would not cover your conference or event but asked for follow-up information. That's your primary list.

Next, write a 20-second radio statement, or edit a radio audio news release from the tape of the press conference. Call the radio stations that didn't attend. Contact those on your primary list first, then the others. Your pitch could be as follows:

> *Hello. This is Harry Kwan of Plains City Solar Energy Company. I'm sorry you weren't able to be at our press conference this morning. I've got quite a statement from Governor Kousoulas. Do you want to run a tape now, or do you need a voice-level test first?*

The reporter or news director may ask you to read the statement or play the tape twice. The first time you read it, he will adjust his equipment to get the best recording level, and the second time he will record. If it is newsworthy, and they are not swamped with material that day, many radio stations will use your statement uncut. It's certainly worth trying.

Your next step is to write a one-page press release summarizing the announcement made at your press conference or describing your special event. This should be sent to the newspaper and TV reporters who didn't attend. If you have any visual material you can reproduce easily for the TV stations, it's worth including. If you recorded your press conference or media event on videotape, and you have a video production house that can work *fast*, you could even edit a video news release from your footage and distribute it to television stations.

You will have to work quickly in order to meet deadlines: This applies especially if you had some coverage and wish to expand it. Once the stations or papers that did attend have run your story, others are less likely to; it's already stale news. So, this is no time for writer's block or introspection. You should have prepared all your material, made your calls, and delivered your stories by 3:00 P.M., at the latest. After that, you're entitled to a leisurely lunch with cocktails.

Publicity at Trade Shows

Trade shows draw journalists by the dozens, and if it's a major show, you can bet that every important writer, editor, and reporter in the industry will be there, looking for news. Help them find it, and you can get great publicity for your business or organization, whether you're exhibiting or not—but you have to plan ahead of time.

Start by contacting the trade show's management firm at least six weeks before show time. The company may have a list of journalists who have preregistered for the exhibition. Sometimes the list is available only to exhibitors, but even if you won't have a booth, it can't hurt to ask. If you can't get a list from the manager, call your key contacts at the major trade magazines in your industry to find out who will be covering the show.

Once you have a list, read through it and ask yourself what information you have—and what news pegs you can develop—that will interest these journalists. Offer them interviews with any of your company's experts who will attend the show, and if you will be exhibiting or introducing new products, let journalists know by sending them a tip sheet several weeks ahead of time.

You should also ask the exhibition's management these questions:

- Are there pressrooms available at the show? What equipment will they have for journalists? If you know that the trade journalists you work with will need equipment that won't be provided to cover your story, you can arrange to have it on hand.
- Can exhibitors display their press kits in the pressroom? Can you send your kits ahead? Who will receive them? Will the management firm take responsibility for the kits? These policies will vary from one show manager to another.
- Does the show management notify the press of new product announcements to be made at the show? How does the firm handle this? What lead time is needed? Will that announcement be more effective than you can be, or can you do it better on your own?
- Is there a daily show publication? Will it include stories on new product announcements to be made at the show? What is the lead time?
- Has the management reserved rooms at show headquarters for press conferences and interviews with journalists? What facilities are available? Is there a charge for using them? Will these rooms meet your needs, or do you have to rent your own space at the exhibition headquarters for press conferences and journalist interviews?

Finally, don't be swayed by the popular perception that you must exhibit in order to get publicity at a trade show. Joel Strasser of Dorf & Stanton Technology Communications cites a case in which one of his clients was *not* exhibiting at a major trade show. "We found that there are a good number of editors who are interested in talking with the company even if they don't exhibit, so we set up press interviews in a hospitality suite."

Unplanned Visits from Reporters

Hopefully you will never have a fire, a strike, an explosion, an accident, or a major crime that brings the press, full of questions, to your doorstep without an invitation. Even if you think it could never happen to your organization or business, remember, the *Titanic* was supposed to be unsinkable. Emergencies are difficult for the publicist, and if you want to cope with them well, you must plan ahead. So *you* ought to think through how to handle emergency situations.

Anticipating Emergencies

You should develop a written emergency plan and give your staff, volunteers, or members copies. Be sure the plan includes a list of officers, executives, staff, or volunteers who must be notified in case of an emergency. Also be certain that everyone knows that *you* must be called at once, immediately after the fire department or the police. This means that you will need a pager and a cell phone, and you must have them with you and activated at all times, even in the small hours of the night and when you're on vacation.

Says public relations executive Ravelle Brickman, "If somebody gets murdered in your facility or there's a fire or major accident at your premises, it will be all over the news. Unless you, the publicist, are at the scene of the emergency to give the media your organization's story, reporters will rely on the police version and rumors. You want to be sure you get your organization's version to the media while the story is hot. The next day may well be too late. So you must know media deadlines and get your story to the press in time."

Replying to Questions

Your emergency plan should limit the number of people who can talk with the media during a disaster. This is a time when too many cooks will really ruin the broth. Aside from you, the publicist, only one or two officers or executives should be designated to make statements to reporters. Other staff or volunteers should be told to refer journalists' questions to authorized spokespeople, and you should explain to the staff why it's so important that they don't talk with media people.

Even though you and others authorized to speak may be rushing around trying to find out exactly how many people were killed and injured in an explosion at your organization's headquarters, you must talk to reporters. Let's suppose a reporter tries to collar you and ask questions. Because you're frantic, you start to get angry. You want to tell him to go to hell, but instead you say, "No comment." That isn't a very good idea. "No comment" sounds as if you have something to hide, and it may mean that the reporter will turn to other, possibly less accurate, sources for information. And those sources may be biased.

If you don't have any information, tell them you don't know yet but you'll let them know just as soon as you find out. Try to anticipate questions, and start working on answers immediately. If rumors are having a field day, you should deflate them as soon as you can—with facts. Although you may not be able to tell the press everything you know about the emergency or disaster because of legal problems, do not lie to the press. It will only cause you more problems later.

Don't ever guess about what happened, the cause of an accident, or the size of losses. Say that you don't know yet, or that losses appear to be large or small, but cover yourself by using that word *appear*, since you may be overlooking something. Also, even though you should try to answer reporters' questions honestly, don't volunteer information they haven't asked for.

You may want to give the press a written statement, but first check it with your lawyer. In the confusion surrounding an emergency situation, such a statement often helps reporters write accurate stories. Of course, you can't leave it at that; you will still have to try to answer questions.

Checklist—When the Media Visit

1. Do you really need to call a press conference?
2. Does your subject demand a question-and-answer session?
3. Does your press kit cover all the angles, thereby making a question-and-answer press conference unnecessary?
4. Do you know whether the journalists you work with prefer press conferences, press releases, or one-on-one product demonstrations?
5. Does the subject of your media event demand a particular location?
6. Is there a city with the best media resources for your press conference?
7. Will there be reporters in that city who are familiar with your subject matter?
8. Is the local press friendly to your organization, business, cause, or industry?
9. Does the city you're considering have network news bureaus?
10. Are there wire service bureaus in that town?

11. Which part of town is most convenient for reporters?

12. Will journalists have immediate access to the press conference site without cumbersome security procedures?

13. If you're expecting major television and radio coverage, have you looked at the sound and lighting systems in the room you're going to use?

14. Does your invitation let television news directors know that your press conference room has adequate lighting for their cameras?

15. If you're expecting television coverage, have you worked out lighting arrangements that will make you look your best?

16. Are the doorways and halls in the building wide enough for television equipment?

17. Are there enough heavy-duty circuits for TV lights?

18. Should you have your press conference on location, rather than at a hotel or in your office?

19. If your media event will be outdoors, have you planned for shelter from bad weather, crowd control, noise control, and adequate lighting?

20. Is your event or press conference scheduled at a time that meets the deadlines of most of the media?

21. Have you avoided conflicts with major holidays and events?

22. Are your press conference and special event invitations neatly typed and limited to one page with wide margins?

23. Do they include the "who," "when," "where," "why," "how," and "what"?

24. Have you included a one-paragraph summary, the names of the speakers, a brief blurb on each of them, the location, time, and date, and travel directions if needed?

25. Have you included the exact addresses on your website where journalists can find in-depth and background information?

26. Have you listed the picture and video possibilities, and times for each of them?

27. Have you sent your invitations to the reporters who actually cover your subject?

28. Did the AP Daily Budget editor and the UPI Daybook editor get invitations?

29. Do you know which reporters hate reminder calls?

30. Have you practiced your reminder call pitch so you can describe your press conference or event—and why each journalist's readers will want to know about it—in 15 words or fewer?

31. Did you make reminder telephone calls to the reporters you invited between 8:00 and 9:00 A.M. on the morning of the event?

32. Have you made a list of reporters who said they couldn't come but want follow-up materials?

33. Have you planned to use visual aids at your press conference?

34. Have you rehearsed your speaker?

35. Have you trained him to speak in 10- to 20-second sound bites?

36. Have you worked with him to pare his opening remarks down to five minutes or less?

37. Is your spokesperson ready to answer every possible question, fair and foul?

38. Will you attend the special events and press conferences you arrange?

39. Will you, or someone on your staff, personally greet all reporters as they arrive?

40. Have you limited the number of people attending from your organization?

41. Do you have a press packet for each reporter in a handy location at your event or press conference?

42. Does the packet include a basic release; a backgrounder or longer release; a copy of the speaker's statement; background information on your business, organization, industry, product, or cause; and any relevant documents?

43. Have you considered whether any of this material can be posted on your website instead of handed out in your press packet?

44. Does your press packet include a short list of documents with background information, and the exact URLs where they can be found on your website?

45. Have you thought about how you'll handle your competition or your opposition if they appear at your media event?

46. Have you listed all the things that can go wrong at your media event, and how you'll handle them if they do?

47. Is someone available during your media event to answer the telephone at the number listed on your invitation?

48. Have you taped your press conference?

49. Have you considered archiving your tape on your website so that your staff, stockholders, dealers, distributors, or members can view or listen to it later?

50. Have you planned to call the person staffing the telephone to find out if there are any messages?

51. Have you written a 20-second radio statement or edited a radio audio news release from your audiotape to release to radio reporters who didn't attend?

52. Have you called them and offered the statement or audio news release?

53. Have you written a one-page press release based on the announcement made at the conference or event?

54. Have you delivered this to the print and broadcast journalists who didn't attend, along with your press kit?

55. If you recorded your media event on videotape, have you offered video news releases to major television journalists who didn't attend?

56. Have you delivered the tapes by messenger, satellite, or overnight courier, and included your press kit?

57. Have you contacted trade show managers at least six weeks ahead of show time to find out which journalists have preregistered?

58. What news pegs can you offer to induce these journalists to interview you and your staff at the exhibition?

59. Can you provide experts from your organization for journalists to interview at the show?

60. Do you have a room available that is suitable for the interviews?

61. Have you sent journalists a tip sheet several weeks before show time to let them know what news you will have to offer?

62. Have you found out what arrangements the show has for receiving and exhibiting your press kits?

63. Have you found out how the show's management notifies reporters of new products to be introduced at the show?

64. Can you get coverage in the show's daily publication?

65. Does your organization have an emergency media plan?

66. Does everyone you work with know which staff and executives to notify in an emergency?

67. Does the plan designate the people from your organization who can talk to the media in an emergency or disaster?

68. Do staff members know why it's important not to talk to the media in a crisis?

69. Do all staff members have your cell phone and pager numbers so they can contact you in an emergency?

Making Controversy Positive

O h boy! Did you put your foot in it! You mentioned, in passing, that your company wants to dump harmless chemical wastes into the river. Perhaps an investigative reporter discovered that your solar energy information center used government funds for well-intentioned research that just did not produce any results. Or maybe you're trying to cope with a blizzard of news stories about a design problem with one of your products that has resulted in serious injuries and even deaths.

Whatever the case, your telephone is ringing nonstop, and reporters are jumping through your doors and windows, pointing microphones in your face and asking questions. Oh! the questions. You don't know how to answer them. It's like a bad dream. Whatever you say, you get deeper and deeper into a sticky morass.

Should you run for cover and blanket yourself with a patchwork of "no comments" the moment you smell controversy? According to public relations executive Richard Weiner, that's what has happened in the past. "Public relations people tended to be timid or cowardly with regard to taking a

361

position on controversial issues. Public relations people traditionally said, 'Don't make waves, you can't get the last word in, try to be evasive, and don't be interviewed.'"

But it doesn't work. John and Jane Q. Public aren't dumb, and they know when an organization involved in a controversy is being evasive. Reporters aren't dumb either. If they don't feel you're leveling with them in a controversial situation, they'll go to other sources. And those other sources just may be your opposition, or your competition.

Handling Controversy

To handle controversy coolly, you need to distinguish between healthy controversy and really detrimental publicity. Your next task is to learn how to make advance preparations for coping with bad publicity, when to act and when to remain silent, how to reply to attacks when such action is called for, and how to handle difficult questions from the media. This chapter guides you through that process.

The Positive Side of Controversy

Controversy is not necessarily bad. A good, healthy controversy can, under some circumstances, give you the chance to reach large numbers of people with your organization's point of view. And while under other circumstances it can be more serious, it's almost never the end of the world.

Irving Rimer, vice president for public information for the American Cancer Society, describes it this way: "Controversy can be one of the best things in the world for an organization. If you take a look at the big stories in cancer, they're primarily issue oriented. Cigarette smoking: front-page story. Should the federal government step up its war against cancer? Fraught with controversy."

Rimer continues, "You will not fall apart, no matter how tough the opposition is, if you have done a good job over the years. You have to remember a basic truism: people get tired of conflict. They don't want it to last forever. And they will forget it."

Even if your organization is small and you don't feel very powerful, you may do better than you would expect if you find yourself involved in a controversy that gets media coverage. Says public relations executive

Richard Weiner, "Quite often the little guys include a lot of very intelligent people who by virtue of their intelligence and numbers, aside from the rightness of their cause, are quite able to succeed. On environmental and other public issues, the press and the media tend to side with the little guy." At the same time, the big guy who responds with candor—and persuasive arguments—will get heard, too.

Being Prepared

One fine way to avoid many controversies and a lot of bad publicity is to make sure your organization or business is not busily hiding skeletons in the closet. Nevertheless, there are times when organizations with the cleanest closets in town and nothing to hide find themselves suddenly caught up in a maelstrom of controversy. And, yes, it could happen to you!

If you have any inkling that you will be involved in controversial issues, have facts and figures ready at all times. If your opposition or competition issues a statement, and the press calls you for comment, you must be able to provide your own clear, factual, persuasive statement with little or no warning. In fact, if the press does not call you, you should call them to offer your response as soon as you learn of your opponent's manifesto.

To be ready at all times, follow these recommendations:

- Maintain a good file system with continually updated information drawn from opinion polls, trade and technical magazines, professional and trade associations, material from press clipping bureaus, and whatever other sources you can tap. This will help you respond to attacks with factual answers that can blow the offensive to smithereens.
- Ask yourself all the leading, difficult, tricky questions that the nastiest reporter could concoct. You could even have a panel of colleagues role-play aggressive reporters. Then practice answering them in front of a tape recorder or video camera so that you can calmly analyze your answers afterward.
- It's a very good idea to show the answers you develop to your lawyer, who can help ensure that they can't harm you from a legal point of view. If you're ever faced with difficult, hostile questions in an emergency situation, you'll be glad you did this exercise. Professional help in dealing with the media is listed under "Training" in Chapter 13.

- Know how you can contact journalists quickly in an emergency, even after hours when main switchboards are closed. At minimum, you'll need the telephone numbers for direct lines to newsrooms to reach reporters. If your organization or business has frequent emergencies and crises, you may want to subscribe to one of the 24-hour news wire or broadcast fax services listed in Chapter 13.
- You may also want to make contact with a satellite media tour operator equipped to respond to an emergency within hours. As *Public Relations Journal* points out, a satellite tour "can turn around crisis communication problems in an afternoon, presenting [your] point of view directly to 25 major markets."
- You should know the direct-dial phone number, E-mail address, and fax number for every journalist on your critical list.
- You'll need to know what the press is saying about you, and your emergency situation, on a daily basis. And you must monitor discussions about your organization on the Internet. Several clipping services can give you same-day, almost instantaneous updates on coverage of your product, issue, or organization. (See Chapter 13.)

Journalists expect publicists to do such preparation, and well-prepared publicists are respected. Couple that with honesty, and a publicist can earn a reputation that's worth his weight in gold.

In addition, don't overlook the value of working out a common plan for counterattack within your field. You may find that other members of your trade or professional association are just as enmeshed in controversy as you are. In fact, trade associations are often formed because controversy has hit an industry.

"I think it's very important to find out who your allies are," says Irving Rimer, ". . . and not go in alone. Most issues are not focused on a single [organization], but a broad interest." He further advises: "One of the first steps is to list all the people who have this similar interest. See if you can get together and work out a common cause. The very fact that there's a unity of interest makes your position with the media stronger. It also gives you the opportunity to seek out the best spokesman."

To Act or Not to Act

When it comes to controversial situations, you have to think strategically. You have to determine, says Rimer, if you have "a problem that will last for a period of time, that is going to have an impact, and you have to do something about it." If the problem will go away quickly on its own, you should probably ignore it. Ask yourself whether a reaction from your organization or business would only feed the fires of contention or if it would make a real contribution to an honest debate.

Responding to Attacks

If the attack is coming from a newspaper or broadcaster, *The Publicist* advises the following:

> There are at least five things you can do when a publication or broadcaster says something untrue or distorted about [you]. In escalating order, they are:
> 1. Nothing.
> 2. Write a letter to the journalist who reported and/or wrote the story.
> 3. Write a letter to the editor of the medium, but not for publication.
> 4. Write a letter to the editor for publication.
> 5. Issue a reply, not only to the medium which published the statement but to other media as well.
>
> In a surprising number of cases, number one is the best course. . . . Complaining about errors which are important to [you and your colleagues] but which seem trivial to the press and the public really accomplishes nothing aside from making you . . . feel better. Since you must repeat the misstatement at least partially in your reply, you may actually reinforce it. . . .
>
> When you must reply, do so in writing rather than by telephone or in person. This enables you to marshal your arguments more calmly. . . . Concentrate upon your positive points, rather than a detailed rebuttal of the misstatements. The medium's audience probably will not remember the original story anyway. Never repeat the misstatement in detail. . . . Never attribute bad motives to the medium or question its integrity.

If you're attacked in a newspaper article, and you decide to respond, it's a fairly straightforward matter, according to Gil Cranberg, a professor at the University of Iowa. Writing in *Masthead*, he says, "Most newspapers routinely give the targets of attacks by the papers' own writers an opportunity to respond."

However, if the verbal assault is committed by a syndicated columnist, Cranberg points out, you may want to find out the names of *all* the papers that carry that columnist, so you can offer your response to each and every one of them.

If you are the subject of attack in a syndicated column, you should write a rebuttal and send it to the syndicate. Draw on as many facts as you can to make a calm and reasoned counterargument. If you can include additional supporting data or documents to help you make your case, by all means, do so! Then contact the newspaper in which you saw the attack, and find out the syndicate's address. Mail your response to the syndicate, asking that it be distributed to the editors at all newspapers that carried the column, and ask the syndicate to confirm that this was done. Include a copy of the column and the date it ran to help the syndicate identify it.

If this does not produce results, and you want to try again, write a letter to the columnist, explaining that you contacted the syndicate's office but have received no response. Ask the newspaper that published the column or the syndicate that distributed it for the columnist's office address, which is usually different from the syndicate's.

If an attack is the work of discredited cranks who are keeping themselves well hidden, they will often become remarkably quiet if you let the media know who is at the storm center of this hurricane of words, and why they have been discredited.

Somewhere in the real world about midway between Chelm and Plains City, a neighborhood recreation center found itself the target of letters to the editor and talk show call-ins complaining about the immoral goings-on at the teen drop-in center. The letters and calls, it turned out, were coming from the family of one person, a former maintenance man with an alcoholism problem who had been dismissed when several teenagers and adults complained that they saw him drinking on the job. When his role was brought to light, not only did the letters and calls stop, but also the neighborhood paper wrote an editorial supporting the recreation center's activities and ran a feature story about the drop-in center.

Handling Controversies Under Negotiation

When you have had a meeting with your opposition and have come to an agreement over a controversy, issue a press release immediately. If you wait, your opponents could release material you don't agree with. Even though you thought you and they saw eye to eye at the meeting, that might not have been the case. If they get to the media first, you'll be on the defensive, not a good place to be in a controversy. Even if you are under attack, always be positive. Try to make it look as though you are the one who has taken the bull by the horns.

"The reply is never as effective as the attack," says Irving Rimer. "It doesn't get the same prominence, and it doesn't have the media's support."

Answering Difficult Questions

Admitting your problems to the press? Acknowledging to a reporter that there's another point of view besides your own? You say that sounds like suicide? Well, it isn't. You should not volunteer information about problems your organization or business is having, but when a reporter asks you difficult questions, she probably already has some information. In that case, the more human and helpful you are, the more understanding and receptive she's likely to be. To put it another way, *you* are in command of the situation if you reveal the bad news yourself, rather than waiting for a journalist to unearth it.

"I don't think it's a terrible thing to show some aspect of the organization that isn't as good as you'd like it to be. That, to me, establishes more credibility than anything else," says Cindy Loose of the *Staten Island Register*.

Tom Callaghan of the *Birmingham News* advises, "We'd like you to be straightforward about your shortcomings. If we ask you if it's true that people say this about you, or if we ask you about the negative points about your program, don't try to cover them up or evade them. Be willing to talk about those arguments and say, 'Yes, but . . .' or, 'We see their side, but we have to do this.'"

There are, however, some occasions when, for legal reasons, you cannot answer a question. Or you simply don't know the answer yet. Just as in the case of a disaster, tell journalists that you can't comment for legal reasons, and then take a moment to let them know what those reasons are. Or tell them you don't know the answer yet, but you'll let them know as soon as you do. Be sure to let them know exactly what you're doing to find out that answer.

You may be pulled in two directions in a situation like this. Newton N. Minow, a lawyer who teaches media relations at Northwestern University's Kellogg School of Management, explains why in an article in the *New York Times*. "Generally, lawyers tell executives to shut up while public relations people tell them to communicate. . . . We want to teach students to balance the conflicting advice." It can be quite a balancing act, especially in a crisis situation. That's why you should discuss this matter thoroughly with your organization's top executives and board of directors, and decide on clear guidelines before they are needed.

In your discussion, be sure to point to the ongoing damage to public opinion—and perhaps profitability—caused by the poor handling of controversies and emergencies by some of America's largest corporations. For example, the CEO of a major petroleum company appeared unconcerned when a huge oil spill fouled some of the most environmentally sensitive areas on earth. In a similar case, the head of an international chemical manufacturer couldn't seem to grasp the seriousness of a major industrial disaster. The petroleum producer and the chemical company sustained major damage to their public images because the media are quick to pick up disaster stories in which the organization's spokesperson is not candid and concerned, or in which the spokesperson denies that anything is wrong when the evidence clearly shows a problem.

Even when legal considerations prevent you from speaking, never cut off a reporter with "No comment." Even if you are called at home after midnight, "No comment" is one of the worst of all possible responses. Cindy Loose explains, "It's always wrong because it's going to appear in the paper that you said, 'No comment.' And anytime you say that, it's like pleading the Fifth Amendment. Even if you feel that a reporter is out to get you, if you say something, at least he can present some part of your picture. If you say nothing, you're certainly not going to get a fair shake. I'll always go to another source if the story is important enough. And that source is probably going to be one that is antagonistic to the organization."

Remember that a reporter's job is *not* to take what a publicist says at face value. She must question and probe what you tell her, even in non-controversial situations. Her job is to analyze the news. And she knows that your allegiance is to your organization first and foremost, which is as it should be. She expects you to do your job, and you should expect the same from her.

It is possible to evade questions in order to present positive material first, and then to answer the troublesome points later. Let's say that a neighborhood recreation center was taken over by a new director three months ago, and it has come to light that there is a severe drug problem there. A reporter talks with the new director, and every time she mentions the drug problem, he answers by describing another good program his center runs.

Loose's response to that situation is, "I want people to answer my questions. So it would be very irritating to me. If he inundates me with good stuff, I'm susceptible like anybody else, and I might pick up a point or two. But I want my questions answered, and I'll feel very irritated if I think I'm being evaded."

If, after evading questions for a while, the director says, "Yes, we have a drug problem. There's been one here for years. Since I've taken over I've done this and this to deal with it. We are quite concerned about it and we especially want community input to help solve it," Loose says her response would be positive.

"He'd probably get a better story out of it than if he just kept evading my questions. If I'm really interested in the drug problem, I'm going to talk to kids who have been in his program. I'm going to talk to people who are complaining about his program. I'm going to get all the worst possible information. The question is whether he's going to give me information easily and I'm going to be satisfied with that, so I'm not going to look for his worst critics who will do him much more damage than if he just admitted the problem to begin with."

If you don't know the answer to a reporter's question, admit it. Joyce Michels of the *Billings Gazette* gives the following advice: Say you don't know, but you'll find out. Ask when the reporter needs the information, and be sure you let her know by the deadline. Even if you can't come up with an answer, don't leave her hanging. Describe the steps you took to try to get the answer, and why you can't come up with it. She'll think more highly of you if you level with her.

If you are asked a question about a trade secret, be straightforward with the reporter. Explain that the material is confidential and you don't want your competitors to know about it, so you can't answer her question. She'll understand: after all, journalism is competitive, too.

If a question has legal overtones, refer the reporter to your lawyer. There may be times, particularly in controversies involving possible legal claims, when you cannot admit your organization's shortcomings. Never say anything that could be used to help establish liability in a lawsuit. If you tell a reporter that you can't answer the question because it involves potential litigation, she should accept that if she's a pro, especially if you let her know that she can contact your lawyer for a statement. Be sure you warn your lawyer that the reporter may be calling, so he can have a statement ready.

If controversy pounces on you out of the blue, try for a little breathing space so you can collect your wits and words. Listen to the reporter. Take notes. Say nothing. Ask when she needs to know. Ask for her telephone number and name. Promise to call back with an answer. You now have time to put on your thinking cap, create a careful statement, and anticipate any other questions the reporter may have up her sleeve, but make certain you call back well before her deadline.

This discussion has assumed that reporters are asking honest, straightforward questions. Unfortunately, there are irresponsible, and even dishonest, reporters who will grab a controversy and try to sensationalize it. "Keep in mind," says public relations executive Nan Hohenstein, "that the media often want to present both extremes, not both sides. Ideally, it's best to answer the question, but too often the questions are not structured to accommodate your answer, or to give a comprehensive or insightful answer. They are structured to elicit a sixty-second answer, a yes or no, a paint yourself in the corner answer. Because most people can't think as fast as electronic impulses, it's permissible to give *your* answer, even if it doesn't quite match the question."

How Some Actual Controversies Were Handled

Cindy Loose of the *Staten Island Register* describes how one college president might have undermined his own position. Loose called a private college that was having a little trouble with contract negotiations with the union. According to Loose:

> *They fired a lot of people. The college claimed they were fired because it had financial problems, when it's pretty clear they were let go because negotiations were coming soon, and the college wanted to keep the union down.*
>
> *I called the union people. They were very cooperative. They had a story they wanted to give me. Then I called the president of the college, and I asked him a*

simple question: "Are you in a state of financial emergency?" Now that's a tough question because if he says yes it looks bad for the college, but if he says no, he's screwing with his union negotiations.

He got very angry. Instead of answering me, he just said, "I won't answer any questions relating to that." So I asked about something indirectly related. He hung up on me.

Now when I write that story, the only information I have to go on is whole sheaves of material from the union. But I've got absolutely nothing from the college, only "No comment." How do you think that story is going to come out?

And I'm willing to bet that after the story appears, the president of the college is going to complain. He's going to say "You didn't tell my side." My response to him is that I didn't have his side. How can I tell his side if I don't know what it is?

The following anecdote illustrates how Irving Rimer took charge of a potentially negative situation and preserved the reputation of his institution:

In West Virginia, one of the leading papers was doing a story on the salaries paid to top executives in nonprofit agencies. They wanted the salaries of the executives in the American Cancer Society, and there was a problem getting the information at the state level. Finally the newspaper demanded them directly from us, so I said, "Let's tell them. But let's also tell them what these people do and give them some news ideas along with the information."

I called the reporter and said, "I'm going to give you these salaries, but let me tell you what these people do. Dr. Bauscher, our senior vice-president of research, makes so much. He's the man behind the whole interferon story you've been writing about."

The reporter said, "Oh, that's the one I did last week."

"Yes," I said, "he's the brains behind it; he's the organizer behind it. And our chief executive makes so much per year. He is responsible for an organization that uses two million volunteers and has 2,500 local chapters. He's also responsible for what happens to the $146 million we raised last year." And that's exactly what happened in the story. Instead of just giving him the salaries, I gave him the story behind the salaries.

I think the principle is that if you raise money from the public, you are responsible to the public. If a responsible member of the press is asking for facts, then you should oblige. With understanding and interpretation, you can turn the story around.

In some cases it may not be worthwhile or wise to respond to an attack. Irving Rimer again describes one such case:

> *The American Cancer Society was confronted with ten consecutive programs on WNEW-TV in New York, moderated by Gabe Pressman. Night after night he attacked the Society, the National Cancer Institute, and the whole philosophy behind the cancer control program. Now we had agreed to participate in these programs with our best representatives, but Mr. Pressman's skill and editing overwhelmed them.*
>
> *Volunteers and staff members get most upset by this kind of criticism. It makes them uncomfortable. Representing their interest, we had a meeting with station management in which we were very critical of what took place. We asked that they correct the situation.*
>
> *They told us we could have a half-hour program, but we would be interviewed by Mr. Pressman, and he would have an opportunity to state his views. We thought that would be a useless exercise. As the station manager said to us, "You know we've done a lot of good programs about cancer." Which is true. So that wasn't worth pursuing beyond providing assurances to our own people.*

In another situation, a corporate executive at Cordis Dow managed to turn unfounded rumors into positive publicity for his company. Cordis Dow Corporation manufactures artificial kidneys. Its clipping service started sending the company short news stories urging public-spirited citizens to save computer price codes, pop can tops, or even tea bag tags, which could be exchanged for free dialysis time for needy kidney disease victims.

There was only one problem. When Robert E. Biel, manager of corporate communications for Cordis Dow, tried to find out where and how the tags, tops, and codes could be redeemed, he came to a series of dead ends. The Kidney Foundation had never heard of the campaign, hospitals had no information, and even the experts were puzzled. But the rumors persisted, and stories continued to surface in newspapers from Nashville to Newport.

"I started a one-man campaign to try to stamp out the rumor," says Biel. Cordis Dow tackled the problem through a "blitz" of the news media, hoping to stop the unintentional hoax. The company felt that if people were willing to spend time trying to help kidney disease patients, their efforts should not be fruitless.

Since a successful kidney transplant is the best way to treat kidney failure, Cordis Dow's publicity material explained how people can arrange to donate their kidneys after death. Cordis Dow loses a customer when a kidney patient gets a transplant because the patient no longer needs artificial kidneys, so this was a truly public spirited program.

The president of Cordis Dow sent a letter to the editors of the 70 largest newspapers in the country. A day or two later, Biel heard that the Associated Press was going to put the story on the wire.

Biel contacted the AP reporter working on the story and supplied him with more information. He sent a Mailgram to the editors who had been sent letters, alerting them to the forthcoming wire service story. He also communicated with the Kidney Foundation, which sent reinforcing letters to the 70 editors.

The story got extensive coverage in newspapers from coast to coast. Before Biel's blitz, Cordis Dow was receiving three to five clips a month about kidney dialysis collections. After the story ran, that dropped off to one clipping every two or three months. The whole campaign cost less than $500.

The moral here is that if you tackle a controversial situation with an imaginative, carefully conceived plan that allows you to take the initiative and deal with journalists truthfully, you have an excellent chance to turn a potentially disastrous situation into positive publicity for your organization.

Checklist—Handling Controversy

1. Are you prepared with facts and figures so you can respond to an attack quickly?
2. Have you written down lists of leading, difficult, tricky, and nasty questions that reporters could ask you in a controversial situation?
3. Have you come up with answers to them?
4. Did you discuss these answers with your lawyer?
5. Have you taped your spokesperson answering these questions and helped him make his delivery as believable as possible?

6. Do you know the direct telephone lines and fax numbers for news-rooms, so you can reach them after hours, when switchboards are closed?

7. Have you considered using a 24-hour fax broadcast or E-mail service, or a news wire, to handle emergency communications with the media?

8. Do you know the E-mail addresses for reporters on your media list?

9. Do you have a way to track what the press says about you on a daily basis in a crisis situation? Does that include tracking for both on-line and off-line media?

10. Have you considered finding a satellite media tour operator who can produce a tour in a few hours in an emergency situation?

11. Do you know who your allies are?

12. Have you considered working with others in your industry or field on a common plan for counterattacking your critics?

13. Will the controversy you face go away on its own?

14. Should you ignore it?

15. Will a response only serve to fuel the fires or reinforce wrong information?

16. Will your counterattack make a real contribution to an honest debate?

17. Is your response based on compelling facts and persuasive logic?

18. Can you bolster your response with documents or other supporting evidence?

19. Do you have these documents available on your website, so reporters can access them easily?

20. Even if you have been attacked, can you make it look as if *you're* the initiator of the debate?

21. Have you avoided restating misconceptions and wrong information?

22. Have you asked the publication or broadcaster for an opportunity to respond to an attack?

23. If the attack came from a syndicated columnist, have you contacted the syndicate and asked for an opportunity to rebut it?

24. If that didn't work, did you contact the columnist at his office address?

25. Can you discredit attackers by exposing their hidden motives?

26. If you've negotiated an agreement with your opposition, have you made sure that *you* can issue a release announcing the agreement before the other side does?

27. Have you figured out how to discuss your organization's shortcomings in the most positive light possible?

28. Have you discussed with your lawyer the circumstances in which you absolutely cannot talk about a problem with the press?

29. Have you asked your counsel for advice in handling that type of situation without alienating the media?

30. Is your lawyer willing and able to handle media questions on these matters?

31. Does your lawyer understand why being candid with the media can pay dividends that can't be measured in dollars?

32. Have you discussed this issue with your organization's executives and board of directors and developed crystal-clear guidelines for spokespeople?

33. Have you removed the term "no comment" from your vocabulary?

34. Do you understand why a reporter *must* question what you say, especially in a controversial situation?

35. If a reporter is adversarial, can you respond to her questions with *your* answers in order to paint a positive picture—and then deal with the problem candidly?

36. Can you admit that you don't know the answer to a reporter's question—and then offer to find out for her?

37. Are you confident enough to tell a reporter that you can't discuss trade secrets?

38. When a reporter asking controversial questions calls you out of the blue, can you gain time by listening rather than responding, and offering to call the reporter back later?

12

Solving Problems with the Media

Y ou've sent out 87 press releases, 12 feature article summaries, and a dozen public service spots. But nothing has happened. Not a column inch in the paper, not a call from a reporter, not a single word on the air. What do you do now?

Whatever you do, don't despair! If you view this as a challenge, you have a fighting chance of turning the situation around. On the other hand, if you let anger overwhelm you, and vow to get even, or take on the media, you're sure to lose. "Declaring war on the press, tempting as it may sometimes be, is a game you can't win," says Stratford P. Sherman, writing in *Fortune* magazine.

The first part of that challenge is to look long and hard at yourself, your organization, or your business and ask yourself these questions:

- How can you make your publicity material more interesting? Can you add facts and figures? Anecdotes? A local angle?
- Is your competition getting coverage? If so, what are their news pegs? Can you develop similar news pegs for your material?

- If none of your competition is getting "ink" or airtime, can you join with them in trying to get coverage for a forgotten industry or cause? This could break the ice and make it easier to get coverage later.
- Are there breaking news stories or newsworthy trends you can tie into?
- Have you followed all the recommendations in this book? Yes, that's time-consuming, and no, it isn't easy. But, if you want the media to cover your story, you have to be willing to pay your dues.

If you are not getting the coverage you would like, or if it is not as complete or accurate as it should be, you have to solve the problem yourself. Recent court decisions have weakened the power of the Federal Communications Commission (FCC) to help you deal with broadcasters—and there wasn't a whole lot that could be done even before that. Moreover, the government never has regulated newspapers or magazines, so what it comes down to is this: If you want to be a publicist, you have to rely on persuasion—and excellent publicity material. Combined with some of the techniques in this chapter, persuasiveness and excellence will open doors that are otherwise impervious to all the angry firepower you can muster.

Some tips for handling problems with the media follow. Under any circumstances, no matter how angry you are, remember that the person you are talking with is also human. Approach him with an attack, and he will react defensively. He will try to justify what he's done to explain why he can't help you. And once he has said he won't be able to work with you, it's hard for him to reverse himself because he'll lose face. On the other hand, if you approach a reporter or public service director with a request for help, you've set up a situation in which he can become a problem solver. Many people like that role, since it provides a boost to their self-esteem. And helpers are not as likely to feel defensive.

Make sure that your protests are well thought out and presented in a constructive way. You'll need to go back to that reporter, editor, or public service director for future coverage. "You have to recognize that there's always a tomorrow, and you shouldn't burn your bridges," says Robert Cummings of the *Maine Sunday Telegram*.

Using National Publicity as a Tool

Sometimes your organization, association, or business just can't generate much interest in the local media. But a thousand miles away, you become the out-of-town expert, and national media give you lots of play. If that happens, great! Keep copies of any newspaper clippings, and show these to your local editors and broadcasters to help convince them that you are newsworthy. And if you're lucky, the word about your out-of-town media coverage will travel to your hometown by wire service!

As public relations executive Richard Weiner points out, "In some cases you're not able to get publicity in your local area, and then you get an article in *Time*, and the local media seek you out. Publicity begets publicity."

You can also try getting coverage on the Internet. Web-based journalists are under the pressure of continual deadlines, and they have a voracious appetite for solid stories. Since good stories are often syndicated from one Internet news source to another, you can get considerable exposure from Web-based news media. And this could tilt the balance in your favor, because many brick-and-mortar journalists monitor the Web for story ideas. Chapter 6 has more information on Internet publicity.

How to Handle Inaccurate Coverage

"Reporting, because it's done by people, is not always objective," says Tom Callaghan of the *Birmingham News*. Good reporters recognize this fact of life. As S. Griffin Singer, city editor of the *San Antonio Light* explains, "Sometimes we need our knuckles rapped. Maybe we've dropped the ball, or made mistakes. If we've got a problem, we need to know about it. And it's the same with the material the publicist turns in. If he has misled us, or there was a mistake in information . . . I would complain."

So, you see, it's a two-way street. Before you call the newsroom to complain that the station has blown the story on your new microminiature widget, your Rotary Club's anticrime program, or the impact of your state's new legislation on the gadget industry, switch roles for a minute. Think about how you'd react if the newsroom were calling to chew *you* out for botching your press release.

When you feel that the media have given you inaccurate coverage, you have to determine if the problem involves an *error* of fact or an *interpretation* of the facts that differs from yours.

Errors of fact are easier to manage. Present the correct factual information with as much documentation as you can muster, and try to persuade the journalist involved to do a correction.

A journalist with a different point of view from yours, however, presents a challenge. You can make your task easier by explaining up front that there is a difference of opinion involved and that you'd like a chance to present yours to him and, ultimately, to his audience. Explain your point of view briefly, and back it up with as many facts as possible. Present reasons why his listeners, viewers, or readers will want to be aware of your viewpoint. Be careful not to attack the reporter personally; in fact, the more you refer to his *interpretation* and contrast yours with it, the more legitimate you sound. Finally, ask the reporter if he can help you get coverage for your side of the story.

When your story has been poorly covered, or the information is inaccurate, see if you can develop a new angle and add new material before you call the reporter. That will save his ego; he can run a "new" second story with the correct information, without having to admit he made an error. For the *Boise Statesman*'s Randy McCarthy, that new slant can be decisive: "There's not really much I can do to rectify it after we've already done it. If we have an angle to camouflage the mistake, and we could get back into the story on a second shot, I'll try to do that."

Some reporters will be willing to rectify mistakes in print or on the air even without a new angle. KGW-TV has a "general rule" on this, says Larry Badger: "The reporter who did the particular story with the problem corrects it on the air."

Many reporters will respond positively to a caller who presents another point of view that has not gotten ink or airtime. If, for example, KRAE-AM's Ralph Graczak gets a call from someone who says, "You didn't cover our side of the story," he turns on the tape recorder and asks the caller to tell his side, right then and there. So, if you plan to call a broadcaster, prepare a brief, 20- or 30-second statement. Then you'll be ready if he offers to roll the tape.

If you can't work out a solution with the reporter involved, you should probably let the matter drop, unless the story is going to have a major, serious, and continuing impact on your business or organization. In that case you may want to see if you can arrange a meeting with the managing editor, the editorial board, or the news assignment editor. Explain to them that you'd like an opportunity to present your organization's side of the story. Let them know that you want to work with them to avoid any future problems. Some stations and newspapers will be receptive; some won't.

Help from the Federal Communications Commission

Although the courts may weaken Federal Communications Commission regulation of broadcasting further, as of May 2000, FCC regulations offered limited help with the three following problems:

- You have been attacked on a broadcast.
- You are a political candidate denied equal access to broadcast time.
- You can *prove* that news coverage of your business, organization, or cause has been deliberately falsified.

But don't count on the FCC to solve your coverage problems for you, even if the courts leave the agency's remaining powers intact. The FCC moves slowly. You, as a publicist, must move fast.

"Before complaining to the Commission, complain to the station," advises the FCC. "We encourage negotiations between candidates and stations . . . and have found that many disputes can be settled in that way . . . When you do file a complaint with the Commission, send a copy to the station . . . at the same time . . . thus saving time in settling the complaint."

So, once again, it's up to you to get what you want by persuasion and negotiation. Sure, you can cite FCC regulations to add weight to your argument, but the power of your presentation will come from your ability to convince broadcasters that you have a valid argument—and that their listeners will want to know about it.

FCC Rules on Personal Attack

According to the FCC, "When, during the presentation of views on a controversial issue of public importance, an attack is made upon the honesty, character, integrity or like personal qualities of an identified person or group, a licensee must provide a script, tape or accurate summary (if a script or tape is not available) of the attack to the persons or group attacked. Likewise, when a licensee, in an editorial, endorses or opposes a candidate for public office, the licensee must provide the other qualified candidate[s] for the same office (if endorsement of a candidate) or the candidate opposed in the editorial with a script or tape of the editorial."

The FCC requires a broadcaster to notify a person or organization that has been attacked of the date, time, and name of the program within a reasonable time and in no event later than one week from the attack. You must be offered a "reasonable" opportunity to personally respond to the attack on the air. And, if the original attack was made during prime time, you should insist that your reply time is not at midnight.

The personal-attack rule does not apply if the comments were made during a newscast, a news interview, or on-the-spot coverage of a news event. Nonetheless, you still may want to ask the station for a chance to reply. The personal-attack rule also does not apply if the comments concerned foreign groups or foreign public figures; occurred during uses by legally qualified candidates; or were "made by legally qualified candidates, their authorized spokespersons, or those associated with them in the campaign, on other such candidates, their authorized spokespersons or persons associated with the candidates in the campaign."

The FCC's Policies on Fraudulent News Coverage

Under some circumstances, the FCC will act on complaints that news programming has been "distorted, slanted, rigged, or staged." It must have hard evidence that this was done deliberately by a station, and that evidence must come from somewhere other than the newscast itself.

As an FCC fact sheet explains: "The Commission is barred by law from censoring broadcast material. Also, the FCC does not attempt to substitute its judgment for that of the broadcaster in the selection and presentation of material for programs of news and comment. As a public trustee, the broadcaster may not engage in intentional and deliberate falsification (distorting, slanting, rigging, staging) of the news. Therefore, the Commission does act appropriately to protect the public interest in this important respect where we have received extrinsic evidence of such rigging and slanting."

13

Sources and Services for Publicists

The following directory gives you some idea of the books, information, and services available to publicists. Many of the firms listed are in New York, the nation's public relations capital. Check your city's yellow pages for local firms to widen your choices.

No prices are given here. Contact each service for complete information, including current fees. Be sure you understand exactly what you will get for your money; always ask for written estimates and descriptions of services. Whenever you can, compare the prices and promises of two or three services before you sign on the dotted line.

This is not a complete list. If your curiosity is whetted and you want to know more about publicity resources, more information is available at Jack O'Dwyer's website (http://www.odwyerpr.com), which is an encyclopedia of useful information about services and sources for publicists. Several other Web pages with useful links for publicists are listed in the "Websites" section.

All the URLs mentioned in this chapter are live on this book's website (http://www.publicityhandbook.com). If you hate typing in links, go to the website and just click on them! Books and directories that don't have contact information are available through the large on-line book-sellers. Use the ISBN (International Standard Book Number) to find the title quickly on-line.

Audio and Video News Releases

Gourvitz Communications, Inc.
729 Seventh Avenue, 15th Floor, New York, NY 10019, (212) 730-4807.

Complete production and distribution facilities for video news releases, using Gourvitz's script or yours. The company can deliver video crews for any project in the world on one day's notice. All crews and technical people have broadcast experience. VNRs can be mailed to stations on cassettes or delivered by satellite.

Medialink
708 Third Avenue, Ninth Floor, New York, NY 10017, (212) 682-8300, (800) 843-0677—with production affiliates worldwide; http://www.medialink.com.

Medialink's dedicated transmission network is used exclusively for satellite media tours, video news releases, and public service spots. The company offers complete planning, consulting, and delivery services for video news releases but does not produce them. Says Medialink, "We are the nation's professional *distributor* of VNRs, not the manufacturer."

The company's nationwide news-wire service, used solely to alert network and local television newsrooms to video news releases available for booking in advance, is tied in to the Associated Press wire.

MG Productions, Inc.
216 E. 45th Street, New York, NY 10017-3374, (212) 682-4725; http://www.mgproductions.com; E-mail: info@mgproductions.com.

Full-service scripting, production, editing, and distribution house. MG's creative approach has won numerous awards. MG distributes VNRs on cassettes or by satellite transmission. Distribution and usage reports are computerized.

On the Scene Productions

5900 Wilshire Boulevard, Suite 1400, Los Angeles, CA 90036,
(323) 930-1030; New York: (212) 715-0800; Chicago: (312) 644-6170;
http://www.onthescene.com; E-mail: info@onthescene.com.

From scouting the location through distributing your video news
release on cassettes or by satellite, On the Scene Productions handles
video news releases from start to finish. The company specializes in
shooting on location (which can produce more compelling stories that
get better airplay).

PCS Broadcast Services Division of DWJ Television

1 Robinson Lane, Ridgewood, NJ 07450, (212) 697-2765,
(201) 445-1711, extension 141.

PCS and its parent company are among the largest producer-
distributors of video news releases. They will write the script and do all the
production, distribution, and tracking for video news releases and their
radio counterpart, audio news releases. VNRs are distributed by satellite,
fiber, tape, and other methods. ANRs are distributed by telephone feeding,
satellite, and notification of newsrooms to call DWJ's automated feeding
system. They are leaders in incorporating Internet promotion of these
releases. PCS also produces, distributes, and tracks radio and TV feature
programs.

PR Newswire

810 Seventh Avenue, New York, NY 10019, (212) 596-1500,
(800) 832-5522; http://www.prnewswire.com.

Distributes video news releases to traditional broadcasters and digi-
tizes them for Internet distribution. Off-line broadcasters can preview
VNRs on PR Newswire's website.

West Glen

1430 Broadway, Ninth Floor, New York, NY 10018, (212) 921-2800;
635 N. Michigan Avenue, Suite 600, Chicago, IL 60611, (312) 751-4274;
595 Market Street, Suite 2500, San Francisco, CA 94105, (415) 495-1455;
1155 Connecticut Avenue NW, Suite 300, Washington, D.C. 20036,

(202) 331-9454; 2220 S. Arbutus Court, Lakewood, CO 80228, (303) 914-9382; http://www.westglen.com; E-mail: info@westglen.com.

West Glen will counsel you on the story angle and scripting of your video news release, provide full-service production and editing for studio and on-location stories, and then book and track usage of your VNR. The in-house database includes information on each station's subject and format preferences, as well as technical requirements.

West Glen uses both internal and outside monitoring sources to report on how your VNR was used by television stations, and encodes VNRs digitally to aid in tracking. In many markets the company can provide videotaped "clippings." Also distributes VNRs produced by others, with consultation available on newsworthiness and editing. Distribution is by both satellite and mailed videocassettes, with West Glen advising which method is best on a case-by-case basis. West Glen distributes VNRs in the United States and abroad.

In addition, West Glen specializes in rereleasing evergreen video news releases (containing material that will not quickly become dated) to cablecasters, through which they get an additional audience. West Glen can also create a library of your prerecorded 5- to 30-minute television features and lend them to broadcasters on a regular basis.

West Glen distributes radio ANRs on CD, reel-to-reel, or cassette tapes.

Books and Tapes

The Associated Press Stylebook and Briefing on Media Law
Goldstein, Norm, editor. Associated Press. ISBN: 0917360192.

Organized in a dictionary format, an A-to-Z listing of guides to capitalization, abbreviation, punctuation, spelling, numerals, and usage. Use this stylebook, and your copy will be acceptable to all AP newspapers and broadcasters. Also includes information on photo captions, media law, and avoiding libel, as well as a list of all AP bureaus. Available in larger bookstores.

The Copywriter's Handbook
Bly, Robert W. Henry Holt. ISBN: 0805011943.

How to write effective publicity and promotion copy, by one of the nation's leading freelance copywriters. Includes information on how to write persuasively and how to make sure you're communicating, along with dozens of tips and techniques to make the writing task easier and more productive. Particularly useful if you need to go beyond publicity writing to turning out copy for newsletters, direct mail, brochures, and ads.

The Crisis Counselor

Caponigro, Jeffrey, R. NTC Business Books, (800) 323-4900. ISBN: 0809224909.

Provides a list of 15 crises that can strike any business, and seven simple rules for preparing to handle them in advance. Includes detailed suggestions for crisis management.

The Critical Issues Audit

Sopow, Eli. Issue Action Publications, Inc. ISBN: 001386904X.

This workbook takes you through a series of self-administered tests that show you where your organization is vulnerable. Helps you prepare to deal with these areas before the media focus on them.

Effective Crisis Planning (videotape)

Public Relations Society of America, Video Library, 33 Irving Place, New York, NY 10003, (212) 995-2230; http://www.prsa.org.

Three experts discuss and explain the principles and techniques of preparing a crisis plan for an organization.

Effective Planning and Budgeting for Public Relations Programs (videotape)

Public Relations Society of America, 33 Irving Place, New York, NY 10003, (212) 995-2230; http://www.prsa.org.

Features tips and techniques to help you enhance your skills for planning budgets that stay on track.

The Elements of Business Writing

Bly, Robert W., and Gary Blake. MacMillan Distribution. ISBN: 0020080956.

A thorough refresher course on writing clearly in a compact book that's easy to read. You'll probably use it as a daily reference.

Great News Photos and the Stories Behind Them
Faber, John. Dover Publications. ISBN: 0486236676.

A collection of 140 famous news photos from 1855 to 1976, and the stories of how they were shot. It will help you understand what makes a good piece of publicity art.

Public Relations Writing
Bivins, Tom. NTC/Contemporary Publishing Group, (800) 323-4900. ISBN: 0844203513.

Practical guidelines for producing publicity material and press kits, and information on desktop publishing applications for publicists. Includes case studies and assignments.

How to Write, Speak, and Think More Effectively
Flesch, Rudolf, and Salvatore Raimondo. New American Library. ISBN: 0451167635.

A helpful book about how to write plain English and how to test your writing for readability. Every publicist should read—and reread—this gem!

Media Relations/Crisis Management (Public Relations Body of Knowledge Abstracts)
Public Relations Society of America, 33 Irving Place, New York, NY 10003, (212) 995-2230; http://www.prsa.org.

A comprehensive collection of abstracts from books, journals, and articles on both media relations and crisis management, conveniently categorized for quick reference. Available in printed form or on diskettes.

NTC's Mass Media Dictionary
NTC Business Books, (800) 323-4900. ISBN: 084423186X.

A comprehensive dictionary of more than 20,000 technical terms, from *abaxial lens* to *zapping*, used in television, radio, journalism, publishing, graphic arts, advertising, and public relations. Related entries are cross-referenced. This dictionary can help you understand what the experts are really saying.

Pictures for Organizations
Douglis, Philip N. Lawrence Ragan Communications, Inc.,
316 N. Michigan Avenue, Suite 300, Chicago, IL 60601, (800) 878-5331;
E-mail: cservice@ragan.com.

Written especially for house publication editors, this book will be
highly valuable to publicists who either take their own pictures or work
with photographers to get publicity shots. Crammed with practical tips
about using photography to communicate.

Power Public Relations
Saffir, Leonard. NTC Business Books, (800) 323-4900.
ISBN: 0658000608.

How public relations strategies can be used to change public perceptions of your organization.

Public Relations in the Marketing Mix
Goldman, Jordan. NTC Business Books, (800) 323-4900.
ISBN: 0844230847.

An in-depth discussion of how to determine what kinds of public relations an organization needs, techniques for writing a public relations plan
and presenting it to management, the considerations involved in selecting
public relations vehicles, and how to deal with problem situations.

Public Relations Law (**videotape**)
Public Relations Society of America, 33 Irving Place, New York, NY
10003, (212) 995-2230; http://www.prsa.org.

Information about laws that affect publicity, including copyright, trade-
marks, confidentiality, financial reporting requirements for public corporations, and the right to privacy.

Public Relations Workbook
Simon, Raymond, and Joseph Zappala. NTC Business Books,
(800) 323-4900. ISBN: 0844236675.

How you can work with your organization's marketing and advertising departments to create powerful integrated marketing.

Publicity and Media Relations Checklists
Yale, David R. NTC Business Books, (800) 323-4900;
http://www.publicityhandbook.com. ISBN: 0844232181.

Fifty-nine proven checklists help you apply what you've learned in *The Publicity Handbook*. Yale guides you through the process, step-by-step, showing you exactly what to think about and write down. By the time you're finished, you have a complete publicity plan for your organization and every project you tackle. You'll save time, win attention, and maximize exposure with every public relations and publicity contact. Several checklists from the book are posted on the website.

Reporting for the Media
Fedler, Fred, John R. Bender, Lucinda Davenport, and Paul E. Kostyu. HBJ College & School Division. ISBN: 0155037242.

A detailed textbook for beginning journalists, with chapters on style, leads, features, and the use of quotations, coupled with comprehensive exercises. Useful for publicists who want to improve their writing skills.

State of the Art Marketing Research
Breen, George E., A. B. Blankenship, and Alan Dutka. NTC Business Books, (800) 323-4900. ISBN: 0844234435.

Oriented toward marketing research, this book covers the basics of conducting your own surveys. The techniques described will help you do the research you need for your publicity program.

Value-Added Public Relations
Harris, Thomas L. NTC Business Books, (800) 323-4900. ISBN: 0844234117.

Dozens of case histories show how some of the nation's most successful marketers have used public relations techniques to give added power and persuasion to their marketing messages.

Webcasting Handbook
West Glen, 1430 Broadway, Ninth Floor, New York, NY 10018, (212) 921-2800; http://www.westglen.com; E-mail: info@westglen.com.

The West Glen *Webcasting Handbook,* published on-line, is a plain-English introduction to this important publicity tool. It's available at the company's website, at this URL: http://www.medialink.comwebcast/index.html.

Webster's New World Dictionary of Media and Communications, *2nd Edition*
Weiner, Richard. IDG Books Worldwide. ISBN: 0028606116.

Publicists must be familiar with technical terms from many industries—including broadcasting, printing, television, and video—to understand what the experts are saying. This single source for definitions of terms such as *baby kicker, B-roll, duckfoot, gobo,* and *niffnoff* includes more than 30,000 definitions from 27 fields related to publicity.

Writing for the Media
Pesmen, Sandra. NTC Business Books, (800) 323-4900.
ISBN: 0844230766.

A guide to writing for the media that can help get your releases and feature articles published. Includes more than 50 examples and exercises.

Content Syndicators

These Web-based services syndicate your content to websites and E-zines. Since several recent studies have shown that good content makes a website more attractive, or "sticky," and gets viewers to return, website proprietors are interested in adding solid material to their sites. You can usually include a link to your website in the articles you submit to these sites. For more information about this new Web-based publicity opportunity, see the listing for ContentBiz.Com under "Newsletters and Magazines."

Isyndicate.com
iSyndicate, Inc., 455 Ninth Street, San Francisco, CA 94103, (415) 896-1900; http://www.isyndicate.com.

The service can make your content available to more than 247,472 websites, by posting headlines that are linked to the complete text on your site. You have to apply and get approval first.

MediaPeak.com

(602) 532-7218; http://mediapeak.com; story submissions:
mailto:submitnews@aol.com; E-mail: mediapeak@mindspring.com.

An on-line service that provides free content to on-line publishers.
More than 2,000 on-line publishers subscribe to the E-mail service, which
provides free, reprintable news and articles for use in the publishers' websites and E-zines. Content is archived on the website, so publishers can
access it at any time. The site welcomes unsolicited press releases, news,
feature article submissions, and story pitches. Particular interests are business, marketing, E-commerce, Internet issues and news, computer news,
politics, inspirational material, and book reviews. A list of other syndica-
tion services is provided on the website.

NET Designs

434 Winchester Street, Prince George, VA 23875, (804) 733-2843;
http://www.certificate.net/wwio/.

Software that lets you self-syndicate content to other websites. You
use the software to handle distribution, but you set the terms of usage:
fee-based or free.

Directories of Experts

ExpertSource

Business Wire, 40 E. 52nd Street, 19th Floor, New York, NY 10022,
(212) 752-9600, (800) 221-2462; http://www.businesswire.com.

ExpertSource helps journalists quickly and easily find experts for
authoritative analysis, insights, and commentary about news and feature
stories. Journalists submit queries seeking experts for specific editorial
projects. ExpertSource searches its proprietary database of academic and
industry experts and quickly responds with a roster of prospective interview candidates.

ProfNet

100 North Country Road, Suite C, Setauket, NY 11733, (631) 941-3736,
(800) PROFNET; http://www.profnet.com.

ProfNet provides journalists and authors convenient access to expert sources. Reporters phone, fax, or E-mail their queries to ProfNet. Four times daily, ProfNet sends these queries to publicist members by E-mail.

The Yearbook of Experts, Authorities, and Spokespersons

Broadcast Interview Source, 2233 Wisconsin Avenue, Suite 406, Washington, DC 20007-4104, (202) 333-4904, (800) YEARBOOK; http://www.yearbook.com.

Used by more than 5,000 journalists to find experts and spokespeople, with both paper-based and on-line versions. If you want journalists to contact you when they're working on stories in your field, consider a paid listing here.

Discussion Groups and Mailing Lists

There are dozens of mailing lists of interest to publicists. Here are some of the best, with thanks to Barbara Croll Fought, associate professor at the S. I. Newhouse School of Public Communications at Syracuse University, and Robin Marshall, APR, of Hieran Publishing, for sharing their recommendations.

Airwaves

To subscribe: subscribe@airwaves.com. In the body of the message, type: subscribe airwaves firstname lastname.

This list is a daily digest of the newsgroup rec.radio.broadcasting. It is moderated and is aimed at radio professionals.

Broadcast (BRDCST-L)

To subscribe: listserv@unlvm.unl.edu. In the body of the message, type: subscribe brdcst-l firstname lastname.

A list for professionals and academics covering all subjects in TV, radio, and cable. Features postings on news but also covers topics of interest to people in management, sales, or public relations.

CompuServe Information Service

5000 Arlington Centre Boulevard, Columbus, OH 43220, (800) 848-8990; http://www.compuserve.com.

CompuServe's Public Relations and Marketing Forum is one of the oldest discussion groups around. Good discussions abound here. You don't have to be a CompuServe member to lurk, but if you want a voice in this forum, you have to join to post messages. To preview the Forum, go to the website and click on the Forums link to look up the specific forum.

Computer-Assisted Reporting (NICAR-L)

To subscribe: listproc@missouri.edu. In the body of the message, type: subscribe nicar-l firstname lastname.

Information on computer-assisted reporting (CAR) run by the National Institute of Computer-Assisted Reporting at the University of Missouri. Helpful group for trading information, leads, and techniques among reporters doing CAR.

Computer-Assisted Research (CARR-L)

To subscribe: listserv@ulkyvm.louisville.edu. In the body of the message, type: subscribe carr-l firstname lastname.

The best list around for journalists. Although its focus is computer-assisted research and reporting (how to find data and software programs, as well as how to use data in stories), it covers many journalism topics. List owner Elliott Parker, a Central Michigan University professor, feeds the list with wonderful tips and posts that you won't find in other places. It's an active list, so expect 15 messages a day!

Digital News

To subscribe: digital_news-request@rtndf.org. In the subject line (not the body of the text), type: subscribe.

Part of the "News in the Next Century" project of the Radio-Television News Directors association. Covers implications of new technology for news, and the future of the news business.

Edupage

To subscribe: listproc@educom.unc.edu.

A digest from newspaper coverage of media issues and information technology.

Freelance Journalists

To subscribe: majordomo@mlists.net. In the body of the message, type: subscribe freelance-journalists firstname lastname.

Here's where freelance journalists share ideas and exchange information. Run by Katim Touray.

Freelance Journalists' Usenet Group

alt.journalism.freelance.

A source for finding freelance writers for your publicity materials.

Freelance Photographers' Usenet Group

alt.journalism.photo.

A good place to learn photojournalism tips and tricks, and a resource for finding a local photojournalist for freelance work.

The Internet Public Relations Discussion List (I-PR)

http://www.audettemedia.comi-public_relations/.

I-PR is a free twice-weekly E-mail newsletter and discussion list moderated by publicist Adam Sherk. Topics covered include publicity strategy and implementation for the Internet, on-line media relations, case studies from subscribers, and news from major publicity trade shows and seminars.

Investigative Reporting (IRE-L)

To subscribe: listproc@lists.missouri.edu. In the body of the message, type: subscribe ire-l firstname lastname.

This active list covers discussions related to investigative reporting. Most posters are involved in the professional organization Investigative Reporters and Editors (IRE).

Journalism and Religion List (JREL-L)

To subscribe, send a request and brief description of yourself and your interest to jrel-l-owner@iclnet.org.

For reporters and editors on the religion beat; operated by Tim Morgan, associate editor, *Christianity Today* magazine.

National Conference of Editorial Writers (NCEW-L)

To subscribe, send an E-mail message requesting to be added to pfiske@netusa.net, including your name, your professional affiliation, and a brief description of your interest in the list.

Discussions among editorial page writers, editors, and others involved with editorials or op-eds. Includes print and broadcast journalists, as well as professors and students.

National Press Photographers Association (NPPA-L)

To subscribe: listserv@cmuvm.csv.cmich.edu. In the body of the message, type: subscribe nppa-l firstname lastname.

A discussion group for visual communicators, news photographers and editors, system operators, and graphics editors. Covers print and electronic media.

News Librarians (NEWSLIB)

To subscribe: listproc@ripken.oit.unc.edu.

Primarily for news librarians, but includes journalists and researchers. Good for tips on where to find information, especially on the Internet.

Online News

To subscribe: majordomo@marketplace.com.

Extensive discussions about on-line publications.

Online Writing

To subscribe: http://www.planetarynews.comonline-writing.

Another group run by Steve Outing, along with Amy Gahran, a Web content developer. This group branched off from Online News to focus specifically on writing for on-line media, including the Web, E-mail publications, and intranets.

PRFORUM

To subscribe: listserv@listserv.iupui.edu. In the body of the message, type: subscribe prforum.

The most popular public relations mailing list. Covers strategies, contacts, and issues in public relations.

PRSA Listserv

Public Relations Society of America, 33 Irving Place, New York, NY 10003, (212) 995-2230; http://www.prsa.orgppc/listserv.html.

An on-line discussion group for publicists and public relations professionals that is open to anyone, both members and nonmembers of PRSA.

Public Information Officers Working in Academia (PIONET)

To subscribe: listproc@mlist.access.digex.net. In the body of the message, type: subscribe pionet firstname lastname.

This discussion is geared to public information officers in colleges and universities. Topics range from executing special events to working with reluctant faculty researchers. This group formerly focused on science writing but is much broader now.

Radio Forum

To subscribe: majordomo@sojourn.com. In the body of the message, type: subscribe radio-forum e-mail-address.

Covers all aspects of radio, from music, to sales, to management, to engineering. Designed for anyone who works in radio.

Shoptalk (TV News)

To subscribe: listserv@listserv.syr.edu.

A must-read for people interested in TV news.

Small Shop PR Agency

To subscribe: smallshoppragency-subscribe@onelist.com. Leave message blank.

From OneList (http://www.onelist.com), which also hosts several other PR- and communications-related lists; you can visit the site and do a search for lists of interest to you.

Society of Professional Journalists (SPJ-L)

To subscribe: listserv@psuvm.psu.edu. In the body of the message, type: subscribe spj-l firstname lastname.

An active list run by the nation's oldest journalism organization. Includes SPJ chapter updates and covers a wide range of topics and current events in the news. Frequented mostly by journalists. Very active.

Steve Outing's Online News

To subscribe: http://www.planetarynews.comonline-news.

This forum discusses interactive media and the on-line news industry. Great for writers, editors, and new media content producers.

WIREPHOTO-L

To subscribe: listserv@pressroom.com. In the body of the message, type: subscribe wirephoto-l firstname lastname.

A discussion of wire service photography and photographers. Subscribers include wire photographers, stringers, and picture editors. Topics include technology, ethics, working conditions, coverage problems, and photojournalism.

Fax News Distribution Services

Bacon's Information, Inc.

332 S. Michigan Avenue, Chicago, IL 60604, (800) 621-0561; http://www.baconsinfo.com.

Direct Media Services, Inc.

200 Park Avenue South, #1401, New York, NY 10003, (212) 375-0002.

Fast-Fax, Media Distribution Services

307 W. 36th Street, New York, NY 10018-0230, (800) MDS-3282; http://www.mdsconnect.com; E-mail: services@mds-newyork.com.

Medialink

708 Third Avenue, New York, NY 10017, (212) 682-8300; http://www.medialink.com.

PIMS

21 Penn Plaza, New York, NY 10001, (212) 279-5112; http://www.pimsinc.com; E-mail: mryan@pimsinc.com.

PR Newswire

810 Seventh Avenue, New York, NY 10019, (212) 596-1500, (800) 832-5522; http://www.prnewswire.com.

Mat Services

Mat services take your press release or feature story and pictures, print them in easily reproducible form (called "mats" or "reproduction proofs"), and send them out to newspapers. Busy editors at smaller papers often use the entire article, with the art, because it saves time. And since they can use the reproduction proofs directly, without typesetting, they save money. Many corporations, trade associations, and nonprofit organizations use this method to get the message to readers exactly as they wrote it.

When you contact a mat service, ask for samples, and find out whether the fee includes providing you with clippings.

Associated Release Service, Inc.
43 N. Canal Street, Chicago, IL 60606, (312) 726-8693;
E-mail: assocrel@aol.com.

This service, specializing in theme page placements, will prepare and distribute your release in typeset form to 8,100 suburban and community daily and weekly newspapers, as well as all daily papers worldwide. All or part of the list can be used. Clippings are provided as part of service.

Derus Media Service, Inc.
7702 S. Cass Avenue, #110, Darien, IL 60561-5080, (630) 960-4690.

Derus will write a feature story based on your material and send out glossy reproduction proofs to more than 8,000 daily and weekly papers in the United States. All or part of the list can be used. You can send out a regular column series topped by a standing headline, or opt for a specially made crossword puzzle based on your firm's product or service or your organization's cause. Derus can also send proofs to Canadian papers and send Spanish-language material to Hispanic publications in the United States. Clippings are provided as part of the service for U.S. papers.

Metro Associated Services, Inc.
33 W. 34th Street, New York, NY 10001, (212) 947-5100,
(800) 223-1600; http://www.metrocreativegraphics.com.

Metro sends out reproduction proofs of monthly feature sections, each one with a theme, such as Home Improvement, Mother's Day Gift Guide, or Food and Cooking. Each section includes stories from several organizations. The proofs are distributed to 7,000 daily and weekly papers.

North Americas Precis Syndicate, Inc.
350 Fifth Avenue, Suite 6500, New York, NY 10118, (212) 867-9000;
http://www.napsnet.com.

Your release or a release adapted from your material is sent to 1,500 suburban dailies and 8,500 weeklies, in ready-to-print form. Staff writers include a home economist, former reporters and editors, and public relations and advertising professionals, all of whom specialize in preparing stories that editors can use. NAPS promises at least 100 placements per release, and clippings are provided as part of the fee. The company guarantees satisfaction or will do another release at no cost.

Media Directories

You can save your fingers from doing a lot of walking by buying a few good media directories. Each directory has its own strong points. If your publicity is regional, national, or international in scope, you will need more than one of them.

All-in-One Directory
Gebbie Press, PO Box 1000, New Paltz, NY 12561-0017, (845) 255-7560; http://www.gebbie.com.

A compact directory with 23,000 listings for daily and weekly papers; radio and TV stations; consumer, business, and trade magazines; farm publications; the black and Hispanic press; and more. Available in printed, bound form or on floppy disks for the IBM-PC or Macintosh.

All-Links
http://www.all-links.comnewscentral/.

An index of more than 3,500 newspapers worldwide that have an on-line presence, with links to their websites.

Bacon's Media Directories
Bacon's Information, Inc., 332 S. Michigan Avenue, Chicago, IL 60604, (312) 922-2400, (800) 621-0561; http://www.baconsinfo.com.

Ten directories, which together provide detailed information on more than 400,000 editorial contacts at nearly 60,000 print, broadcast, and on-line media outlets in the United States, Canada, Mexico, and the Caribbean. Available in electronic and print format. Individual titles include:

- *Newspaper and Magazine*
- *Radio, Television, and Cable*
- *Media Calendar*
- *Internet Media*
- *International Media*
- *New York Publicity Outlets*
- *Metro California Media*
- *Business Media*
- *Computer and Hi-Tech Media*
- *Medical and Health Media*

Burrelle's Media Directories
Burrelle's, 75 E. Northfield Avenue, Livingston, NJ 07039, (973) 992-6600, (800) 631-1160; http://www.burrelles.com.

Publishers of directories, including more than 300,000 U.S. contacts among them. The individual titles are:

- *Daily Newspapers*
- *Non-Daily Newspapers*
- *News Services and Feature Syndicates*
- *Magazines and Newsletters*
- *Radio Stations and Programming*
- *Television Stations and Programming*
- *Local Cable Systems*

CorporateNews.com
1642 Kelliwood Oaks Drive, Suite 100, Katy, TX 77450, (281) 599-9200; (877) 763-4257; http://www.corporatenews.com.

Here you'll find a Web-based directory of 30,000 on-line and off-line media outlets, from daily papers to E-zines. Listings are updated continuously. All E-mail addresses are provided by the media. Allows you to add journalists from your own lists, create customized lists on-line in minutes, and distribute press releases to your list electronically. Also, you can create an on-line pressroom for your organization, hosted by Corporate News.com.

Directory of Women's Media

National Council for Research on Women, 11 Hanover Square,
New York, NY 10005, (212) 785-7335.

Listings for more than 700 periodicals and 100 women's presses and publishers, as well as other types of women's media.

EdCals

311 Arsenal Street, Watertown, MA, 02472-2700, (617) 374-9300;
http://www.edcals.com.

This site, which is jointly operated by Bacon's Information, Inc., and MediaMap, is a search engine for editorial calendars for both print and Web media. You can search thousands of continuously updated editorial calendars with more than 120,000 upcoming stories and special issues from nearly every leading U.S. magazine and newspaper, both print and Web-based. Story listings include in-depth information, and the service E-mails updates to you every week to make sure you're on top of crucial changes in upcoming stories. You can search by topic and date range.

Editor and Publisher International Yearbook

Editor & Publisher, 11 W. 19th Street, New York, NY 10011-4234,
(212) 675-4380; http://www.mediainfo.com.

A wealth of newspaper facts and figures, organized in seven sections. Listings for daily, national, weekly, black, religious, foreign-language, and college newspapers in the United States. The foreign section covers newspapers in Canada, Europe, the Caribbean, Central America, Mexico, South America, Africa, the Middle East, Asia, the Far East, Australia, New Zealand, and the Pacific Ocean territories.

Also includes listings for wire and photo services, syndicates, newspaper-distributed magazine sections, mat services, and clipping bureaus.

EzineSeek

http://www.ezineseek.com.

A directory of E-zines in which you'll find such titles as *Teacher's Network Teacher Talk* and *Electronic Broadcaster*. Includes sample issues on-line.

Ezines Plus

http://www.ezinesplus.com.

A directory of family-friendly E-zines, with topics such as food and health, crafts, pets, and gardening.

Hispanic Media and Markets

Standard Rate & Data Service, 1700 Higgins Road, Des Plaines, IL 60018-5605, (847) 375-5000, (800) 851-7737; http://www.srds.com.

Profiles of more than 2,200 Hispanic newspapers, consumer and business publications, and broadcast stations. Although this publication is heavily oriented to advertisers, publicists will also find it useful. Updated quarterly.

Hudson's Newsletter Directory

H&M Publishers, 4 W. Market Street, PO Box 311, Rhinebeck, NY 12572, (845) 876-2081.

Lists more than 4,900 major subscription newsletters worldwide and gives details on acceptance of press releases and key contact names. Cross-indexed by subject.

International Directory of New Age and Alternative Publications

Sunstar Publications, Ltd. ISBN: 1887472185.

Latin American Media Directory

International Media Center. ISBN: 0965639908.

Here's information on daily Spanish- and Portuguese-language newspapers, all radio and television networks, plus major independent Spanish or Portuguese stations. The listings include addresses, telephone and fax numbers, websites, E-mail addresses, key personnel, circulation, and broadcast audience size. Listings are in English and Spanish.

Low Bandwidth

http://www.disobey.comlow.

A directory of E-zines from *Appellate Decisions Noted* to *Weight Loss Coach News*, and everything else in between.

MediaMap

311 Arsenal Street, Watertown, MA, 02472-2700, (617) 374-9300;
http://www.mediamap.com.

This unusually thorough media directory includes more than 200,000
off-line and on-line editorial contacts and is updated continuously on-line.
MediaMap is particularly strong in several industries: high tech, business
and finance, health care, automotive, arts and entertainment, fashion and
beauty, and hospitality and travel. In addition, you'll find contact information for foreign correspondents in the United States. Listings include an
overview of each publication and information on its audience, circulation,
editorial profile, editorial preferences, editorial calendar, and lead time. The
MediaMap database can be integrated into the service's publicity management software. See the MediaManager listing under "Software."

The MIT List of Radio Stations on the Internet

http://wmbr.mit.edu/stations/list.html.

Links to the Web pages of more than 9,000 stations worldwide. If the
station has an audio feed, you can link to that, too. The site is technically
oriented and doesn't give the addresses or phone numbers for the stations,
but you can go to the Web pages for that information. This site lists broadcast stations only; it does not list Internet-only stations, but it does identify broadcasters that are live on the Net. The site is searchable by
geographic area, call letters, and format. It will soon also include E-mail
addresses for the stations listed.

National Directory of Magazines

Oxbridge Communications, Inc., 150 Fifth Avenue, Suite 302, New York,
NY 10011, (212) 741-0231.

Lists and describes all magazines published in the United States and
Canada.

National Hispanic Media Directory

WPR Publications. ISBN: 1889379174.

Oxbridge Directory of Newsletters

Oxbridge Communications, Inc., 150 Fifth Avenue, Suite 302, New York,
NY 10011, (212) 741-0231.

Includes complete editorial information for more than 20,000 U.S. and Canadian newsletters, categorized by subject.

Travel Media Directory
Scott American Corporation, PO Box 88, West Reading, CT 06896-0088, (203) 938-2955; http://www.scottamerican.com.

Covers hundreds of consumer and trade media outlets worldwide. Includes columnists, radio and TV programs, and travel Internet sites with editorial content. Printed on demand when you order it, so the listings are up-to-the-minute.

Ulrich's International Periodicals Directory
R. R. Bowker. ISBN: 0835242307.

Washington News Media Contacts Directory
H&M Publishers, 44 W. Market Street, PO Box 311, Rhinebeck, NY 12572, (845) 876-2081.

Listings include Washington, D.C., newspapers, news bureaus, news services and syndicates, radio and TV stations, and specialized newsletters.

Willings Press Guide
Hollis Directories Ltd., Harlequin House, 7 High Street, Teddington, Middlesex, United Kingdom TW11 8EL, 011-44181-977-7711; http://www.hollis-pr.co.uk.

This two-volume set gives you more than 20,000 entries within the United Kingdom and approximately 30,000 entries internationally. Most entries include E-mail and Web addresses, circulation, summary of contents, target audience, and language of publication. Available in print, on-line, and CD-ROM versions.

Writer's Market
Writer's Digest Books, 1507 Dana Avenue, Cincinnati, OH 45207, (513) 531-2222; http://www.writersdigest.com; E-mail: writersdig@fwpubs.com.

A directory of magazines interested in articles written by freelance writers. Gives information about length, as well as editorial requirements, interests, and needs. Helpful for publicists who want to approach magazine editors with story ideas.

Yahoo! Radio Networks
http://dir.yahoo.comnews_and_media/radio/networks/.

Links to Web pages for radio networks, from ABC Radio to Z-Spanish Radio Network.

Yahoo! Radio Programs by Category
http://dir.yahoo.comnews_and_media/radio/programs/.

Links to Web pages for radio programs, sorted by categories ranging from Automotive to Travel. Each category is broken down further, with the Music section subdivided into Blues, Celtic, Christian, Country & Western, and nine others. A good tool for becoming familiar with individual programs, as opposed to the MIT directory, which is station-oriented.

Media Lists on Labels and Computer Diskettes

All-in-One Directory
Gebbie Press, PO Box 1000, New Paltz, NY 12561-0017, (845) 255-7560; http://www.gebbie.com.

23,000 listings for daily and weekly papers; radio and TV stations; consumer, business, and trade magazines; farm publications; the Black and Hispanic press; and more. Available on floppy disks for the IBM or Macintosh, or in printed, bound form.

Bacon's **Media Lists**
Bacon's Information, Inc., 332 S. Michigan Avenue, Chicago, IL 60604, (312) 922-2400, (800) 621-0561; http://www.baconsinfo.com.

Custom-selected lists on labels, with names of editors, reporters, news directors, and public service directors. The database includes 60,000 media outlets and nearly 400,000 editorial contacts at magazines, newspapers, broadcasters, and wire services. The lists are based on a daily-updated computer file and are available on pressure-sensitive labels, as ASCII files on diskette, or by E-mail, ready to be imported into your software. Same-day turnaround is available.

Editor and Publisher International Yearbook

Editor & Publisher, 11 W. 19th Street, New York, NY 10011-4234, (212) 675-4380; http://www.mediainfo.com.

Listings for daily, national, weekly, black, religious, foreign-language, and college newspapers in the United States. The foreign section covers newspapers in Canada, Europe, the Caribbean, Central America, Mexico, South America, Africa, the Middle East, Asia, the Far East, Australia, New Zealand, and the Pacific Ocean territories. Available on labels or diskettes.

Media Selects

Broadcast Interview Source, 2233 Wisconsin Avenue, Suite 406, Washington, DC 20007-4104, (202) 333-4904, (800) YEARBOOK; http://www.yearbooknews.com.

Three directories give you up-to-date contact information for the most influential journalists in the United States in print, broadcast, and on-line media. You can reach decision makers at the wire services, syndicates, top 50 daily newspapers, major television and radio talk shows, and most influential business, financial, and consumer magazines, as well as syndicated columnists. Listings include more than 600 of the most influential radio and television talk show hosts, producers, and talent bookers in the United States. Contact information provides name, title, show name, station, address, telephone, and fax number. Listings are for regularly scheduled shows that welcome outside sources.

- *Power Media Selects*: Wire services, newspapers, magazines.
- *Talk Show Selects*: The nation's top talk show hosts and producers on TV, radio, and cable.
- *Web Selects*: The most influential media and search engines on-line.

Media Tours (Also see "Satellite Media Tours")

Daybook.com

Broadcast Interview Source, Inc., 2233 Wisconsin Avenue NW, Washington, DC 20007, (202) 333-4904, (800) YEARBOOK; http://www. yearbook.com.

An interactive calendar of today's events, both virtual and real-world, which posts your media alerts for a fee. Journalists, who can register for a daily or weekly E-mail update of headlines, can filter the content so they get only materials of interest to them.

Interviewtour.com
Broadcast Interview Source, Inc., 2233 Wisconsin Avenue NW, Washington, DC 20007, (202) 333-4904, (800) YEARBOOK; http://www. yearbook.com.

Let the media know you're available to appear on talk shows on short notice, by listing your topic with Interviewtour.com.

West Glen
1430 Broadway, Ninth Floor, New York, NY 10018, (212) 921-2800; 635 N. Michigan Avenue, Suite 600, Chicago, IL 60611, (312) 751-4274; 595 Market Street, Suite 2500, San Francisco, CA 94105, (415) 495-1455; 1155 Connecticut Avenue NW, Suite 300, Washington, DC 20036, (202) 331-9454; 2220 S. Arbutus Court, Lakewood, CO 80228, (303) 914-9382; http://www.westglen.com; E-mail: info@westglen.com.

Radio media tours are booked ahead and taped live, with your spokesperson linked to the stations by telephone. Another effective method of distribution is Radio Express, a hot-line service that lets stations preview and tape prerecorded stories right over the phone.

News Wires

These private services are wired to newsrooms at major newspapers, magazines, broadcast stations, and websites worldwide. For a fee, they will transmit your copy over their wires, exactly as you wrote it, directly into newsrooms, in minutes. This can increase the impact of your material, and it can be critical when time is limited.

News wires are particularly important for publicists who have to meet requirements for prompt disclosure in cases in which news may impact their organizations' stock prices.

Most wire services have interconnecting arrangements and can send your copy over other circuits. If you're going to use a private wire service, staff your telephones for two or three hours after the material is sent out on the wire, so you can answer any questions editors may have.

Business Wire

40 E. 52nd Street, 19th Floor, New York, NY 10022, (212) 752-9600, (800) 221-2462; 44 Montgomery Street, 39th Floor, San Francisco, CA 94104, (415) 986-4422, (800) 227-0845; http://www.businesswire.com. Offices in Atlanta, Boston, Charlotte, Chicago, Cincinnati, Cleveland, Dallas, Denver, Detroit, Florida, Houston, Los Angeles, Minneapolis, Nashville, Newport Beach, Philadelphia, Phoenix, Portland, Sacramento, San Antonio, San Diego, Seattle, Silicon Valley, Washington, D.C., and Brussels, Belgium.

Business Wire's national circuit includes 2,000 newsrooms across the country. Your release can be distributed to the entire circuit or on a state or regional basis. Business Wire has more than a dozen special circuits, including ethnic media, sports and entertainment news, a financial disclosure circuit, and full-text posting to on-line databases, search engines, and news sites. The service can transmit news photos by wire and can transmit your release to international news wires for worldwide coverage. The analyst wire reaches key players in the investment community.

Canada NewsWire (CNW)

http://www.newswire.ca.

CNW sends full-text news releases over a dedicated network, with simultaneous delivery of news releases directly into the editorial systems of media, news agencies, and the financial community in Canada.

Collegiate Presswire

1191 Valley Road, Suite 2, Clifton, NJ 07013, (888) 621-7721; http://www.cpwire.com; E-mail: info@cpwire.com.

Collegiate Presswire distributes press materials to more than 450 college media outlets by E-mail, fax, and the Internet. Its news feed goes directly to influential publications in the higher education market, including the *Chronicle of Higher Education* and *Education Daily*, the College Press Network, ScreamingMedia.com, and Student.com.

Internet News Bureau

(541) 318-8633, (888) 699-6939; http://www.newsbureau.com.

This service specializes in Web-related news or launches. Covers on-line and off-line print and broadcast media. Press release writing services are also available.

Internetwire

5757 W. Century Boulevard, Suite 391, Los Angeles, CA 90045, (310) 846-3600; http://www.internetwire.comrelease.

Daily E-mail distribution to 24,000 journalists at top daily and national newspapers, technology and business periodicals, major television and radio stations, financial analysts, and industry researchers. Also distributes your news by PointCast, NetCaster, Active Channels, and WorldFlash to major news sites on the Web. International distribution is included. No word-count restrictions or membership fees.

PR Newswire

810 Seventh Avenue, 35th Floor, New York, NY 10019, (212) 596-1500, (800) 832-5522; http://www.prnewswire.com. Nearly 40 bureaus across the world, including 29 in the United States: Atlanta, Austin, Boston, Charlotte, Chicago, Cleveland, Dallas, Denver, Detroit, Houston, Los Angeles, Miami, Minneapolis, Nashville, Orange County, Philadelphia, Phoenix, Pittsburgh, Portland, St. Louis, Salt Lake City, San Diego, San Francisco, San Jose, Seattle, Tampa, Tulsa, Washington, D.C., Brazil, France, Germany, Hong Kong, and the United Kingdom.

PR Newswire reaches more than 22,000 media recipients via wire, fax, and E-mail in addition to about 30,000 journalists through on-line media websites. A 24-hour operation, it offers immediate access to local, national, and international circuits, translations for international distributions, and delivery to more than 1,240 websites and databases such as LEXIS-NEXIS. PR Newswire offers special circuits and services such as:

- North American Disclosure (NAD) service to reach the business press and financial community in the United States and Canada. All NAD wire distributions satisfy U.S. disclosure requirements.
- EntertaiNet, geared exclusively for entertainment editors.
- Feature News Service for early-morning delivery of your feature story to the appropriate editor in 1,000 U.S. newsrooms.
- Satellite and Web transmission of photos.

Wieck Photo DataBase, Inc.
PO Box 59408, Dallas, TX 75229, (972) 392-0888;
http://www.wieckphoto.com.

In addition to U.S. and worldwide distribution on the Associated Press and other wire services, Wieck offers ImageLink, which enables the media to download high-resolution, publication-ready images from your website.

Newsgroup and Mailing List Search Engines

Dejanews
http://www.deja.com/usenet.

Deja.com offers access to approximately 35,000 Usenet newsgroups through its Usenet Discussion Service. A "power search" feature lets users customize searches and look for specific messages by author, date, forum, subject, or language. In addition, a "thread digest" feature allows users to quickly view an entire "discussion thread"—the current message, any message replies, and any previous messages. You can access newsgroups directly through Dejanews. For more information about the site's capabilities, go to http://www.deja.comcorp/press_usenet.shtml.

E-Groups
http://www.egroups.com.

Hosts more than 90,000 mailing lists, including 868 devoted to marketing. Some have just a few members, but others are quite large.

Liszt
http://www.liszt.com.

One of the best places to find relevant mailing lists and learn more about how they operate is Liszt, a directory of 90,095 mailing lists. Liszt can help you find mailing lists that may interest you and tell you how to get more information about them, so you avoid joining by trial and error. For help with list searching, go to http://www.liszt.comhelp.html. Newcomers to the world of lists should read Liszt's helpful introduction at http://www.liszt.comintro.html. In addition, you'll find directories of 30,000 Usenet discussion groups and 25,000 IRC chat channels. IRC channels are based on the Internet and are very similar to chat rooms on the commercial on-line services. There are hundreds of them, many of which are highly specialized.

Meta-List.net

http://www.meta-list.net.

This multilingual site lets you search 235,032 newsletters and discussion lists in 13 languages from English to Turkish. You can subscribe to any list right from the site.

Tile.net

This site has three different directories:

http://tile.net/lists/about.html is a directory of E-mail discussion groups and mailing lists on the Internet. The listing is searchable, and entries are also sorted by name and description.

http://tile.net/news is a searchable directory of Usenet newsgroups, with a link to each group, statistics on the amount of traffic and use, and a direct link to the frequently asked questions document for each group. Listings are by newsgroup hierarchy, as well as by description.

http://tile.net/ftp/about.html is a directory of anonymous FTP sites, the bulletin boards of the Internet, which are a rich resource of information on thousands of topics. You can search for them by contents, country, or site name.

Newsletters and Magazines

It's a good idea to ask for a sample copy of publications with which you're unfamiliar, or check one in your library before you subscribe. Or visit the publication's website, which may have sample copies or articles.

Bulldog Reporter

Infocom Group, 5900 Hollis Street, Suite R2, Emeryville, CA 94608, (510) 596-9300; http://www.infocomgroup.com.

Bulldog Reporter, the media-placement newsletter for publicists, keeps your media database current with contact updates. Helps you hone your pitching skills through journalist interviews on how to successfully place stories with the most influential business media in the nation.

Communication World

International Association of Business Communicators, One Hallidie Plaza, Suite 600, San Francisco, CA 94102, (415) 544-4700; http://www.iabc.com.

This award-winning publication is full of highly useful information about publicity and communication techniques, as well as the latest developments in the field.

ContentBiz.Com

http://www.contentbiz.com.

This free E-letter covers the business of syndicating content, primarily to websites and E-zines. If you have publicity material that has solid content, you could find out how to distribute it to vast new markets, and you may even be able to generate income.

Fast Forward

West Glen, 1430 Broadway, Ninth Floor, New York, NY 10018, (212) 921-2800; http://www.westglen.com; E-mail: info@westglen.com.

A free newsletter loaded with practical information about how to develop and produce video news releases, satellite media tours, audio news releases, public service spots, and other electronic publicity.

i-PR (Interactive Public Relations)

Xpress Press News Service, 4741 Sarazen Drive, Hollywood, FL 33021, (954) 989-3338, (800) 713-7701; http://www.xpresspress.com/ipr/html.

i-PR is a free monthly electronic newsletter that includes a continual flow of helpful Internet-based articles and resources for publicists. To see the past issues and subscribe, go to http://www.xpresspress.comipr.html.

Jack O'Dwyer's Newsletter

J. R. O'Dwyer Company, Inc., 271 Madison Avenue, New York, NY 10016, (212) 679-2471; http://www.odwyerpr.com.

A weekly report with information on new publications, staff changes, placement tips and opportunities, innovative publicity campaigns and programs, legal aspects of publicity, and more.

Liquid Media

MediaMap, 311 Arsenal Street, Watertown, MA, 02472-2700,
(617) 583-1367; http://www.mediamap.com.

A weekly E-newsletter reporting trends, editorial moves, and industry news for all sectors of the media.

Media Relations Report

Lawrence Ragan Communications, Inc., 316 N. Michigan Avenue,
Suite 300, Chicago, IL 60601, (312) 960-4100, (800) 878-5331;
http://www.ragan.com; E-mail: cservice@ragan.com.

A biweekly newsletter that combines nuts-and-bolts how-to articles with updates on journalists' needs and pitching opportunities.

O'Dwyer's PR Services Report

J. R. O'Dwyer Company, Inc., 271 Madison Avenue, New York, NY
10016, (212) 679-2471; http://www.odwyerpr.com.

A monthly magazine with the latest on how to hire and make the best use of publicity services, as well as new sources and techniques for publicists. Regular columns cover video news releases, legal issues, publicity photo placement, and accounting for publicists, among other topics. Articles from back issues are archived at the website.

pr reporter

PR Publishing Company, Dudley House, PO Box 600, Exeter, NH
03833-0600, (603) 778-0514; http://www.prpublishing.com;
E-mail: prr@publishing.com.

This weekly newsletter covers the broader field of public relations, including public affairs, employee relations, and investor relations. Recent articles of interest to publicists include information on how publicists can align their programs with top management's objectives and get seats at the boardroom table, strategies for controlling intrusive reporters, examples of press kits that cut through the clutter, and the decreasing length of network news sound bites.

Ragan's Interactive Public Relations
Lawrence Ragan Communications, Inc., 316 N. Michigan Avenue, Suite 300, Chicago, IL 60601, (312) 960-4100, (800) 878-5331; http://www.ragan.com; E-mail: cservice@ragan.com.

A monthly newsletter that teaches publicists how to use the Internet and other technologies to do media relations, PR, marketing, investor relations, and community relations.

Ragan's Public Relations Journal
Lawrence Ragan Communications, Inc., 316 N. Michigan Avenue, Suite 300, Chicago, IL 60601, (312) 960-4100, (800) 878-5331; http://www.ragan.com; E-mail: cservice@ragan.com.

This bimonthly journal focuses on publicity strategy and the issues facing publicists. Topics include how to appraise campaigns and programs and convince senior management of their importance, as well as the latest innovations in media relations and how PR professionals are using them.

Tactics
Public Relations Society of America, 33 Irving Place, New York, NY 10003, (212) 995-2230; http://www.prsa.orgtactics/tac0600.html.

A monthly newspaper covering trends and hands-on how-to information for publicists. Cover stories go behind the scenes to reveal the public relations issues connected to crises, media events, and new product launches. Highlights are available on-line.

Travel Publicity Leads
Scott American Corporation, PO Box 88, West Reading, CT 06896-0088, (203) 938-2955; http://www.scottamerican.com.

Devoted to worldwide travel editorial placement opportunities. Includes a yearly editorial calendar listing.

WebPR
MediaMap, 311 Arsenal Street, Watertown, MA, 02472-2700, (617) 583-1367; http://www.mediamap.com.

A weekly E-newsletter aimed at demystifying the Web as a working medium for publicists. Also covers personnel changes at major sites such as ABCNews.Com and Adweek Online, so you can keep your journalist contacts up-to-date.

On-Line Pressrooms and Press Kits

CorporateNEWS.com

1642 Kelliwood Oaks Drive, Suite 100, Katy, TX 77450, (281) 599-9200, (877) 763-4257; http://www.corporatenews.com.

If your organization doesn't have the staff to develop a pressroom for your website, CorporateNEWS.com can create one for you. Although it will be based on the company's site, it will include your logo and can be easily linked to your own website.

InternetPressKit.Com

(949) 852-3999; http://internetpresskit.com.

InternetPressKit.Com creates on-line press kits. They can be interactive, multimedia presentations including text, graphics, photos, video, and audio. They can also include links to your organization's website.

Press Books

Package Publicity Services, Inc.

158 West 27th Street, #908, New York, NY 10001, (212) 255-2872.

Publishes press books and related promotional material for more than 2,000 major Broadway plays. Use these collections of suggested press releases, background information on playwrights, and copies of reviews to give you ideas for your community theater publicity campaign. For best results, contact the service as far ahead as possible.

Press Clipping Services

In addition to letting you know when and where your press releases, feature stories, fillers, broadcast publicity, and Internet publicity have been used, clipping services can help you keep track of what's going on in your field or industry. You can even use them to find out what kinds of coverage your competition is getting. If you like, they can also help you monitor proposed regulations and legislation that will affect your business or organization.

Because clipping services, like human beings, are not perfect, some publicists use two or three services to make sure they get most of the articles they're interested in. You may want to experiment to find the best way to meet your needs.

Many clipping services still have staff who actually read thousands of publications and send you paper clippings. However, Web-based services scan electronic versions of newspapers and magazines, as well as dispatches from the wire services, news websites, mailing lists, Usenet discussion groups, and Internet radio, and automatically "clip" any item that mentions the keywords you specify. You get your "clippings" in electronic form.

Each clipping service includes different publications, wire services, websites, discussion groups, and broadcasts. You'll have to find out if prospective services cover your key media outlets, as well as if that coverage is full-text or just the highlights.

When you choose an off-line clipping service, find out if it offers limited service for just your city or state, if that's what you want. Some services operate on a regional or national basis and charge you accordingly, even if that coverage is too broad for you. Also check with your state press association; a number of them offer inexpensive local clipping services. If you don't know how to find your state's association, call the managing editor of the largest daily in your area. He's sure to know.

Some of the larger clipping bureaus also offer services that analyze your clippings for editorial slant, product or keyword mentions, number of readers reached, and photos used.

Bacon's Information, Inc.

332 S. Michigan Avenue, Chicago, IL 60604, (312) 922-3127,
(800) 621-0561; http://www.baconsinfo.com;
E-mail: clipping@baconsinfo.com.

Provides clippings from thousands of trade, business, and consumer magazines and virtually every daily and weekly newspaper in the United States and Canada, as well as 3,000 news websites and hundreds of daily TV news programs. Bacon's can also provide clippings on any subject you specify, from Abrasives to Zen Buddhism.

The Clipping Analysis Service transforms your hard-to-manage press clippings into clear, concise reports that measure the effectiveness of your publicity campaigns.

Clippings can be delivered in your choice of hard-copy or on-line format. In addition to the outlets cited, the on-line service includes hundreds of niche-specific portals. On-line delivery is by E-mail, which includes a summary of the article and a direct link to it.

Burrelle's Press Clipping Service

75 E. Northfield Road, Livingston, NJ 07039, (973) 992-6600, (800) 631-1160.

At Burrelle's, they read 17,587 daily, Sunday, and weekly U.S. newspapers, trade journals, consumer magazines, and the dispatches from major news wires. Canadian and foreign coverage is available. They monitor all network TV and radio news and public affairs programming, plus local TV news and public affairs programs in major metro areas, with typed transcripts available.

Burrelle's NewsExpress service reads 74 major U.S. daily papers, as well as 63 major business and news magazines. Clippings from those publications and transcripts of network TV and radio broadcasts are delivered to you by fax—before 9:00 A.M. the day they appear. Burrelle's Cyber Talk service monitors Web user groups, chat rooms, forums, and more. The Web Clips service includes monitoring of websites, especially those that are related to print publications.

In addition, you can receive analysis reports of your clippings based on a variety of factors. Burrelle's can also archive your clippings and publicity materials on optical disks for fast retrieval and space-saving storage.

CyberAlert

Foot of Broad Street, Stratford, CT 06515, (203) 375-7200; http://www.cyberalert.com.

CyberAlert searches more than 2,000 on-line news sources every four to six hours. The service also searches Web publications, websites, message boards, and Usenet newsgroups once each day. The reports, which are E-mailed to you daily, include direct links to each mention. CyberAlert's software eliminates duplicates and lets you manage your clippings.

EWatch Internet Monitoring

1120 Avenue of the Americas, Fourth Floor, New York, NY 10036, (800) 748-3737; http://www.ewatch.com.

Coverage includes thousands of editorial-based sites on the Web, more than 63,000 Usenet groups and electronic mailing lists, and hundreds of public discussion areas on AOL and CompuServe. WebWatch alerts you when changes are made on sites you have selected. Line-by-line additions and deletions are flagged for easy spotting.

Intellinews

http://www.intellinews.com.

This inexpensive service notifies you by E-mail whenever a post is made to a selected newsgroup that covers a topic or issue in which you are interested. You specify the keywords. The service covers more than 100,000 groups and will consider adding groups that you want to monitor.

Luce Online Inc.

6617 N. Scottsdale Road, Suite 204, Scottsdale, AZ 85250, (800) 518-0088; www.luceonline.com; E-mail: info@luceonline.com.

In-depth coverage of the on-line editions of the top 100 U.S. daily newspapers, wire services, business magazines and journals, and trade publications, plus major broadcast and general news and information websites. Full-text articles delivered in real time on the day of publication. Items are sent by fax or E-mail or are posted to a news website created specifically for you.

Luce Press Clipping Service

420 Lexington Avenue, New York, NY 10170, (212) 687-2945, (800) 528-8226; http://www.lucepress.com.

Provides coverage of every daily and virtually every weekly newspaper in the United States, plus the AP, UPI, Dow Jones, and Reuters news wires, as well as more than 6,000 trade and consumer magazines.

Luce can provide transcripts or videotapes of all regularly scheduled national network TV news shows, and many regularly scheduled local TV news and talk shows in major metro areas. The AM Newsbreak service delivers clippings to you by fax on the morning they appear in the nation's top news sources. The clipping analysis service can provide you with reports analyzing your media coverage, on paper or computer disk.

WebClipping.com

276 Canal Street, Seventh Floor, New York, NY 10013, (212) 965-1900; http://www.webclipping.com.

WebClipping is an Internet-based monitoring and clipping service that alerts you when your organization, product, or service appears anywhere on the Web. The service monitors 30 search engines, more than 14,000 local, national, and international publications on-line, and Usenet messages.

Professional Organizations

Association for Women in Communications

1244 Ritchie Highway, Suite 6, Arnold, MD 21012-1887, (410) 544-7442; http://www.womcom.org.

An organization of professional women in the communication field, including radio, television, newspapers, publishing, advertising, marketing, and public relations. Attending local meetings is a good way to meet journalists and other publicists. Although the organization is primarily for women, men should check to see what it offers them. Write for information about the chapter nearest you.

International Association of Business Communicators (IABC)

One Hallidie Plaza, Suite 600, San Francisco, CA 94102, (415) 544-4700; http://www.iabc.com.

A worldwide network for communication professionals, with affiliates in more than 40 countries. With dozens of chapters across the United States, IABC offers a chance to meet—and learn from—other communicators. Services to members include workshops and classes, as well as a subscription to the award-winning publication *Communication World.* The organization includes internal communicators (who aim their work at their companies' employees) as well as publicists.

Issue Management Council

207 Loudoun Street SE, Leesburg, VA 20175-3115, (703) 777-8450;
http://www.issuemanagement.org.

A professional membership organization for publicists who manage issues. Offers conferences, publications, and on-line advice for members.

National Association of Government Communicators

10301 Democracy Lane, Suite 203, Fairfax, VA 22030, (703) 691-0377;
http://www.nagc.com.

A national not-for-profit professional network of federal, state, and local government employees who disseminate information within and outside government. Its members are editors, writers, graphic artists, video professionals, broadcasters, photographers, information specialists, and agency spokespersons.

Public Relations Society of America (PRSA)

33 Irving Place, New York, NY 10003, (212) 995-2230;
http://www.prsa.org.

An organization of public relations men and women in business, government, PR agencies, and large nonprofit organizations. PRSA emphasizes professional development and publishes a *Code of Professional Standards for the Practice of Public Relations.* The organization has more than 113 chapters throughout the United States. Write for information about the chapter nearest you.

Public Relations Student Society of America

33 Irving Place, New York, NY 10003, (212) 995-2230;
http://www.prssa.org.

The student affiliate of the Public Relations Society of America has 216 chapters on college campuses across America. Internship programs for qualified members offer students a chance to get practical, on-the-job public relations and publicity experience. The website lists scholarships and job opportunities.

Public Service Spot Production and Distribution

Gourvitz Communications, Inc.

729 Seventh Avenue, 15th Floor, New York, NY 10019, (212) 730-4807.

Complete production and distribution facilities for public service spots, using the company's script or yours. Gourvitz handles both radio and TV spots. Write for sample storyboards and scripts.

Medialink

708 Third Avenue, Ninth Floor, New York, NY 10017, (212) 682-8300, (800) 843-0677—with production affiliates worldwide; http://www.medialink.com; E-mail: info@medialink.com.

A full-service PSA production facility, Medialink will write, tape, distribute, and report on the usage of your public service spots.

MG Productions, Inc.

216 E. 45th Street, New York, NY 10017-3374, (212) 682-4725; http://www.mgproductions.com; E-mail: info@mgproductions.com.

MG Productions handles public service spots from concept to script, production, and editing. The company also handles distribution, available on a local, regional, or national basis. PSA scripts can be localized and can be produced in English, Spanish, Japanese, and Chinese versions. MG has won national and international awards for its film and video productions.

PCS Broadcast Services Division of DWJ Television

1 Robinson Lane, Ridgewood, NJ 07450, (212) 697-2765, (201) 445-1711, extension 141.

PCS Broadcast Services will write the script and do all the production, distribution, and tracking for radio and television public service spots, or will handle distribution, tracking, and reporting for spots produced by others. The database helps the company send the preferred format to each station and choose broadcasters based on actual PSA usage. The company also can select national and regional cable networks, as well as local cable systems, that use PSAs.

West Glen

1430 Broadway, Ninth Floor, New York, NY 10018, (212) 921-2800;
635 N. Michigan Avenue, Suite 600, Chicago, IL 60611, (312) 751-4274;
595 Market Street, Suite 2500, San Francisco, CA 94105, (415) 495-1455;
1155 Connecticut Avenue NW, Suite 300, Washington, DC 20036,
(202) 331-9454; 2220 S. Arbutus Court, Lakewood, CO 80228,
(303) 914-9382; http://www.westglen.com; E-mail: info@westglen.com.

West Glen can write, produce, distribute, and track television and radio
public service announcements and will guarantee that your spot will be
aired. Also offers consulting on script development and creative. West
Glen's annual survey of PSA directors at TV and radio stations keeps the
company on top of trends in usage preferences and content preferences.
The media contacts and station usage history database is updated daily. All
TV PSAs distributed by West Glen are digitally encoded, so tracking
reports are highly accurate. West Glen can help businesses find suitable
nonprofit partners, which can help boost PSA placements. The company
distributes PSAs produced by others, as well.

Publicity Distribution Services

If you are mailing releases and feature stories on a statewide, regional, or
national basis, you may find it worthwhile to use one of these press release
distribution services. In addition to the companies listed, a number of state
press associations offer localized service at reasonable rates. If you don't
know where to find your state press association, call your local library and
ask the reference librarian to check for you.

Bacon's Information, Inc.

332 S. Michigan Avenue, Chicago, IL 60604, (312) 922-2400;
(800) 621-0561; http://www.baconsinfo.com.

Bacon's will print your release or press kit, duplicate your photos, and
use its database of 400,000 media contacts by name to develop a customized
distribution list for each release. The company handles the stuffing, seal-
ing, stamping, addressing, and sorting, too.

You can reach the Black and Hispanic press, every daily and weekly
newspaper in the United States, all broadcast stations, and 8,400 U.S. and

Canadian magazines. International distribution is available. Bacon's can also set up and maintain your organization's list on its computer.

Media Distribution Services, Inc. (MDS)

307 W. 36th Street, New York, NY 10018, (212) 247-4800;
(800) MDS-3282; http://www.mdsconnect.com;
E-mail: services@mds-newyork.com. Service centers in Atlanta,
San Francisco, Boston, Los Angeles, Washington, D.C., Minneapolis, and
Chicago.

You provide the camera-ready copy, and MDS will print, address, stamp, and mail your publicity material for you. The company also has a simultaneous fax delivery service. The computerized database, which contains more than 200,000 editors and other key media contacts by name, helps you reach as many as 50,000 print and broadcast media in the United States and Canada. You can use more than 2,500 editorial and geographic classifications to target your publicity mailing to just the right journalists.

The database, updated with as many as 1,000 changes daily, includes all daily, weekly, and college newspapers, TV and radio stations, cable and broadcast networks, business and consumer magazines, wire services, syndicated columnists, and even major freelance writers.

Media Information's PRNet

25 Charter Gate, Quarry Park Close, Moulton Park, Northampton, United Kingdom, 011-01604-670-550; http://www.prnet.co.uk.

Media Information is a British company that distributes news to the United Kingdom's journalism community. PRNet will place your release in a searchable database, which journalists then consult for stories. The site records usage for you. There's also a journalist's forum in which reporters seek stories and information, along with a press contacts database.

Newstips, Inc.

13830 Braeburn Lane, Novelty, OH 44072, (440) 338-8400;
http://www.newstips.comabout.html.

The weekly Newstips Electronic Editorial Bulletin reaches journalists covering the computer industry, who get it by fax or E-mail. Each issue is a collection of brief, newsy tidbits about Newstips client companies, intended as news hooks or story starters for reporters.

North Americas Precis Syndicate, Inc.

350 Fifth Avenue, Suite 6500, New York, NY 10118, (212) 867-9000; http://www.napsnet.com.

This company will write and produce brief audio and video news releases and distribute them to 6,000 radio stations and 1,000 television stations.

The URLwire

(423) 637-2438; http://www.urlwire.com;
E-mail: ericward@urlwire.com.

The oldest E-mail news release service on the Web, URLwire is best used for announcing website launches, Web-based promotions or events, and Web and Internet software and services. It specializes in distributing news about website content. Recipients are editors who write about the Web in print, on-line, and on television and radio, all over the world. The service matches news to editor-interest profiles. In order to make sure each item really fits every subscriber's interests, owner Eric Ward hand-matches them. Ward is highly selective; you must E-mail him a synopsis of your news before he'll agree to distribute it.

Xpress Press

4741 Sarazen Drive, Hollywood, FL 33021, (954) 989-3338,
(800) 713-7701; http://www.xpresspress.com;
E-mail: info@xpresspress.com.

Xpress Press could be viewed as the publicity equivalent of permission marketing, in which someone chooses to receive marketing materials. When journalists subscribe to Xpress Press, they supply a profile of their beat. As with any form of permission marketing, they can always unsubscribe. Express Press distributes publicity material to newspapers, magazines, and their on-line counterparts, as well as Web-based news organizations and wire services. Xpress Press subscribers include more than 9,000 journalists covering 400 news beats in 36-plus countries. The service has several circuits, including Internet and Technology, Business News, General Interest and Feature News, and the Software Wire.

Satellite Media Tours

Medialink

708 Third Avenue, Ninth Floor, New York, NY 10017, (212) 682-8300, (800) 843-0677—with production affiliates worldwide; http://www.medialink.com.

Medialink's transmission network is dedicated to satellite media tours, video news releases, and public service spots. The company offers complete planning, consulting, and delivery services for satellite media tours. A nationwide news-wire service, used to alert network and local television newsrooms to satellite media tours available for booking in advance, is tied into the Associated Press wire.

On the Scene Productions

5900 Wilshire Boulevard, Suite 1400, Los Angeles, CA 90036, (323) 930-1030; New York: (212) 715-0800; Chicago: (312) 644-6170; http://www.onthescene.com; E-mail: info@onthescene.com.

On the Scene Productions specializes in arranging, producing, and distributing satellite media tours shot on location, often producing more dramatic results (and higher media interest) than tours done from a studio. The company can schedule a tour within 48 hours in a crisis situation.

Although it can and does work with virtually any subject matter, the company has extensive experience in the publishing and entertainment industries.

PR Newswire

810 Seventh Avenue, New York, NY 10019, (212) 596-1500, (800) 832-5522; http://www.prnewswire.com.

PR Newswire coordinates all technical aspects of your satellite media tour, including studio production, satellite transmission, and monitoring. Alerts are sent to broadcast newsrooms through the proprietary AP Express network and to all national media through the wire and the Web.

West Glen

1430 Broadway, Ninth Floor, New York, NY 10018, (212) 921-2800;

635 N. Michigan Avenue, Suite 600, Chicago, IL 60611, (312) 751-4274;

595 Market Street, Suite 2500, San Francisco, CA 94105, (415) 495-1455;

1155 Connecticut Avenue NW, Suite 300, Washington, DC 20036,

(202) 331-9454; 2220 S. Arbutus Court, Lakewood, CO 80228,

(303) 914-9382; http://www.westglen.com; E-mail: info@westglen.com.

West Glen arranges every aspect of your tour, including the development of broadcast press advisories, scheduling of interviews, booking satellite and studio time, distribution of B-roll, and ensuring that the tour runs smoothly. As many as 20 interviews can take place within two or three hours. Interviews can be aired live or taped for future use. The company can digitally encode SMTs so that they can be tracked and provides "airchecks" to show you how you appeared on the air. Tours can be done from the studio or live on the scene. The company also can help you develop news pegs and content that has the best chance of getting aired.

Software

MediaManager Publicity Productivity Tools

MediaMap, 311 Arsenal Street, Watertown, MA, 02472-2700,

(617) 374-9300; http://www.mediamap.com.

MediaManager lets you create and save customized lists by beat. Includes MediaMap profiles, contact preferences, and your notes from past calls, as well as information about 120,000 upcoming stories on editorial calendars across America. Use it to contact the media by E-mail, fax, broadcast fax, wire service, and even snail mail. The software lets you send materials to each contact based on preference. Use it to schedule callbacks and other future actions.

PRality

Vocus, Inc., 4235 Forbes Boulevard, Lanham, MD 20706,

(800) 345-5572; http://www.vocus.com.

Software tools for publicists help you generate targeted media lists, issue news releases, and capture and report on news clips, as well as track all press inquiries. Offered in networked or Web-based versions, which don't require software installations or updates. You can see a demonstration of the software at http://www.prality.com.

PRtrak

TrakWare Inc., 10500 Northwest Freeway, #110, Houston, TX 77092, (800) 846-5831; http://www.trakwareinc.com.

PRtrak software lets you calculate the value of your print and broadcast publicity. Since you can do both qualitative and quantitative valuations, PRtrak can be a valuable tool for interpreting publicity budgets to top managers. The software reports results by project, client, media type, and date. The valuations are based on audience data and advertising rates provided by Arbitron, NielsenTV, MMR, and SRDS.

Targeter

Media Distribution Services, Inc., 307 W. 36th Street, New York, NY 10018, (800) MDS-3282; http://www.mdsconnect.com.

Targeter software includes a media contact list of 200,000 editors and other key contacts in your personal computer, and daily updates (with up to 1,000 changes a day) by E-mail. You'll be able to print out media lists, run mailing labels, and look up media contacts 24 hours a day. Also available in a networked version.

Surveys

Roper-Starch Organization

205 E. 42nd Street, New York, NY 10017, (212) 599-0700; http://www.roper.com; E-mail: info@www.roper.com.

Offers Limobus, a "tack-on" service that includes your questions in the company's regular surveys of a nationally representative sample of 2,000 adults. In-home, in-person surveys are conducted every six to eight weeks. Since you're paying for just a small part of the survey, this can be a cost-effective way to get your questions answered. The company also designs and implements full-scale custom studies.

Training

Douglis Visual Workshops
Phil Douglis, 2505 E. Carol Avenue, Phoenix, AZ 85028, (602) 493-6709;
E-mail: pnd1@home.com.

Workshops about communicating with pictures, for newsletter and magazine editors, as well as publicists. Sessions include skills and techniques of photojournalism, principles of visual communication, how to avoid clichés, editing photos, and hands-on experience. These two-and-a-half-day sessions are offered twice a year in Sedona, Arizona.

Institute for Crisis Management Workshops
400 Missouri Avenue, Suite 101, Clarksville, IN 47129,
(812) 284-8351; http://www.crisisexperts.comworkshops.htm.

Small-group training exercises for executives and consultants who will have the responsibility for managing responses to the media during emergencies and crises.

International Association of Business Communicators (IABC)
One Hallidie Plaza, Suite 600, San Francisco, CA 94102, (415) 544-4700;
http://www.iabc.com.

Offers communication workshops and classes on a national, international, and local basis. Contact the IABC for complete information, and be sure to ask about sessions sponsored by local and regional chapters in your area.

Persuasive Presentation Techniques
Communispond Division of Frontline Group, Inc., 52 Vanderbilt Avenue, New York, NY 10017, (212) 972-4899; 676 Saint Clair Street, Chicago, IL 60611, (312) 787-0484; 160 Sansome Street, San Francisco, CA 94104, (415) 392-6600; London: 011-44-20-7405-3800; Boston: (617) 621-7088; Detroit: (248) 948-9700; Dallas: (214) 665-9488; Newport Beach: (949) 851-9200; Frontline Group's Headquarters—Nashville: (615) 301-2100; http://www.communispond.com or www.frontline-group.com.

A variety of public and private workshops and corporate programs teach you how to present persuasively, eliminate nervousness, think clearly under pressure, and control adversarial discussions. The company also conducts public and corporate programs on varied persuasion skills, such as dialoguing, negotiating, and writing.

Videotaping and on-the-spot coaching allow you to see yourself as others see you and to note your progress. Available in major cities (see www.communispond for details) or at your organization's facility. Workshops can be adapted to your organization's requirements.

Public Relations on the Internet

Mitchell Friedman Communications, PO Box 460642, San Francisco, CA 94146-0642, (415) 824-1466; http://www.mitchellfriedman.com; E-mail: mfctalk@mitchellfriedman.com.

Training programs and classes on how to use the Internet for public relations and publicity, as well as media interview skills. Programs are available at your facilities.

Strategic Media Relations Conference

Lawrence Ragan Communications, Inc., 316 N. Michigan Avenue, Suite 300, Chicago, IL 60601, (312) 960-4100, (800) 878-5331; http://www.ragan.com; E-mail: cservice@ragan.com.

Covers news peg development as well as Web-based publicity and crisis management.

Webcasting and Web Conferences

PlaceWare

PlaceWare Web Conferencing, 295 N. Bernardo, Mountain View, CA 94043, (888) 526-6170; www.placeware.com.

Web conferencing software lets you incorporate PowerPoint presentations, software demonstrations, and even notes that you make on your electronic white boards. The audio portion of the conference is handled by an old-fashioned conference call.

PR Newswire

810 Seventh Avenue, 35th Floor, New York, NY 10019, (212) 596-1500, (800) 832-5522; http://www.prnewswire.com.

Live or archived Webcasts of conference calls for the expanded Internet audience, which includes institutional and individual investors. PR Newswire publicizes conference calls by distributing an announcement over the wire to on-line services, databases, and websites with a link back to the live or archived call. All conference calls are archived for 90 days on PR Newswire's website.

PRWebcast.com

2220 Superior Viaduct, Third Floor—Front, Cleveland, OH 44113-2382, (216) 623-1900.

Produces live and on-demand Webcasts and handles the streaming media for you. Also produces multimedia Internet press releases.

WebEx

100 Rose Orchard Way, San Jose, CA 95134, (408) 435-7000; http://www.webex.com.

Pay-per-use Web conferencing with or without audio. The company can provide telephone hookups, and conferences don't require much lead time. WebEx conferences can include PC-based presentations, software demonstrations, document sharing, video, guided website tours, electronic white-board input, and documents. Attendees can annotate or comment on shared documents, and the conference leader can allow any attendee to present. Since this system is Web based, you don't have to buy software.

West Glen

1430 Broadway, Ninth Floor, New York, NY 10018, (212) 921-2800;
635 N. Michigan Avenue, Suite 600, Chicago, IL 60611, (312) 751-4274;
595 Market Street, Suite 2500, San Francisco, CA 94105, (415) 495-1455;
1155 Connecticut Avenue NW, Suite 300, Washington, DC 20036,
(202) 331-9454; 2220 S. Arbutus Court, Lakewood, CO 80228,
(303) 914-9382; http://www.westglen.com; E-mail: info@westglen.com.

West Glen can plan and produce live and on-demand Webcasts, including multimedia production and interactive components. West Glen's staff takes care of digital encoding, video streaming, pitching and distribution to on-line news sites, and follow-up reporting of usage. The company also handles Webcast website hosting and can develop cyber media tours, with prebooked interviews as part of the Webcast.

Websites

About Public Relations, with Jeff Domansky
http://publicrelations.about.com/careers/publicrelations/?once=true&.

An information source for publicists, including articles and case studies collected from dozens of publications. You'll find sections on crisis communications, investor relations, media directories, and E-zines, along with more than 800 links to other resources for publicists.

O'Dwyer's PR Daily
O'Dwyer's, 271 Madison Avenue, New York, NY 10016, (212) 679-2471; http://www.odwyerpr.com.

One of the most complete on-line directories of publicity-related services. Offers 1,121 listings, from Awards Programs to Video News Releases. Also includes breaking news in the public relations field and a searchable database of 550 PR firms.

Online Public Relations
C/o Robert Marston and Associates, 485 Madison Avenue, New York, NY 10022-5896, (212) 371-2200; http://www.online-pr.com.

Dedicated to helping you deliver better, faster, and less-expensive on-line PR, this site has hundreds of links to media, research sites, directories, PR resources, and on-line training.

PR Central
EMMI, Inc., 708 Third Avenue, Suite 205, New York, NY 10017; http://www.prcentral.com.

Includes The Body of Knowledge, an extensive, searchable on-line library of case histories and articles concerning the field of public relations.

Public Relations Society of America PR Services Directory

Public Relations Society of America, 33 Irving Place, New York, NY 10003, (212) 995-2230; http://www.prsa.org/ppc/sdir1299.html.

An on-line directory of services for the publicist, from Audio News Releases to Webcasting.

Public Service Advertising Research Center

http://www.psaresearch.com.

An on-line information library dedicated to public service advertising. Includes articles sorted by category, case studies, and organizations involved in public service spots.

The Publicity Handbook

http://www.publicityhandbook.com.

The website for this book includes clickable links for all the URLs mentioned in this chapter, with regular updates. Training exercises for new publicists help them understand how journalists look at press releases and search for news pegs. Work sheets, which you can download and print out, help you apply what you've learned in this book. And if you're looking for a media directory, this site has one of the most complete listings anywhere, with clickable links to the source.

Index